IFP/LOS ANGELES INDEPENDENT FILMMAKER'S MANUAL

SECOND EDITION

IFP/LOS ANGELES INDEPENDENT FILMMAKER'S MANUAL

SECOND EDITION

Eden H. Wurmfeld
Nicole Laloggia

ELSEVIER

AMSTERDAM • BOSTON • HEIDELBERG • LONDON
NEW YORK • OXFORD • PARIS • SAN DIEGO
SAN FRANCISCO • SINGAPORE • SYDNEY • TOKYO
Focal Press is an imprint of Elsevier

Focal Press

Focal Press is an imprint of Elsevier
200 Wheeler Road, Burlington, MA 01803, USA
Linacre House, Jordan Hill, Oxford OX2 8DP, UK

Recognizing the importance of preserving what has been written, Elsevier prints its books on acid-free paper whenever possible.

Library of Congress Cataloging-in-Publication Data
Application submitted.

British Library Cataloguing-in-Publication Data
A catalogue record for this book is available from the British Library.

ISBN: 0-240-80585-2

For information on all Focal Press publications
visit our Web site at www.focalpress.com

03 04 05 06 07 08 10 9 8 7 6 5 4 3 2 1
Printed in the United States of America

The following figures are used with permission from Honthaner, Eve. *The Complete Film Production Handbook.* Boston: Butterworth–Heinemann, 1997.

Figure 7–4 (call sheet); Figure 7–9 (mileage log); Figure 7–12A (raw stock inventory form); Figure 7–12B (daily raw stock log); Figure 7–14 (location agreement); Figure 7–19 (purchase order); Figure 7–24 (daily cost overview)

The following figures are used with permission from the Screen Actors Guild, Los Angeles, CA.

Figure 7–6 (Exhibit G form); Figure 7–7 (SAG Taft-Hartley report); Figure 7–8 (SAG extra Taft-Hartley report); Figure 7–28 (SAG sign-in sheet); Figure 7–29 (SAG freelance contract); Figure 7–30 (SAG daily contract)

The following figures are used with permission from Screenplay Systems (for Movie Magic Budgeting & Scheduling), Burbank, CA.

Figure 5–1 (*Swingers* strip board [days 1–9]); Figure 5–2 (*Swingers* shooting schedule); Figure 5–3 (*Swingers* one-line schedule [days 1–9]); Figure 5–4 (*Swingers* day-out-of-days sheets [cast, extras, and props]); Figure 6–1 (sample budget form); Figure 6–2 (*Swingers* budget); Figure 6–3 (*Swingers* actualized budget); Figure 6–4 (sample budget 1); Figure 6–5 (sample budget 2); Figure 6–6 (sample budget 3); Figure 6–7 (sample budget 4 for *Kissing Jessica Stein*); Figure 7–2 (*Swingers* chart of accounts)

". . . what's really needed in producing is basically unrealistic optimism despite complete evidence to the contrary . . . Which is probably very similar to the definition of being absolutely crazy—you know, it's like refusal to accept the evidence that the world is not as you dream it to be . . ."

—*Ted Hope, Producer,* American Splendor, 21 Grams

Dedicated to Michael S. Wurmfeld, who taught us to dream while keeping our feet planted in reality.

CONTENTS

INTRODUCTION

When we were approached by IFP/Los Angeles (then IFP/West) to write a book about producing an independent film, we set out to create the manual we would have liked to have had early on. This manual, a step-by-step guide for the line producer, provides suggestions, examples, ideas, advice, tips, and rules that have worked for us. In it, we address some of the many questions filmmakers have asked us since our work on the film *Swingers*. We strove to structure the manual so that it will read in chronological order as you make your movie. Because it is common that the line producer on an *independent* film wears many hats and may also be the producer, we have also included some information that does *not* fall within the parameters of the line producer's responsibilities *per se* but is information we would have liked to have had when we were making various films.

In addition to this brass tacks information, we have included firsthand perspectives from some luminaries of the independent film world that we hope will both guide and inspire you. You can find the interviews *associated with quotes in the book* on the companion CD-ROM.

Keep in mind that there is no "right" way to make an independent movie. There is no formula. It is possible, however, to find a method to the madness. The bulk of the line producer's work occurs during pre-production. Strategy and overview are the big-picture essentials; organization and detail are the day-to-day essentials. We hope this book will guide you through both aspects of your work.

ACKNOWLEDGMENTS

Writing this manual has been an inspiring, rewarding, and challenging experience. (It has also been a test of our patience, will, and discipline!) We are most grateful for the opportunities, experience, and newfound knowledge it has afforded us.

We would like to express our sincere gratitude to Dawn Hudson and Michael Harrison of IFP/Los Angeles for their confidence in us and for giving us the opportunity to share our experiences and our knowledge. Their encouragement and enthusiasm were remarkable, and we thank them from the bottom of our hearts.

We would also like to express our gratitude and appreciation to all of the interviewees for their time and support: Tom Bernard, Peter Broderick, Michelle Byrd, Jon Favreau, Geoffrey Gilmore, Ted Hope, Marcus Hu, Ang Lee, Kasi Lemmons, Scott Mosier, Mira Nair, Mark Pogachefsky, John Sloss, Kevin Smith, Billy Bob Thornton, Christine Vachon, and Gary Winick. They have all been inspirational, and their experience and wisdom have helped to give this manual life.

We would like to thank Jack Ofield for tackling the enormous task of reviewing an early draft of the first edition, and providing us with suggestions, advice, and revisions that were pivotal in helping us organize and focus this manual.

We would like to thank Entertainment Partners (creator of the Movie Magic Scheduling and Budgeting programs) for allowing us the use of their products and forms and for their overall support. We are grateful to them for making film scheduling and budgeting easy and efficient, and therefore making our lives easier and saving us on many occasions.

We also thank all the staff of Focal Press who have made this book a reality. We are thankful for all of the wonderful resource guides and filmmaking handbooks to which we often referred both while working and writing this manual. (See Appendix A.) They have taught us much, and we are grateful to their authors. Thankfully, most of them now have Web sites too!

We would like to express our utmost appreciation and gratitude to Alex Blumberg, Kristen Brainard, Sean Cole, Laura Gabbert, Katherine Hellmouth, Mark Litwak, and Justin Schein. Their time, advice, generosity, knowledge, support, and encouragement have been invaluable. And thank you to Miles Ketley and Fox Searchlight for granting us permission to utilize the *Kissing Jessica Stein* materials included here.

We continue to be grateful to everyone who helped us on the first edition: Kiersta Burke, Michael Donaldson, Charles Herman-Wurmfeld, Julianne Kelley, George LaVoo, Sheila Levine, Doug Liman, Sean Mahoney, and the faculty, staff, and students at the UCLA School of Film and Television.

To our parents: Y'all must have had a screw loose when you raised us to believe we could take on such feats! With some luck and your unconditional encouragement, we did it. Your support, advice, and belief in us kept us going. We love you.

1 BEFORE YOU BEGIN

"Don't rush. Write a good script. Make sure it's something . . . . Let friends read it . . . . And get some other opinions."

—*Marcus Hu, Strand Releasing*

Before you begin official pre-production on your film, there are some important considerations to take into account that too often get overlooked. Making a movie requires a tremendous amount of hard work and a lot of money. The script is the fundamental building block to a successful film. Make sure the script represents the story you want to tell and that it is solid. One way to get some outside perspective is to select three trusted readers, who are not your relatives or friends and who are experienced at reading scripts, and ask them to give their honest opinion about your treatment or script. Are the characters interesting? Is the story engaging? Is there an audience for this film?

Another useful tool in gaining distance from your material enough to see if it is "working" is to conduct a staged or table reading, and we cannot stress enough what a valuable tool this can be. On *Kissing Jessica Stein*, we used readings as a three-pronged strategy: First, the readings served as a development tool, allowing us to hear what was and was not working in the script. Second, the readings functioned as a fundraising tool; that is, we invited potential investors to these readings, who aided us in securing a significant portion of our budget. Third, the readings served as rehearsal time, as several of the actors who participated in the readings were cast in the film and gained familiarity with the material through the readings (of course, the leads Helen and Jessica had written the parts for themselves, so their parts were "cast" from the outset).

Do not start pre-production without a realistic budget. Run the budget numbers to ensure that you can get your film through production and out of post-production. To give your script the best chance possible, you must assess the true needs of your film. Can you make the movie with the resources you have? If the answers is no, put this project on the back burner and find a different script. The negative repercussions of shooting a film without the proper resources for capturing the story at hand or to complete the film seem obvious—but just in case, we will say for the record that more likely than not the result of failing to obtain these resources will be a film that does not serve you (i.e., does not lead to other work) and that financially puts you in the red (be it other people's money or your own). Suffice it to say that this is not the best place to find oneself. In Chapters 4, 5, and 6 you will find detailed cost considerations as they relate to the script—but, in short, the fewer locations, stunts, special effects, extras, and so on needed to execute your story, the less it will cost you to make your film.

Give some thought to when you will shoot your film. Weather, for example, is a significant factor that should be taken into consideration. Does the film in question require rain or shine, or both? Is it largely an exterior daytime shoot? Will it be too hot or too cold to shoot it in the summer or winter, depending on the city in which you are shooting? In cold weather, productions tend to move more slowly. Equipment and film stock will be affected by extreme cold. Days are shorter in the winter, which means less light. For example, on *Swingers*, since one of the points of the story is that it is sunny in Los Angeles almost every day, to have shot in January might have been problematic in that we did not have the time or resources to arrange our production schedule around the weather. We were much safer to shoot in the summer, when Los Angeles is typically sunny every day.

Finally, if one of your goals is to travel to specific festivals with your film, you may want to plan your shoot according to the festival submission deadlines. Although there are festivals all year round, many people have their heart set on festivals such as Sundance, Telluride, Toronto, or Berlin. We caution people against rushing any aspect of the process based on a single festival deadline. However, because everyone seems to do it anyway, we feel it is important to mention. Further, will the needs of your film (equipment, crew, locations, and so on) be available at the time of year you plan to shoot? Ask yourself if you can you afford to work for little money and dedicate all of your time to your film.

2 THE SCRIPT

"The Swingers *script opened and closed with a helicopter shot. On low-budget films, those types of things get axed out fast. It's a compromise, but it's not a problem. It doesn't change the story. You just have to get creative."*

—Jon Favreau, writer, actor, and co-producer, Swingers

Although we come from a background of line producing, we never tell writers to think about the budget while they are writing. It causes too many creative roadblocks. During the first several passes, the writer should focus on making the script as rich as he or she dares. Then, reality must set in: You may not be able to secure the $10 million you had hoped for. You may have to work with $50,000 or $500,000. Remember, good films can be made for this amount of money. It is the line producer's job to read through the script with an eye toward the budget. It is the line producer's job to make the film as true to the script as possible for the money available. It is also the line producer's job to insist on changes if there is no way to achieve something within the available budget. Adjustments may need to be made to the script. For example, in the original *Swingers* script, Jon Favreau opened the film with a helicopter montage shot of Hollywood. We decided we could capture the essence of that opening scene by using photographs of Hollywood nightclubs shot with a 35-mm still camera long after principal photography had wrapped. This was a compromise that everyone agreed could be made without sacrificing the feel or the essence of the story.

On *Swingers*, it was clear that the scripted Los Angeles bars were essential to the story. We felt we could not go outside L.A. or to a stage to shoot the bar scenes and expect the movie to look and feel the way it should. In addition, it would have been much more costly to have shot on a stage dressed to look like a bar. The only compromise we made was substituting for a few scripted bars other bars that would agree to rental fees in line with our limited funds for this type of thing. For example, if you know L.A. well you will see that we shot the exterior of a bar called The Room and used the interior of the 3 of Clubs. We could not film at The Room based on our budget. On the other hand, the scripted Treasure Island Casino in Las Vegas was not essential to the overall feel of the film. We simply needed a casino, so we shot at one we could afford.

The *Swingers* script had a daunting number of extras for a low-budget film. They could not be eliminated because they were part of the look and feel of the movie. We decided to shoot in the bars while they were open to the public. This way, the bars did not lose money, and willing barflies and members of the crew served as our extras. We were careful to secure personal releases from all of them. (See Figure 7–2 for an example of a release form.)

On *Kissing Jessica Stein*, two months before we began shooting we asked the writers to make a "budget" pass on the script. We created a list of all budget-related elements that had to be taken into consideration for the new pass, and made some suggestions about how they might be implemented. We let the writers try to find answers that changed the story as little as possible, while enabling us to shoot the script on what had become a very low budget. Examples of the types of items on our list were: reducing the number of locations, eliminating potentially expensive or difficult-to-secure locations (such as a metroliner train or an airplane), and reducing the number of extras a given scene might require. One example of how the *Kissing Jessica Stein* script changed is that in the original script each of Jessica's bad dates occurred in a different locale—a restaurant, a cafe, a park, and so on. Our low-budget solution was to make all of her dates occur in one restaurant, which we thought justified by the notion that she might well take all of her first dates to the same place.

As a line producer, you must be creative when reading the script and making decisions with the writer and producer about rewrites. Your job is to figure out how to best capture a scene for the money you have. It is ultimately your job to assess what is affordable and what is not. Some sacrifices usually need to be made to accommodate a low-budget shoot. Changes may or may not require a rewrite. If rewrites prove necessary, be sensitive and tactful. The writer has invested a great deal of time, energy, and passion in the script and may be not be happy, willing, or agreeable when you ask for certain changes. Explain that your motivation is financial. Once all changes have been made to the script, you will have what is called the "white copy," the initial shooting script.

THE OPTION/PURCHASE AGREEMENT

The option/purchase agreement has many purposes. It should be used to obtain the rights to a previously written work (script, book, article) with the ultimate goal of turning it into your movie. Generally, you will use it first to option a script (or any literary property), not buy it outright. This gives you the right to develop the material, shop it around, and see if it is viable without spending the money it would cost to purchase the material. Typically, you option a property for 12 months, via a contract that contains a renewal clause. When and if you secure financing for the work, you can exercise your option to purchase the script in accordance with the terms of your option/purchase agreement.

If you do not have an option/purchase agreement or at least an attachment to the material you are working to produce, you may find yourself in a quandary: you may have done a great deal of work on the project and then be without the rights to make it. If you protect yourself from the outset you will avoid the difficulties that can arise if tensions and conflicts of interest occur among the parties making the film. Some key negotiation points are the length and cost of the option, the purchase price, the buyer's right to make changes to the material and own those changes, how many rewrites the initial option period includes, the credit granted to the writer, and the net profit participation of the writer. Figures 2–1 and 2-2 show sample option/purchase agreements

SAMPLE OPTION 1

DATE

Re: "Script"

Dear Owner/Writer:

The following is a proposed draft of the agreement reached between Producer and Producer (hereinafter referred to as "Producer") and Owner/Writer (hereinafter referred to as "Owner") with respect to the acquisition by Producer of an exclusive option to purchase (the "Option") motion picture, television, and allied rights in and to the screenplay written by Owner entitled "Script" (the "Work").

1. Option: Owner hereby grants to Producer the Option for a period of twelve (12) months to commence upon the date of signature ("Initial Option Period"). In consideration of the grant of such Option, Producer shall pay to Owner the sum of _________ Dollars, payable upon execution of this agreement, which payment shall be applicable against the purchase price set forth herein.

2. Setup Bonus (Second Option Period): If (but only if) prior to the expiration of the Initial Option Period, Producer enters into a written agreement with a third-party financial entity for the development of a motion picture based on the Work, Producer shall pay to Owner the sum of _________ Dollars. Such payment, which shall not be applicable against the purchase price set forth herein, shall be deemed to extend automatically the Initial Option Period for a period of twelve (12) additional months, commencing upon the expiration of the Initial Option Period (the "Second Option Period").

3. Purchase Price: If Producer elects to exercise the Option, it shall do so by written notice to Owner prior to the expiration of the applicable option period (it being understood, in any event, that commencement of principal photography of the initial version of the Work produced hereunder [the "Picture"] shall be deemed an exercise of the Option) and shall pay the Owner the following amounts:

Figure 2–1 Option/purchase agreement 1

A. Fixed Compensation. The fixed purchase price for exercising the option (the "Fixed Purchase Price") shall be an amount equal to two and one-half percent (2 1/2 percent) of the final approved cash production budget of the Picture, excluding any overhead charged by a principal financier, completion guaranty fees, deferred payments, finance costs, unspent portion of any contingency, and the fixed portion (i.e., the noncontingent portion) of the purchase price, it being further understood that the Fixed Purchase Price shall in no event be less than _________ Dollars nor more than _________ Dollars. The fixed purchase price shall be paid to Owner at a time and in a manner mutually agreed upon between Owner and Producer. Producer shall, in good faith, make every effort to make payment upon commencement of principal photography, however, the parties agree that such payment shall not be made if determined that it would forestall completion of the Picture.

B. Contingent Writer Compensation-Profit Participation. The contingent writer compensation for exercising the option shall be an amount equal to five percent (5 percent) of one hundred percent (100 percent) of the net profits of the Picture to Owner for sole "Screenplay by" credit in connection with such picture. For the purposes hereof, "net profits" shall be defined, computed, and payable in the same manner as for Producer.

C. Contingent Writer/Director Compensation-Profit Participation. The contingent writer/director compensation for exercising the option shall be an amount equal to ten percent (10 percent) of one hundred percent (100 percent) of the net profits of the Picture to Owner for sole "Directed by" and sole "Screenplay by" credit in connection with such picture. In the event that Owner directs said picture, he shall receive "A film by" credit in connection with such picture.

D. Contingent Writer/Actor/Director Compensation-Profit Participation. The contingent writer/actor/director compensation for exercising the option shall be an amount equal to fifteen percent (15 percent) of one hundred percent (100 percent) of the net profits of the Picture to Owner for sole "Screenplay by," "Directed by," and "Starring" credit in connection with such picture.

4. Subsequent Versions:

A. Sequels and Remakes: Fifty percent (50 percent) of the purchase price, and profit participation set forth in paragraph 2 hereof with respect to each sequel; thirty-three and one-third percent (33 1/3 percent) of such purchase price, and profit participation with respect to each remake.

B. Television Series: A royalty (the "Applicable Royalty") of Two Thousand Five Hundred Dollars ($2,500.00) with respect to each new 30-minute episode produced, and Three Thousand Dollars ($3,000.00) with respect to each new one-hour episode produced. With respect to spin-offs, one-half (1/2) the applicable royalty; with respect to generic spin-offs, one-third (1/3) the applicable royalty. With respect to each of the first five domestic reruns of any such episode, Producer shall pay to Owner twenty percent (20 percent) of the initial royalty paid.

C. MOW/Miniseries: $25,000 per hour pro rata.

5. Credit: Although this agreement is not subject to WGA jurisdiction, WGA credit determination standards shall be used in determining the writing credit to be afforded to Owner in connection with the Picture, and Owner shall be afforded such credit wherever the WGA requires such credit to be given. Anything herein to the contrary notwithstanding, in the event the WGA is willing to conduct a credit determination with respect to the Picture, the parties agree to submit to same.

6. Further Revision of Work: In the event Producer requires any further revision or polish of the Work after delivery of the Work, Owner shall be guaranteed the right to write the revisions or polish thereof that Producer requires (provided Owner is available to do so in accordance with Producer's reasonable time requirements).

7. Rights Granted and Reserved: The Option and purchase agreement is for the exclusive, perpetual, and worldwide theatrical motion picture, television, allied, and subsidiary rights in and to the Work, and all elements thereof, including theatrical motion picture, television (whether filmed, taped, or otherwise recorded, and including series rights), cassette and other compact devices, sequel, remake, and advertising rights (including 7,500-word excerpts and synopses publication rights); all rights to exploit, distribute, and exhibit any motion picture or other production produced hereunder, in all media whether now known or hereafter devised; merchandising, soundtrack, music publication, and exploitation rights; the right to use Owner's name on or in connection with the exploitation of the rights granted hereunder; and all other rights customarily contained in connection with option and literary purchase agreements, which shall be binding upon and inure to the benefit of the parties

(continued)

Figure 2–1 Option/purchase agreement 1 (continued)

hereto and their successors, representatives, assigns, and licensees. Owner reserves all publishing rights in the Work (but same shall not prevent Producer from authorizing publication of "the making of"-type books); all interactive game rights therein; and all live stage rights therein (subject to a 7/10 year holdback).

8. Representations and Warranties: Owner represents and warrants that Owner has the right to enter into this agreement and grant the rights herein granted; that the Work is original with Owner; and that to the best of Owner's knowledge no part thereof will infringe upon the property rights, rights of privacy, or any other rights of any parties, nor does any part of the Work constitute a libel, slander, or defamation of any party. Owner makes no representations or warranties with respect to any material that may be included in any version of the Work produced hereunder by Producer that was not contained in the Work, and Producer agrees to indemnify and hold harmless Owner from and against any damages (including reasonable attorney's fees) sustained by Owner as a result of any such material included in such version that was not contained in the Work or resulting from the production, distribution, and exploitation of any version of the Work produced hereunder.

9. Payments to Owner: Subject to Section 3(A), all sums due to Owner hereunder shall be made by checks payable to Owner at rule ______________________________

10. More Formal Agreements: The parties will enter into more formal agreements, if any (which may be negotiated in good faith between the parties), as may be necessary to more fully effectuate the purposes and intents of the foregoing, incorporating all the terms herein, together with such additional provisions as are customary in the entertainment industry in agreements of this nature, including but not limited to ownership of the Picture, force majeure, editing rights (inclusion of commercial inserts and logos), and waiver of equitable relief. Until the execution of such more formal agreements, however, this document shall be deemed binding upon the parties hereto.

AGREED TO AND ACCEPTED:

Producer:

Producer/Producer

By: ______________________________

Its

____

Its

Owner:

Owner/Writer

____

Owner/Writer

SS# ______________________________

Figure 2–1 Option/purchase agreement 1 (continued)

from actual deals we have made. Note that these are not "standard" agreements. We have included them because they reflect the flexibility of the independent filmmaking world.

The terms of the option/purchase agreement are negotiable and should reflect the needs and resources of the parties involved. Strange things can happen when money is lost or gained, so it is best to establish the terms up front. When you sign the option, agree on what the purchase price will be. Usually, the purchase price amounts to about 2.5 percent of the production budget. The purpose here is to agree beforehand so that no misunderstandings arise if you sell your "no-budget" film for $3 million. When a script is optioned, it gives the buyer the exclusive right to shop the material. It is like entering into a monogamous relationship. If you are the writer and you sign an

SAMPLE OPTION 2

DATE

Re: "SCRIPT"

Dear Owner/Writer:

The following is a proposed draft of the agreement reached between Producer and Producer (hereinafter referred to as "Producer") and Owner/Writer (herein after referred to as "Owner") with respect to the acquisition by Producer of an exclusive option (the "Option") on motion picture, television, and allied rights in and to the screenplay written by Owner entitled "Work" (the "Work").

1. Option: Owner hereby grants to Producer the Option for a period of six (6) months to commence upon the date of signature ("Initial Option Period"). In consideration of the grant of such Option, Producer shall pay to Owner the sum of One (1) Dollar, payable upon execution of this agreement, which payment shall be applicable against the purchase price hereafter set forth.

2. Setup Bonus (Second Option Period): If (but only if) prior to the expiration thereof, Producer enters into a written agreement with a third-party financial entity for the development of a motion picture based on the Work, Producer shall pay to Owner the sum of _________ Dollars. Such payment, which shall not be applicable against the purchase price herein set forth, shall be deemed to extend automatically the Initial Option Period for a period of twelve (12) additional months, commencing upon the expiration of the Initial Option Period (the "Second Option Period").

3. Purchase Price:

A. Fixed Compensation. If Producer elects to exercise the Option, it shall do so by written notice to Owner prior to the expiration of the applicable option period (it being understood, in any event, that commencement of principal photography of the initial version of the Work produced hereunder [the "Picture"] shall be deemed an exercise of the Option). Further, payment of the fixed purchase price, which shall be an amount equal to two and one-half percent (2 1/2 percent) of the final approved cash production budget of the Picture, excluding any overhead charged by a principal financier, completion guaranty fees, deferred payments, finance costs, unspent portion of any contingency, and the fixed portion (i.e., not the contingent portion) of the purchase price, it being further understood that such purchase price shall in no event be less than _________ Dollars nor more than _________ Dollars, which payment shall be made upon commencement of principal photography. Producer agrees that if, at the time they exercise the Option, the final approved production budget of the Picture has not been determined, it shall pay to Owner upon such exercise the minimum amount of the fixed purchase price and shall pay any further amount due upon the determination of such final approved cash production budget.

B. Contingent Compensation - Profit Participation. An amount equal to five percent (5 percent) of one hundred percent (100 percent) of the net profits of the Picture if Owner receives sole "Screenplay by" credit in connection with such picture, reducible to two and one-half percent (2 1/2 percent) of the net profits of the Picture if Owner receives shared "Screenplay by" credit. For the purposes hereof, "net profits" shall be defined, computed, and payable in the same manner as for Producer.

4. Consulting Services of Owner. If, but only if, Producer actually produces the Picture, Producer agrees to engage Owner as a creative consultant. Owner shall be paid _________ Dollars per week during principal photography of the Picture, but in any event, Owner shall be paid no less than _________ Dollars nor more than _________. The Owner/Consultant's transportation and accommodations to production locations shall be paid for by Producer.

5. Subsequent Versions:

A. Sequels and Remakes: Fifty percent (50 percent) of the purchase price, and profit participation set forth in paragraph 2 hereof with respect to each sequel; thirty-three and one-third percent (33 1/3 percent) of such purchase price, and profit participation with respect to each remake. It is further understood that in the event Owner receives sole

(continued)

Figure 2–2 Option/purchase agreement 2

"Screenplay by" credit with respect to the Picture, Owner shall be given the opportunity to write all such remakes or sequels (if any) upon terms to be negotiated in good faith between the parties, but in no event on terms less favorable to Owner than those set forth in this agreement.

B. Television Series: A royalty (the "Applicable Royalty") of Two Thousand Five Hundred Dollars ($2,500.00) with respect to each new 30-minute episode produced, and Three Thousand Dollars ($3,000.00) with respect to each new one-hour episode produced. With respect to spin-offs, one-half (1/2) the applicable royalty; with respect to generic spin-offs, one-third (1/3) the applicable royalty. With respect to each of the first five domestic reruns of any such episode, Producer shall pay to Owner twenty (20 percent) percent of the initial royalty paid.

C. MOW/Miniseries: $25,000 per hour pro rata.

6. Credit: Although this agreement is not subject to WGA jurisdiction, WGA credit determination standards shall be used in determining the writing credit to be afforded to Owner in connection with the Picture, and Owner shall be afforded such credit wherever the WGA requires such credit to be given. Anything herein to the contrary notwithstanding, in the event the WGA is willing to conduct a credit determination with respect to the Picture, the parties agree to submit to same.

7. Further Revision of Work: In the event Producer requires any further revision or polish of the Work after delivery of the Work. Owner shall be guaranteed the right to write the revisions or polish thereof that Producer requires (provided Owner is available to do so in accordance with Producer's reasonable time requirements), for a fee to be negotiated in good faith between the parties. In the event Producer sets up the Picture with a third party (i.e., studio or independent film company), Owner/Writer shall be granted the right to write any revisions or polishes thereof agreed upon by all parties.

8. Rights Granted and Reserved: The option and purchase agreement is for the exclusive, perpetual, and worldwide theatrical motion picture, television, allied, and subsidiary rights in and to the Work, and all elements thereof, including theatrical motion picture, television (whether filmed, taped, or otherwise recorded, and including series rights), cassette and other compact devices, sequel, remake, and advertising rights (including 7,500-word excerpts and synopses publication rights); all rights to exploit, distribute, and exhibit any motion picture or other production produced hereunder, in all media whether now known or hereafter devised; merchandising, soundtrack, music publication, and exploitation rights; the right to use Owner's name on or in connection with the exploitation of the rights granted hereunder; and all other rights customarily contained in connection with option and literary purchase agreements, which shall be binding upon and inure to the benefit of the parties hereto and their successors, representatives, assigns, and licensees. Owner reserves all publishing rights in the Work (but same shall not prevent Producer from authorizing publication of "the making of"-type books); all interactive game rights therein; and all live stage rights therein (subject to a 7/10 year holdback).

9. Representations and Warranties: Owner represents and warrants that Owner has the right to enter into this agreement and grant the rights herein granted; that the Work is original with Owner and that to the best of Owner's knowledge no part thereof will infringe upon the property rights, rights of privacy, or any other rights of any parties, nor does any part of the Work constitute a libel, slander, or defamation of any party. Owner makes no representations or warranties with respect to any material that may be included in any version of the Work produced hereunder by Producer that was not contained in the Work, and Producer agrees to indemnify and hold harmless Owner from and against any damages (including reasonable attorney's fees) sustained by Owner as a result of any such material included in such version that was not contained in the Work or resulting from the production, distribution, and exploitation of any version of the Work produced hereunder.

10. Payments to Owner. All sums due to Owner hereunder shall be made by checks payable to Owner at________.

11. More Formal Agreements: The parties will enter into more formal agreements, if any (which may be negotiated in good faith between the parties), as may be necessary to more fully effectuate the purposes and intents of the foregoing, incorporating all the terms herein, together with such additional provisions as are customary in the entertainment industry in agreements of this nature, including but not limited to ownership of the Picture, force majeure, editing rights

Figure 2–2 Option/purchase agreement 2 (continued)

(inclusion of commercial inserts and logos), and waiver of equitable relief (all of which such additional provisions are deemed incorporated herein). Until the execution of such more formal agreements, however, this document shall be deemed binding upon the parties hereto.

AGREED TO AND ACCEPTED:

Producer:

Producer/Producer

By: ______________________

Its

____

Its

Owner:

Owner/Writer

____

Owner/Writer

SS# ______________________

Figure 2–2 Option/purchase agreement 2 (continued)

option/purchase agreement with another party, you cannot pitch your script to other people or companies during the term of the agreement.

The cost of the option is different from the purchase price. Usually, a much smaller sum is paid for the option itself. Depending on the circumstances, the option price can be any mutually agreed-upon sum, from $1 on up. Figure 2–1 shows a deal we made with a writer who wanted to direct and star in the film. We agreed as producers to do everything in our power to effectuate that, but we also felt it was important to have some flexibility in the event we could not garner the necessary financing with a first-time director who was also an unknown actor. Therefore, we created three possible scenarios (sections 3B, C, and D in the agreement). We also agreed to give the writer the right to execute any and all script changes and a setup bonus. None of these things is necessarily standard. However, the agreement worked for the situation, time, place, and people involved.

In Figure 2–2, the option period is for only six months. The writer wanted to remain involved in the project, and we satisfied that request by granting him a paid consultant position on the film in the event the picture went into production (paragraph 4). We also gave him the right to all rewrites if the film were to be produced (paragraph 7) and the right to first negotiation as the writer on any sequel or remake (paragraph 5A).

Each situation is unique, and part of the negotiation process is determining what makes sense for the project and the parties involved. You want to be generous, but you also want to be savvy. Be careful that none of the points you are agreeing to will make the project unattractive to potential investors or talent. For example, you do not want to give up 75 percent of net profit or an executive producer credit and not have those cards to play when you need them down the line (for other talent, investors, or others). The option/purchase agreement will probably be the first in a long line of deals and agreements you will need to make. Do not give up too much of the pie at this early stage. As you will see from the sample agreements included here, we have strayed from the norm when and where it worked for the parties involved.

Appendix A: Resource Guide at the back of this book lists guidebooks to legal issues and contracts in the entertainment industry. We recommend you work with a reputable lawyer, but if you cannot make that arrangement it is possible to navigate through this on your own. Be thorough. Read as much as you can. Many standard legal contracts exist that protect all parties involved. It is advisable to let the system work for you and have the proper paperwork in place.

REGISTRATION WITH THE WRITERS GUILD OF AMERICA

Registering your script with the Writers Guild of America (WGA) serves as a record of the script's completion date and protects your original work and ideas. It is an easy process that can now be done online, in person, or by mail. We cannot stress enough the importance of taking these easy steps. It will protect your idea or your script and it is the professional thing to do. It is so easy, there is no excuse not to do it. Registration of your script (treatment, synopsis, outlines, and written ideas) with the WGA through The Writers Guild's Registration Service (or Intellectual Property Registry) is available to members and nonmembers of the Guild.

Submission Requirements for WGA Registration

The following are the requirements for submission of a script to the WGA for intellectual property registration.

- An unbound copy of the script
- A cover sheet with the title and the writer's full legal name
- The writer's Social Security number, return address, and telephone number (if there is more than one writer, you must choose one)
- A check for (currently) $20 for nonmembers or $10 for members

When you receive your registration number, enter it on the front page of your script. The term of registration is five years, which can be renewed. Only the registrant has access to the registration information, and will need to present a photo ID for access or renewal. On the West Coast, the WGA is located at:

WGA, West, Intellectual Property Registry
7000 W. Third St.
Los Angeles, CA 90048
Phone: 323/782-4500; fax: 323/782-4803

On the East Coast, the WGA is located at:

WGA, East, Intellectual Property Registry
555 W. 57th St.
New York, NY 10019
Phone: 212/767-7800; fax: 212/582-1909

Online Registration

The Writers Guild of America West Intellectual Property Online Registry is found at the following address:

https://www.writersguild.org/webrss/dataentry.asp

The following are procedures to be followed for WGA online registration:

- Fill in material details and registrant/author(s) information and other required fields. (Authors *cannot* be added to an existing registration once it is submitted.)
- Browse and select the file to be submitted. (File names must be limited to 35 characters or less for uploading.) When submitting online, the preferred file formats are ASCII, PDF (Adobe Acrobat), Word, Final Draft, and Movie Magic Screenwriter 2000. You will be prompted to select the file on your hard drive that you wish to register. Note that only one file for each online registration request will be accepted. Currently the file size limit is 10 MB.
- Submit your registration request.

It is important to note that online registrations are effective immediately and cannot be changed in any way once submitted. Online processing prices are the same as mail and in-person submissions. Once submitted, you will receive a registration certificate in the mail several weeks later.

COPYRIGHT

Registration with the WGA does not take the place of copyright. Copyright protects "original works of authorship," and the copyright claimant can be the author or the owner of exclusive rights to the work. Registering your script with the U.S. Copyright Office in Washington, D.C. is easy and the forms can now be printed from their Web site (*www.loc.gov/copyright/*). Again, this is an easy step to take and a worthwhile one. Hopefully, you will never run into the problems that can arise when and if someone steals your idea, but copyright and WGA registration really do protect you. Furthermore, chain of title, should you ever sell the property, will require copyright registration, so you might as well get it over with. Submission requirements are as follows:

- A completed and signed Form PA (See Figures 2–3 and 2–4.)
- A check for $30 payable to the Register of Copyrights
- One copy of the script

These three items should be submitted in one envelope to:

The Library of Congress
Copyright Office
101 Independence Avenue, S.E.
Washington, D.C. 20559–6000

Registration is effective the day the Copyright Office receives your submission, but you may not receive paperwork for up to 16 weeks. When you make a production deal, secure financing from a bank, or deliver your film to a distribution company, evidence of the chain of title will be required. At a minimum, you will have to provide a certificate of copyright, the option/purchase agreement, and the writer's agreement if there is one. (See Appendix A: Resource Guide for sources of assistance with copyright law.)

Filling Out Application Form PA

Detach and read these instructions before completing this form.
Make sure all applicable spaces have been filled in before you return this form.

BASIC INFORMATION

When to Use This Form: Use Form PA for registration of published or unpublished works of the performing arts. This class includes works prepared for the purpose of being "performed" directly before an audience or indirectly "by means of any device or process." Works of the performing arts include: (1) musical works, including any accompanying words; (2) dramatic works, including any accompanying music; (3) pantomimes and choreographic works; and (4) motion pictures and other audiovisual works.

Deposit to Accompany Application: An application for copyright registration must be accompanied by a deposit consisting of copies or phonorecords representing the entire work for which registration is made. The following are the general deposit requirements as set forth in the statute:

Unpublished Work: Deposit one complete copy (or phonorecord).

Published Work: Deposit two complete copies (or one phonorecord) of the best edition.

Work First Published Outside the United States: Deposit one complete copy (or phonorecord) of the first foreign edition.

Contribution to a Collective Work: Deposit one complete copy (or phonorecord) of the best edition of the collective work.

Motion Pictures: Deposit *both* of the following: (1) a separate written description of the contents of the motion picture; and (2) for a published work, one complete copy of the best edition of the motion picture; or, for an unpublished work, one complete copy of the motion picture or identifying material. Identifying material may be either an audiorecording of the entire soundtrack or one frame enlargement or similar visual print from each 10-minute segment.

The Copyright Notice: For works first published on or after March 1, 1989, the law provides that a copyright notice in a specified form "may be placed on all publicly distributed copies from which the work can be visually perceived." Use of the copyright notice is the responsibility of the copyright owner and does not require advance permission from the Copyright Office. The required form of the notice for copies generally consists of three elements: (1) the symbol "©", or the word "Copyright," or the abbreviation "Copr."; (2) the year of first publication; and (3) the name of the owner of copyright. For example: "© 1995 Jane Cole." The notice is to be affixed to the copies "in such manner and location as to give reasonable notice of the claim of copyright." Works first published prior to March 1, 1989, **must** carry the notice or risk loss of copyright protection.

For information about requirements for works published before March 1, 1989, or other copyright information, write: Information Section, LM-401, Copyright Office, Library of Congress, Washington, D.C. 20559-6000.

PRIVACY ACT ADVISORY STATEMENT Required by the Privacy Act of 1974 (P.L. 93-579)
The authority for requesting this information is title 17, U.S.C., secs. 409 and 410. Furnishing the requested information is voluntary. But if the information is not furnished, it may be necessary to delay or refuse registration and you may not be entitled to certain relief, remedies, and benefits provided in chapters 4 and 5 of title 17, U.S.C.

The principal uses of the requested information are the establishment and maintenance of a public record and the examination of the application for compliance with legal requirements.

Other routine uses include public inspection and copying, preparation of public indexes, preparation of public catalogs of copyright registrations, and preparation of search reports upon request.

NOTE: No other advisory statement will be given in connection with this application. Please keep this statement and refer to it if we communicate with you regarding this application.

LINE-BY-LINE INSTRUCTIONS

Please type or print using black ink.

1 SPACE 1: Title

Title of This Work: Every work submitted for copyright registration must be given a title to identify that particular work. If the copies or phonorecords of the work bear a title (or an identifying phrase that could serve as a title), transcribe that wording *completely* and *exactly* on the application. Indexing of the registration and future identification of the work will depend on the information you give here. If the work you are registering is an entire "collective work" (such as a collection of plays or songs), give the overall title of the collection. If you are registering one or more individual contributions to a collective work, give the title of each contribution, followed by the title of the collection. For an unpublished collection, you may give the titles of the individual works after the collection title.

Previous or Alternative Titles: Complete this space if there are any additional titles for the work under which someone searching for the registration might be likely to look, or under which a document pertaining to the work might be recorded.

Nature of This Work: Briefly describe the general nature or character of the work being registered for copyright. Examples: "Music"; "Song Lyrics"; "Words and Music"; "Drama"; "Musical Play"; "Choreography"; "Pantomime"; "Motion Picture"; "Audiovisual Work."

2 SPACE 2: Author(s)

General Instructions: After reading these instructions, decide who are the "authors" of this work for copyright purposes. Then, unless the work is a "collective work," give the requested information about every "author" who contributed any appreciable amount of copyrightable matter to this version of the work. If you need further space, request additional Continuation Sheets. In the case of a collective work, such as a songbook or a collection of plays, give the information about the author of the collective work as a whole.

Name of Author: The fullest form of the author's name should be given. Unless the work was "made for hire," the individual who actually created the work is its "author." In the case of a work made for hire, the statute provides that "the employer or other person for whom the work was prepared is considered the author."

What is a "Work Made for Hire"? A "work made for hire" is defined as: (1) "a work prepared by an employee within the scope of his or her employment"; or (2) "a work specially ordered or commissioned for use as a contribution to a collective work, as a part of a motion picture or other audiovisual work, as a translation, as a supplementary work, as a compilation, as an instructional text, as a test, as answer material for a test, or as an atlas, if the parties expressly agree in a written instrument signed by them that the work shall be considered a work made for hire." If you have checked "Yes" to indicate that the work was "made for hire," you must give the full legal name of the employer (or other person for whom the work was prepared). You may also include the name of the employee along with the name of the employer (for example: "Elster Music Co., employer for hire of John Ferguson").

"Anonymous" or "Pseudonymous" Work: An author's contribution to a work is "anonymous" if that author is not identified on the copies or phonorecords of the work. An author's contribution to a work is "pseudonymous" if that author is identified on the copies or phonorecords under a fictitious name. If the work is "anonymous" you may: (1) leave the line blank; or (2) state "anonymous" on the line; or (3) reveal the author's identity. If the work is "pseudonymous" you may: (1) leave the line blank; or (2) give the pseudonym and identify it as such (example: "Huntley Haverstock, pseudonym"); or (3) reveal the author's name, making clear which is the real name and which is the pseudonym (for example: "Judith Barton, whose pseudonym is Madeline Elster"). However, the citizenship or domicile of the author **must** be given in all cases.

Dates of Birth and Death: If the author is dead, the statute requires that the year of death be included in the application unless the work is anonymous or pseudonymous. The author's birth date is optional, but is useful as a form of identification. Leave this space blank if the author's contribution was a "work made for hire."

Author's Nationality or Domicile: Give the country of which the author is a citizen, or the country in which the author is domiciled. Nationality or domicile **must** be given in all cases.

Nature of Authorship: Give a brief general statement of the nature of this particular author's contribution to the work. Examples: "Words"; "Coauthor of Music"; "Words and Music"; "Arrangement"; "Coauthor of Book and Lyrics"; "Dramatization"; "Screen Play"; "Compilation and English Translation"; "Editorial Revisions."

Figure 2–3 Instructions for filling out Form PA

3 SPACE 3: Creation and Publication

General Instructions: Do not confuse "creation" with "publication." Every application for copyright registration must state "the year in which creation of the work was completed." Give the date and nation of first publication only if the work has been published.

Creation: Under the statute, a work is "created" when it is fixed in a copy or phonorecord for the first time. Where a work has been prepared over a period of time, the part of the work existing in fixed form on a particular date constitutes the created work on that date. The date you give here should be the year in which the author completed the particular version for which registration is now being sought, even if other versions exist or if further changes or additions are planned.

Publication: The statute defines "publication" as "the distribution of copies or phonorecords of a work to the public by sale or other transfer of ownership, or by rental, lease, or lending"; a work is also "published" if there has been an "offering to distribute copies or phonorecords to a group of persons for purposes of further distribution, public performance, or public display." Give the full date (month, day, year) when, and the country where, publication first occurred. If first publication took place simultaneously in the United States and other countries, it is sufficient to state "U.S.A."

4 SPACE 4: Claimant(s)

Name(s) and Address(es) of Copyright Claimant(s): Give the name(s) and address(es) of the copyright claimant(s) in this work even if the claimant is the same as the author. Copyright in a work belongs initially to the author of the work (including, in the case of a work made for hire, the employer or other person for whom the work was prepared). The copyright claimant is either the author of the work or a person or organization to whom the copyright initially belonging to the author has been transferred.

Transfer: The statute provides that, if the copyright claimant is not the author, the application for registration must contain "a brief statement of how the claimant obtained ownership of the copyright." If any copyright claimant named in space 4 is not an author named in space 2, give a brief statement explaining how the claimant(s) obtained ownership of the copyright. Examples: "By written contract"; "Transfer of all rights by author"; "Assignment"; "By will." Do not attach transfer documents or other attachments or riders.

5 SPACE 5: Previous Registration

General Instructions: The questions in space 5 are intended to show whether an earlier registration has been made for this work and, if so, whether there is any basis for a new registration. As a general rule, only one basic copyright registration can be made for the same version of a particular work.

Same Version: If this version is substantially the same as the work covered by a previous registration, a second registration is not generally possible unless: (1) the work has been registered in unpublished form and a second registration is now being sought to cover this first published edition; or (2) someone other than the author is identified as copyright claimant in the earlier registration, and the author is now seeking registration in his or her own name. If either of these two exceptions apply, check the appropriate box and give the earlier registration number and date. Otherwise, do not submit Form PA; instead, write the Copyright Office for information about supplementary registration or recordation of transfers of copyright ownership.

Changed Version: If the work has been changed, and you are now seeking registration to cover the additions or revisions, check the last box in space 5, give the earlier registration number and date, and complete both parts of space 6 in accordance with the instructions below.

Previous Registration Number and Date: If more than one previous registration has been made for the work, give the number and date of the latest registration.

6 SPACE 6: Derivative Work or Compilation

General Instructions: Complete space 6 if this work is a "changed version," "compilation," or "derivative work," and if it incorporates one or more earlier works that have already been published or registered for copyright or that have fallen into the public domain. A "compilation" is defined as "a work formed by the collection and assembling of preexisting materials or of data that are selected, coordinated, or arranged in such a way that the resulting work as a whole constitutes an original work of authorship." A "derivative work" is "a work based on one or more preexisting works." Examples of derivative works include musical arrangements, dramatizations, translations, abridgments, condensations, motion picture versions, or "any other form in which a work may be recast, transformed, or adapted." Derivative works also include works "consisting of editorial revisions, annotations, or other modifications" if these changes, as a whole, represent an original work of authorship.

Preexisting Material (space 6a): Complete this space and space 6b for derivative works. In this space identify the preexisting work that has been recast, transformed, or adapted. For example, the preexisting material might be: "French version of Hugo's 'Le Roi s'amuse'." Do not complete this space for compilations.

Material Added to This Work (space 6b): Give a brief, general statement of the **additional** new material covered by the copyright claim for which registration is sought. In the case of a derivative work, identify this new material. Examples: "Arrangement for piano and orchestra"; "Dramatization for television"; "New film version"; "Revisions throughout; Act III completely new." If the work is a compilation, give a brief, general statement describing both the material that has been compiled **and** the compilation itself. Example: "Compilation of 19th Century Military Songs."

7,8,9 SPACE 7, 8, 9: Fee, Correspondence, Certification, Return Address

Deposit Account: If you maintain a Deposit Account in the Copyright Office, identify it in space 7. Otherwise leave the space blank and send the fee of $20 with your application and deposit.

Correspondence (space 7): This space should contain the name, address, area code, and telephone number of the person to be consulted if correspondence about this application becomes necessary.

Certification (space 8): The application cannot be accepted unless it bears the date and the **handwritten signature** of the author or other copyright claimant, or of the owner of exclusive right(s), or of the duly authorized agent of the author, claimant, or owner of exclusive right(s).

Address for Return of Certificate (space 9): The address box must be completed legibly since the certificate will be returned in a window envelope.

MORE INFORMATION

How to Register a Recorded Work: If the musical or dramatic work that you are registering has been recorded (as a tape, disk, or cassette), you may choose either copyright application Form PA (Performing Arts) or Form SR (Sound Recordings), depending on the purpose of the registration.

Form PA should be used to register the underlying musical composition or dramatic work. Form SR has been developed specifically to register a "sound recording" as defined by the Copyright Act—a work resulting from the "fixation of a series of sounds," separate and distinct from the underlying musical or dramatic work. Form SR should be used when the copyright claim is limited to the sound recording itself. (In one instance, Form SR may also be used to file for a copyright registration for both kinds of works—see (4) below.) Therefore:

(1) **File Form PA** if you are seeking to register the musical or dramatic work, not the "sound recording," even though what you deposit for copyright purposes may be in the form of a phonorecord.

(2) **File Form PA** if you are seeking to register the audio portion of an audiovisual work, such as a motion picture soundtrack; these are considered integral parts of the audiovisual work.

(3) **File Form SR** if you are seeking to register the "sound recording" itself, that is, the work that results from the fixation of a series of musical, spoken, or other sounds, but not the underlying musical or dramatic work.

(4) **File Form SR** if you are the copyright claimant for both the underlying musical or dramatic work and the sound recording, *and* you prefer to register both on the same form.

(5) **File both forms PA and SR** if the copyright claimant for the underlying work and sound recording differ, or you prefer to have separate registration for them.

"Copies" and "Phonorecords": To register for copyright, you are required to deposit "copies" or "phonorecords." These are defined as follows:

Musical compositions may be embodied (fixed) in "copies," objects from which a work can be read or visually perceived, directly or with the aid of a machine or device, such as manuscripts, books, sheet music, film, and videotape. They may also be fixed in "phonorecords," objects embodying fixations of sounds, such as tapes and phonograph disks, commonly known as phonograph records. For example, a song (the work to be registered) can be reproduced in sheet music ("copies") or phonograph records ("phonorecords"), or both.

Figure 2–3 Instructions for filling out Form PA (continued)

FEE CHANGES
Registration filing fees are effective through June 30, 1999. For information on the fee changes, write the Copyright Office, check http://www.loc.gov/copyright, or call (202) 707-3000. Beginning as early as January 1, 2000, the Copyright Office may impose a service charge when insufficient fees are received.

FORM PA
For a Work of the Performing Arts
UNITED STATES COPYRIGHT OFFICE

REGISTRATION NUMBER

PA PAU

EFFECTIVE DATE OF REGISTRATION

Month Day Year

DO NOT WRITE ABOVE THIS LINE. IF YOU NEED MORE SPACE, USE A SEPARATE CONTINUATION SHEET.

1
TITLE OF THIS WORK ▼

PREVIOUS OR ALTERNATIVE TITLES ▼

NATURE OF THIS WORK ▼ See instructions

2
a NAME OF AUTHOR ▼ — DATES OF BIRTH AND DEATH Year Born ▼ Year Died ▼

Was this contribution to the work a "work made for hire"? M Yes M No — AUTHOR'S NATIONALITY OR DOMICILE Name of Country OR { Citizen of ▶ / Domiciled in ▶ — WAS THIS AUTHOR'S CONTRIBUTION TO THE WORK Anonymous? M Yes M No Pseudonymous? M Yes M No — If the answer to either of these questions is "Yes," see detailed instructions.

NATURE OF AUTHORSHIP Briefly describe nature of material created by this author in which copyright is claimed. ▼

b NAME OF AUTHOR ▼ — DATES OF BIRTH AND DEATH Year Born ▼ Year Died ▼

Was this contribution to the work a "work made for hire"? M Yes M No — AUTHOR'S NATIONALITY OR DOMICILE Name of Country OR { Citizen of ▶ / Domiciled in ▶ — WAS THIS AUTHOR'S CONTRIBUTION TO THE WORK Anonymous? M Yes M No Pseudonymous? M Yes M No — If the answer to either of these questions is "Yes," see detailed instructions.

NATURE OF AUTHORSHIP Briefly describe nature of material created by this author in which copyright is claimed. ▼

c NAME OF AUTHOR ▼ — DATES OF BIRTH AND DEATH Year Born ▼ Year Died ▼

Was this contribution to the work a "work made for hire"? M Yes M No — AUTHOR'S NATIONALITY OR DOMICILE Name of Country OR { Citizen of ▶ / Domiciled in ▶ — WAS THIS AUTHOR'S CONTRIBUTION TO THE WORK Anonymous? M Yes M No Pseudonymous? M Yes M No — If the answer to either of these questions is "Yes," see detailed instructions.

NATURE OF AUTHORSHIP Briefly describe nature of material created by this author in which copyright is claimed. ▼

NOTE
Under the law, the "author" of a "work made for hire" is generally the employer, not the employee (see instructions). For any part of this work that was "made for hire" check "Yes" in the space provided, give the employer (or other person for whom the work was prepared) as "Author" of that part, and leave the space for dates of birth and death blank.

3
a YEAR IN WHICH CREATION OF THIS WORK WAS COMPLETED — This information must be given ◀ Year in all cases.
b DATE AND NATION OF FIRST PUBLICATION OF THIS PARTICULAR WORK — Complete this information ONLY if this work has been published. Month ▶ Day ▶ Year ▶ ◀ Nation

4
COPYRIGHT CLAIMANT(S) Name and address must be given even if the claimant is the same as the author given in space 2. ▼

See instructions before completing this space.

TRANSFER If the claimant(s) named here in space 4 is (are) different from the author(s) named in space 2, give a brief statement of how the claimant(s) obtained ownership of the copyright. ▼

APPLICATION RECEIVED
ONE DEPOSIT RECEIVED
TWO DEPOSITS RECEIVED
FUNDS RECEIVED
DO NOT WRITE HERE OFFICE USE ONLY

MORE ON BACK ▶ • Complete all applicable spaces (numbers 5-9) on the reverse side of this page. • See detailed instructions. • Sign the form at line 8.

DO NOT WRITE HERE
Page 1 of ____ pages

EXAMINED BY — FORM PA
CHECKED BY
☐ CORRESPONDENCE Yes
FOR COPYRIGHT OFFICE USE ONLY

DO NOT WRITE ABOVE THIS LINE. IF YOU NEED MORE SPACE, USE A SEPARATE CONTINUATION SHEET.

5
PREVIOUS REGISTRATION Has registration for this work, or for an earlier version of this work, already been made in the Copyright Office?
M Yes M No If your answer is "Yes," why is another registration being sought? (Check appropriate box.) ▼
a. M This is the first published edition of a work previously registered in unpublished form.
b. M This is the first application submitted by this author as copyright claimant.
c. M This is a changed version of the work, as shown by space 6 on this application.
If your answer is "Yes," give: Previous Registration Number ▼ Year of Registration ▼

6
DERIVATIVE WORK OR COMPILATION Complete both space 6a and 6b for a derivative work; complete only 6b for a compilation.
a Preexisting Material Identify any preexisting work or works that this work is based on or incorporates. ▼

See instructions before completing this space.

b Material Added to This Work Give a brief, general statement of the material that has been added to this work and in which copyright is claimed. ▼

7
DEPOSIT ACCOUNT If the registration fee is to be charged to a Deposit Account established in the Copyright Office, give name and number of Account.
Name ▼ Account Number ▼

CORRESPONDENCE Give name and address to which correspondence about this application should be sent. Name/Address/Apt/City/State/ZIP ▼

Area code and daytime telephone number ▶ ( ) Fax number ▶ ( )
Email ▶

8
CERTIFICATION* I, the undersigned, hereby certify that I am the (check only one) ▼
M author
M other copyright claimant
M owner of exclusive right(s)
M authorized agent of ____ Name of author or other copyright claimant, or owner of exclusive right(s) ▲

of the work identified in this application and that the statements made by me in this application are correct to the best of my knowledge.

Typed or printed name and date ▼ If this application gives a date of publication in space 3, do not sign and submit it before that date.

Date ▶

Handwritten signature (X) ▼
x

9
MAIL CERTIFICATE TO
Name ▼
Number/Street/Apt ▼
City/State/ZIP ▼

Certificate will be mailed in window envelope

• Complete all necessary spaces
• Sign your application in space 8
1. Application form
2. Nonrefundable $20 filing fee in check or money order payable to Register of Copyrights
3. Deposit material
Library of Congress
Copyright Office
101 Independence Avenue, S.E.
Washington, D.C. 20559-6000

*17 U.S.C. § 506(e): Any person who knowingly makes a false representation of a material fact in the application for copyright registration provided for by section 409, or in any written statement filed in connection with the application, shall be fined not more than $2,500.
July 1998—250,000
PRINTED ON RECYCLED PAPER
U.S. GOVERNMENT PRINTING OFFICE: 1998-432-381/00,013

Figure 2–4 Form PA

3 FINANCING

"The point is, don't give up. Don't be the person who says, I wrote this, I want to make it, I want to be in it, this is the only way to do this, because the bottom line is, if I had not taken the opportunity to make the movie [Swingers] *the way we did it, it would never have happened. I was able to enjoy probably more creative control as a co-producer on this film—being able to be in the editing room, picking the music, the people, the wardrobe—than if I were the director, much less a first-time director working with a studio or a mini-studio. They would have never given me the amount of control that I had in this situation. So by not worrying about the credit or the money, I ended up getting the film that I wanted."*

—*Jon Favreau, on* Swingers

Getting your picture financed is not easy, and the process may cause you to reconsider many aspects of making a movie. We have found the financing process to be frustrating and difficult, but we also believe the process itself is as important as the product and that there is much to be learned from it. The time you spend securing financing for your film can be one of the most trying and overwhelming periods of the filmmaking process. It is important to remain open to various options and to not cling to a specific idea of how you want to get your film made.

DANCING WITH A DOUBLE-EDGED SWORD

Financing is a catch-22. You cannot secure financing without having talent attached, and you cannot get commitments from talent unless you have financing. Ideally, you pursue both simultaneously and hope that you will find either the financier who loves the project and wants to be involved or the actor who loves the piece and is willing to grant you permission to use his or her name to help finance the piece.

On *Swingers*, we had a difficult time for this very reason. We knew the cast we wanted, but unfortunately few people knew of Vince Vaughn, Jon Favreau, Ron Livingston, Patrick Van Horn, or Alex Desert at the time. In meeting after meeting, executives suggested the movie might be viable if the role of Trent could be cast with a bankable star. We stuck to our guns, but none of those production companies ultimately wanted to finance the picture. The good news is that everyone is looking for a good role and a viable project, so it is feasible—if you are prepared and persistent and if your material is good—that you will find financing for your film.

The *Kissing Jessica Stein* story was almost identical to *Swingers*. Everyone who read the script loved it, and we had companies indicate interest in purchasing the script outright with the idea of producing it with stars. This was not an option, in that Juergensen and Westfeldt had written the project as a vehicle for themselves. Our original budget was over $2 million, and we ended up completing a rough cut for $720,000 and finishing an answer print for $950,000. The delivery expense, including music licenses, brought the total budget to $1.1 million.

THE PITCH

At every stage of making your film, people will ask you what your movie is about. You may find yourself pitching your film to your best friend or to a banker, so you want to be able to give a compelling thumbnail sketch of your film. The pitch is a boiled-down description of what your film is about. It is imperative that you nail down the pitch that works for your project. Pitching is an art, not a science. Think carefully about your pitch, and work on it; you may have little more than one minute to pique someone's interest.

Your pitch should be vivid, concise, animated, and distinct. It should be both memorable and easily repeatable. Your pitch should describe the genre of the film, the key characters, and the general story line. It should also describe the turning points at the ends of the first and second acts. Practice your pitch on your friends and colleagues before you go into a meeting. Make sure it hits the necessary points but is not too long. It is always better to leave people wanting more and asking follow-up questions than bored out of their skulls, wondering when your pitch will end.

Think of your pitch in terms of the game of telephone: Your message needs to travel well. More likely than not, when you pitch your project to an executive he or she in turn will have to pitch it to someone else—a colleague, a boss, a banker. If your pitch is vivid, memorable, and clear, it will pass the telephone test. Remember, you do not need to be true to all of the details of your story. The key is to aim for what will draw the listener in and leave him or her wanting to know more. High-concept stories are usually the easiest to pitch, and character-driven tales are the most difficult to sum up.

OPTIONS FOR FINANCING INDEPENDENT FILMS

Domestic Production-Distribution Deal

If you can make a domestic production-distribution deal (P-D deal) with a company, the money you receive for domestic rights should cover from 40 to 60 percent of your budget. The more money the company gives you, the more creative control it will want. Some of the key negotiating points on a P-D deal are the minimum prints-and-advertising (P&A) expenditure, the advance, above-the-line fees, and the release date. Increasingly, the role of the P&A expenditure figures largely in the success of any film. If you make a P-D deal, make sure the company handles films like the one you intend to make and that they can get it out to the public in a way that makes sense. Remember, if you relinquish certain rights when you make your deal, you may have little control over whether and how the film is released.

Equity Financing

Equity financing is hard cash invested by a company or an individual—a family member, friend, or professional investor—in exchange for credit, profit points, or both. It is a high-risk investment. People invest equity in films for a myriad of reasons, including experience in the film business, financial gain, and film credit. Companies that invest equity in pictures are constantly soliciting material in an attempt to find their next project.

Swingers was financed through straight equity by a few silent investors. This is in many ways a great way to finance a film because it typically allows for greater creative control than studio or mini-major financing. If you are raising equity to finance your film, you will need to form a limited liability company (LLC) or a limited liability partnership (LLP) to protect the investors. This structure literally limits the liability of the investors to the amount of money they have put into your film. For more information on how to establish an LLC or LLP, refer to the legal manuals cited in Appendix A: Resource Guide, or consult an attorney. It should be noted that the laws regarding LLCs differ from state to state. It is essential that you or your attorney know about the regulations of the state in which you are establishing the LLC, as well as the Securities and Exchange Commission (SEC) regulations regarding investor offerings. These details can be read about in books dealing with entertainment law (see Resource Guide: Appendix A: Resource Guide) and/or can be gleaned from your attorney, who should be knowledgeable in this arena. (If he or she is not, that should raise a red flag.)

Foreign Presales

With foreign presales, you sell the rights to your picture on a territory-by-territory basis before actually shooting the film. How much money you can presell your film for depends on the packaging of the film (that is, which elements are attached and the foreign value of those elements) and on the territory itself. To capitalize your picture through foreign presales, you should hire a foreign sales agent to assist you. Foreign sales agents run the gamut in terms of the types of films they handle. Find an agent who handles films along the lines of the one you are trying to make, both in terms of budget and genre. By attending film markets and exploiting his or her contacts, the agent will secure sales agreements with various foreign territories. He or she will take a percentage—usually 10 to 15 percent for straight presales and up to 25 percent if you want an advance from the agent. The agent will also charge you for the cost of attending a given market.

You will want to negotiate with your agent a cap on the expenses you are responsible for, to ensure that you do not absorb too many of his or her costs, thereby negating the value of the sale. You can use these presale contracts as collateral on a bank loan, or if your film is extremely low budget you may be able to shoot it for the small advance you receive from your presales. Consult IFP/LA (Independent Feature Project, Los Angeles chapter) or your local chapter for a list of foreign sales agents.

Gap Financing

When you have raised most of the capital needed to cover the full cost of your picture, the remaining amount is called the gap. Gap financing is a common but expensive way to finance a picture. Approach a bank that does gap financing. Be prepared to provide them with any presale contracts and guaranteed equity investment contracts as well as your budget, business plan, and proof of chain of title, to name a few of the required items. The bank will determine whether you are eligible for a gap loan and, depending on the assessed risk involved, will let you know how much it will cost you. You pay both interest on the loan (typically either LIBOR or prime plus 2 percent) and a flat fee to the bank. The killer on a gap deal is that you continue to pay interest on the loan until it is paid back, and that duration is unknowable because it is contingent on further foreign sales or on performance of the picture at the box office.

Beg, Borrow, Steal

Depending on the budget of your film, it is conceivable to piece together money through personal savings, credit cards, and donations from family members and friends. Generally speaking, we cannot say it is a bad idea to invest your own money in your movie. If you believe in the project and you have some cash, there is no reason not to. Just be aware that you may not get it back.

As for credit cards, use them only as a last resort. Credit card money is expensive money. Annual interest can be as high as 18 percent, which really adds up. Going into credit card debt is not a decision to be made without careful thought.

When asking loved ones, family members, and friends for money to make your movie, be up front about the risk of the investment. If you present it as a sure thing that they will be paid back in full, you run the risk of burning bridges with people you care about. Establishing an LLC or an LLP is just as important when the money belongs to family and friends. This legal entity will protect any assets they own beyond the investment they have made in the film and will show them that you are serious.

On *Kissing Jessica Stein* we ended up with approximately forty equity investors. We had one investor who put in 50 percent of the budget, and the rest came in drips and drabs. Each share in the company cost $2,500. At first we thought we would never make it, with such small increments. But it all adds up. Some investors purchased a partial share, whereas many purchased more than one share. Low and behold, we raised $950,000 this way. The final money for post-production was raised by showing a rough cut to a post-production lab, which decided that they would do all the work in-kind, in exchange for the number of shares commensurate with the cost of the work they had done.

ASKING PEOPLE TO WORK FOR FREE OR ON A DEFERRAL BASIS

If your funds are short, you may want to consider going back through your budget to determine what changes and adjustments can be made. (See "When Your Budget Estimate Is Way Too High" in Chapter 6.) Although it is not ideal to ask people to work for little or no money, it may be the only way to make your movie. We have been involved with productions on which everyone worked for free. It is possible to find a committed crew willing to work for little or no money. The key is to find people who really want and need the experience. Find people who are eager to learn grip work, for example, and match them up with an affable, experienced key grip who can talk to them about the various aspects of the job. Figure out which shoot days will be the most complicated and would benefit from a more experienced crew. Ask production-savvy crew people to donate one day of their time to cover these shoot days.

On *Swingers*, we paid all of the crew members $300 per week. We made no exceptions. We informed each potential crew member about the pay and the hours at the beginning. We also told them what we could provide (good meals; experience; a cool, friendly working environment) and asked them to decide if it was feasible to work for $300 per week for the duration of the show. We made deferral agreements with everyone, which guaranteed that they would be better compensated if the film sold.

Deferrals create good will and signify to the crew that if there is money made they will share the wealth. Typically, the deferral amount is the difference between what the crew member was actually paid and what the crew member would have been paid on a higher-budget independent project. A small premium is attached to compensate the crew member for contributing his or her time at a cut rate. (See the deferral clause in Figure 7.16.) On *Swingers*, we were lucky and were able to make good on all of the deferral agreements. This is an exception, however, and people are skeptical about ever seeing a deferred payment. If you do go this route, make it clear that there is no guarantee that the deferral will be paid. Of course, the reputations of the line producer and the producer are enhanced when deferred payments are actually made.

COMPLETION FUNDS

If you have raised enough money to get through production but do not have enough for post-production, you will need to raise completion funds. If your footage is good, you may think it will be easier to raise money than before you had something to show, but do not be fooled by this thinking. Securing financing based on unedited dailies is a tough row to hoe. Even experienced film people who say they know how to look at a rough cut usually do not. *Swingers* was rejected from Sundance on a rough cut submission. Granted, what was submitted was full of black holes, had no music, and looked little like the film that was released. The point is that even when a significant amount of editing has been completed it is not always possible for people to imagine the finished film. On the other hand, having something to show that demonstrates the look and feel of the piece can be useful.

Should you find yourself in the position of having an unfinished film, the good news is that there are resources exclusively tagged for completion financing. One good way to find out what is available to you, both regionally and nationally, is through organizations such as Independent Feature Project (IFP) or the Film Arts Foundation (FAF). If you do not have such organizations in your town, try the public library, local university or college libraries, local community foundations, bookstores, and the film commission in your city or state. Some companies are specifically interested in assisting low-budget projects get out of the can and onto the screen.

SUPPORT MATERIALS FOR FINANCING

Although it is most desirable to have potential investors read your script in its entirety, this is not always the first step. You may be asked to provide a synopsis, a treatment, or other supporting materials, so it is best to have them ready. Compile a development kit. The very process of generating these materials will force you to address important questions about your project. It will help prepare you for meetings. In your development kit, you may want to include a synopsis, biographies of key personnel, the budget top sheet, and details of your financing plan or strategy.

How these materials are written should be indicated in part by who your readership will be. For example, if you are targeting film-savvy people—either mini-majors or production companies—your approach should be very different than if you are targeting "uncles and orthodontists" who may have little to no background knowledge about the film business.

The Synopsis

The synopsis should grab the reader. It is a brief written description of what your script is about, not a scene-by-scene breakdown. As with the pitch, the objective of the synopsis is to provide a sense of the story, enticing readers to read the script. Writing a good synopsis is not easy, especially when you are close to the material. Remember, you do not have to be true to every plot detail. Inevitably, you will have to leave some things out. Ask someone you trust to read the draft of your synopsis for both style and content. Try to limit your synopsis to one or two pages. The following is an example of a synopsis.

> Kissing Jessica Stein *is a fresh take on the subject of sex and the single girl. When we first meet Jessica—a sensitive but neurotic New York journalist—she is at the end of her emotional rope. Her brother's engaged, her best friend's pregnant, she hasn't dated in a year, and she can't sleep.*
>
> *After an optimistic but nightmarish dating spree, she happens upon an intriguing personal ad, whose only drawback is that it's in the "women seeking women" section. On a daring whim, she decides to answer it. She meets funky downtown hipster Helen Cooper for drinks, and to her surprise they click instantly. Their evening of banter, connection, and heated debate culminates in a kiss that confounds and intrigues even the reluctant Jessica.*
>
> *With conventional gender roles absent, the two women proceed to muddle through an earnest but hilarious courtship, making up the rules as they go.* Kissing Jessica Stein *is a modern romantic comedy that breaks all the rules—it blurs the lines between friendship and romantic love, and finds the funny, surprising, and ultimately poignant overlap between the two.*

Treatment

A treatment is different from a synopsis in that it is a longer, more detailed outline of the script. It maybe anywhere from 5 to 10 pages, depending on the subject matter and the audience for which you are writing. Generally, you would submit a treatment to an executive or potential investor only in the event it was requested. For the purpose of your development kit, a synopsis will suffice.

Biographies of Key Personnel

People need to know with whom they will be going into business. You should present yourself in an honest and professional way—one that shows your best side, as in the following biography of Jon Favreau, written in 1998. Include bios of the writer, director, and producer. Should there be cast attachments to your project, include them as well.

> *After establishing himself as an actor and writer of considerable import with the acclaimed hipster comedy* Swingers, *Jon Favreau is poised to follow up that success with several upcoming projects, both as an actor and director.*

> *Favreau was most recently seen in this summer's hit, the Dreamworks/Paramount thriller* Deep Impact, *directed by Mimi Leder.* Deep Impact *traces the effort of the Earth's people to prevent an impending asteroid collision and to brace for its potentially cataclysmic results. Favreau plays an astronaut opposite Robert Duvall, Morgan Freeman, and Vanessa Redgrave.*
>
> *Favreau will next be seen opposite Christian Slater and Cameron Diaz in the Interscope and Ballpark co-production* Very Bad Things. *Written and directed by Peter Berg, this black comedy follows the spiraling mayhem that ensues as a group of friends turn on each other after a bachelor party goes horribly wrong. The Polygram release is due in theaters this November.*
>
> *Favreau will follow with a career-defining turn as the title character in the MGM biopic* Marciano, *which is currently filming on location in Toronto, Canada. Written and directed by Charles Winkler, the film will chronicle Rocky Marciano's rise to fame in the heavyweight boxing arena. Costarring George C. Scott,* Marciano *is set for a 1999 release.*
>
> *Based on his personal Hollywood experience, Favreau wrote, developed, and co-produced* Swingers, *a project for his friends and him to star in. Shot on a micro-budget, the film ultimately resulted in a record-breaking distribution deal with Miramax.* Swingers *opened to critical and audience acclaim, prompting the Chicago Film Critics Association to give Jon a nomination for Most Promising Actor in 1997.*
>
> *Born and raised in Queens, New York, Jon did everything from cleaning garage vents in Hell's Kitchen to working for an investment banking firm on Wall Street before deciding to become an actor. He moved to Chicago to pursue a career in improv comedy and live theater, supporting himself as a cartoonist. It was during this time that David Anspaugh cast him in a starring role in Tristar's* Rudy, *which marked Jon's film debut.*

Budget Top Sheet

A realistic budget shows that you have done your homework. (See Chapter 6.) It tells people that you can focus on more than the aesthetics of your film. You must compile your budget from true numbers. You must break down all of the elements of your script and prepare a preliminary schedule to come up with a budget that is in the realm of possibility. (See Chapters 4 and 5.) For the development kit, the top sheet of the budget—which reflects the categories and their totals but does not show line-item detail—is sufficient.

Project Status

Include a tentative schedule for pre-production, production, post-production, film completion, and so on, as well as some of your cast and crew ideas, especially as they relate to the film's budget, the script's genre, and the film's potential return. As with the budget, it is essential to show potential investors that you have thought through some basic elements of making and distributing your film. Let investors know who the niche audience for your film is and why the material is timely. If there are relevant press clippings on members of your team or other source materials (such as an article on the specific genre) pertinent to your project, include them as well.

Presentation counts for a lot, but do not spend excessive amounts of money compiling your development kit. The most important thing is that the materials be informative, well written, and presented in a professional manner.

Figure 3–2 shows an example of a business plan we recently put together. The target audience for this plan is the equity financier, be it friends and family or the slightly more savvy business person interested in investing in a film. This plan would not be submitted to a bank or mini-major studio for financing.

ORGANIZATIONS AND OTHER RESOURCES

If you are having difficulty orienting yourself in the world of film finance, contact a few of the organizations that support filmmakers. You will find that many provide valuable information and resources. In addition to IFP, organizations in many cities have libraries full of resource materials, grant applications, lists of people seeking work on films, and more. Most of these support organizations also have Web sites, which can be useful and can help you determine if a trip into their office will be worth your time. By tapping into your local film network, you may be able to secure hard cash, find a crew, or even just receive moral support.

The Sundance Institute offers several programs that are helpful to independent filmmakers, ranging from a producers' conference, which takes place every summer, to the writer and director labs that take place twice a year in Utah. Although attending a writers' workshop may not appear to be a way to raise money, in a circuitous way it is. The Sundance workshop is prestigious, and people will respond positively when you tell them you have participated. You will meet other filmmakers and receive invaluable feedback on your script.

FILM FINANCING CONFERENCES

Film financing conferences can be tremendously useful. Two that we have attended are the Cinemart at Rotterdam and No Borders in New York City. Some conferences, such as these, are competitive. You have to submit an

UNNAMED FILM

Writer/Director:
Will Geiger

Producers:
Nicole Shay LaLoggia & Eden H. Wurmfeld

Figure 3–2 Business Plan

TABLE OF CONTENTS

(continued)

Figure 3–2 Business Plan (continued)

UNNAMED MOVIE

EXECUTIVE SUMMARY

Unnamed Movie reunites the award-winning producing team that created the indie hit *Swingers*. Producers Nicole LaLoggia and Eden Wurmfeld rejoin to create another quality indie film with award-winning writer/director Will Geiger. Wurmfeld and LaLoggia have produced winning films that pay back investors 1200 percent (*Swingers*) and 125 percent (*Kissing Jessica Stein*) of their initial investment. Geiger's first feature *Ocean Tribe* also paid back 100 percent of investors' money. The producers are implementing the same financial strategy they implemented on the production of *Swingers* and *Kissing Jessica Stein*. The minimum capitalization of Unnamed Movie, LLC is $4 million.

While independent films have been around for decades, it was only in the late 1980s that indies came into the fore in a more significant way. Over the last 15 years we have witnessed a significant shift in American film-going audiences with the sleeper successes and record-breaking sales at the box office of such notables as the recent *Y Tu Mama Tambien, Monsoon Wedding, Kissing Jessica Stein, Adaptation,* and *My Big Fat Greek Wedding.* Audiences today are more savvy and sophisticated; they are demanding thought-provoking films. The shift in audience demand has been proven by box office returns for indie films in 2002, which were at an unprecedented high. "I think that there is a big, smart, upscale audience out there," said Peter Rice, head of Fox Searchlight, a foremost distributor of specialized fare. The above-named films are among some of last year's successes that demonstrate audience appreciation of innovative filmmaking (see chart in Industry Overview).

Unnamed Movie incorporates all the elements of great storytelling, weaving a complex and moving tale. Among the themes explored in *Unnamed Movie* are the ethics of war, Catholicism, the women's liberation movement, conservative politics clashing with an emergent liberal view, infidelity, abuse and love. *Unnamed Movie* is a poignant and humorous story of a family's growing pains in 1972 America, based on the true-life story of writer/director Will Geiger as he came of age in the South as the son of an undercover F.B.I. agent. The film combines familiar elements from such past successes as *Stand By Me, What's Eating Gilbert Grape* and *The Great Santini.*

SYNOPSIS

UNNAMED MOVIE synopsis goes here.
see Kissing Jessica Stein example synop, Figure 6–7.

THE TEAM

Unnamed Movie re-teams the award-winning producing duo that created the indie hit *Swingers.* Nicole LaLoggia and Eden Wurmfeld team to create another quality indie film, using the same fund-raising model and financial strategy they implemented in producing *Swingers* and *Kissing Jessica Stein,* while harnessing the creative talents of award-winning writer/director Will Geiger.

WRITER/ DIRECTOR

Writer/Director Will Geiger was born in New Rochelle, New York, and lived in various parts of the U.S. as the son of an undercover F.B.I. agent. While moving from town to town, he developed a strong passion for writing, photography, and theater. He attended the University of California, Irvine as a theater major where he studied with renowned professor and author Robert Cohen. After directing and acting in various university productions, Will was accepted to the theater program at the prestigious Royal Academy of Dramatic Arts (R.A.D.A.) in London, where he studied acting with some of England's finest. Upon completion of R.A.D.A., he moved from London to Rome, Italy where he became fluent in Italian and worked as director of the Italian television series *Family Business.*

Will returned to the U.S., where he wrote and directed many short films including *In Love and War,* which won awards at festivals in the U.S. and abroad including the Silver Plaque Award at the Chicago Film Festival.

Figure 3–2 Business Plan (continued)

Ocean Tribe, his first feature film, was shot in 24 days with a budget of $380,000. The film tells the story of four friends who journey from Bodega, California to Baja, Mexico with a dying friend on one last surfing expedition. *Ocean Tribe* premiered at the Los Angeles Independent Film Festival winning Will the award for Best Director. The film received critical acclaim in *Variety, The Hollywood Reporter, The Los Angeles Times, American Cinematographer, Detour* and the *L.A. Weekly*. The film also won the Grand Prize award at the Charleston International Film Festival and Best Drama at the Houston International Film Festival. Mike Medavoy's Phoenix Pictures picked up the U.S. rights while J&M Entertainment acquired foreign territories. The film played in many countries in Europe and Asia, and was on the top ten lists of several reviewers in Japan.

Will was invited by Seattle International Film Festival to take part in the *Fly Filmmaking* program. The festival gives a filmmaker two rolls of 16mm film and two days to make a short film with a small local crew and local actors. Will's resulting short film *Red Man* was about a dying Native American and his search for a burial ground amidst the concrete jungle of Seattle. *Red Man* is currently playing on the Independent Film Channel.

Geiger's credits include an adaptation of *Hi Dharma* for MGM, a story of five bank robbers who are stranded in a Buddhist monastery with a group of Tibetan monks. His romantic comedy *Elvis and Anabelle* has been optioned by Hawk Koch and Ascendant Pictures (*Frequency, Primal Fear*). Elijah Wood is attached to star.

Will has citizenship in the U.S. and Italy and is a legal resident of Canada. He is represented by the William Morris Agency and Principato-Young Management.

PRODUCERS

NICOLE LALOGGIA

Nicole LaLoggia began her film career in 1993 in development. During the past ten years, Nicole's work has both contributed to and reflected the great resurgence of the independent film. Nicole quickly found her niche in physical production while on location with director Doug Liman's first feature film, *Getting In*, shooting in Raleigh-Durham, North Carolina. Since then, Nicole has developed, produced, line produced, post-produced, marketed, sold, and taught about nearly every aspect of independent filmmaking.

Nicole's first solo producer credit is on the critically acclaimed independent film *Swingers*. Principal photography on the $275,000 indie began on August 31, 1995. In February 1996, less than sixth months later, Miramax Films acquired *Swingers* worldwide distribution rights for an advance cost of $5 million.

Nicole and her fellow filmmakers traveled the festival circuit with *Swingers*, beginning with its world premiere at the Venice Film Festival only one year to the date from the start of principal photography. The film had its American premiere at Telluride and went on to the Toronto Film Festival and elsewhere with nearly universally positive press and ultimately great audience success. *Swingers* became a benchmark for the course study of independent film. Moreover, its video and DVD releases put *Swingers* on nearly every college student's "TEN BEST" list where it remains firmly entrenched to this day almost a decade later. In 1997, the *Swingers*' team was awarded the MTV award for Best New Filmmakers.

In 1998, Nicole and Eden Wurmfeld, penned the IFP/West Independent Filmmaking Manual published by Focal Press. The writers are currently updating and revising the book in advance of its second edition printing later this year (see more info in Wurmfeld's bio, pg. 7).

Between 1999 and 2001, Nicole produced two more films, collaborating again on one with Doug Liman and Eden Wurmfeld. Nicole also produced and collaborated creatively on two commercials for high-profile political figures in the North Carolina area. In 2001, Nicole was asked to teach a producer series at the North Carolina School of the Arts during Intensive Arts organized by Dale Pollack, the school's Dean. Nicole continues to be in touch with many of the faculty and students, guiding them through finishing their course work and advising them on employment and internships in the professional film arena.

(continued)

Figure 3–2 Business Plan (continued)

Nicole has taught seminars and classes at both the UCLA and USC Schools of Film, and participated in film making panels for IFP/Los Angeles, IFP/New York, and The AFI School of Film. She frequently prepares schedules and budgets for upcoming films.

EDEN WURMFELD

Eden Wurmfeld began her feature producing career in 1994 on her brother's experimental feature *Fanci's Persuasion*. This led to her work on Doug Liman's directorial debut *Swingers* (production manager). The success of the experience on *Swingers* led to not only another collaboration with Doug Liman and Nicole LaLoggia (*See Jane Run*), but also to a co-writing venture with *Swingers* producer Nicole LaLoggia. In 1998, Wurmfeld and LaLoggia penned The IFP/West Independent Filmmaker's Manual (Focal Press), the definitive "how to" manual on independent filmmaking. The book is now a staple in film school classrooms and production offices across the country – it's a "cookbook" on how to make an indie film. They are currently updating and revising the book, which will have its second edition printing in 2003.

Eden went on to produce her third 35mm feature with the award-winning *Kissing Jessica Stein* released by Fox Searchlight in March of 2002. Eden is currently developing a television show *Bringing Up Mom*, with Brillstein Grey. Eden's documentary, *Sunset Story*, on which she is a co-producer, was granted ITVS funding for 2002, and will be airing on PBS this year, with its world premiere screening at the Tribeca Film Festival in May, 2003.

Additionally, Eden programs The Digital Center at the Sundance Film Festival, a forum dedicated to merging new technology with the visual arts. She has participated on numerous panels at The IFP Los Angeles Film Festival, The AFI Film Festival, among others. After the success of *Kissing Jessica Stein*, she was named one of Variety's "10 Producer's to Watch for 2002," (see Press Clippings) was a finalist for the Independent Spirit Awards Motorola Producer's Award, 2003.

Wurmfeld is committed to creating entertaining films with relevant social messages. She is an avid bicycle rider, yogi, and Russophile. She lives in native New York City with her husband, award-winning documentary filmmaker Justin Schein.

INDUSTRY OVERVIEW

While independent films date back to B movies and poverty-row production companies, it was only in the late 1980s that independent films came into the fore in a more significant way, creating a niche alongside studio blockbusters in the marketplace. Independent films have increasingly taken over even more market share of box office returns. Each of the top 10 specialized films of 2002 grossed more than $10 million, according to Nielsen EDI Inc., a box-office tracking firm[(1)]. With audiences demanding smarter fare, the mandate for thought-provoking films, often thought of as art-house pictures, has grown significantly.

It is known throughout the industry that studio financed films must recoup four to seven times their cost before they show a profit. While any investment is a risk, the potential for a greater return on an independent film far exceeds that of a studio produced film. *Coming to America*, starring Eddie Murphy, grossed $300 million and never showed a profit. *Swingers*, the critically acclaimed independent hit of 1996 was made for $250,000 and was acquired for distribution by Miramax for $5 million dollars. Last year's *My Big Fat Greek Wedding* was made for $5 million dollars and had a box-office gross of over $200 million. *Kissing Jessica Stein* was made for under $1 million dollars and grossed $7 million at the box office.

The numbers show that quality independent cinema is often significantly more lucrative than the blockbuster films that studios pour tens of millions and more into making. Since the expensive studio paradigm is proving increasingly problematic from an economic standpoint, the demand for indie production and acquisition is on a steady rise. The

[1] Nielsen defines "specialized" as films that played in fewer than 500 theaters in their first three weeks and fewer than 1,500 theaters in weeks four through six.

Figure 3–2 Business Plan (continued)

performance of 2002's specialized films — which range from such easily accessible feel-good fare as *Greek Wedding* to more challenging offerings such as *Y Tu Mamá También* — has given studios the financial incentive to make and distribute more smaller-budget movies (see chart, pg. 9).

The following chart demonstrates the higher return on investment of successful independents over their more expensive studio counterparts. Last year, specialized films accounted for nearly 7 percent of the market — a 3 percent increase from 2001.

Return on Investment Comparison

Title/Distributor	Global Box Office ($ in MM)	Project Budget	Return on Investment (%)
The Champs			
My Big Fat Greek Wedding (IFC Films)	$273.8	$5.0	5376
The Full Monty (Fox Searchlight)	243.7	3.5	6862
The Blair Witch Project (Artisan Entertainment)	155.4	0.04	443986
Monster's Ball (Lions Gate Films)	34.9	4.0	773
The Usual Suspects (Gramercy Pictures)	25.8	6.0	330
Chasing Army (Miramax)	14.7	0.3	5780
When the Cat's Away (Sony Classics)	7.6	0.3	2433
In the Company of Men (Sony Classics)	2.9	0.2	1328
Red Inks			
Father's Day (WB)	36.2	65.0	–44
Turbulence (MGM/Rysher)	28.6	65.0	–48
Rosewood (WB)	15.2	31.0	–51
U-Turn (Sony)	10.2	19.0	–46
Hamlet (Sony/Castle Rock)	1.3	24.0	–95

BOX OFFICE GROSSES

The following chart details the box office grosses of films that are similar in subject matter and genre to *Unnamed Movie.*

Relevant Box Office Grosses

Film
Stand By Me
Billy Elliott
In the Bedroom
Monster's Ball
October Sky
The Sandlot
Sling Blade
The War
Hope and Glory
What's Eating Gilbert Grape
My Dog Skip

(continued)

Figure 3–2 Business Plan (continued)

PRODUCTION STRATEGY

The first step to the success of any film is determining a solid production strategy that will result in a finished film with elements that can be profitably exploited. The success of a film is based largely upon its box office receipts; therefore producers must build solid strategies in both the production and distribution phases. "If they are made at the right cost, then that is a very good business and a satisfying business to be in," said Jeff Blake, president of worldwide marketing and distribution for Sony. Our production strategy on *Unnamed Movie* incorporates several key factors: keeping the budget as low as possible, while within union rules and regulations; putting as much money on the screen as possible while keeping the "above the line" costs lower than on most films; attracting name cast.

CAST

One of the first questions asked about any film is "Who's in it?" Attaching name actors will add a valuable element serving to increase the potential market value of the finished product. In *Unnamed Movie* the complex character role of Harry, as well as that of Kate are both fantastic opportunities for more established actors to showcase their talents. Actor Sew and Sew has expressed serious interest in playing the role of Harry and has taken meetings and given script notes to Director Will Geiger. Actresses Blank and Blank are eager to play the role of Kate. The eldest brother Michael, as well as the roles of James and Fig provide exciting casting opportunities for younger rising talent or breakout new talent. The production team has not committed to any of the above cast and is working with casting director Blank (*credit, credit, credit,* among others), who will help guide the team to the most appropriate bankable talent.

BUDGET & SHOOTING STRATEGY

The current budget for *Unnamed Movie* is $4 million (See attached Budget Top Sheet, pg. 14). For that money *Unnamed Movie* will have a 30 day union shoot in a right-to-work state such as North Carolina or Georgia. It also includes a completion bond, which is an insurance policy for the investors that the film will be completed, as well as a contingency of ten percent. The producer's first choice for shooting is on location in North Carolina. The North Carolina Film Commission offers studio support and shooting facilities, equipment, and experienced crew. The geography of the state provides the right look for *Unnamed Movie.* Producer Nicole LaLoggia worked on her first movie in North Carolina and also taught at the North Carolina School of the Arts. She remains in contact with local crew and unions.

DISTRIBUTION STRATEGY

The most electrifying moment for anyone involved in a film is when he or she sees his or her contributions brought to the light of the big screen. Often getting there is an exciting and harrowing journey in itself. Today, independent filmmaking is a global business of marketing and distribution, with many films being sold for exploitation in theatrical release, video/DVD, cable and other ancillary markets. The sole purpose of cable outlets such as The Sundance Channel

Figure 3–2 Business Plan (continued)

and The Independent Film Channel, is to showcase and promote independent films. The Independent Film Channel was launched in 1994 and is available in **67 million homes and has 27 million subscribers** The Sundance Channel was launched in 1996, and is now available in all markets throughout the U.S. via cable and direct-to-home satellite in 65 million homes and has 16 million subscribers.

FESTIVAL CIRCUIT

As independent films have grown increasingly popular, film festivals like Sundance Film Festival in Park City, Utah, Toronto Film Festival, and Los Angeles Film Festival (the LA Film Festival is run by the same non-profit organization—IFP/Los Angeles—that publishes this book) have flourished. With the intense media coverage that these festivals garner, the spotlight is on independent film. Distributors often act quickly, trying to buy a film before a competitor. Largely, distributors are at festivals for this purpose – to acquire films that will make up their release slate for the coming year. Harvey Weinstein, President of Miramax Pictures, insisted that Miramax had already beaten the competition to the punch at Sundance in 1995 by acquiring the film *Picture Bride* before the festival even began. "I hate to disappoint my peers, but I think we already have the No. 1 movie that was going to be here," Weinstein said with a smile.

The festival circuit is showcasing quality films and helping create a buzz in advance of a film's release. Such notable indies as *Far From Heaven*; *In the Bedroom*; *Sex, Lies and Videotape; El Mariachi; Clerks; The Brothers McMullen; Slingblade; Blair Witch Project; Girlfight*; and *Boys Don't Cry* (to name a few) have all been acquired by distributors and created positive buzz from festivals including Toronto, Sundance, Los Angeles, and Cannes.

Traveling the festival circuit will be the best road for *Unnamed Movie* to gain exposure and secure a sale. Will Geiger successfully steered his first feature, *Ocean Tribe*, into 15 film festivals including the Los Angeles Independent Film Festival (now the IFP Los Angeles Film Festival) where the foreign rights were sold within hours of its premiere screening with a six-figure advance. *Kissing Jessica Stein* sold to Fox Searchlight following its world premiere screening at the Los Angeles Film Festival. With the elements we have in place, we expect to have great success with *Unnamed Movie* at the major North American festivals.

ACQUIRING A DISTRIBUTOR

The 1990s saw the birth of a new breed of independent distributor. Companies like Gramercy/USA (*The Big Lebowski, Being John Malkovich, Pitch Black*), Fox Searchlight (*The Full Monty, Brothers McMullen, Waking Ned Devine*), and Miramax (*Good Will Hunting, Scary Movie, Cider House Rules*) have made a name for themselves by distributing highly profitable independent films. With the talents of award-winning director Will Geiger and the producing team, two major stars and a compelling story, we are confident we will secure a distribution deal.

The team has engaged John Sloss' Cinetic Media to act as a producer's representative[2] for *Unnamed Movie*. Cinetic will guide the team of *Unnamed Movie* through the complex landscape of securing a sale; shepherding our project through negotiation (in partnership with Sloss Law Office P.C.), servicing delivery to a distributor and overseeing collection. Cinetic principals will attend all major festivals with *Unnamed Movie*, supervising screenings and meetings. Wurmfeld partnered with Cinetic on the successful *Kissing Jessica Stein* sale. Among Cinetics' 2002 sales are *Tadpole* and *Personal Velocity*, which each sold at Sundance.

2 Someone who works exclusively to secure distribution for feature motion pictures and other content.

(continued)

Figure 3–2 Business Plan (continued)

BUDGET TOP SHEET

UNNAMED MOVIE
(First Pass 1/15/03)

PRODUCERS:
Nicole LaLoggia/Eden Wurmfeld
WRITER/DIRECTOR: Will Geiger
SAG BASIC AGREEMENT (Favored Nations)
IATSE 491/TEAMSTER
LOCATION: North Carolina

6 WEEKS PREP
30 SHOOTING DAYS = 6/5 DAY WEEKS
16 WEEKS POST

Account #	Category Title	Page	Total
600–00	STORY	1	$28,942
610–00	PRODUCER	1	164,100
620–00	DIRECTOR	1	73,890
630–00	CAST	2	125,062
640–00	ALT TRAVEL & LIVING	3	43,820
650–00	**ALT FRINGES**		**70,827**
	TOTAL ABOVE THE LINE		**506,641**
700–00	EXTRA TALENT	4	52,530
705–00	PRODUCTION STAFF	5	192,046
710–00	CAMERA	7	134,411
715–00	ART/SET DRESSING	8	144,840
720–00	SET CONSTRUCTION	9	0
725–00	SET OPERATIONS	9	135,349
730–00	ELECTRICAL	11	113,558
735–00	STUNTS/SPECIAL EFFECTS	12	14,200
750–01	PROPERTIES/PICTURE VEHICLES	12	71,724
755–00	WARDROBE	13	78,756
760–00	MAKEUP & HAIRSTYLISTS	14	58,361
765–00	PRODUCTION SOUND	14	56,699
770–00	TRANSPORTATION	15	256,902
775–00	LOCATION EXPENSE	17	303,462
785–00	PRODUCTION FILM & LAB	20	163,300
790–00	TESTS	20	5,080
795–00	LIVESTOCK/WRANGLERS	21	5,250
798–00	SECOND UNIT SHOOTING	21	0
799–00	**TOTAL FRINGES**		**500,896**
	TOTAL SHOOTING PERIOD		**2,287,364**
800–00	EDITING	21	174,000
810–00	MUSIC	22	262,600
820–00	POST PRODUCTION SOUND	23	106,000
840–00	TITLES & OPTICALS	23	35,000
860–00	LABORATORY PROCESSING	23	50,600
	TOTAL FRINGES		**45,926**
	TOTAL COMPLETION PERIOD		**674,126**

Figure 3–2 Business Plan (continued)

910–00	ADMINISTRATIVE EXPENSES	24	78,400
920–00	PUBLICITY/EPK	25	8,000
	TOTAL FRINGES		**2,496**
	TOTAL OTHER		**88,896**
925–00	Bond: 3.00 percent		106,711
928–00	INSURANCE: 2.00 percent		71,141
930–00	Contingency: 10.00 percent		355,703
	TOTAL ABOVE-THE-LINE		**506,641**
	TOTAL BELOW-THE-LINE		**3,050,386**
	TOTAL ABOVE- & BELOW-THE-LINE		**3,557,027**
	GRAND TOTAL		**4,090,580**

CASE STUDY

The *Kissing Jessica Stein* producers learned a great deal from the experience of making the film with equity financing outside the more established Hollywood system.

Kissing Jessica Stein ("KJS") was conceived by two largely unknown actresses determined to create substantial, complex roles for themselves in an industry driven slavishly by "name" actors. Because they were not "names" they were forced to develop the story and script entirely outside the Hollywood studio system. This turned out to be a blessing in disguise.

What the KJS producers discovered as they developed the material was that while Hollywood might not be interested in the film they were assembling, audiences definitely were. The producers raised money through countless readings with "civilians" – regular folks who were excited by the story and interested in helping the film come to fruition. This enabled the filmmakers to maintain creative control and execute their original vision for the film.

The producers raised straight equity by selling shares in a limited liability company created for the exclusive purpose of making the movie. The idea was to keep costs as low as possible, making the potential upside as high as possible. The film was completed for just under $1 million. The film grossed $7 million in domestic box office and has already grossed over $3 million internationally. It is currently in release worldwide and has already surpassed films such as *Chasing Amy* in the United Kingdom. Thus far, *Kissing Jessica Stein* investors have earned back 125 percent of their investment. Many investors remarked that with the market being where it is, *Kissing Jessica Stein* ended up being a better bet for their money than the stock market itself!

FINANCIAL STRUCTURE

There are myriad ways in which to finance a film. In an effort to keep costs on *Unnamed Movie* down, our goal is to raise at least 50 percent of the financing through straight equity.

EQUITY INVESTMENT

Equity investors share the risk and the advantage of the huge upside potential of a successful independent film. But equity investment in the film industry is always a high-risk venture. The possibility always exists for any project to fall short of expectations. The investor must be fully advised of this and realize there are no guarantees herein made explicit or implied.

The following is an outline of distribution of cash-flow upon the sale of *Unnamed Movie*. Naturally, this should be relied on as guide. Investment documents should be read carefully and, as with any investment, you may wish to consult with an attorney or tax advisor.

(continued)

Figure 3–2 Business Plan (continued)

After *Unnamed Movie* is sold, the profit structure will work as follows:

- **1st monies in** go to pay back investors. Investors will recoup 120 percent of their investment (e.g. a $100,000 investment will yield $120,000);
- **2nd monies in** pay back deferrals (items in the budget secured on loan which require a deferred payment). Deferrals on *Unnamed Movie* will not exceed $200,000;
- **3rd monies in** represent profit, each dollar of which will be distributed 50/50 between Unnamed Movie, LLC and the investors.

(See Flow Chart, pg. 17)

EQUITY ACCOUNT

The monies raised during development of *Unnamed Movie* will be held in escrow by the producers' law firm Herman, Shay & Sons. See investment document instructions for details.

Once the company is officially capitalized, pre-production can begin. The minimum capitalization for *Unnamed Movie, LLC* is $4.0 million dollars. If the producers fail to raise the money required to officially capitalize the company and begin shooting the film, all monies will be returned to the investors plus interest.

Below is a guide of how investors will be paid revenue from *Unnamed Movie, LLC.* Investment documents should be read carefully and, as with any investment, you may want to consult with an attorney or tax advisor:

Figure 3–2 Business Plan (continued)

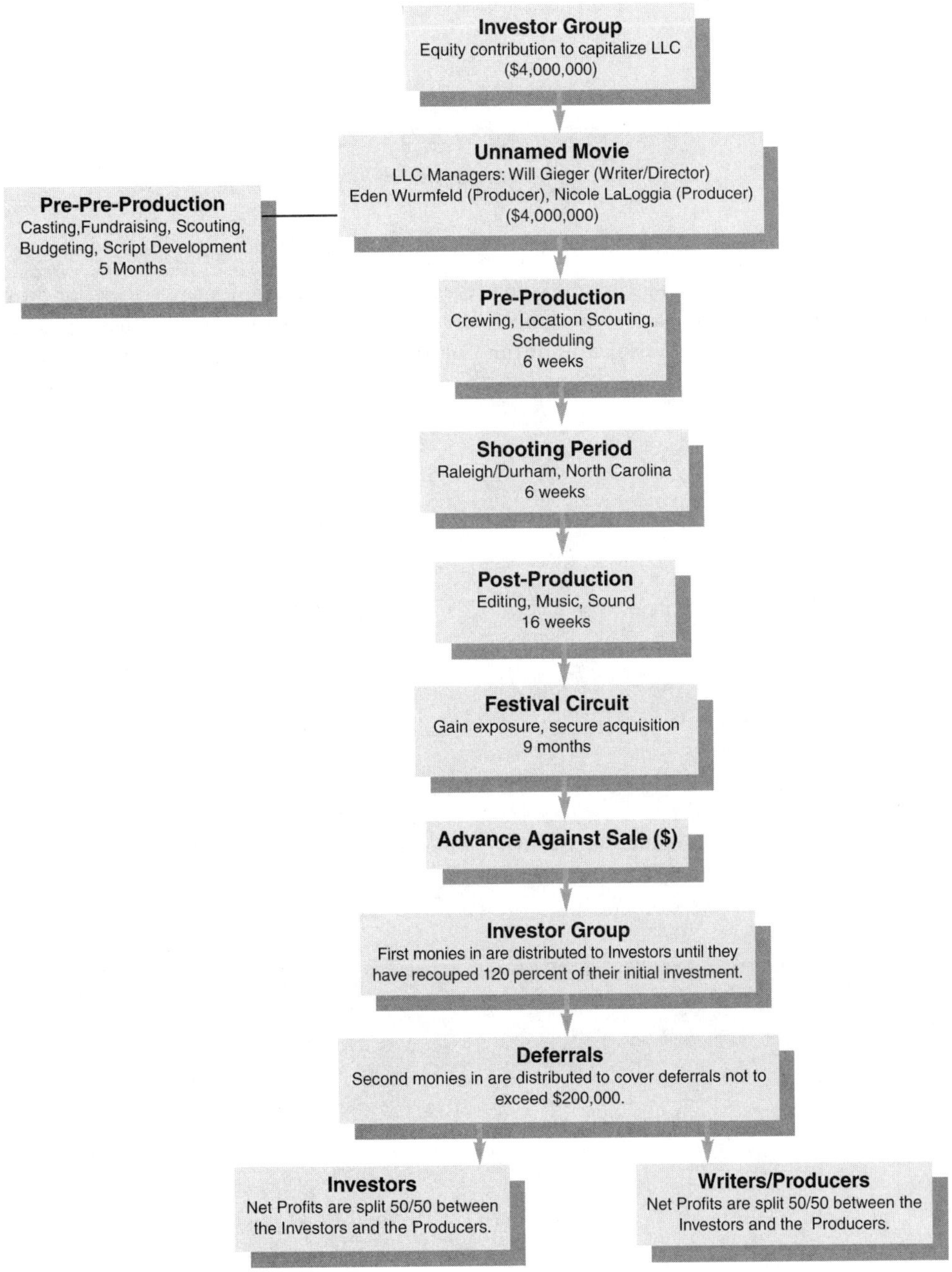

(continued)

Figure 3–2 Business Plan (continued)

PRESS CLIPPINGS

KISSING JESSICA
STEIN

This page would serve as a cover sheet to your press clippings.

Pages to follow would be press clippings from Kissing Jessica Stein. Then another cover sheet for Swingers press clippings would follow. If you have no previous films to draw press from, consider using other relevant press – for example, if you've won an award, or done theater or run a business previously that got some press attention.

Figure 3–2 Business Plan (continued)

application and be accepted in order to attend. The application may require supporting materials you have included in your development kit.

The benefit of attending a film financing conference is that it affords you the opportunity to meet industry professionals and to pitch your project. If you are new to the business, your learning curve at a financing conference will be huge. In addition to private meetings, there are seminars about various aspects of the film business, and in the evening there are social gatherings that are useful for networking. The fee for participating in a conference can range from $350 to $500.

By and large, deals are rarely signed at these conferences. Do not go expecting to come home with a suitcase full of production money. We have, however, had meetings and made contacts at these conferences that have resulted in fruitful business relationships. For example, following a conference that took place in January of 1996 we signed a deal with an Alliance Atlantis in September of that year. Much of the time in those interim months was spent in meetings, forwarding supporting materials on the project, and then, finally, negotiating the contract.

AFM

Founded in 1981, the American Film Market (AFM) is currently the largest motion picture trade event in the world. Unlike a film festival, the AFM is a marketplace where leaders in motion picture production and distribution, directors, agents, writers, lawyers, bankers, and trade groups convene to network and make deals. The AFM is an annual Hollywood gathering for the motion picture industry and has become a pivotal destination for independent filmmakers and business people from all over the world. Participants may view more than 600 screenings of approximately 400 films—the majority of them world or U.S. premieres. Titles range from big budget blockbusters that will be released by the major studios in the United States to lower budget art and genre films recognized at international film festivals. Many say that Sundance, while technically not a market, is the best marketplace for American independent films.

WHERE THERE'S A WILL, THERE'S A WAY

Don't give up. If you continually hit the same barriers in the film financing process, try to glean something positive from this negative. Why isn't anyone interested? Why are you getting negative feedback? Part of what allows independent filmmaking to continue to flourish is the will and the passion we all have for the films we make. You will find the resources to make your first film—and your second and your third. Remember, where there's a will, there's a way.

4 BREAKING DOWN A SCRIPT

The first step to scheduling and budgeting a film is breaking down the script. This must occur before engaging in pre-production. Breaking down the script will enable you to account for all of the film's needs (props, characters, locations, picture vehicles, extras, special effects, and so on), and the breakdown will serve as the framework for both your schedule and your budget. If you have a detailed breakdown to refer to, you will be able to budget the film accurately and target any potential budgetary concerns. Your breakdown will also be helpful to your department heads later on.

This chapter explains how to break down a script using Movie Magic Scheduling. We use this computer program ourselves and recommend it highly, but you can accurately break down a film without it. The program is costly, but the time, money, and frustration it will save you are well worth the cost. Whether you purchase Movie Magic Scheduling or not, Ralph Singleton's manual *Film Scheduling* (Los Angeles, Lone Eagle Publishing, 1984) is an extremely useful reference if you are new to the process.

Before you begin, make a copy of the script, and find a ruler and a highlighter or a blue pen. You can also color-code your breakdown by element: characters, locations, costumes, extras, and so on. Begin by going through the script page by page. Identify the elements required in each scene. Highlight or underline the props, characters, locations, extras, vehicles, stunts, and other elements you will need to shoot the scene. Also note the time of day and whether the location is an interior or exterior. Movies are usually not shot sequentially for budget, cast, and location scheduling reasons. Because scenes are almost always shot out of order, it is important to identify the needs of each scene individually.

Next, mark each scene's length in the right-hand margin. Scene length is indicated in eighths of a page. An eighth of a page equals approximately 1 inch of type. Any scene that is less than 1 inch of type is considered 1/8 of a page. In Figure 4–1, for example, scene 11 is counted as 1/8 of a page. Any scene that is one page long is counted as "1 page," not "8/8." For scenes longer than one page, mark them "1 2/8," not "10/8." This is important for scheduling purposes. It will help you calculate the amount of time required to shoot each scene and the amount of time you will need for each cast member, location, and piece of equipment.

You may be able to shoot only one or two scenes a day, depending on the length and complexity of the scene. In an average day, you may be able to shoot four to five pages. Each film has specialized needs and, depending on those needs, the number of pages shot per day will vary. For example, a dialogue-driven scene usually takes less time to shoot than an action-driven scene.

To illustrate the process, we broke down a few pages from Jon Favreau's screenplay for *Swingers* so that you can see what to look for (see Figure 4–1). We entered all of the elements we marked from each scene in the script into Movie Magic Scheduling's breakdown sheets (see Figure 4–2). The software program can then easily translate this breakdown into your schedule. You will also be able to strip-board the film with the assistant director and compile your day-out-of-days sheets for the characters and any other elements, all of which are addressed in Chapter 5.

Let's look at the marked-up script pages from *Swingers* (see Figure 4–1) and note what has been identified in each scene. In scene 11, we marked that it is an exterior (EXT) night shot of the Vegas strip (location). There is a detail shot of the dice (props) on the character Trent's car tire (picture vehicle). The car settles into a casino driveway (set). The car, dice, tire, Vegas strip, and casino driveway must all be provided before we can film this scene, so they have been underlined in the script. No actors are required for this particular scene. The audience will assume that the characters are in the car, but the shot does not require their presence. (The director may want them to be present during filming, however.) The scene length is approximately 1/8 of a page.

Next, we noted that scene 12 is an exterior night shot (same night as scene 11) of the Treasure Island Casino valet area on the Vegas strip. Note that two characters, Mike and Trent, are present and that the shot must reveal their buffed shoes and vintage threads. Trent leans on his car. He wears a zoot suit and sports a pocket chain. He tosses the keys to the valet, and the characters enter the casino. That is the entire shot. We have underlined the props, costumes, vehicles, characters, and locations that will be needed. The scene is approximately 2/8 of a page.

We followed this process for scenes 13 and 14. Scene 13 is 3/8 of a page. Note that scene 14 is two pages long. Because it is mostly dialogue, it can be shot during the same shoot day as the other casino scenes. It is likely that these scenes will follow each other sequentially when scheduling because the character Mike will be on the set. We entered the underlined information from the script into Movie Magic Scheduling's breakdown sheets to be certain that we accounted for the needs of each scene (see Figure 4–2). Each breakdown sheet represents one scene.

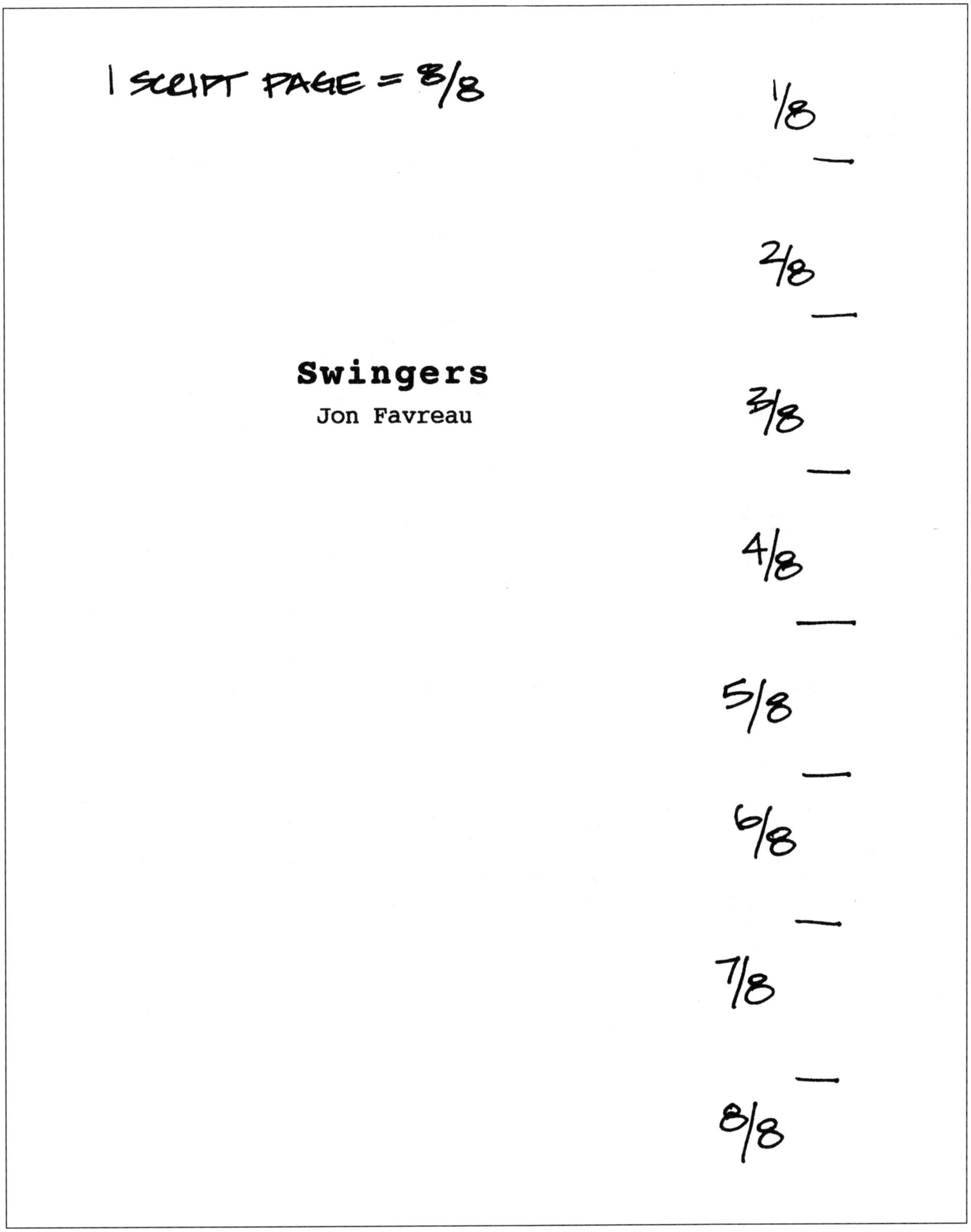

1 SCRIPT PAGE = 8/8

1/8

2/8

Swingers

Jon Favreau

3/8

4/8

5/8

6/8

7/8

8/8

Figure 4–1 Marked-up script pages from Swingers

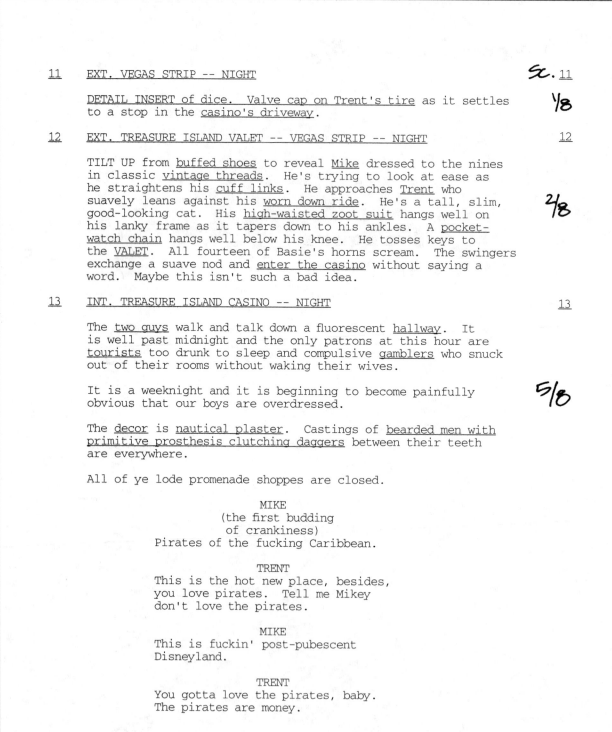

11 EXT. VEGAS STRIP -- NIGHT Sc. 11

DETAIL INSERT of dice. Valve cap on Trent's tire as it settles to a stop in the casino's driveway. 1/8

12 EXT. TREASURE ISLAND VALET -- VEGAS STRIP -- NIGHT 12

TILT UP from buffed shoes to reveal Mike dressed to the nines in classic vintage threads. He's trying to look at ease as he straightens his cuff links. He approaches Trent who suavely leans against his worn down ride. He's a tall, slim, good-looking cat. His high-waisted zoot suit hangs well on his lanky frame as it tapers down to his ankles. A pocket-watch chain hangs well below his knee. He tosses keys to the VALET. All fourteen of Basie's horns scream. The swingers exchange a suave nod and enter the casino without saying a word. Maybe this isn't such a bad idea. 2/8

13 INT. TREASURE ISLAND CASINO -- NIGHT 13

The two guys walk and talk down a fluorescent hallway. It is well past midnight and the only patrons at this hour are tourists too drunk to sleep and compulsive gamblers who snuck out of their rooms without waking their wives.

It is a weeknight and it is beginning to become painfully obvious that our boys are overdressed. 5/8

The decor is nautical plaster. Castings of bearded men with primitive prosthesis clutching daggers between their teeth are everywhere.

All of ye lode promenade shoppes are closed.

MIKE
(the first budding
of crankiness)
Pirates of the fucking Caribbean.

TRENT
This is the hot new place, besides,
you love pirates. Tell me Mikey
don't love the pirates.

MIKE
This is fuckin' post-pubescent
Disneyland.

TRENT
You gotta love the pirates, baby.
The pirates are money.

Figure 4–1 Marked-up script pages from Swingers *(continued)*

Swingers

14 INT. TREASURE ISLAND CASINO -- THE CLASSY SECTION -- NIGHT 14

Mike is at a blackjack table with Trent at his side. The game has paused to observe the newcomers as Mike draws a billfold out of his breast pocket. They're pulling it off with only slightly noticeable effort.

MIKE
I don't know. I guess I'll start with three hundred in, uh, blacks.

Mike tries to hand the DEALER a handful of twenties after counting them twice.

DEALER
On the table.

MIKE
Sorry?

DEALER
You have to lay it on the table.

8/8

MIKE
Uh, I don't want to bet it all.

The other players grow impatient.

DEALER
You're not allowed to hand me money, sir. You'll have to lay it on the table if you want me to change it.

MIKE
(hastily laying down the bills)
Oh...right.

The dealer lays out the bills such that the amount is visible to the camera encased in the black glass globe overhead.

DEALER
Blacks?

MIKE
Huh?

DEALER
You want this in black chips.

MIKE
Sure, that'll be fine.

The dealer chirps out an unintelligible formality and the PIT BOSS chirps the response.

(continued)

Figure 4–1 Marked-up script pages from Swingers *(continued)*

Swingers

14 CONTINUED: 14

Trent and Mike stare at the pit boss ten feet away.

The dealer plunks down the measly THREE CHIPS which represent Mike's entire cash reserve. Not quite the effect he had hoped for.

The swingers stare at the chips. The players stare at the swingers. The dealer stares at the pit boss.

MIKE (CONT'D)
Do you have anything smaller?

DEALER
Yes, but I'm afraid this table has a hundred dollar minimum bet. Perhaps you'd be more comfortable at one of our lower stakes tables.

8/8

The dealer indicates a FIVE DOLLAR TABLE across the room where a disheveled DEALER deals to a BLUEHAIR, a BIKER, and a COUPLE in matching Siegfried & Roy tee shirts.

The swingers look back to the dealer who is now flanked by the pit boss.

The tense silence is broken by...

CHRISTY
Drinks?
(then to Trent)
How about you, Cap'n?

Trent looks over to see that it's the same WAITRESS who flashed him a smile earlier.

MIKE
Yes, I'll have a scotch on the rocks, please. Anything will do. As long as it's not a blend, of course. Any single malt. A Glenlivit or Glenfiddich, perhaps. Maybe a Glengowen. Any "Glen".

CHRISTY
(under her breath)
One scotch on the rocks.

She leaves.

2 pages total scene #14

Figure 4–1 Marked-up script pages from Swingers *(continued)*

52 INT. MIKE'S APARTMENT -- LATER THAT NIGHT 52

Mike opens the door and flicks on the lights in his sparsely furnished single.

He drops his keys on the table and makes a bee line to the answering machine.

He pushes the button.

ANSWERING MACHINE
(synthesized voice)
She didn't call.

Mike collapses into his futon and lights a smoke.

Beat.

He pulls out the COCKTAIL NAPKIN. He stares at the number.

He looks at the clock. 2:20 AM.

He looks at the napkin.

He thinks better of it, and puts the napkin away. 8/8

Beat.

He takes out the napkin and picks up the phone.

ANSWERING MACHINE (CONT'D)
(synthesized voice)
Don't do it, Mike.

MIKE
Shut up.

He dials.

It rings twice, then...

NIKKI
(recorded)
Hi. This is Nikki. Leave a message.
(beep)

MIKE
Hi, Nikki. This is Mike. I met you tonight at the Dresden. I, uh, just called to say I, uh, I'm really glad we met and you should give me a call. So call me tomorrow, or, like, in two days, whatever. My number is 213-555-4679.
(MORE)

(continued)

Figure 4–1 Marked-up script pages from Swingers *(continued)*

Swingers

52 CONTINUED: 52

MIKE (CONT'D)
(beep)

Mike hangs up.

Beat.

He dials again.

NIKKI
(recorded)
Hi. This is Nikki. Leave a message.
(beep)

MIKE
Hi, Nikki. This is Mike, again. I just called because it sounded like your machine might've cut me off before I gave you my number, and also to say sorry for calling so late, but you were still there when I left the Dresden, so I knew I'd get your machine. Anyway, my number is...
(beep)

8/8

Mike calls back right away.

NIKKI
(recorded)
Hi. This is Nikki. Leave a message.
(beep)

MIKE
213.555.4679. That's all. I just wanted to leave my number. I don't want you to think I'm weird, or desperate or something
(he regrets saying it immediately)
...I mean, you know, we should just hang out. That's it. No expectations. Just, you know, hang out. Bye.
(beep)

He hangs up.

Beat.

He dials.

NIKKI
(recorded)
Hi. This is Nikki. Leave a message.
(MORE)

Figure 4–1 Marked-up script pages from Swingers *(continued)*

Swingers

52 CONTINUED: (2) 52

NIKKI (CONT'D)
(beep)

MIKE
I just got out of a six year relationship. Okay? That should help explain why I'm acting so weird. It's not you. It's me. I just wanted to say that. Sorry.
(pause)
This is Mike.
(beep)

He dials again. There's no turning back.

NIKKI
(recorded)
Hi. This is Nikki. Leave a message.
(beep)

MIKE
Hi, Nikki. This is Mike again. Could you just call me when you get in? I'll be up for awhile, and I'd just rather talk to you in person instead of trying to squeeze it all...
(beep)

8/8

He dials yet again.

NIKKI
(recorded)
Hi. This is Nikki. Leave a message.
(beep)

MIKE
Hi, Nikki. Mike. I don't think this is working out.
I think you're great, but maybe we should just take some time off from each other. It's not you, really. It's me. It's only been six months...

NIKKI
(live, in person. she picks up the line)
Mike?

MIKE
Nikki! Great! Did you just walk in, or were you listening all along?

(continued)

Figure 4–1 Marked-up script pages from Swingers *(continued)*

Swingers

52 CONTINUED: (3) 52

NIKKI
(calmly)
Don't call me ever again.

MIKE
Wow. I guess you were home...
(click)

3/8

She hung up on him.

He's frozen.

He hangs up.

Beat.

Beat.

Beat.

3 3/8 total
scene # 52

Figure 4–1 Marked-up script pages from Swingers *(continued)*

SWINGERS
Breakdown Sheet

Page 1

Sheet: **1** I/E: **EXT** Set: **CASINO DRIVEWAY** D/N: **Night**

Scenes: **11** Pages: **1/8**

Synopsis: **DETAIL INSERT OF TRENT'S CAR PULLING INTO CASINO DRIVEWAY**

Location: **TREASURE ISLAND CASINO**

Sequence: Script Day: **1** Script Page: **11**

Vehicles TRENT'S CAR **Props** 15. DICE ON VALVE CAP	

(continued)

Figure 4–2 Breakdown sheets 1 through 5 for Swingers

SWINGERS Page 2

Breakdown Sheet

Sheet: **2** I/E: **EXT** Set: **CASINO DRIVEWAY** D/N: **Night**

Scenes: **12** Pages: **2/8**

Synopsis: **TRENT & MIKE EXIT CAR AT VALET STAND, TOSS VALET KEYS, ENTER**

Location: **TREASURE ISLAND CASINO**

Sequence: Script Day: **1** Script Page: **11**

Cast Members

1. MIKE
2. TRENT
22. VALET

Extras

1. BACKGROUND GAMBLERS

Vehicles

TRENT'S CAR

Props

15. DICE ON VALVE CAP
20. KEYS

Costume

BUFFED SHOES
CUFF LINKS
POCKET CHAIN
VALET UNIFORM
ZOOT SUITS

Figure 4–2 Breakdown sheets 1 through 5 for Swingers *(continued)*

SWINGERS Page 3

Breakdown Sheet

Sheet: **3** I/E: **INT** Set: **CASINO HALLWAY** D/N: **Night**

Scenes: **13** Pages: **3/8**

Synopsis: **MIKE & TRENT WALK AND TALK DOWN THE CASINO HALLWAY**

Location: **TREASURE ISLAND CASINO**

Sequence: Script Day: **2** Script Page: **11**

Cast Members

1. MIKE
2. TRENT

Extras

1. BACKGROUND GAMBLERS
2. TABLE DEALERS
3. TOURISTS
4. CASINO WAITRESSES

Props

25. NAUTICAL DECOR

Costume

CASINO WAITRESS OUTFITS
CUFF LINKS
POCKET CHAIN
ZOOT SUITS

Music

CASINO MUZAK IN BACKGROUND

Sound

GAMBLING CHIPS
SLOT MACHINES

Special Equipment

SLOT MACHINES

Security

SECURITY IN CASINO

(continued)

Figure 4–2 Breakdown sheets 1 through 5 for Swingers *(continued)*

SWINGERS Page 4

Breakdown Sheet

Sheet: **4** I/E: **INT** Set: **BLACKJACK TABLE - CASINO** D/N: **Night**

Scenes: **14** Pages: **4**

Synopsis: **MIKE & TRENT AT THE BLACKJACK TABLE**

Location: **TREASURE ISLAND CASINO**

Sequence: Script Day: **2** Script Page: **14**

Cast Members

1. MIKE
2. TRENT
7. BLUE HAIR
12. BIKER
14. GAMBLING HUSBAND
15. GAMBLING WIFE
16. DEALER
19. PIT BOSS
23. WAITRESS

Extras

1. BACKGROUND GAMBLERS
4. CASINO WAITRESSES

Props

6. BILLFOLD
13. COCKTAILS
17. ENCASED CAMERA
18. GAMBLING CHIPS
24. MONEY

Costume

CASINO WAITRESS OUTFITS
CUFF LINKS
POCKET CHAIN
SIEGFRIED & ROY T-SHIRTS
ZOOT SUITS

Music

CASINO MUZAK IN BACKGROUND

Sound

GAMBLING CHIPS
SLOT MACHINES

Security

SECURITY IN CASINO

Figure 4–2 Breakdown sheets 1 through 5 for Swingers *(continued)*

SWINGERS Page 5
Breakdown Sheet

Sheet: **5** I/E: **INT** Set: **CASHIER'S WINDOW - CASINO** D/N: **Night**

Scenes: **15** Pages: **5 4/8**

Synopsis: **MIKE COLLECTS HIS MONEY; TRENT & MIKE TALK**

Location: **TREASURE ISLAND CASINO**

Sequence: Script Day: **3** Script Page: **18 - 24**

Cast Members
1. MIKE
2. TRENT
8. CHRISTY

Extras
1. BACKGROUND GAMBLERS
2. TABLE DEALERS
5. ATMOSPHERE EXTRAS
6. CASHIER

Props
9. CIGARETTES
12. COCKTAIL NAPKIN
13. COCKTAILS
18. GAMBLING CHIPS
24. MONEY

Costume
CASINO WAITRESS OUTFITS

Music
CASINO MUZAK IN BACKGROUND

Sound
GAMBLING CHIPS
LAUGHING, TALKING
SLOT MACHINES

Security
SECURITY IN CASINO

Figure 4–2 Breakdown sheets 1 through 5 for Swingers *(continued)*

5 SCHEDULING

In the first edition of this book, this chapter was strictly about scheduling your movie—how to break down your script and arrive at an accurate shooting schedule. All of that information on film scheduling remains, but because we have received a number of questions about scheduling as it relates to the filmmaking process as a whole, we decided that some of those questions should be addressed here.

If you are planning on creating an LLC or LLP for the making of your film, you want to allow enough time before official pre-production to get paperwork in place. Therefore, if pre-production is set to begin July 15, you may want to file the papers for your LLC by June 1. You will then wait to receive a Federal Identification number, within several days which you will need to open your bank account and to begin the signatory process with any guild.

If you are fundraising over a longer period (6 to 24 months) you may want to put the money you raise into an escrow account. An LLC or LLP is costly to maintain (there are minimum yearly taxes) and there is no reason to have it open if you are months away from needing to spend the money you are raising. Many attorneys who work in independent film offer escrow service to their clients for a nominal fee (much less than the annual fees required to have an LLC open).

To really get pre-production rolling, you will need to have your Federal ID number, which is only issued once your LLC has been officially established. Therefore, give yourself at least four to six weeks before official pre-production is to begin, to register your company and get your Federal ID number assigned. This number is required for you to open a bank account or sign Screen Actors Guild (SAG) paperwork. If you start spending money before your bank account is officially open, keep track of expenses and reimburse yourself. This, however, should not be a problem, as long as you have your entity officially created.

How long script development and fundraising will take depends on many factors. Whether you are green-lighting yourselves (because you have come up with the money needed) or are getting the green light from a mini-major studio or other company, the *most important thing* is to be confident that your script is in place *before* you begin shooting. The only way to really know this is to have workshopped and edited your script extensively beforehand.

SCHEDULING YOUR FILM SHOOT

Breaking down your script will allow you to determine how much time you will need at each location, how many weeks or months you will need for filming, and for how many days or weeks to schedule each actor. It will also help you devise an order for filming that makes sense. Once you have determined this order, you will have the shooting schedule. The schedule will be the guideline for your budget.

We refer to scheduling as preliminary at this point because it is the job of the first assistant director (first AD) to arrive at a more formal schedule once the availability of the actors has been determined and locations begin to fall into place. By referring to the preliminary schedule, you will also be able to assess with department heads the costs specific to each department. Department heads will have an idea of when filming will take place at each location, the order in which the scenes will be shot, and when their work must be ready for each scene.

Keep in mind that the shooting schedule is always subject to change, even during filming. However, for the line producer, preliminary scheduling is a necessary step to budgeting a film and is the basis on which you will secure cast, crew, locations, extras, equipment, and so on.

If you will be using Movie Magic Scheduling to schedule your film, the program will automatically translate the information entered into your breakdown sheets into a shooting schedule, a one-line schedule, a strip board, and day-out-of-days sheets for the actors and any other elements you specify. The program will assign all of the elements (characters, props, and so on)

ID numbers so that you can quickly reference them from any format in which you are working. All of this can be done by hand, but it is far more efficient if you have a computer program.

When scheduling your shoot, sort scenes by location, interior/exterior, actors, and day/night. Add day breaks or banners where desired so that you are shooting a reasonable number of pages per day. (Movie Magic Scheduling's *Script Breakdown and Scheduling Reference Manual* will show you how to add day breaks within the strip board.) When grouping scenes, take into consideration both location and actor availability. Try to schedule all of an actor's scenes together. This will work best after you have grouped all locations and are able to determine which actors are needed at each location, and when. Some actors may be needed for a few scenes only, so you may want to try to schedule those scenes either first or last, depending on the time of day, to avoid keeping actors waiting.

What you are trying to achieve is a clustering of each location (scheduling all of the scenes to be filmed at a given location within the same time frame) and a clustering of the actors who are needed at that location. Sometimes this works, and sometimes it does not. Ideally, you want to avoid having to return to any location after you have wrapped there It is too costly and not always logistically possible to return to a location. On low-budget shows, shooting all scripted scenes for a single location at one time is usually more cost effective than trying to schedule all of an actor's scenes at one time, but you need to weigh the location's cost versus the actor's cost. When actors' fees outweigh the cost of returning to a location, you should prioritize the actors' schedules over the location if possible. This is more likely to happen on larger-budget shoots for which the actors are being paid larger fees.

If you will not be returning to any of the locations, actors are often put on hold because they most likely will be needed at other locations. A hold takes place over one or more days when the actor is not required for filming but remains available to you. SAG requires that you pay actors for hold days, even though they are not actually shooting. Placing an actor on hold prohibits him or her from taking other work that may interfere with your filming schedule. (SAG rules are discussed in Chapter 7.) Union rules guide your schedule to an extent, even on low-budget independent films. Regardless of whether you have a SAG cast, you should be mindful of SAG rules.

Arrange your schedule so that you give the cast and crew proper turnaround time. For example, do not schedule a night shoot that you estimate will wrap at 5 A.M. preceding a day shoot for which there is a 10 A.M. call. This would make the turnaround five hours; SAG and union rules require that there be a 12-hour turnaround.

If yours is a SAG film, you will need to provide SAG with a copy of your schedule, a day-out-of-days for the principal cast, and a budget. (See "About the Cast Checklist" in Chapter 7 for more about SAG rules and requirements.) As you budget, certain schedule changes may become apparent based on cast and location availability and on cost considerations. Remember, you can rearrange the schedule as necessary.

THE STRIP BOARD

Movie Magic Scheduling will translate the information from your breakdown sheets into strips you can group into days. The strips can then be printed out, individualized, and placed into a board called a strip board. You can rearrange and organize each strip within the board in an order that takes into consideration cost, cast, locations, and other important factors. These strips can be produced on a computer or bought at film supply houses (e.g., Enterprise Stationers in Los Angeles) and are usually 14 to 15 inches long. For a feature film, you will need approximately six to eight panels in your board.

You may use colored strips (indicating day or night, interior or exterior scenes) or black-and-white strips, depending on the needs of the film. (Movie Magic Scheduling has color-coding options for your strip board, enabling you to print out your strips in color if you have a color printer.) Usually, shows with multiple characters, stunts, locations, special effects, voiceovers, extras, and similar elements use strips of different colors to represent the film's various needs. *Swingers* is a dialogue-driven piece, and its needs were fairly simple; color-coded strips were not essential.

The headboard, or header, that appears on the strip board contains reference information, such as the film title, the director, the producers, the line producer, the AD, and so on. Fill in the information in the spaces provided. Each character will appear with his or her corresponding ID number, which you will assign when entering each character into the breakdown sheets. You can assign any other elements an ID number or a letter (for example, *M* = music) and the element will be referenced by its ID number or letter on any strip for which it is relevant. Remember, each strip represents a scene.

If there are 103 scenes in the script, there will be 103 strips.

Examine the sample *Swingers* strip board shown in Figure 5–1. (The sample strip board shows just nine days of shooting and does not reflect the actual order in which *Swingers* was filmed.) From the top of the first strip, trace the following:

- The breakdown sheet number for each scene is the first number listed. Scene 11, described in the first strip, can be found on sheet 1.
- The page count of each scene is the second number given. Scene 11 is 1/8 of a page.
- The shoot day on which the scene is to be shot is listed third.
- Next, the strip indicates whether the scene is an interior or exterior scene, and the location and the time of day of the scene are described. If a scene is an exterior night shot, it will ideally be filmed at night. If the scene is an interior night shot, it could be filmed during the day. This is called filming day for night. The scene number is also given in this box.
- Below the location and the scene number, the characters that appear in the scene are listed by ID number. For instance, on the second strip, for scene 12, ID numbers 1 and 2 are found in the boxes that correspond to Mike and Trent on the headboard. Therefore, Mike and Trent are needed in scene 12. Mike is always referenced as ID number 1, and Trent is always ID number 2.
- A brief description of the scene is found at the bottom of each strip for easy reference.
- Day breaks ("End of Day 1") are found at the end of a clustering of scenes to be shot on a given day. Insert day breaks into your schedule after you have sorted the strips by location, day/night, cast, interior/exterior scenes, and so on. The date on which the scenes will be shot and the total number of pages for that day are also listed in the day break portion of the strip board.

SHOOTING SCHEDULE AND ONE-LINE SCHEDULE

Figures 5–2 and 5–3 show the shooting schedule and the one-line schedule that correspond to the nine-day strip board shown in Figure 5–1. The schedules and the day-out-of-days sheets will help you to budget the costs of the film accurately. For the purposes of this book, we will be scheduling and budgeting for a SAG cast and operating within SAG parameters.

Examine the *Swingers* shooting schedule (see Figure 5–2). The schedule is broken down into shoot days, and the scenes to be shot each day are listed. The scenes appear in the order in which they will be shot, and the scene lengths are combined so that the total number of pages to be shot on a given day is listed. For example, the total number of pages to be shot on shoot day 2 is 6 5/8 pages. This is the combined total length of scenes 14 and 16. When possible, try to order scenes sequentially that are to be shot at the same location.

A brief description of each scene is included in the shooting schedule so that you can quickly identify the scenes to be shot without having to refer to the script. The actors required for a particular scene can be easily determined from their ID number, and the AD will be able to determine appropriate call times for both actors and crew to avoid costly and unnecessary overtime and to give them a proper turnaround.

Examine shoot day 7. Scenes 65 and 35 are both interior scenes at the Hollywood Hills Diner. Scene 65, however, is an interior day shot, and scene 35 is an interior night shot. Because the director wanted to film scene 65 at a booth in the diner by a window, daylight was required, and due to our minimal lighting package and small crew, we could not shoot night for day, which is often done to accommodate both the schedule and the budget. We scheduled scene 65 to be shot first in the late afternoon while it was still daylight, and scene 35 was scheduled for later, when it was dark outside. We kept a couple of factors in mind when scheduling shoot day 7: we estimated the amount of time required to set up for and shoot scene 65 while it was still daylight out, and we set our call time as close as possible to when it would become dark outside while still allowing enough time to film scene 65 so that we could give our cast and crew a proper turnaround and avoid overtime.

On *Swingers*, we scheduled several scenes to be shot each day, and we were able to shoot approximately six to eight script pages per day because *Swingers* is a dialogue-driven piece. For instance, the opening shot of the film requires only two principal cast members, Mike and Rob (shoot day 8, scene 2). They have a one-on-one conversation at a booth in the Hollywood Hills Diner. Although the scene is two pages long, it was shot fairly quickly and on the same day as all of the other diner scenes.

Although dialogue scenes typically do not take as long to film as action scenes, do not underestimate the time needed for these scenes. Give the director and the actors the time they need to get the scene right and to feel comfortable with the performance. The number of

SWINGERS

Director:

Producer:

Asst. Director:

Script Dated:

Sheet Number:		1	2	3	5		4	6		17	18	7		8	10
Page Count:		1/8	2/8	3/8	5 4/8		4	2 5/8		1 1/8	3 3/8	2 6/8		4 1/8	3 3/8
Shoot Day:		1	1	1	1		2	2		3	3	3		4	4
		EXT - CASINO DRIVEWAY - Night Scs. 11	EXT - CASINO DRIVEWAY - Night Scs. 12	INT - CASINO HALLWAY - Night Scs. 13	INT - CASHIER'S WINDOW - CASINO - Nig Scs. 15	— End Of Day 1 – 9/5/95 — 6 2/8 pgs.	INT - CASINO BLACKJACK TABLE - Night Scs. 14	INT - COFFEE SHOP - CASINO - Night Scs. 16	— End Of Day 2 – 9/6/95 — 6 5/8 pgs.	EXT - ALLEYWAY BEHIND BAR - Night Scs. 33	INT - HOLLYWOOD CLUB - BAR - Night Scs. 34	INT - LANDLUBBER LOUNGE - TREASUR Scs. 17	— End Of Day 3 – 9/7/95 — 7 2/8 pgs.	INT - MIKE'S APARTMENT LIVING ROOM Scs. 3	INT - MIKE'S APARTMENT LIVING ROOM Scs. 52
Character	**No.**														
MIKE	1		1	1	1		1	1		1	1	1		1	1
TRENT	2		2	2	2		2	2				2			
ROB	3									3	3				
SUE	4														
CHARLES	5										5				
BARTENDER	6										6	6			
BLUE HAIR	7						7	7							
CHRISTY	8				8							8			
DELIVERY MAN	9														
GIRL WITH CIGAR	10														
BALD GUY CREW (5)	11														
BIKER	12						12								
COFFEE SHOP WAITRESS	13							13							
GAMBLING HUSBAND	14						14								
GAMBLING WIFE	15						15								
DEALER	16						16								
GIRL WITH BABY	17														
LISA	18											18			
PIT BOSS	19						19								
THREE-YEAR-OLD	20														
TWO BEAUTIFUL GIRLS	21														
VALET	22		22												
WAITRESS	23						23								
BABY	24														
CASHIER	25														
DINER WAITRESS	26														
Extras:			E:1	E:4	E:4		E:2	E:1		E:1	E:1	E:1			
Prepared by:		DETAIL INSERT OF TRENT'S CAR PULLING INTO CASINO DRIVEWAY	TRENT & MIKE EXIT CAR AT VALET STAND, TOSS VALET KEYS, ENTER CASINO	MIKE & TRENT WALK AND TALK DOWN THE CASINO HALLWAY	MIKE COLLECTS HIS MONEY; TRENT & MIKE TALK		MIKE & TRENT AT THE BLACKJACK TABLE	TRENT & MIKE ORDER FOOD; TALK ABOUT GIRLS; ARRANGE TO MEET GIRLS		MIKE & ROB WALK DOWN ALLEY TO BAR ENTRANCE	MIKE & ROB ORDER DRINKS AND MEET UP WITH CHARLES AT HOLLYWOOD CLUB	MIKE & TRENT MEET CHRISTY & HER FRIEND LISA AT LOUNGE		MIKE PLAYING MESSAGES FOR EX'S CALL; TRENT TELLS MIKE IT'S VEGAS	MIKE CALLING NIKKI, LEAVING PATHETIC MESSAGES

Figure 5–1 Swingers strip board (days 1 through 9)

Description	Elements	Cast	Set / Scenes	Day	Pages	Strip
— End Of Day 4 – 9/8/95 — 7 4/8 pgs.						
MIKE WAKES; MICHELLE AND LORRAINE CALL		1	INT - MIKE'S BEDROOM - Morning Scs. 64	5	4 2/8	12
MIKE LOOKING AT LORRAINE'S CARD		1	INT - MIKE'S APARTMENT LIVING ROOM Scs. 63	5	3/8	11
MIKE LOOKS TERRIBLE; ROB COMES TO CHEER HIM UP		3, 1	INT - MIKE'S APARTMENT LIVING ROOM Scs. 54	5	3 1/8	9
— End Of Day 5 – 9/11/95 — 7 6/8 pgs.						
SUE, TRENT, & MIKE PLAY VIDEO GAMES AT SUE'S		9, 4, 2, 1	INT - SUE'S LIVING ROOM - Night Scs. 30	6	3	13
TRENT & SUE TORMENT MIKE WITH DELIVERY MAN		4, 2	INT - SUE'S LIVING ROOM - Night Scs. 31	6	2/8	14
MIKE PAYING DELIVERY MAN; SUE & TRENT GIVE HIM A HARD TIME		9, 4, 2, 1	INT - SUE'S DOORWAY - Night Scs. 32	6	1 3/8	15
SUE & TRENT & BALD GUY CREW PLAY VIDEO GAMES; MIKE SHOWS UP		11, 4, 2, 1	INT - SUE'S LIVING ROOM - Night Scs. 56	6	1 1/8	16
— End Of Day 6 – 9/12/95 — 5 6/8 pgs.						
MIKE TELLS TRENT HE'S OVER MICHELLE; GIRL WITH BABY	E:2	20, 17, 2, 1	INT - DINER TABLE - Day Scs. 65	7	2 5/8	22
RESERVOIR DOGS 360-DEGREE TABLE SHOT OF THE SWINGERS		5, 4, 3, 2, 1	INT - HOLLYWOOD HILLS DINER - ROUN Scs. 35	7	1 6/8	20
— End Of Day 7 – 9/13/95 — 4 3/8 pgs.						
ROB & MIKE TALK	E:2	3, 1	INT - DINER TABLE IN WINDOW - Night Scs. 2	8	2	19
TRENT ON TOP OF TABLE	E:2	4, 3, 1	INT - DINER TABLE - Night Scs. 52	8	2 4/8	21
— End Of Day 8 – 9/14/95 — 4 4/8 pgs.						
THE SWINGERS ENTER THE PARTY; EVERYTHING STOPS	E:1	5, 4, 3, 2, 1	INT - CHATEAU MARMONT BUNGALOW LI Scs. 38	9	3/8	23
THE SWINGERS FIX THEMSELVES DRINKS	E:1	5, 4, 3, 2, 1	INT - BAR AREA OF PARTY - Night Scs. 39	9	6/8	24
TRENT & SUE ARE SCOUTING THE LADIES	E:1	4, 2	INT - LIVING ROOM OF PARTY - Night Scs. 40	9	2/8	25
ROB & MIKE ARE SCOUTING TWO BEAUTIFUL GIRLS; THEY GO TO SPEAK WITH THEM	E:1	21, 3, 1	INT - LIVING ROOM - PARTY - Night Scs. 41	9	1 4/8	26

(continued)

Figure 5–1 Swingers *strip board (days 1 through 9) (continued)*

TRENT & SUE PRETEND NOT TO LOOK AT GROUP OF GIRLS; TALK ABOUT GIRLS	E:1																		10						4	3	2	1	INT - LIVING ROOM - PARTY - Night Scs. 42	9	2	27
TRENT TALKING WITH GIRL WITH CIGAR; REST OF SWINGERS LOOKING ON	E:1																		10					5	4	3	2	1	INT - LIVING ROOM - PARTY - Night Scs. 43, 44, 45 ALL CONTINUOUS	9	2 6/8	28
— End Of Day 9 – 9/15/95 — 7 5/8 pgs.																																

Figure 5–1 Swingers *strip board (days 1 through 9) (continued)*

SWINGERS Page 1

Shooting Schedule

SHOOT DAY #1 -- Tue, Sep 5, 1995

Scene #11 **EXT - CASINO DRIVEWAY - Night** 1/8 Pgs.

DETAIL INSERT OF TRENT'S CAR PULLING INTO CASINO DRIVEWAY

Props
15. DICE ON VALVE CAP

Vehicles
TRENT'S CAR

Scene #12 **EXT - CASINO DRIVEWAY - Night** 2/8 Pgs.

TRENT & MIKE EXIT CAR AT VALET STAND, TOSS VALET KEYS, ENTER CASINO

Cast Members
1. MIKE
2. TRENT
22. VALET

Extras
1. BACKGROUND GAMBLERS

Props
15. DICE ON VALVE CAP
20. KEYS

Vehicles
TRENT'S CAR

Costume
BUFFED SHOES
CUFF LINKS
POCKET CHAIN
VALET UNIFORM
ZOOT SUITS

Scene #13 **INT - CASINO HALLWAY - Night** 3/8 Pgs.

MIKE & TRENT WALK AND TALK DOWN THE CASINO HALLWAY

Cast Members
1. MIKE
2. TRENT

Extras
1. BACKGROUND GAMBLERS
2. TABLE DEALERS
3. TOURISTS
4. CASINO WAITRESSES

Security
SECURITY IN CASINO

Props
25. NAUTICAL DECOR

Music
CASINO MUZAK IN BACKGROUND

Costume
CASINO WAITRESS OUTFITS
CUFF LINKS
POCKET CHAIN
ZOOT SUITS

Sound
GAMBLING CHIPS
SLOT MACHINES

Special Equipment
SLOT MACHINES

(continued)

Figure 5–2 Swingers *shooting schedule (days 1 through 9)*

SWINGERS
Shooting Schedule

Page 2

Scene #15 **INT - CASHIER'S WINDOW - CASINO - Night** 5 4/8 Pgs.
MIKE COLLECTS HIS MONEY; TRENT & MIKE TALK

Cast Members
1. MIKE
2. TRENT
8. CHRISTY

Extras
1. BACKGROUND GAMBLERS
2. TABLE DEALERS
5. ATMOSPHERE EXTRAS
6. CASHIER

Props
9. CIGARETTES
12. COCKTAIL NAPKIN
13. COCKTAILS
18. GAMBLING CHIPS
24. MONEY

Music
CASINO MUZAK IN BACKGROUND

Costume
CASINO WAITRESS OUTFITS

Sound
GAMBLING CHIPS
LAUGHING, TALKING
SLOT MACHINES

Security
SECURITY IN CASINO

END OF DAY #1 - 6 2/8 Total Pages

SHOOT DAY #2 -- Wed, Sep 6, 1995

Scene #14 **INT - CASINO BLACKJACK TABLE - Night** 4 Pgs.
MIKE & TRENT AT THE BLACKJACK TABLE

Cast Members
1. MIKE
2. TRENT
7. BLUE HAIR
12. BIKER
14. GAMBLING HUSBAND
15. GAMBLING WIFE
16. DEALER
19. PIT BOSS
23. WAITRESS

Extras
1. BACKGROUND GAMBLERS
4. CASINO WAITRESSES

Props
6. BILLFOLD
13. COCKTAILS
17. ENCASED CAMERA
18. GAMBLING CHIPS
24. MONEY

Music
CASINO MUZAK IN BACKGROUND

Costume
CASINO WAITRESS OUTFITS
CUFF LINKS
POCKET CHAIN
SIEGFRIED & ROY T-SHIRTS
ZOOT SUITS

Sound
GAMBLING CHIPS
SLOT MACHINES

Security
SECURITY IN CASINO

Figure 5–2 Swingers *shooting schedule (days 1 through 9) (continued)*

SWINGERS
Shooting Schedule

Page 3

Scene #16 — **INT - COFFEE SHOP - CASINO - Night** — 2 5/8 Pgs.
TRENT & MIKE ORDER FOOD; TALK ABOUT GIRLS; ARRANGE TO MEET GIRLS

Cast Members
1. MIKE
2. TRENT
7. BLUE HAIR
13. COFFEE SHOP WAITRESS

Extras
5. ATMOSPHERE EXTRAS

Props
3. ASHTRAYS
9. CIGARETTES
10. CIGARS
14. COFFEE CUPS
16. DINER FOOD
23. MENUS

Costume
CASINO WAITRESS OUTFITS

Security
SECURITY IN CASINO

Music
CASINO MUZAK IN BACKGROUND

END OF DAY #2 - 6 5/8 Total Pages

SHOOT DAY #3 -- Thu, Sep 7, 1995

Scene #33 — **EXT - ALLEYWAY BEHIND BAR - Night** — 1 1/8 Pgs.
MIKE & ROB WALK DOWN ALLEY TO BAR ENTRANCE

Cast Members
1. MIKE
3. ROB

Extras
7. DOORMAN

Costume
POCKET CHAIN

Special Equipment
EXTRA DOLLY TRACK

Scene #34 — **INT - HOLLYWOOD CLUB - BAR - Night** — 3 3/8 Pgs.
MIKE & ROB ORDER DRINKS AND MEET UP WITH CHARLES AT HOLLYWOOD CLUB

Cast Members
1. MIKE
3. ROB
5. CHARLES
6. BARTENDER

Extras
8. BAR PATRONS

Props
3. ASHTRAYS
4. BEER BOTTLE
13. COCKTAILS

Music
BAR MUSIC

Set Dressing
SINATRA PHOTO

Costume
BLACK LEATHER JACKET
BLACK TURTLENECK

Security
SECURITY AT DOOR OF BAR

Mechanical FX
SMOKE MACHINE

(continued)

Figure 5–2 Swingers *shooting schedule (days 1 through 9) (continued)*

SWINGERS
Shooting Schedule

Page 4

Scene #17 — **INT - LANDLUBBER LOUNGE - TREASURE ISLAND CASINO - Night** — 2 6/8 Pgs.
MIKE & TRENT MEET CHRISTY & HER FRIEND LISA AT LOUNGE

Cast Members
1. MIKE
2. TRENT
6. BARTENDER
8. CHRISTY
18. LISA

Extras
5. ATMOSPHERE EXTRAS

Props
5. BEER BOTTLES
9. CIGARETTES
10. CIGARS
13. COCKTAILS

Makeup
THEATRICAL MAKEUP
WIG

Music
BAR MUSIC

Costume
ACID-WASHED CLOTHES-GIRLS

Sound
LAUGHING, TALKING

END OF DAY #3 - 7 2/8 Total Pages

SHOOT DAY #4 -- Fri, Sep 8, 1995

Scene #3 — **INT - MIKE'S APARTMENT LIVING ROOM - Night** — 4 1/8 Pgs.
MIKE PLAYING MESSAGES FOR EX'S CALL; TRENT TELLS MIKE IT'S VEGAS

Cast Members
1. MIKE

Props
2. ANSWERING MACHINE
29. PHONE
35. WALL CALENDAR

Set Dressing
ARMCHAIR
COUCH
LAMP
REFRIGERATOR
TABLE

Notes
TRENT IS OFF-SCREEN

Scene #52 — **INT - MIKE'S APARTMENT LIVING ROOM - Night** — 3 3/8 Pgs.
MIKE CALLING NIKKI, LEAVING PATHETIC MESSAGES

Cast Members
1. MIKE

Props
2. ANSWERING MACHINE
11. CLOCK
12. COCKTAIL NAPKIN
20. KEYS
29. PHONE

Set Dressing
ARMCHAIR
COUCH
FUTON
LAMP
TABLE

Sound
ANSWERING MACHINE SOUNDS
EXTERIOR STREET NOISE
PHONE DIAL TONE & RING

(continued)

Figure 5–2 Swingers *shooting schedule (days 1 through 9) (continued)*

SWINGERS
Shooting Schedule

Page 5

END OF DAY #4 - 7 4/8 Total Pages

SHOOT DAY #5 -- Mon, Sep 11, 1995

Scene #64 — **INT - MIKE'S BEDROOM - Morning** — 4 2/8 Pgs.
MIKE WAKES; MICHELLE AND LORRAINE CALL

Cast Members
1. MIKE

Props
2. ANSWERING MACHINE
11. CLOCK
27. PEN
29. PHONE
35. WALL CALENDAR

Set Dressing
ARMCHAIR
COUCH
FUTON
LAMP
REFRIGERATOR
TABLE

Costume
MIKE'S PJs

Scene #63 — **INT - MIKE'S APARTMENT LIVING ROOM - Night** — 3/8 Pgs.
MIKE LOOKING AT LORRAINE'S CARD

Cast Members
1. MIKE

Props
2. ANSWERING MACHINE
11. CLOCK
22. LORRAINE'S CARD
29. PHONE

Set Dressing
ARMCHAIR
COUCH
LAMP
TABLE

Scene #54 — **INT - MIKE'S APARTMENT LIVING ROOM - Night** — 3 1/8 Pgs.
MIKE LOOKS TERRIBLE; ROB COMES TO CHEER HIM UP

Cast Members
1. MIKE
3. ROB

Props
2. ANSWERING MACHINE
8. BROWN BAG
9. CIGARETTES
19. GREETING CARDS
26. ORANGE JUICE
28. PEPPERONI
29. PHONE
32. SEMOLINA
33. SWISS ARMY KNIFE

Set Dressing
ARMCHAIR
COUCH
FUTON
LAMP
TABLE

END OF DAY #5 - 7 6/8 Total Pages

(continued)

Figure 5–2 Swingers *shooting schedule (days 1 through 9) (continued)*

SWINGERS
Shooting Schedule

Page 6

SHOOT DAY #6 -- Tue, Sep 12, 1995

Scene #30 **INT - SUE'S LIVING ROOM - Night** 3 Pgs.
SUE, TRENT, & MIKE PLAY VIDEO GAMES AT SUE'S

Cast Members
1. MIKE
2. TRENT
4. SUE
9. DELIVERY MAN

Props
1. 12-PACK OF BEER
3. ASHTRAYS
5. BEER BOTTLES
9. CIGARETTES
24. MONEY
29. PHONE
30. PIZZA BOXES
31. SEGA HOCKEY GAME

Special FX
VIDEO GAME FOOTAGE ON TV

Makeup
SUE'S VARGA GIRL TATTOO

Set Dressing
CHAIRS
COUCH
TABLE
TV
WALL POSTERS

Costume
DELIVERY UNIFORM
L.A. KINGS HOCKEY JERSEY
POCKET CHAIN

Sound
WRESTLING COMMOTION

Scene #31 **INT - SUE'S LIVING ROOM - Night** 2/8 Pgs.
TRENT & SUE TORMENT MIKE WITH DELIVERY MAN

Cast Members
2. TRENT
4. SUE

Props
3. ASHTRAYS
5. BEER BOTTLES
9. CIGARETTES
29. PHONE
30. PIZZA BOXES
31. SEGA HOCKEY GAME

Set Dressing
COUCH
CHAIRS
TABLE
TV
WALL POSTERS

Sound
WRESTLING COMMOTION

Notes
COMMOTION FROM OS

Scene #32 **INT - SUE'S DOORWAY - Night** 1 3/8 Pgs.
MIKE PAYING DELIVERY MAN; SUE & TRENT GIVE HIM A HARD TIME

Cast Members
1. MIKE
2. TRENT
4. SUE
9. DELIVERY MAN

Props
1. 12-PACK OF BEER
3. ASTHRAYS
5. BEER BOTTLES
9. CIGARETTES
24. MONEY
29. PHONE
30. PIZZA BOXES
31. SEGA HOCKEY GAME

Set Dressing
COUCH
CHAIRS
TABLE
TV

(continued)

Figure 5–2 Swingers *shooting schedule (days 1 through 9) (continued)*

SWINGERS

Shooting Schedule

Page 7

Scene #56 **INT - SUE'S LIVING ROOM - Night** 1 1/8 Pgs.

SUE & TRENT & BALD GUY CREW PLAY VIDEO GAMES; MIKE SHOWS UP

Cast Members
1. MIKE
2. TRENT
4. SUE
11. BALD GUY CREW (5)

Props
3. ASHTRAYS
5. BEER BOTTLES
9. CIGARETTES
30. PIZZA BOXES
31. SEGA HOCKEY GAME

Set Dressing
CHAIRS
COUCH
TABLE
TV
WALL POSTERS

Makeup
TATTOOS

END OF DAY #6 - 5 6/8 Total Pages

SHOOT DAY #7 -- Wed, Sep 13, 1995

Scene #65 **INT - DINER TABLE - Day** 2 5/8 Pgs.

MIKE TELLS TRENT HE'S OVER MICHELLE; GIRL WITH BABY

Cast Members
1. MIKE
2. TRENT
17. GIRL WITH BABY
20. THREE-YEAR-OLD

Extras
4. CASINO WAITRESSES
9. DINER PATRONS

Props
14. COFFEE CUPS
16. DINER FOOD

Makeup
CLUB STAMPS

Music
DINER BACKROUND MUSIC

Additional Labor
WELFARE WORKER FOR MINOR

Scene #35 **INT - HOLLYWOOD HILLS DINER - ROUND TABLE - Night** 1 6/8 Pgs.

RESERVOIR DOGS 360-DEGREE TABLE SHOT OF THE SWINGERS

Cast Members
1. MIKE
2. TRENT
3. ROB
4. SUE
5. CHARLES

Props
9. CIGARETTES
16. DINER FOOD
24. MONEY

Special Equipment
EXTRA DOLLY TRACK

Notes
NO ATMOSPHERE EXTRAS

END OF DAY #7 - 4 3/8 Total Pages

(continued)

Figure 5–2 Swingers *shooting schedule (days 1 through 9) (continued)*

SWINGERS
Shooting Schedule

Page 8

SHOOT DAY #8 -- Thu, Sep 14, 1995

Scene #2 — **INT - DINER TABLE IN WINDOW - Night** — 2 Pgs.
ROB & MIKE TALK

Cast Members
1. MIKE
3. ROB

Extras
4. CASINO WAITRESSES
9. DINER PATRONS

Props
14. COFFEE CUPS
16. DINER FOOD

Music
DINER BACKROUND MUSIC

Sound
LAUGHING, TALKING

Scene #52 — **INT - DINER TABLE - Night** — 2 4/8 Pgs.
TRENT ON TOP OF TABLE

Cast Members
1. MIKE
3. ROB
4. SUE

Extras
4. CASINO WAITRESSES
9. DINER PATRONS

Props
7. BREAKFAST FOOD
14. COFFEE CUPS
23. MENUS

Makeup
TRENT LOOKS DRUNK

END OF DAY #8 - 4 4/8 Total Pages

SHOOT DAY #9 -- Fri, Sep 15, 1995

Scene #38 — **INT - CHATEAU MARMONT BUNGALOW LIVING ROOM - Night** — 3/8 Pgs.
THE SWINGERS ENTER THE PARTY; EVERYTHING STOPS

Cast Members
1. MIKE
2. TRENT
3. ROB
4. SUE
5. CHARLES

Extras
10. PARTY GUESTS

Props
5. BEER BOTTLES
9. CIGARETTES
10. CIGARS
13. COCKTAILS

Greenery
PLANTS

Set Dressing
COUCH

Costume
TRENDY BACKPACKS

Special Equipment
EXTRA DOLLY
SLOT MACHINES

Security
SECURITY AT PARTY

Notes
PARTY IS HIP AND PACKED

(continued)

Figure 5–2 Swingers *shooting schedule (days 1 through 9) (continued)*

SWINGERS
Shooting Schedule
Page 9

Scene #39 **INT - BAR AREA - PARTY - Night** 6/8 Pgs.
THE SWINGERS FIX THEMSELVES DRINKS

Cast Members
1. MIKE
2. TRENT
3. ROB
4. SUE
5. CHARLES

Extras
10. PARTY GUESTS

Props
9. CIGARETTES
10. CIGARS
13. COCKTAILS
21. LIQUOR BOTTLES

Music
PARTY MUSIC

Sound
LAUGHING, TALKING

Security
SECURITY AT PARTY

Scene #40 **INT - LIVING ROOM - PARTY - Night** 2/8 Pgs.
TRENT & SUE ARE SCOUTING THE LADIES

Cast Members
2. TRENT
4. SUE

Extras
10. PARTY GUESTS

Props
4. BEER BOTTLE
9. CIGARETTES
10. CIGARS
13. COCKTAILS

Costume
COMBAT BOOTS
SHORT SEXY DRESSES
TRENDY BACKPACKS

Sound
LAUGHING, TALKING

Music
PARTY MUSIC

Security
SECURITY AT PARTY

Notes
PARTY IS HIP AND PACKED

Scene #41 **INT - LIVING ROOM - PARTY - Night** 1 4/8 Pgs.
ROB & MIKE ARE SCOUTING TWO BEAUTIFUL GIRLS; THEY GO TO SPEAK WITH THEM

Cast Members
1. MIKE
3. ROB
21. TWO BEAUTIFUL GIRLS

Extras
10. PARTY GUESTS

Props
9. CIGARETTES
13. COCKTAILS

Music
PARTY MUSIC

Costume
MIDRIFF TOPS
STRETCH BELLBOTTOMS
TRENDY BACKPACKS

Sound
LAUGHING, TALKING

Security
SECURITY AT PARTY

Notes
PARTY IS HIP AND PACKED

(continued)

Figure 5–2 Swingers *shooting schedule (days 1 through 9) (continued)*

SWINGERS
Shooting Schedule

Page 10

Scene #42 | **INT - LIVING ROOM - PARTY - Night** | 2 Pgs.
TRENT & SUE PRETEND NOT TO LOOK AT GROUP OF GIRLS; TALK ABOUT GIRLS

Cast Members
1. MIKE
2. TRENT
3. ROB
4. SUE
10. GIRL WITH CIGAR

Extras
10. PARTY GUESTS

Security
SECURITY AT PARTY

Props
5. BEER BOTTLES
9. CIGARETTES
10. CIGARS
13. COCKTAILS

Music
PARTY MUSIC

Costume
TRENDY BACKPACKS

Sound
LAUGHING, TALKING

Scene #43,44,45
ALL CONTINUOUS | **INT - LIVING ROOM - PARTY - Night** | 2 6/8 Pgs.
TRENT TALKING WITH GIRL WITH CIGAR; REST OF SWINGERS LOOKING ON

Cast Members
1. MIKE
2. TRENT
3. ROB
4. SUE
5. CHARLES
10. GIRL WITH CIGAR

Extras
10. PARTY GUESTS

Security
SECURITY AT PARTY

Props
5. BEER BOTTLES
9. CIGARETTES
10. CIGARS
12. COCKTAIL NAPKIN
13. COCKTAILS
27. PEN

Music
PARTY MUSIC

Costume
TRENDY BACKPACKS

Sound
LAUGHING, TALKING

END OF DAY #9 - 7 5/8 Total Pages

Figure 5–2 Swingers *shooting schedule (days 1 though 9) (continued)*

SWINGERS

Page 1

ONE - LINE SCHEDULE

Shoot Day #1 -- Tue, Sep 5, 1995

Scs. 11 EXT **CASINO DRIVEWAY** **Night** 1/8 pgs.
DETAIL INSERT OF TRENT'S CAR PULLING INTO CASINO DRIVEWAY
ID:

Scs. 12 EXT **CASINO DRIVEWAY** **Night** 2/8 pgs.
TRENT & MIKE EXIT CAR AT VALET STAND, TOSS VALET KEYS, ENTER CASINO
ID: 1, 2, 22

Scs. 13 INT **CASINO HALLWAY** **Night** 3/8 pgs.
MIKE & TRENT WALK AND TALK DOWN THE CASINO HALLWAY
ID: 1, 2

Scs. 15 INT **CASHIER'S WINDOW - CASINO** **Night** 5 4/8 Pgs.
MIKE COLLECTS HIS MONEY; TRENT & MIKE TALK
ID:1, 2, 8

End Day #1 -- Total Pages: 6 2/8

Shoot Day #2 -- Wed, Sep 6, 1995

Scs. 14 INT **CASINO BLACKJACK TABLE** **Night** 4 pgs.
MIKE & TRENT AT THE BLACKJACK TABLE
ID:1, 2, 7, 12, 14, 15, 16, 19, 23

Scs. 16 INT **COFFEE SHOP - CASINO** **Night** 2 5/8 pgs.
TRENT & MIKE ORDER FOOD; TALK ABOUT GIRLS; ARRANGE TO MEET GIRLS
ID:1, 2, 7, 13

End Day #2 -- Total Pages: 6 5/8

Shoot Day #3 -- Thu, Sep 7, 1995

Scs. 33 EXT **ALLEYWAY BEHIND BAR** **Night** 1 1/8 pgs.
MIKE & ROB WALK DOWN ALLEY TO BAR ENTRANCE
ID:1, 3

Scs. 34 INT **HOLLYWOOD CLUB - BAR** **Night** 3 3/8 pgs.
MIKE & ROB ORDER DRINKS AND MEET UP WITH CHARLES AT HOLLYWOOD
CLUB ID:1, 3, 5, 6

Scs. 17 INT **LANDLUBBER LOUNGE - TREASURE ISLAND** **Night** 2 6/8 pgs.
MIKE & TRENT MEET CHRISTY & HER FRIEND LISA AT LOUNGE
ID:1, 2, 6, 8, 18

End Day #3 -- Total Pages: 7 2/8

Shoot Day #4 -- Fri, Sep 8, 1995

Scs. 3 INT **MIKE'S APARTMENT LIVING ROOM** **Night** 4 1/8 pgs.
MIKE PLAYING MESSAGES FOR EX'S CALL; TRENT TELLS MIKE IT'S VEGAS
ID:1

Scs. 52 INT **MIKE'S APARTMENT LIVING ROOM** **Night** 3 3/8 pgs.
MIKE CALLING NIKKI, LEAVING PATHETIC MESSAGES
ID:1

(continued)

Figure 5–3 Swingers *one-line schedule (days 1 through 9)*

SWINGERS

ONE - LINE SCHEDULE

Page 2

END OF DAY #4 -- Total Pages: 7 4/8

Shoot Day #5 -- Mon, Sep 11, 1995

Scs. 64	INT	**MIKE'S BEDROOM** MIKE WAKES; MICHELLE AND LORRAINE CALL ID:1	**Morning**	4 2/8 pgs.
Scs. 63	INT	**MIKE'S APARTMENT LIVING ROOM** MIKE LOOKING AT LORRAINE'S CARD ID:1	**Night**	3/8 pgs.
Scs. 54	INT	**MIKE'S APARTMENT LIVING ROOM** MIKE LOOKS TERRIBLE; ROB COMES TO CHEER HIM UP ID:1, 3	**Night**	3 1/8 pgs.

End Day #5 -- Total Pages: 7 6/8

Shoot Day #6 -- Tue, Sep 12, 1995

Scs. 30	INT	**SUE'S LIVING ROOM** SUE, TRENT, & MIKE PLAY VIDEO GAMES AT SUE'S ID: 1, 2, 4, 9	**Night**	3 pgs.
Scs. 31	INT	**SUE'S LIVING ROOM** TRENT & SUE TORMENT MIKE WITH DELIVERY MAN ID: 2, 4	**Night**	2/8 pgs.
Scs. 32	INT	**SUE'S DOORWAY** MIKE PAYING DELIVERY MAN; SUE & TRENT GIVE HIM A HARD TIME ID: 1, 2, 4, 9	**Night**	1 3/8 pgs.
Scs. 56	INT	**SUE'S LIVING ROOM** SUE & TRENT & BALD GUY CREW PLAY VIDEO GAMES; MIKE SHOWS UP ID: 1, 2, 4, 11	**Night**	1 1/8 pgs.

End Day #6 -- Total Pages: 5 6/8

Shoot Day #7 -- Wed, Sep 13, 1995

Scs. 65	INT	**DINER TABLE** MIKE TELLS TRENT HE'S OVER MICHELLE; GIRL WITH BABY ID: 1, 2, 17, 20	**Day**	2 5/8 pgs.
Scs. 35	INT	**HOLLYWOOD HILLS DINER - ROUND TABLE** RESERVOIR DOGS 360-DEGREE TABLE SHOT OF THE SWINGERS ID: 1, 2, 3, 4, 5	**Night**	1 6/8 pgs.

End Day #7 -- Total Pages: 4 3/8

Shoot Day #8 -- Thu, Sep 14, 1995

Scs. 2	INT	**DINER TABLE IN WINDOW** ROB & MIKE TALK ID: 1, 3	**Night**	2 pgs.

(continued)

Figure 5–3 Swingers *one-line schedule (days 1 through 9) (continued)*

SWINGERS Page 3

ONE - LINE SCHEDULE

Scs. 52	INT	**DINER TABLE** TRENT ON TOP OF TABLE ID: 1, 3, 4	**Night**	2 4/8 pgs.

End Day #8 -- Total Pages: 4 4/8

Shoot Day #9 -- Fri, Sep 15, 1995

Scs. 38	INT	**CHATEAU MARMONT BUNGALOW LIVING** THE SWINGERS ENTER THE PARTY; EVERYTHING STOPS ID: 1, 2, 3, 4, 5	**Night**	3/8 pgs.
Scs. 39	INT	**BAR AREA - PARTY** THE SWINGERS FIX THEMSELVES DRINKS ID: 1, 2, 3, 4, 5	**Night**	6/8 pgs.
Scs. 40	INT	**LIVING ROOM - PARTY** TRENT & SUE ARE SCOUTING THE LADIES ID: 2, 4	**Night**	2/8 pgs.
Scs. 41	INT	**LIVING ROOM - PARTY** ROB & MIKE ARE SCOUTING TWO BEAUTIFUL GIRLS; THEY GO TO SPEAK WITH THEM ID: 1, 3, 21	**Night**	1 4/8 pgs.
Scs. 42	INT	**LIVING ROOM - PARTY** TRENT & SUE PRETEND NOT TO LOOK AT GROUP OF GIRLS; TALK ABOUT GIRLS ID: 1, 2, 3, 4, 10	**Night**	2 pgs.
Scs. 43, 44, 45 ALL CONTINUOUS	INT	**LIVING ROOM - PARTY** TRENT TALKING WITH GIRL WITH CIGAR; REST OF SWINGERS LOOKING ON ID: 1, 2, 3, 4, 5, 10	**Night**	2 6/8 pgs.

End Day #9 -- Total Pages: 7 5/8

Figure 5–3 Swingers *one-line schedule (days 1 through 9) (continued)* pages you will be able to shoot each day will depend on the lighting needs in a particular location, the type of camera being used (how easily it can be moved around), the amount of equipment present on the set, the size of the space you are filming in, how large the crew is, how many actors are present in each scene, how many extras are needed, and other factors. If the script has a fair amount of action, stunts, extras, or special effects (requiring more setup time), the number of pages shot per day will be much less. It is important to keep these things in mind when scheduling the film, and your AD will be most helpful here.

As the line producer, it is your job to keep the show moving forward at a steady pace, while being careful not to overwork anyone. If you anticipate that it will take only a portion of a shoot day to shoot all scenes in a given location, schedule other scenes that require a different location on that same day. This new location should ideally be near the first location. When you move locations within the same day, it is called a company move day. According to the *Swingers* sample shooting schedule, shoot day 3 was a company move day. The day began in the alley behind a bar called The Room, and the production moved to a bar called The 3 of Clubs, which served as the Hollywood Bar. We needed an exterior shot of Mike and Rob entering the bar, so we used the alley of The Room and actually shot the interior bar scenes at The 3 of Clubs. Company moves must be carefully factored into your schedule and well planned. Although they require time and organization, they can save you time and money in the long run. (See Chapter 7 for more on company move days.)

The one-line schedule is merely a shortened version of the shooting schedule. It does not list props, set dressing, wardrobe, vehicles, or similar elements, and it refers to characters by ID number only. The one-line schedule lists each day's scenes in the order in which they will be shot, indicates whether each scene is an interior or exterior, gives the scene location, and shows the total number of pages to be shot each day. The one-line schedule is easier to refer to than the shooting schedule, especially for department heads.

DAY-OUT-OF-DAYS SHEETS

The day-out-of-days sheet indicates which days each of the actors, extras, vehicles, props, and other elements are required and will help you properly budget and schedule for production. Movie Magic Scheduling allows you to generate a day-out-of-days for any of the elements required in the film. Sample day-out-of-days sheets are reproduced in Figure 5–4. They show the principal cast, extras, and props required for the first nine shoot days for *Swingers* and correspond to the sample schedules. Examine the sample day-out-of-days for the principal cast. All of the characters are listed in the order in which they appear in the script, referenced by an ID number assigned to them in the breakdown sheets. Read the day-out-of-days as if it were a graph. The letter codes are defined as follows.

- *SW* stands for "start work" and appears in the box that corresponds to the actor's first day of work.
- *WF* is "work finish" and is placed in the box that corresponds to the actor's last day of work.
- *SWF* stands for "start work finish." When this code appears, the actor starts and finishes work on the same day. He or she should be paid as a day player, according to SAG rules and rates.
- *H* means that a hold has been placed on the actor. You may hold an actor for a day, a week, or more, until he or she is needed again. Keep in mind that under most SAG contracts you must pay actors for hold days, so it is important to schedule their workdays as consecutively as possible.
- *W* stands for "work." Every day an actor is scheduled to work, a W appears in the box corresponding to that date.
- *T* indicates a travel day for the actor. You must pay actors for travel days as if they were regular workdays, according to SAG rules and rates.
- *R* indicates a rehearsal day for the actor. Rehearsals must be carefully planned with the appropriate actors and the director. Rehearsal days are typically paid as normal workdays, according to SAG rules.
- A slash mark (/) or a blacked-out box indicates a holiday or a production day off. Slash marks (/) are usually used with actors who have already begun filming.

The following information can be derived from the day-out-of-days sheet for the *Swingers* cast:

- Mike started work on Tuesday, September 5, shoot day 1, and worked every day until the production was off on Saturday, September 9, and Sunday, September 10. Mike finished work on Friday, September 15, shoot day 9. He had no hold or travel days during this period.
- Trent started work on Tuesday, September 5, shoot day 1. He was on hold on Friday, September 8; Monday, September 11; and Thursday, September 14. He finished work the next day, shoot day 9.
- Lisa started work and finished work on Thursday, September 7, shoot day 3.

September	Day of Month:	5	6	7	8	9	10	11	12	13	14	15	Rehearse	Travel	Work	Hold
	Day Of Week:	Tu	W	Th	F	Sa	Su	M	Tu	W	Th	F				
	Shooting Days:	1	2	3	4			5	6	7	8	9				
1.	MIKE	SW	W	W	W			W	W	W	W	WF			9	
2.	TRENT	SW	W	W	H			H	W	W	H	WF			6	3
3.	ROB			SW	H			W	H	W	W	WF			5	2
4.	SUE								SW	W	W	WF			4	
5.	CHARLES			SW	H			H	H	W	H	WF			3	4
6.	BARTENDER			SWF											1	
7.	BLUE HAIR		SWF												1	
8.	CHRISTY	SW	H	WF											2	1
9.	DELIVERY MAN								SWF						1	
10.	GIRL WITH CIGAR											SWF			1	
11.	BALD GUY CREW (5)								SWF						1	
12.	BIKER		SWF												1	
13.	COFFEE SHOP WAITRESS		SWF												1	
14.	GAMBLING HUSBAND		SWF												1	
15.	GAMBLING WIFE		SWF												1	
16.	DEALER		SWF												1	
17.	GIRL WITH BABY									SWF					1	
18.	LISA			SWF											1	
19.	PIT BOSS		SWF												1	
20.	THREE-YEAR-OLD									SWF					1	
21.	TWO BEAUTIFUL GIRLS											SWF			1	
22.	VALET	SWF													1	
23.	WAITRESS		SWF												1	
24.	BABY															
25.	CASHIER															
26.	DINER WAITRESS															

	Day of Month:	Holiday	Loop	Start	Finish	TOTAL
	Day Of Week:					
	Shooting Days:					
1.	MIKE			9/5	9/15	9
2.	TRENT			9/5	9/15	9
3.	ROB			9/7	9/15	7
4.	SUE			9/12	9/15	4
5.	CHARLES			9/7	9/15	7
6.	BARTENDER			9/7	9/7	1
7.	BLUE HAIR			9/6	9/6	1
8.	CHRISTY			9/5	9/7	3
9.	DELIVERY MAN			9/12	9/12	1
10.	GIRL WITH CIGAR			9/15	9/15	1
11.	BALD GUY CREW (5)			9/12	9/12	1
12.	BIKER			9/6	9/6	1
13.	COFFEE SHOP WAITRESS			9/6	9/6	1
14.	GAMBLING HUSBAND			9/6	9/6	1
15.	GAMBLING WIFE			9/6	9/6	1
16.	DEALER			9/6	9/6	1
17.	GIRL WITH BABY			9/13	9/13	1
18.	LISA			9/7	9/7	1
19.	PIT BOSS			9/6	9/6	1
20.	THREE-YEAR-OLD			9/13	9/13	1
21.	TWO BEAUTIFUL GIRLS			9/15	9/15	1
22.	VALET			9/5	9/5	1
23.	WAITRESS			9/6	9/6	1
24.	BABY					
25.	CASHIER					
26.	DINER WAITRESS					

(continued)

Figure 5–4 Swingers day-out-of-days sheets (cast, extras, and props) (continued)

September	Day of Month:	5	6	7	8	9	10	11	12	13	14	15	Rehearse	Travel	Work	Hold
	Day Of Week:	Tu	W	Th	F	Sa	Su	M	Tu	W	Th	F				
	Shooting Days:	1	2	3	4			5	6	7	8	9				
1.	BACKGROUND GAMBLER	SW	WF												2	
2.	TABLE DEALERS	SWF													1	
3.	TOURISTS	SWF													1	
4.	CASINO WAITRESSES	SW	W	H	H			H	H	W	WF				4	4
5.	ATMOSPHERE EXTRAS	SW	W	WF											3	
6.	CASHIER	SWF													1	
7.	DOORMAN			SWF											1	
8.	BAR PATRONS			SWF											1	
9.	DINER PATRONS									SW	WF				2	
10.	PARTY GUESTS											SWF			1	

	Day of Month:	Holiday	Loop	Start	Finish	TOTAL
	Day Of Week:					
	Shooting Days:					
1.	BACKGROUND GAMBLER			9/5	9/6	2
2.	TABLE DEALERS			9/5	9/5	1
3.	TOURISTS			9/5	9/5	1
4.	CASINO WAITRESSES			9/5	9/14	8
5.	ATMOSPHERE EXTRAS			9/5	9/7	3
6.	CASHIER			9/5	9/5	1
7.	DOORMAN			9/7	9/7	1
8.	BAR PATRONS			9/7	9/7	1
9.	DINER PATRONS			9/13	9/14	2
10.	PARTY GUESTS			9/15	9/15	1

September	Day of Month:	5	6	7	8	9	10	11	12	13	14	15	Rehearse	Travel	Work	Hold
	Day Of Week:	Tu	W	Th	F	Sa	Su	M	Tu	W	Th	F				
	Shooting Days:	1	2	3	4			5	6	7	8	9				
1.	12-PACK OF BEER								SWF						1	
2.	ANSWERING MACHINE				SW			WF							2	
3.	ASHTRAYS		SW	W	H			H	WF						3	2
4.	BEER BOTTLE			SW	H			H	H	H	H	WF			2	5
5.	BEER BOTTLES			SW	H			H	W	H	H	WF			3	4
6.	BILLFOLD		SWF												1	
7.	BREAKFAST FOOD										SWF				1	
8.	BROWN BAG							SWF							1	
9.	CIGARETTES	SW	W	W	H			W	W	W	H	WF			7	2
10.	CIGARS		SW	W	H			H	H	H	H	WF			3	5
11.	CLOCK				SW			WF							2	
12.	COCKTAIL NAPKIN	SW	H	H	W			H	H	H	H	WF			3	6
13.	COCKTAILS	SW	W	W	H			H	H	H	H	WF			4	5
14.	COFFEE CUPS		SW	H	H			H	H	W	WF				3	4
15.	DICE ON VALVE CAP	SWF													1	
16.	DINER FOOD		SW	H	H			H	H	W	WF				3	4
17.	ENCASED CAMERA		SWF												1	
18.	GAMBLING CHIPS	SW	WF												2	
19.	GREETING CARDS							SWF							1	
20.	KEYS	SW	H	H	WF										2	2
21.	LIQUOR BOTTLES											SWF			1	
22.	LORRAINE'S CARD							SWF							1	
23.	MENUS		SW	H	H			H	H	H	WF				2	5
24.	MONEY	SW	W	H	H			H	W	WF					4	3
25.	NAUTICAL DECOR	SWF													1	
26.	ORANGE JUICE							SWF							1	
27.	PEN							SW	H	H	H	WF			2	3
28.	PEPPERONI							SWF							1	
29.	PHONE				SW			W	WF						3	
30.	PIZZA BOXES								SWF						1	
31.	SEGA HOCKEY GAME								SWF					1	1	
32.	SEMOLINA							SWF							1	
33.	SWISS ARMY KNIFE							SWF							1	
34.	TABLE															
35.	WALL CALENDAR				SW			WF							2	

Figure 5–4 Swingers day-out-of-days sheets (cast, extras, and props)

Day of Month: / Day Of Week: / Shooting Days:		Holiday	Loop	Start	Finish	TOTAL
1.	12-PACK OF BEER			9/12	9/12	1
2.	ANSWERING MACHINE			9/8	9/11	2
3.	ASHTRAYS			9/6	9/12	5
4.	BEER BOTTLE			9/7	9/15	7
5.	BEER BOTTLES			9/7	9/15	7
6.	BILLFOLD			9/6	9/6	1
7.	BREAKFAST FOOD			9/14	9/14	1
8.	BROWN BAG			9/11	9/11	1
9.	CIGARETTES			9/5	9/15	9
10.	CIGARS			9/6	9/15	8
11.	CLOCK			9/8	9/11	2
12.	COCKTAIL NAPKIN			9/5	9/15	9
13.	COCKTAILS			9/5	9/15	9
14.	COFFEE CUPS			9/6	9/14	7
15.	DICE ON VALVE CAP			9/5	9/5	1
16.	DINER FOOD			9/6	9/14	7
17.	ENCASED CAMERA			9/6	9/6	1
18.	GAMBLING CHIPS			9/5	9/6	2
19.	GREETING CARDS			9/11	9/11	1
20.	KEYS			9/5	9/8	4
21.	LIQUOR BOTTLES			9/15	9/15	1
22.	LORRAINE'S CARD			9/11	9/11	1
23.	MENUS			9/6	9/14	7
24.	MONEY			9/5	9/13	7
25.	NAUTICAL DECOR			9/5	9/5	1
26.	ORANGE JUICE			9/11	9/11	1
27.	PEN			9/11	9/15	5
28.	PEPPERONI			9/11	9/11	1
29.	PHONE			9/8	9/12	3
30.	PIZZA BOXES			9/12	9/12	1
31.	SEGA HOCKEY GAME			9/12	9/12	1
32.	SEMOLINA			9/11	9/11	1
33.	SWISS ARMY KNIFE			9/11	9/11	1
34.	TABLE					
35.	WALL CALENDAR			9/8	9/11	2

Figure 5–4 Swingers day-out-of-days sheets (cast, extras, and props) (continued)

The day-out-of-days includes a summary page that reflects the total number of workdays, hold days, holidays, and looping days for each actor. According to Figure 5–4, Mike worked a total of nine days. He had no hold days. Trent worked six days and was on hold for three days, totaling nine days of pay. Rob worked five days and was on hold for two days, giving a total of seven days. None of these characters had rehearsal days or travel days during this period.

Refer to the day-out-of-days summary page when budgeting to deter mine how to pay each actor (that is, as a weekly player, a daily player, or a drop-pickup), and to determine which dates to secure locations, certain equipment, vehicles, extras, and so on. (See Chapter 6 for further detail.)

6 BUDGETING

". . . depending on the budget, I cut my cloth to size. I never think epic when I have a peanut, on the one hand, and on the other hand I'm always making epics on a peanut because I'm very practical . . . about what a budget means . . ."

—*Mira Nair, director,* Monsoon Wedding

INTRODUCTION TO BUDGETING

Once you have completed the breakdown and preliminary schedule, you have to run the numbers to ensure that you can make the film you want for the money you have. The budget will tell you how much it will cost to make your film. It will help you keep track of all of the film's needs, and by actualizing the budget you will track money spent and money available. Be certain that you have enough money to get the film both in and out of the can.

Be as precise as possible when budgeting a film. Contact potential vendors to verify any deals you think you may be able to make. Contact the locations you want to secure, and the permit office of the city in which you are shooting, to ascertain all fees involved. If the production will need to travel, get actual quotes from airlines and hotels. Compare quotes from several catering companies, or figure out a creative way to cater the shoot for less money. If the show is nonunion, determine the most cost-effective way to structure crew rates, keeping in mind that you need to be fair to everyone. Call the Screen Actors Guild (if the show is a SAG show) for rates and any financial assurances you will have to pay. The bottom line is that your numbers must be real.

After an initial pass at the budget, go through it again and double check your numbers. Budget extra money for some of the categories and line items, especially those areas in which you are still uncertain about what the actual costs will be. Padding the budget in this way ensures that you will be covered. Have a budget wizard, or someone who has made a low-budget film before and is familiar with the costs you will need to budget for, check and challenge your numbers.

The Budget Is Malleable

The budget is the best assessment of the costs involved in making a movie based on preliminary quotes. The budget is a blueprint. It is not set in stone. Most likely, the money actually spent on each line item will deviate from the original number allocated in the budget. Your budget must be flexible enough to support any unexpected costs. Each category need not conform to its initial allocation. You can use the money saved in one category to cover overages in another. (Try to avoid this, but it is an option.) This is in part why budgets are padded. You will never be able to anticipate everything that might come up, and the needs of the film might change during filming. Almost all independent films could use more money, but the budget is a tool that tells you whether the little you do have will allow you to make the film.

What You Will Need

Before you begin to compile your budget, gather the script, preliminary shooting schedule, day-out-of-days sheets, strip board, calculator, scratch paper, and a pencil. The schedule and day-out-of-days will dictate how long each actor, crew member, piece of equipment, vehicle, location, prop, and so on is needed and will help you budget properly for all of the film's needs.

Using This Manual

As you use this manual for current and future productions, keep in mind that you may have to adjust the budget numbers upward by 10 to 15 percent to accommodate price increases, new union rates, and other market changes.

Generally, the budget formats and the sample figures included in this chapter will provide a helpful yardstick for planning and accounting for a film's costs and needs.

In this chapter, you will find the *Swingers* budget, the *Kissing Jessica Stein* budget, three sample budgets prepared using the Movie Magic Budgeting software, and a $62,000 budget prepared without any budgeting software. Movie Magic Budgeting offers different blank budget forms you can use when compiling a budget (Paramount, Universal, Sony, and HBO, for example). Depending on which budget form you choose, the budget categories and account codes will vary. You might also choose to create your own categories and account codes. The blank Paramount budget form reproduced in Figure 6–1 is the form we used when compiling the four sample budgets. (See the end of Chapter 6, starting on page 110, to review all sample budgets mentioned in this chapter.)

This chapter includes definitions, examples, comparisons, and tips on budgeting the line items found within the sample budgets. It will be most helpful if you read through it once and then refer back to the budgets and line item definitions as you are budgeting, using this manual to help you determine the costs for which you will need to budget. Note that the *Swingers* budget and the sample budgets included here are not final shooting budgets.

A Note About Budgets and Line Items

Every film has different needs, and many of the budget categories and line items included in the forms provided by Movie Magic Budgeting and other budgeting programs may not represent items you will need to account for when budgeting your film. The four sample budgets in this chapter do not always reflect the categories or line items of the blank budget form; each was compiled according to the individual film's needs. In some instances we created new line items and put them in the category that made most sense to us. We assigned them account codes accordingly.

Feel free to create and delete categories and line items as necessary. Do not worry if you need to create a line item you have never seen before. It is important only that you budget for everything required to make the film and that you account for each item in the most appropriate category. This way, the costs will be included within the most appropriate section of the budget (sections such as Above-the-Line Costs, Production, Post-production, and Other). When examining the four sample budgets, you may notice that certain line items are accounted for in different categories or with different account codes. This will happen, and there will be crossovers. Read the explanations of the line items carefully. The definitions provided will help you determine your film's needs and budget properly for its costs.

Budget Structure

Layers

A budget is made up of three layers. The top sheet, the first of the layers, lists the totals for each category and section, as well as the grand total. The second layer is the account level, which lists all line items within each category by account code. The third layer is the detail level of the budget, which is where you will enter any information and equations and break out your rates and costs. A computer program will automatically do the math for you. The detail level is a subaccount of the account category it relates to.

Sections, Categories, and Line Items

Budgets are broken into four sections. In Figure 6–1, the sections are Above-the-Line Costs, Production, Postproduction, and Other. Each section includes categories specific to the section and account codes specific to each category. For example, the Story category is part of the Above-the-Line Costs section and is assigned the account code 600 in Figure 6–1. The categories are further broken down into line items. Each line item is assigned the same three-digit account code as the category to which it belongs, plus a two-digit number specific to it. For example, the subaccount code for the Rights Purchase line item is 600-01. The line items in each category are added to arrive at the total cost of a given category.

Account Codes

All of the sample budgets included in this chapter start with account code 600. Categories 600 through 650 include all above-the-line costs. Above-the-line costs cover the creative components of a film. The Story, Producer, Director, and Cast categories are the large ones, and these categories are broken down into related line items. Categories 700 through 798 include all below-the-line costs. Below-the-line costs cover the manual labor or technical aspects of a film: crew, equipment, locations, props, wardrobe, sound, transportation, and so on. The total cost of the below-the-line section is the total for the shooting period. Categories 800 through 870 include all post-production costs, such as editing and music. The post-production section reflects the total for the completion period of the film.

Categories 910 through 950 include administrative and publicity costs. Below this fourth section is where you will find the budget grand total, and the combined total of the above- and below-the-line sections. You will also see totals for contractual charges and other costs. These other costs, figured as percentages of the overall budget, include the completion bond, contingency, overhead, and insurance. (See "Budgeting Terms and Concepts" later in this chapter.) Except for insurance, these contractual charges are not always amounts that will be spent. Movie Magic Budgeting allows you to set contractual charges that will automatically be applied to the budget.

Using Movie Magic Budgeting

If you will be using Movie Magic Budgeting, refer to the instruction manual. It will save you time by introducing you to all of the features of the program. Keep in mind that account codes, categories, and line items can be created or deleted in any of the budget forms included in the program. Be sure to set all contractual charges so that they will be applied automatically to the budget. You will also need to apply fringes to the budget when appropriate. (See "Budgeting Terms and Concepts" later in this chapter.) Apply fringes to selected line items by calling up the Fringes box and choosing the fringes you want to apply to the selected line items. (The user's manual will tell you how.)

A global, which can be preset, is any variable that will be used consistently throughout the budget. Prep time is already preset in the Global setup box. Adjust the number of weeks to reflect the amount of prep time you will need. For example, if the prep time on the film is five weeks, enter the word *prep* into the column of the Global setup box in which it belongs, and account for it as five weeks in the Weeks column of the setup box. When you type the word *prep* into the detail level of a line item in which you are budgeting for prep time, the program will automatically account for prep time in the unit's field as five weeks and will perform the equation for you. Do the same for shoot and wrap time and other variables. You may change contractual charges, fringes, and globals at any time while you are budgeting.

About the Sample Budgets

The Swingers Budget

A preliminary budget for *Swingers* is reproduced in Figure 6–2, and the top sheet of the actualized budget appears in Figure 6–3. *Swingers* is a dialogue-driven script that was shot primarily in Los Angeles. The cast and crew were local to Los Angeles and were therefore paid as nonunion locals with no per diem. Crew rates were budgeted on flat weekly rates, and no overtime was paid.

Because the actors were friends and the script was shopped for some time before financing was secured, the principal cast had rehearsed and performed readings of the script a number of times before pre-production. Therefore, rehearsal time was not imperative. (In addition, it was an expense the budget could not absorb.) We knew we could shoot multiple scenes in a day because the actors were well rehearsed and the majority of the scenes required few principal actors.

Swingers required numerous extras, a problem we solved by shooting in certain locations while they were open to the public. We posted filming notices and secured personal releases from patrons who appeared in the shot. (See Chapter 8.) No action sequences or stunts were required, and there was no need for any special equipment. We wanted the film to look as real as possible, so we shot in as many actual scripted locations as we could. As a result, the sets required little dressing and fewer props than would have been necessary had we shot on a stage. We used natural light whenever possible and kept our lighting package to a minimum. Using few lights kept the size of the crew and electrical costs down. The small crew also accommodated the size of the spaces we were filming in and enabled us to move quickly and complete the film in three weeks.

We were able to make deals on our equipment, processing, film stock, picture vehicles, and locations that kept the budget down. The difficult part was securing the casino in Las Vegas and transporting the crew, cast, vehicles, and equipment there inexpensively. We needed to provide hotel rooms and per diem to the cast and crew while filming in Las Vegas. (We will tell you how we dealt with these things more specifically when we address line items further in Chapter 8.) The bulk of the money was spent in cast, editing, locations, production staff, and production dailies. By running the initial numbers and considering the deals we were able to make, we knew we could make the film for the money we had.

Sample Budget 1

Sample budget 1, shown in Figure 6–4, is for a character-driven piece that requires mostly interior daytime filming. The budget is based on a local, nonunion crew with flat weekly rates budgeted on a favored-nations basis. Preproduction will be five weeks, and production will be three six-day weeks. (Shooting three six-day weeks rather than four five-day weeks will save money on crew and equipment rentals.) Because of the nonunion status of the crew, six-day weeks do not necessarily have to be paid at time-and-a-half or at a premium rate, as they would on a union show. No overtime has been applied to crew members, though a flat weekly kit rental will be paid to department heads who rent their own supplies to the production. The crew for this show is slightly larger than the crew for *Swingers*. Additions include a production accountant, another (second) second assistant director for two weeks of the shoot to keep the show moving on schedule and to avoid overtime, a lead man, a swing gang member, an extra grip and electrician, and a makeup artist and a hairstylist.

The cast was budgeted based on SAG's low-budget agreement (under $2 million), and overtime was applied to the SAG cast. The film will be shot entirely in Los Angeles (no travel or lodging costs need to be allocated) in preexisting locations, many of which will be open to the public during the shoot, allowing the film to feel real and to save money on having to hire the extras needed in many of the locations. The two most expensive locations will be a bar and a club. Using preexisting locations will also save money on construction costs; stage fees; set, art, and prop rentals and purchases; and strike and rig fees.

Because this picture will be financed through a combination of personal savings and independent investors, only contingency was applied to the budget (at 10 percent), and a bond company will not have to be engaged.

Sample Budget 2

Sample budget 2, shown in Figure 6–5, is for a local, nonunion crew paid on a daily rate. Overtime compensation for the crew is budgeted at 15 percent, and cast overtime at 20 percent. It is a dialogue-driven piece that has more principal characters than *Swingers*, as well as a greater number of locations (16 scripted locales, as opposed to *Swingers*' 15). With the exception of the Brighton Beach boardwalk and a casino in Atlantic City, it takes place in remote rural and suburban areas, in private homes, and in other relatively inexpensive locations.

Because of the nature of the financing for this picture (a combination of equity, foreign sales, and a bank loan), it was necessary to apply all contractual costs to the budget and to engage a bond company. The bond company set parameters for how the budget had to be structured. (See *"Dealing with a Bond Company"* later in this chapter.)

The cast is budgeted primarily on a *favored-nations* basis *(see Glossary)* following the SAG low-budget agreement. The pay scale for the crew is significantly higher than on *Swingers* but is still within low-budget parameters. Crew overtime is budgeted at 15 percent, and although this is low it was all the budget could sustain. Note that deals were made with some key crew people, who were guaranteed higher pay than others (not on a strict favored-nations basis).

Sample Budget 3

Sample budget 3, shown in Figure 6–6, is for a local, nonunion crew paid on a flat weekly rate. However, overtime is accounted for within each crew member's line item and is applied at 20 percent of the total sum of his or her salary for the production period only. The script is set in a small desert town in California and in Las Vegas, neither of which is an expensive location to secure. The number of principal players is larger in this budget than in the *Swingers* budget or sample budget 2. The cast pay (SAG scale), travel, living, and necessary fringes amount to significantly more money in this budget than in the other two.

Sample budget 3 was prepared for fundraising purposes and therefore has not been *actualized. (The film has not been made yet.)* All contractual costs were included because it was likely that with a budget of this level financing would be secured at least partially from a film production company or bank that would require both a contingency and a bond.

Sample budget 4, shown in Figure 6–7, is the *Kissing Jessica Stein* budget. The script is a dialogue-driven romantic comedy, which potentially could be made on the cheap. We shot it in 24 days in New York City and Connecticut. There was no completion bond. All talent and crew worked as locals. We had no paid rehearsal time budgeted. We were, however, able to fly in several actors (such as Jim J. Bullock) for cameos, but the agreement was that they would work as local hires. That way we were not responsible for granting them per diem and hotel. A friend of the project donated airfare, so most of these arrangements were realized due to this fortunate gift. The budget included here is the original budget for the film, which did not include any deliverable items in the event the film sold.

If you compare the *Kissing Jessica Stein* and *Swingers* budgets, there are some fundamental differences that made the *Kissing Jessica Stein* budget higher: (1) we shot factory-unopened film stock, (2) the crew was paid significantly more (even though it was still quite modest pay), and (3) we did not have deferred lab fees for *Kissing Jessica Stein*.

BUDGETING TERMS AND CONCEPTS

This section defines and describes key budgeting terms and concepts that will be helpful to know as you budget your film. All of these terms are also found in the glossary at the back of the book.

Agency Fees

Each cast member must pay his or her agent a 10-percent fee. It is common practice within the industry for the production to pay the agency fee in addition to the actor's salary.

Allow

An allow is money allocated for a given expense, the exact cost of which has not yet been determined. This amount should be based on a deductive reason, not randomly.

Completion Bond

A completion bond is required when a film's financing is secured through an independent film company or a bank. This insurance policy serves as a guarantee to the financing entity that the film will be completed. A completion bond is usually computed at 3 percent of the budget total. The bond company guarantees to pay for any cost overruns, thereby ensuring that the film will be completed. In the event the bond company must actually kick in money to complete the film, it will virtually take over the set and own the film. The bond company can replace the director, the producer, and any crew member it chooses. Not only must the bond company approve the budget before you go into production, but it must also approve the people hired for key crew positions.

Contingency

Contingency was applied to all of the sample budgets at 10 percent, which is usual. Contingency serves as a cushion to protect against the uncertainty involved in making films. Contingency is applied to the below-the-line costs of the budget. A higher contingency may be required for larger-budget films, depending on the nature of the financing.

Favored Nations

This term indicates that a cast or crew member will receive treatment on a par with the best the producer is offering anyone else on the set, but not better. It refers in particular to pay and perks (dressing rooms, travel, accommodations, and so on). We try to run our sets on a favored-nations basis and furnish everyone with an acceptable standard and no one with a lavish standard. Certain established cast or crew members may not accept this approach. Arrangements are always open to negotiation. You may, however, have to meet a particular actor's or crew member's request to keep him or her involved in the project.

Flat Fee

Crew compensation and equipment rentals can be arranged on the basis of a flat fee (as opposed to a daily or weekly rate). There are potential advantages to this arrangement. When you agree to a flat fee, the cost remains the same regardless of how many days or weeks it ultimately takes to complete filming or of how much overtime is worked.

Kit Rental

A kit rental is a fee paid for equipment or supplies a crew member provides to the production. For example, you may have to budget a kit rental fee for a makeup artist who has his or her own makeup supplies. The fee depends on the department and the budget of the show. It can be paid in a lump sum or budgeted for on a weekly basis. The kit rental fee is not subject to payroll taxes.

Overhead

On an independent film, overhead is applied as a percentage of the overall budget. This percentage can range from 1 to 10 percent. Overhead is meant to cover certain pre-production costs, office rental, utility costs, nominal development costs, and out-of-pocket expenses of those who are involved with the project for some time before the film is financed.

Production Insurance

Typically, production insurance is calculated at 2 to 3.5 percent of the budget. All independent films must be insured to secure equipment, locations, transportation, props, wardrobe, cast, crew, and so on, and the policy must be purchased before the production period officially begins. Note in sample budget 2 that the insurance is accounted for in line item 910-08, rather than as a percentage of the budget total, as in the other budgets included here.

Loan-Out Company

A loan-out company is a corporation that "loans" the services of its employee. Certain members of the above- and below-the-line staff may want to be paid as "loan-outs." When hiring a loan-out, the producer (or the producer's payroll company) does not deduct employee payroll taxes or add fringes to the loan-out's pay. Instead, the loan-out company is responsible for absorbing the tax liability on the income. This can be less costly for the production, but in some instances an actor or crew person will require that the production cover the fringes.

A word of warning: If the production does not pay the fringes on a loan-out crew or cast member and the IRS discovers during an audit of the loan-out company that employee taxes were not paid, the IRS could hold the production company responsible for the fringes or the payroll taxes. Any employee paid as a loan-out must provide papers of incorporation, a Federal Identification number or employee identification number (EIN), and proof of workers' compensation insurance so that in the event he or she is hurt on the set the production company will be protected.

Loss and Damage

Loss and damage (L&D) is a line item you should include for almost every department for which you are renting equipment or materials. The most conservative way to handle budgeting for L&D is to set aside an amount in each department's budget equal to the amount of the deductible on the production insurance policy. For example, if your deductible is $1,200, you would budget $1,200 for L&D in each department category. (Insurance deductibles must usually be met on a per-occurrence basis.) What low budgets often reflect is the equivalent of the deductible for the departments for which equipment is costly, such as camera, and less money for departments such as wardrobe. This money ensures that the production will be covered in the event, for example, a lens is broken or a costume is irreparably damaged. You may never use this money, in which case it will be money saved when you actualize your budget.

DEALING WITH A BOND COMPANY

If the financing of your film is such that a completion bond is required, you will have to meet with a bond company representative and "defend" your budget. Prepare for this meeting carefully. The bond company rep will go through your budget line item by line item and ask how you arrived at each cost. If you have allows or flat fees in your budget, you will have to substantiate those numbers with actual quotes from vendors. The bond company will require that you budget overtime for both cast and crew. By and large, bond company reps know a great deal about line producing films and will ask solid questions. The difficult aspect for filmmakers whose budgets require them to "shoot from the hip" is that the bond company cannot approve a budget that is based on deals you think you may be able to secure.

Do not let the bond company get in the way of your making your film, but understand that you will have to abide by its rules and regulations. The bond company will require that you submit daily production reports as well as weekly cost reports. The bond company will require that you have an accountant, and the accountant and an assistant will be instrumental in preparing weekly cost reports.

BUDGETS AND THEIR LINE ITEMS

Items 600-00: Story

Scripts evolve in different ways, and that evolution will dictate how you budget the line items discussed in the following section (taken from the Paramount budget in Figure 6.1). Be certain to adhere to any contractual obligations you may have when budgeting your story costs.

Item 600-01: Rights Purchase

This line item covers the purchase of any underlying rights to property or material, such as the rights to someone's life story or the rights to a story, novel, or play on which the script is based. In sample budget 2 (see Figure 6–5), $50,000 was budgeted for the purchase of the short story on which the script was based. This is relatively high for a low-budget endeavor, but because the story was written by a well-known writer the cost was deemed worthwhile. Negotiate to the best of your ability to keep this number as low as possible.

Item 600-03: Writers

Budget this category if you have a writer-for-hire (as opposed to a spec script), if you anticipate engaging a writer to assist with rewrites during the filming process, or if you have commissioned a writer to pen the script. If you have paid the writer out of your own pocket over the months or years taken to get the project to this point, budget appropriately so that you will be reimbursed the costs. Note that none of the sample budgets has money allocated in this category. None of the independent pictures we have worked on thus far have required that we engage a writer-for-hire.

Item 600-04: Screenplay Purchase

At this stage, you should have an agreement with the writer that spells out the cost of the screenplay when you exercise your option to buy it (See Chapter 2.) Include both the option price and the purchase price in this line item. If it is a percentage of the overall budget with a floor and a ceiling (the floor is the minimum cost, the ceiling the maximum cost), start by entering a middle amount. You will make it more exact when the budget is complete. You will need to apply fringes to this amount unless the writer is a loan-out. Generally, when a significant sum of money will be paid, it makes sense for the writer to incorporate and form a loan-out company to reduce his or her tax burden.

On *Swingers*, the agreement with the writer, Jon Favreau, was a $1,000 fee with contingent compensation guaranteed only if the film was sold. Therefore, in this category we budgeted $1,000 (see Figure 6–2). This was a bare-bones budget, reflecting the least amount of money we could make the movie for. It did not include the amount guaranteed to Favreau if the film sold. Although the amount was specified in his contract, it was not money that had to be paid out of the production budget.

On *Kissing Jessica Stein*, the writers were not compensated for the script up front. We agreed on a deferred script fee. The writers were then paid as actresses and as producers (albeit quite modestly), which was agreeable to all parties. The main objective was to get the film made.

The Writers Guild of America (WGA) currently has several low-budget agreements which are specifically for the purchase of an existing screenplay plus one rewrite. The agreement does not cover development. The contracts apply to films budgeted at $5 million and below, and the low-budget contracts must be requested by the WGA writer. The contracts do mandate that the production company become a signatory to the Guild. If the film budget is between $2 and $5 million, the Guild's basic low budget agreement applies, and for projects over $5 million its high-budget agreement applies. Further information on the specifics of WGA contracts is available at the Guild's Web site at www.*wga.org*. The Web site has a Low Budget Agreement Fact Sheet, which provides a good general overview of the agreements.

Item 600-05: Research

This line item is for research costs for your screenplay. If you are purchasing a screenplay, you probably will not need to budget any money here. If you wrote the script and did the research yourself, or if you commissioned a writer to write the script and do the research, those costs need to be reimbursed.

Item 600-11: Script Copying

Script photocopying costs are budgeted in this line item. For sample budget 2 (see Figure 6–5), 100 script copies were budgeted. Over the course of the development period of this film, at least that many copies were generated.

Items 610-00: Producer

Item 610-01: Executive Producer

If you are raising money, this line item will initially be zero. You do not know what fee the executive producer (if you get one) will take, if any, beyond the money he or she will invest or secure to make the film. On independent pictures, the executive producer credit is often given to people based on various types of involvement. Unless you know for sure you will have an executive producer and what his or her fee will be, leave this line item blank. You can plug in the number later if necessary.

Item 610-02: Producer

Producers' fees depend on the situation and on the overall budget. On *Swingers*, every crew member was paid $300 per week (a favored-nations status), including the producer (see Figure 6–2). The producer is in the budget for a greater number of weeks than anyone else because the producer's job, in effect, spanned the largest time period. Sample budget 2 (see Figure 6–5) has $2,500 allocated for each producer. Originally, this fee was higher, but due to budget limitations the fee was gradually reduced to $2,500. Sample budget 1 (see Figure 6–4) has a $5,000 flat fee for each producer, which if broken down into an hourly rate is still very low pay. Producers on independent films often waive their fees in order to get the movie made. More often than not, when a producer is paid it is either a prenegotiated flat fee or a percentage of the total budget, not a weekly rate (as with *Swingers*).

Item 610-07: Producer's Entertainment

Depending on the type of show you are running and the source of your financing, you may want to allocate some money for entertainment. Will you be taking potential investors or cast members out for lunch? You may want to take department heads to see a film that relates to the film you are making. Even if it is a nominal amount, try to estimate your actual costs realistically. Account for all potential expenses, and add sales tax to purchases.

Item 610-08: Pre-production Expenses

Inevitably, you will have pre-production expenses. If you are going with a bare-bones budget you can leave this line item blank, but everyone will need to eat (you will pick up the tab on meals), the office will need supplies, and you will tip when necessary. You will end up spending the money one way or another, and it is best to account for some expenses here and allow the film to cover these costs if possible.

Items 620-00: Director

Item 620-01: Director

On *Swingers*, everyone worked for a reduced rate and on a favored-nations basis. Note that the director was budgeted for $1,000 (see Figure 6–2). Remember that everything is negotiable. You might find a director who is willing to defer part or all of his or her fee. In sample budget 2 (see Figure 6–5), the director was willing to do anything to get the picture made and agreed to a nominal fee. She was not a director-for-hire. Your primary concern as the line producer is to be certain that those who agree to defer their fees have the financial wherewithal to survive and do the job. If your director is a member of the Directors Guild of America (DGA), you will need to operate within the Guild's rules. The DGA sets minimums for fees and the number of weeks with in which a director must be paid. Contact the DGA for current information. (Newer versions of Movie Magic Budgeting list some of the Guild's rates.)

The DGA has recently created a new low-budget side letter to their basic agreement. This low-budget contract applies to all films made for under $7 million and has four levels, starting with Level 1 (films made for under $1 million) and ending with Level 4 (films produced for $3.5 to 7 million). They are reviewing films with budgets under $500,000 on a case-by-case basis. The DGA's Web site, at *www.dga.org/contracts*, offers a user-friendly breakdown of the low-budget side letter.

Item 620-05: Casting Director

Budget for a casting director if you can afford one. In addition to being a significant creative contributor, the casting director will oversee the casting process, negotiate talent deals, call the Station 12 department of SAG, and facilitate the casting process in other ways. (See Chapter 7 for information on Station 12.) Try to cut a deal with a casting director who will agree to a flat fee. Most casting directors are loan-outs, so it is up to you whether to apply fringes here.

Item 620-08: Casting Expenses

In this line item, budget for casting expenses, including renting a space in which to hold auditions, photocopying script pages (sides), and providing some food and beverages. On *Swingers*, we budgeted $200 (see Figure 6–2). We held auditions in the producer's home and supplied food and drinks. In sample budget 2 (Figure 6–5), $300 was budgeted for casting expenses because it was necessary to rent a space for a nominal fee and provide some beverages and snacks.

Items 630-00: Cast

Item 630-01: Principal Players

Examine your day-out-of-days sheet for your cast. Any actor who is needed for more than three days in a row is considered a principal player and must be budgeted on a weekly rate. On *Swingers*, the core group (Mike, Trent, Rob, and Sue) were all weekly players (see Figure 6–2). The SAG low-budget pay scale at the time was $1,558 (U.S. 1995) per week. In addition to government fringes (which include FICA, SUI, and FUI) you should also include an agency commission of 10 percent of each actor's earnings. (See "Budgeting Terms and Concepts" in this chapter.) If it is a SAG production, the SAG Corp fringe is applied at 13.3 percent (1999). (Rates may change, so verify first.) Although it is not mandatory that the production pay the 10-percent agency fee, it is an expected courtesy. It is safe to assume that government fringes will amount to approximately 18 percent.

Note how the character Rob was accounted for in the *Swingers* budget (see Figure 6–2). We made a mistake here. At the time, we thought it would be less expensive to pay him as a daily player than as a weekly player because he worked few consecutive days. It turned out to be more expensive because Rob was put on hold and the production had to pay for hold days, even though he was not working. (See Chapter 5.) We did not realize this at the time, so we ended up paying the actor more than if we had scheduled him as a weekly player. We also could have budgeted him as a drop-pickup, which means that if we needed him for two days in the beginning of the shoot but not again until the end we could have dropped him and then picked him up again, without paying for hold days between. The risk with a drop-pickup, however, is that the actor is free to take other work in the meantime and could be unavailable to your production when next needed. In current SAG low-budget agreements, the consecutive employment requirement is often waived, so if your budget is low the issue of hold days and of drop-pickups may be irrelevant. Check with SAG in order to budget for your cast properly (*www.sag.org*).

SAG now has several agreements: a low-budget agreement (the budget must be under $2 million), an affirmative-action low-budget agreement (under $2.75 million), a modified low-budget agreement (under $500,000), a limited exhibition agreement (under $200,000), and an experimental film agreement (under $75,000). The SAG Web site, at *www.sagindie.org*, offers comprehensive information about each of the contracts. The *SAG Film Contracts Digest* specifies the parameters of these agreements. When we made *Swingers*, the low-budget agreement was the only contract option in effect. Had we shot only two months later, we would have qualified for the modified low-budget agreement and would have saved about half our cast costs.

All four sample budgets include cast fees based on SAG low-budget scale rates. If you have an actor who demands more than scale, you will have to negotiate his or her fee. If yours is a non-SAG show, you can pay whatever rate you and your cast members agree to. If it is a SAG production but you have an actor who is not yet a member of the Guild, you will have to submit a Taft-Hartley form to the Guild within 15 days from the date of hire. (See Chapter 8.) The Guild will likely charge you a preference claim, which is a penalty for having hired a non-SAG actor, the cost of which is currently $400. (Call SAG to determine the current rate.) Budget for this cost if you anticipate having a mixed cast of SAG and non-SAG members. Make sure your actors just joining the Guild know that they must pay dues no later than within 30 days of their start-work date to be considered SAG members and employable as such.

Item 630-02: Day Players

Examine your day-out-of-days sheet to determine which of your characters will be played by day players. Any actor who works a total of three consecutive days or fewer should be budgeted as a day player. When pre-production begins, you will negotiate with SAG and become a Guild signatory. Only then will you determine what the union scale rates will be at the time of your shoot for the SAG agreement that best fits your project. For now, a quick call to SAG for rates will suffice. You will need to inform SAG of your total budget, along with other information. Do not forget to apply fringes to day players' pay.

Item 630-03: Rehearsal

In sample budget 2 (see Figure 6–5), we separated shoot time and rehearsal time when budgeting principal players and created line item 630-03. We budgeted five cast members for three days of rehearsal. It is fine to include rehearsal time in line item 630-01 instead, adding estimated rehearsal time to the time you have budgeted each actor for filming. Rehearsal time is considered normal work time by the Guild and is paid as such, fringes and all.

In sample budget 3 (see Figure 6–6), the rehearsal time was included in line item 630-01. This is why the first two principal players are budgeted for six weeks of work, whereas the header on the budget states that it is a five-week shoot. The additional week is for rehearsal. Fringes were applied.

Item 630-05: SAG Residuals

Residuals are money earned by an actor when a film sells and plays in foreign territories. SAG has recently started to request that low-budget productions put up money for SAG residuals in advance of filming in addition to the bond. This can be a large sum relative to the overall budget. Although everything is negotiable with SAG, you may want to budget up to $10,000 in this category as a contingency.

Item 630-06: Looping/ADR

Looping, or additional dialogue replacement (ADR), sessions will take place after your shoot has wrapped and you have decided which lines of dialogue need to be rerecorded or added. SAG requires that actors be paid scale (or whatever their agreed-upon rate above and beyond scale) for the days they attend a looping session. It is safe to assume that you will need some of your principal actors (and often day players) for looping, so budget each principal player for at least one day of looping. Most likely, you will not need all of them. Try to negotiate one day of looping into your initial contract with each actor.

Item 630-07: Meal Penalties

All of the sample budgets (see Figures 6–4 to 6–6) have a line item for meal penalties. If your cast is SAG, you will have to pay meal penalties if you work cast members more than six hours in a row without providing a meal. For example, if lunch is served late, you will pay a meal penalty to any actor who breaks for lunch more than six hours after his or her call time. The meal penalty will be figured into the cast time cards and paid as part of their salary. Even if your shoot is nonunion, make every effort to abide by Guild rules. These rules were created in the interest of workers and are important regulations to uphold.

Item 630-08: Overtime

On a SAG production, weekly players are paid for a 44-hour workweek, and daily players are paid for an eight-hour day. If a weekly player works for more than 10 hours in one day, or a day player for more than eight hours, the Guild requires that you compensate the actor for overtime, which is usually paid as time-and-a-half up to 12 hours, and double time for each hour thereafter. Overtime is likely to occur, so budget accordingly.

Item 630-09: Medical Exams

Most companies that provide production insurance require that key cast members have a medical exam before beginning principal photography. The cost of several medical exams is included in all of the sample budgets (see Figures 6–4 to 6–6). The director should be budgeted for an exam as well.

Item 630-20: Side Deals

A side deal is money above and beyond scale that you anticipate paying one or more of your actors. This line item is used to account for any side deals you may make with cameo actors, extras, musicians, and so on. (See the *Swingers* budget, Figure 6–2.)

Items 640-00: Fringes

A fringe is any cost above and beyond a central cost. For example, sales tax, employee taxes, and agency fees are all considered fringes. None of the budgets included here has a fringes category per se; instead, the fringes are built into each relevant category. We have found that this is an easier way to organize the budget because it allows us to see the fringe costs for each line item and the total fringes for each category.

Adjust the fringe rates in Movie Magic Budgeting by choosing the Fringes command under the heading "Setup". When you want to apply fringes to a given line item or category, click on the percent sign in the top middle section of the screen. A box will appear with all established fringe costs. Select the fringe costs that apply to the given line item.

Items 650-00: Travel and Living

Budget here for above-the-line travel and living costs (cast, producers, director, writer, and so on). When a production travels out of town (that is, when it shoots on location), the production is required to pay for the travel and living costs of cast and crew members who travel to work on the show. For example, if you are shooting in Park City, Utah, cast and crew members from Park City are considered local hires, and you need not pay for their travel and living expenses. However, if you need to bring employees from Los Angeles to Park City, Utah, you must provide them with travel, lodging, and a per diem (see Figures 6–5 and 6–6). If the employees in question are members of a union, check with the union for minimum per diem rates. If not, come up with a rate that is sufficient given the local cost of living, for employees to buy meals, do laundry, and so on. Do not forget gratuities and sales tax. Further, cast contracts often stipulate that the production provide certain accommodations (e.g., three-star hotel, a driver, and so on).

Item 650-01: Producer Travel and Producer Living

In the *Swingers* budget (see Figure 6–2), no money was allocated for producer travel because a production van, accounted for in the Transportation category (770-00), took most of the crew and the producer to Vegas. In sample budget 2 (see Figure 6–5), the producers anticipated that the film would be shot on the East Coast but edited in Los Angeles, and they knew that one of the producers would have to make several trips across the country. Therefore, $1,600 was allotted for the travel expenses.

If your production will be traveling to a location where you will have to sleep overnight, you must budget for living accommodations. For the producing unit on *Swingers*, we budgeted three nights in Las Vegas. We secured an inexpensive deal on hotel rooms, which cost us approximately $25 per night. Do not forget sales tax and gratuities.

Item 650-02: Director

In all travel categories, refer to your schedule to determine how many locations above-the-line talent will travel to. Determine the mode of transportation required (plane, train, automobile). Make some phone calls to determine the cost, taking into consideration how each person will, or is required by contract to, travel (first class or economy).

Examine your schedule to determine how long you will be on location. Make some calls to determine what your hotel or motel costs will be. If your director is not a member of the DGA, establish a per diem rate that is reasonable for the locale so that the director can cover such expenses as transportation and food on days off.

Item 650-03: Writer

In each of the four sample budgets (Figures 6–4 to 6–6), the writer was involved in the project in another capacity as well (either as an actor or director), so no extra money was allocated to the writer's travel. (The cost of his or her travel was accounted for under line item 650-02 or 650-06.) If you engage a writer-for-hire and require that the writer be on the set, budget travel and living expenses as you would for the director.

Item 650-06: Cast Travel and Living Expenses and Per Diem

Refer to your schedule to determine which actors need to be where, when, and for how long. Find out the cost of the actors' required mode of transportation. If not stipulated in the actor's contract, budget for the safest and most affordable mode of transportation.

SAG has guidelines about how its members may travel. When you are budgeting your cast, remember that travel days are paid as regular workdays. High-profile actors may have specific requirements about their travel plans. If you do not know yet who your actors will be and how they must travel, pad this line item. If you have cast arriving from a foreign country, do not forget to budget for the necessary work visas and flights.

Examine your schedule and day-out-of-days sheet to determine how many actors will have to travel to distant locations and for how long. Assume that you will give cast members at least one night's rest before they start shooting, and that you may wrap late the day they finish work.

Budget for two extra hotel or motel days and two extra per diem days to cover the beginning and end of their shoot period. The Guild breaks down per diem by breakfast, lunch, and dinner. For example, $60 per diem (1999) is $12 for breakfast, $18 for lunch, and $30 for dinner. Technically, you need to pay per diem only for those meals not provided on the set. If you serve breakfast and lunch on the set and break before a third meal, the per diem cannot be less than $30 but need not be more, pending any other arrangement you have with a given actor. Categories 600-00 through 650-00 cover the above-the-line costs.

Items 700-00: Extra Talent

An extra is anyone who is required in a shot but has no speaking role. Extras are important to the look and feel of a film. Unless your movie is two people sitting in a room for two hours, you will most likely need extras. It is particularly important to hire an extras casting agency if you will be shooting on location. Bringing all of your extras with you will be expensive, and it may be difficult to find extras without the help of a local agency. In general, an extras casting agent will be invaluable if a large number of extras are required. You will also need to compensate extras for any wardrobe you ask them to bring to wear during filming. Compensation will depend on your SAG agreement, as noted by examples in the material that follows.

Item 700-02: Extras and Stand-ins

Examine your day-out-of-days sheet to determine how many extras you will need, where, and for how long. If yours is a SAG show, call SAG for the extras rate. (Rates depend on the state in which you are working.) When you become a SAG signatory, one point of negotiation will be the cost of extras and how many SAG extras you are required to have. (That is, SAG may require you to pay SAG rates for 30 extras who are SAG members, with the remainder of your extras paid whatever rate you agree on.) Under the modified low-budget agreement, extras are not covered at all, and you will need to determine the rate at which you will pay them.

Examine sample budget 2, line item 700-02 (see Figure 6–5). Forty SAG extras were budgeted for one shoot day at the New York SAG rate, which was $102 per day. This met the required number of SAG extras per our negotiated contract. The remaining extras were budgeted at $25 and $40 per day. In sample budget 3 (see Figure 6–6), 30 extras were budgeted at $90 dollars per day for seven days, which was the rate quoted by the Los Angeles SAG office when the budget was compiled, and an additional 20 extras were budgeted at $50 per day for five days.

None of the independent shows we have done thus far has required stand-ins, but it is something to consider if you have name actors. A stand-in would be most appropriate when shooting scenes MOS (without sound), when shooting background shots, or for blocking purposes when you have high-profile actors who should not be required to or are not willing to stand around while the lighting is being tweaked. It may be less expensive to hire stand-ins, and sometimes actors request them. The stand-in rate is usually the same as the extra rate. (Check with SAG for current rates.)

Item 700-03: Welfare Workers/Teachers

If your shoot requires minors to be on the set during the school year, you will need to hire a set teacher. The set teacher can also fulfill the role of welfare worker because he or she ensures that the government's child welfare rules are followed. There are specific rules for employing minors. Secure a copy of the Minors Employment Schedule from SAG for the state in which you are working and contact the Child Labor Laws office. If you have a minor on the set and are shooting during the school year, you must budget for a teacher. If you are shooting during the summer, you may have more flexibility, although a welfare worker will most likely still be required. Use your day-out-of days sheet to determine how many days you will have minors on the set.

Item 700-05: Extras Casting

If you are uncertain while compiling your budget how to deal with extras casting, budget for an extras casting agent. This is particularly important if you will be shooting on location because you will want your extras to be local. Budget 10 percent on top of each extra's salary as an agency fee, and do not forget the fringes.

Item 700-08: Allowances, Car

Figure out how far your extras will be traveling to the set and budget either mileage, currently 30 cents per mile, or gas money. Usually, budgeting for gas costs is somewhat less expensive and can be accounted for in this line item as an allowance.

Items 705-00: Production Staff

Nonunion crew pay may be budgeted either on a weekly or daily rate. On *Swingers*, we budgeted $300 per week as a flat rate. This meant that regardless of how many hours crew members worked their salary remained $300 per week, with no overtime compensation. (We were as careful as possible not to go into overtime.) Often, you will set sliding rates for department heads, seconds, thirds, and production assistants. In sample budget 2 (see Figure 6–5), most key positions were budgeted at a daily rate of $125, seconds at $100, thirds at $80, and production assistants at $50. Unless you make a flat-rate arrangement with your crew, be certain to budget for overtime. Either create a line item and allocate a fixed sum or budget overtime as a percentage (usually 20 percent) of a crew member's shooting period pay. (We prefer the latter.) Crew rates can be structured in various ways on a nonunion show and should reflect your budget level.

Item 705-01: Line Producer/Unit Production Manager

Depending on the production and the budget, you may have a production manager (PM) or a unit production manager (UPM) in addition to a line producer. Often, low-budget films have only a line producer and a coordinator, or a PM and a coordinator but no line producer. Ideally, the production manager is scheduled for the entire pre-production period. The production manager is in charge of below-the-line personnel, equipment, arrangements, and so on, and reports to the line producer who handles both above- and below-the-line matters during pre-production and production. The rates vary significantly depending on the budget level, but on an independent film a PM's rate is rarely higher than $2,000 per week (but may be significantly lower). Do not forget fringes. Determine rates according to what works for your circumstances and your budget.

Item 705-02: Production Coordinator

Budget your production coordinator for one less week of pre-production than your production manager, so that the PM can sort through everything and get organized before the coordinator comes on. Budget the coordinator through production, and for a week of wrap if the budget can sustain this. Having the coordinator scheduled during wrap will help keep the paperwork organized, as the coordinator often makes many of the deals with vendors and should close out those accounts if possible. Note that sample budget 2 (see Figure 6–5) includes a second office coordinator. Although the shoot was short, it took place in two locations far from one another; therefore, it was thought to be worthwhile to have a second production coordinator working at the second production office. Apply all necessary fringes.

Items 705-03, 705-04, and 705-05: Assistant Directors

The assistant director (AD) designs the final shooting schedule and works closely with the director. He or she communicates directly with the actors and the crew, organizes the set, and keeps the production moving on schedule. The AD is also responsible for call sheets, Taft-Hartley reports, Exhibit G forms, production reports, schedule changes, meal breaks, overtime, and accident reports. (See Chapter 8 for more on the AD's responsibilities.) On a low-budget show, budget the AD for about half of the pre-production period, the entire production period, and several days of wrap if affordable. Most of the paperwork that must be completed by the AD department can be completed by the second assistant director (second AD), who is budgeted for in line item 705-04. The second AD works closely with the first AD and usually handles the paperwork for the department. The second AD will also handle talent wrangling, often in conjunction with a key-set production assistant.

Item 705-06: Script Supervisor

The script supervisor or continuity person takes scrupulous notes on each take of every scene shot during production. These notes are essential both for editing purposes as well as for continuity during the shoot itself, in that films most often are not shot chronologically. Therefore, the script supervisor will also work with the wardrobe, set, prop, and makeup departments to ensure the overall continuity of the picture and that the script days are correct.

The script supervisor must do some preparation before production begins. He or she works with the editor, the director, and the AD to prepare. Budget the script supervisor for one week of the pre-production period, for all of production, and for a few days of wrap. The script supervisor needs to organize script notes, meet with the editor, and finalize the continuity notebook, which should include photos of actors and sets, the script supervisor's notes, and lined pages of the script, all of which are essential to the editor. Do not try to get by without a script supervisor. It is essential to have script notes when assembling the film.

Item 705-08: Production Accountant

We have yet to work on an independent picture for which we did not perform the work of the accountant, but if you can afford it even a part-time accountant will be useful in helping to set up your accounting system and vendor accounts so that the show runs as smoothly as possible. The accountant will set up accounts with vendors, prepare crew payroll, and issue checks. Your accountant might be a production employee who works in the production office or someone who works from his or her own office. This person also looks over things, answers your questions, and provides assistance as needed. In the latter case, the production accountant would probably be paid as a loan-out rather than as a crew member. Depending on the nature of your financing and size of your budget, you may be required to have an accountant. In addition to general accounting responsibilities, the production accountant will provide weekly cost reports to your financiers and the bond company.

Item 705-10: Production Assistants

Do not skimp on production assistants (PAs). A low-budget film cannot afford to run off schedule. Provide departments with the support they need. Hiring a PA for a department can be a way to cut back on what would be a higher-paid position in that department. On *Swingers* (see Figure 6–2), we had five PAs on for varying amounts of time. PAs 1 and 2 worked for three and two weeks, respectively, of prep time for the duration of the shoot, and for one week of wrap each. PA 3 worked only for the duration of the shoot.

Item 705-11: Pre-production Expenses

Sample budget 2 (see Figure 6–5) accounts for pre-production costs, meals for the production staff during pre-production, and office supplies in this line item. In sample budget 3 (see Figure 6–6), certain pre-production producer's expenses are included in category 610-08, including such costs as taking an investor out for a meal and watching source films.

Items 710-00: Camera

Try to make a package deal at a rental house for the camera, lenses, and accessories you will need, instead of paying for everything separately. Discuss the package with the director of photography (DP). If you require special camera equipment, rent it overnight or over a weekend on a one-day rate to keep the cost down. Be sure to budget for loss and damage in this category.

Item 710-01: Director of Photography

The DP may require more money than any other below-the-line crew person, but you may be able to negotiate a flat-fee deal with him or her. The DP will need ample time to meet and scout with the director before production and to help design the shooting schedule. The *Swingers* budget (see Figure 6–2) does not include any money for the DP because Doug Liman, who was the director, also photographed the film and waived his fee. All of the sample budgets include nonunion DPs. If you plan to hire a union DP, contact the DGA to find out what your obligations are.

Item 710-02: Operator

None of the budgets provided include money for a camera operator. Shoots the size of the ones exemplified by these budgets cannot always afford, and do not necessarily need, a separate camera operator unless it is a multicamera shoot. Discuss the circumstances of the shoot and the types of shots required with your DP and director to determine their needs. The most important thing is that the DP has the necessary support to do his or her job well.

Item 710-03: First Assistant Cameraperson

The first assistant cameraperson (AC) will need to prepare the camera package at the camera rental house before production (called prepping the camera), and will need to purchase expendables for the camera department. Make certain that sufficient time is budgeted for this. You may want to perform a test or two with the camera and various film stocks. In sample budget 3 (see Figure 6–6), this prep time was budgeted at 6 weeks. In other words, the rate paid to the first AC was prorated based on the weekly flat fee they were to be paid. The AC may pull focus, reload magazines, change lenses, and perform similar tasks. Usually, the DP works regularly with a particular AC or will recommend one for you to hire. If you are shooting in digital, you will want to discuss camera department size and requirements with your DP. You may be able to significantly reduce the size of the camera department, depending on the digital format, how the DP works, and so on.

Item 710–04: Second Assistant Cameraperson

The second AC may need to come on a day or two early to assist the AC in preparing the camera for the shoot, but more often than not he or she can start on the first day of principal photography. The second AC is responsible for filling out camera reports on set and should hand them over to production at the end of every shoot day. Budget a day of wrap so that the second AC can finish any paperwork. Usually, the DP or the first AC can recommend a second AC, who will often pull focus, build the camera help-frame shots, and change lenses. Should you be shooting in mini-DV or some other digital format, the size of your camera department may change. Particularly on DV, you would likely not need a second AC, a loader, and so on.

Item 710-06: Still Photographer

Usable press stills from your shoot are imperative to the success of your film on the festival circuit and for theatrical distribution. Find a capable photographer (even if it is a friend) to take production stills. (Refer to the interviews on the companion CD-ROM.) Make a flat-fee deal with the still photographer, and choose several key shoot days when he or she will photograph on the set. Regardless of the deal you make, you will need to cover the costs of any expendables, film, and processing. Budget accordingly. Do not forget to add sales tax on expendable items and processing.

Item 710-08: Camera Rentals
Speak with the DP and the director before you start calling camera houses for quotes. Get a list of the camera equipment they want. You may have to tell them they cannot have all of it, but the direction on this rental must come from the DP. When calling camera houses for quotes on the camera package, do not forget to tell them the circumstances of your shoot. They may not care, but it may get you the deal you need. Your package, of course, must include ample magazines, batteries, lenses, cable, and so on. The camera equipment will come in protective boxes, but make sure you have a secure place to store the boxes each day.

Item 710-09: Camera Supplies
The camera department will need expendables, such as tape, markers, chamois, and canned air. Either the production can purchase these items (ask the first AC for a list) or the camera department can make the purchases with petty cash. Call around for prices and figure out how much money should be budgeted. Take into consideration the number of weeks you will be shooting. Do not forget to add sales tax to purchases.

Item 710-11: Camera Accessories/Video Equipment
Camera accessories might include a video tap, a SteadiCam, a monitor, and other items the DP may desire. For *Swingers* (see Figure 6–2), very little money was budgeted in this category. We did not have the money for anything that would qualify as an accessory. In sample budget 2 (see Figure 6–5), $250 was allotted in case additional accessories other than those included in the package were needed. In sample budget 3 (see Figure 6–6), the video tap equipment was included with the camera package cost. Try to include the cost of accessories and any video equipment when you are negotiating your deal on the camera package.

Item 710-20: Loss, Damage, and Repair
Because camera equipment is so expensive, budget no less than the deductible on your insurance policy for any loss or damage that may occur, which typically runs between $1,200 and $1,500.

Items 715-00: Set Design

Set design establishes the look and feel of the film. The set design department is responsible for interiors and exteriors, the color of the walls, bedspreads, plants, and vases and the flowers that are in them, for example.

Item 715-01: Production Designer
The production designer is responsible for the overall look of the film. He or she works closely with the art director. Your production designer will need most of the pre-production period to ensure that the sets are ready when you begin production. He or she will scout the locations to determine what is required. On a low-budget shoot, you may have just one person who fills the role of both production designer and art director.

Item 715-02: Art Director
The art director is responsible for helping the production designer conceive and execute the set design. You will need to budget your art director for most of pre-production and for shooting. Most likely, someone else in the department can stay on board to wrap, in conjunction with a production assistant or two, the art department.

Item 715-03: Set Designer/Lead Man
The set designer executes the design created by the art director and the production designer. You may or may not need a set designer, depending on how much money you have, what the production designer wants, and how complicated your sets are. For sample budgets 1 and 2 (see Figures 6–4 and 6–5), production took place on location, not on a stage, which would have required building sets and would have been more costly. Sample budget 3 (see Figure 6–6) does allocate money for set construction. The lead man oversees the set dressing crew, usually referred to as the swing gang.

Items 715-05 and 715-06: Art Rentals and Purchases/Supplies
Budget for rentals and purchases for the art department in these line items. If you have no idea what you will need to purchase and what it will cost, speak with a production designer or an art director to get some ballpark figures. Describe the types of locations, the look of the film, the genre, and so on. Remember to add sales tax to any purchases.

Item 715-07: Research
Even if your script does not require extensive set building, your production designer and art director may need to do some research. Although much of it can be accomplished

online or in a library, you may want to allocate some money for the purchase of special books or for other research activities, such as scouting locations or finding the right stage.

Item 715-10: Box/Car Rentals
Depending on the equipment or materials the members of the set design department will provide, you may need to budget some money for box, or kit, rentals. Ask key crew members how much money is usually paid for their kit and see what type of a deal you can afford to make. A word of caution: if you do not budget any money for kit rentals you may end up upsetting a crew member. When you are asking people to work for less than their usual rates and for long hours, you will want to provide as many perks as you can to make them feel appreciated.

As for car rentals, you should be prepared to pay either mileage or gas for members of the set design department. Inevitably, they have a great deal of driving to do, and their expenses need to be covered. You can also budget for this expense under the Transportation category (770-00).

Items 720-00: Set Construction

Set construction is part of executing the set design. Both your script and your budget will dictate whether or not you will need to budget a separate construction crew. If you plan to film on a stage, set construction can be expensive. Sample budget 3 (see Figure 6–6) is the only budget that has accounted for this expense. The other films were shot in existing apartments, bars, and other locations.

Item 720-01: Construction Labor
If you will be building many sets, you may find that you need a set construction coordinator. This person will oversee set construction and make sure that all the necessary materials are secured, among other tasks. The construction coordinator's function is much the same as that of the production coordinator. You will have to determine with the production designer and the art director whether a construction coordinator is necessary based on your locations and the scope of the construction needed.

Item 720-02: Construction Materials
If you will be constructing sets, call around to get some preliminary quotes on materials, or have your construction coordinator do so. Toward estimating costs, speak with an art director who is experienced in building sets for low-budget productions.

Items 721-00: Set Striking

If a set is built, it must also be deconstructed. There are companies you can hire to come and strike your set. A low-budget alternative is to hire an extra production assistant or two to come on after shooting to strike the set. You cannot expect your crew to strike a set at the end of a long workday. If you have been shooting on a stage, you may need to sweep and repaint it when you are done filming there. An additional truck may be needed to carry the set away. You must budget for all of these expenses.

Item 721-02: Location Striking Costs
This task is similar to set striking. You must leave your locations as you found them. There is some overlap between this line item and cleanup and trash disposal (line item 725-12). You may need assistance, so make sure you budget properly for your costs.

Items 725-00: Set Operations

This category covers the daily workings of your set, including everyone and everything needed for your set to function properly. Ideally, you will hire your department heads and they will bring on the team they usually work with. This is desirable because these teams usually work well together and will enhance your film and the efficiency of the set.

Item 725-01: Key Grip
The key grip, or first company grip, and the gaffer are the cinematographer's key people in creating various lighting effects on the set. On *Swingers*, the key grip had little more than a week of prep time and worked for the duration of the shoot (see Figure 6–2). Often, grips and electricians will not negotiate their rates, which typically range from $400 to $475 for a 10-hour workday, and anything over that is considered overtime. On a low-budget nonunion feature you may be able to negotiate a rate that works for everyone. Establish at the outset whether overtime will be paid. If you can rent your equipment from someone on the crew, it is a good way to boost the allure of the job. Discuss with the key grip the number of crew members he or she feels is required for the show to run smoothly and to best do their job.

Item 725-02: Best Boy Grip
The best boy grip is responsible for dealing with all of the department paperwork, expendables, time cards, and so on. He or she usually begins work a day or two before the shoot, at the earliest. Usually, the key grip will choose the best boy.

Item 725-03: Crane/Dolly Grips
Ask the director and the DP how much crane and dolly work they anticipate. If you will have a crane or a dolly on the set, budget a crane operator who will be in charge of operating this machinery.

The dolly grip works with the camera department and the DP to move the dolly at the speed and for the distance the DP desires. You may be able to use one of the grips you already have on the set if you cannot afford to hire a special person. The primary concern is that there be someone who is solely responsible for operating the dolly, which is essential for both safety and efficiency.

The crane grip is another key technical person. Depending on the type of crane and how sophisticated it is, you may need to hire an outside person who is familiar and comfortable with the equipment. Some cranes come with their own operators.

Item 725-04: Extra Grips/Company Grips
Grips perform a lot of the heavy-duty lifting, hauling, and setup on the set. It is better to budget for more than for less in this line item. If you are unsure, discuss with the key grip what his or her needs are. By and large, when you hire your key grip you are committing to his or her team. It is best to allow the key grip and other top personnel to hire the people they know, trust, and like to work with. This will help ensure your set runs smoothly and on schedule. You may want to bring on more grips for your heavier shoot days (day players). Discuss with the key grip which days could use a few extra grips to ensure that all runs as necessary.

Item 725-05: Camera Dollies
Both dollies and cranes are costly. More likely than not, if your show is low-budget you may not need or be able to afford this special equipment for the duration of the shoot. It will keep your costs down considerably if you rent the equipment only for the days you will use it. If you need a crane once at the beginning of the shoot and not again until the end, you should not pay for a three-week rental.

Item 725-08: Grip Equipment Rentals
The most cost-efficient way to budget for grip rentals is to make a deal with a key grip who owns a grip truck or has his or her own equipment. Otherwise, try to make an all-in deal at a rental house that includes the truck that houses the equipment. If you can secure all of the lighting and grip equipment from one rental house, that is even better. You will find that it is cheaper and easier in terms of pickup and returns. If you are not renting from your key grip, obtain a list of the necessary equipment from him or her.

Item 725-09: Grip Equipment Purchases
Grip purchases can add up, so budget carefully. If you have little idea what to budget, discuss it with the key grip. You may need tape, cloth, gels, and duvetyn, among other things. Do not forget to include sales tax on all purchases. If the key grip has a relationship with a particular vendor, you may be able to purchase expendables at a discount. Your key grip may have his or her own items that can be purchased by the production at a reduced cost.

Item 725-10: Grip Box Rentals
Budget a box rental for the key grip if he or she will be renting items to the production. Do not apply fringes.

Item 725-11: Craft Service
Craft service is absolutely imperative. Keep everyone snacking and happy throughout the shoot day; they all need sustenance. The craft service person will need several days of prep to make purchases. He or she will also need a day or two of wrap for returns and paperwork.

Food always costs more than anticipated. Do not skimp when budgeting for craft service. To keep your crew from mutiny, give the craft service person ample funds to do more than just obtain chips, soda, and salsa. It is important to have healthful snacks, a first aid kit, vitamins, and aspirin on your craft service table. Account for craft service rentals in the production expendables line item (775-07). Tables, thermoses, coffee urns, perhaps a hot plate or two, and chairs will be needed.

Item 725-12: Cleanup and Trash
There may be times when you need to hire someone to come in, clean up, and take garbage away from a location. This is often referred to as cartage. Budgeting this line item will ensure that you do not upset your crew members by making them after a long day work another two hours to clean. It will also ensure that the friend you rented the location from will not want to kill you. You will not always be able to afford cleanup and trash disposal, but the need may well arise and it is best to budget for it.

Item 725-19: First Aid
Have a first aid kit on the set at all times. You can rent one from expendables houses or purchase one. If you will be doing any special effects or stunts, you should budget for an on-set medic as well. The medic will be paid for these supplies. You can budget for the first aid kit in the production expendables line item (910-19).

Item 725-22: Heating/Air-conditioning

Do not forget about the effect the weather will have on the comfort of the cast and crew and on the safety and workability of your equipment. If weather is a potential concern, price out the necessary heating or air-conditioning equipment. Examine your day-out-of-days sheet and figure out how long you will be at a given location that might require a heating or air-conditioning unit. You will be responsible for these costs if you are on a stage or at a location where the heating or air-conditioning will be used.

Item 725-24: Dressing Room Rentals

It may be necessary to budget for a trailer or two if you are shooting outside. You cannot expect your actors to change in the street, and you will need a place to store wardrobe, apply makeup, and style hair. On a low-budget film you may want to rent one vehicle that can serve as a honey wagon, dressing room, and production office, and that is equipped with phones and a bathroom. Trailers or motor homes can be costly, so price them out first. (See "Items 770-00: Transportation.") On larger-budget shows, dressing rooms are usually rented for actors.

Item 725-25: Miscellaneous Expenses

Use this line item to pad the budget (see sample budget 2, Figure 6–5). Unanticipated costs always arise. In sample budget 3 (see Figure 6–6), we allocated money for walkie-talkies and beepers in this line item.

Item 725-30: Location Load and Unload

If you anticipate that any of your locations will be particularly problematic because of heavy set dressing or strict time limitations, you may want to bring on additional PAs to assist with loading and unloading materials and equipment. Their help will ensure that all runs smoothly and on schedule.

Items 730-00: Electrical

In this category you will budget for the electrical department personnel, all electrical equipment rentals and purchases (including a generator), carbons, power, and kit rentals if any. This category may account for a large portion of the budget, depending on the lighting needs of the show and the locations at which you will be filming.

Items 730-01, 730-02, and 730-03: Gaffer, Best Boy, and Electricians

Use these line items to allocate money for the gaffer (730-01), the best boy (730-02), and electricians (730-03). Usually, the gaffer will have a crew with whom he or she likes to work. If the show is nonunion, you will not have to pay union rates, but you may need to budget for overtime (see sample budgets 2 and 3, Figures 6–5 and 6–6).

Try to hire a gaffer with his or her own truck, and budget the cost of the equipment rental in line item 730-08. This will save you money. If not, rent electrical equipment from a vendor with whom your gaffer has a relationship if this allows you to secure a better deal. Determine whether you will be paying the gaffer a kit rental (line item 730-10) for equipment or supplies that he or she provides to the production. From the best boy, obtain a list of expendables that will be needed, and be sure to budget appropriately for electrical purchases (line item 730-09). Add fringes for the electrical crew and sales tax for purchases. When budgeting for loss and damage (line item 730-20), allocate enough money to cover the deductible on your production insurance policy.

Item 730-06: Power

If you are on location or filming on a stage, you may have to cover power costs if they exceed whatever the norm is for the location or stage. Some locations will allow you to tie in for power rather than run power in from a generator. Tying in can be a convenient money saver, but be prepared to cover the cost because a tie-in will typically drive up the electric bill.

Items 735-00: Special Effects

Special effects are often mechanical effects that are shot while filming rather than done optically in post-production, such as an explosion, an earthquake, or the destruction of a building. Special effects of this type can be costly. Call an optical house for quotes. There were no special effects in *Swingers* or in sample budgets 1 or 2 (Figures 6–2 and 6–4 and 6–5, respectively). Sample budget 3 (see Figure 6–6), however, required a shooting star that needed to be optically placed in the film by computer graphics. If you will be creating special effects on the set, you may need to budget for a special effects person (line item 735-01); for special effects equipment rentals (line item 735-08), including trucks to carry equipment, wind machines, smoke machines, rainmakers, models, and electronic devices; and for special effects purchases (line item 735-09) for items that will be destroyed or cannot be secured by rental. Do not forget to add sales tax to any purchases. A firefighter will be needed on the set during any scenes that require special effects. The permit office of the city in which you are filming should be notified, as they will help ensure that the proper officials are present and that guidelines are followed.

Items 740-00: Special Shooting Units

Special shooting units are usually assembled to shoot scenes that do not require actors, such as exterior setups, interior or exterior establishing shots, and special action scenes with stand-ins or stunt doubles. For these types of shots, a smaller crew can be used, which is less costly than shooting with the full crew. Often, special shooting units (called pickups) are scheduled during actual filming or at the end of a shoot. The director, producers, and editor may decide while viewing dailies or during the editing process that additional footage is needed to tell the story. If you budget for a special shooting unit, you will have the money to go back and get the necessary shots. Budget for a small crew, camera, lights, equipment, travel, and permit and site fees. Fringes and sales tax must also be applied.

On *Swingers*, we tacked on two pickup days at the end of the shoot. The director (who was also the director of photography), the first assistant director, the first assistant camera, the second assistant camera, the gaffer, a grip, and a production assistant made up the unit, which was assembled to shoot a few exterior establishing shots without any of our actors. The camera and the crew were still on board because we finished our principal photography in the middle of the week and were still paying for the camera. Therefore, we did not have to budget for a special shooting unit. In sample budget 3 (see Figure 6–6), we budgeted for a three-day second-unit shoot. The script called for exterior shots in the desert that did not require actors. It was cost efficient to shoot these scenes with a smaller crew after principal photography had ended.

Items 745-00: Set Dressing

Set dressing is any decoration or item that occupies a set or is required as background for a scene you are filming. For example, a telephone booth, a desk, curtains, a phone, a plant, and a couch are all set dressing items. These items might also be props if an actor will use or handle them in some way during the scene. In this case, they should be included in the prop department's budget. If you intend to shoot on a stage, you will have to dress it to serve as the scripted location. Had we been unable to secure any of the bars or other locations for *Swingers*, we would have had to shoot on a stage, and our budget would have been much larger in the Set Dressing category. Often, with independent films the Set Dressing and Art Department categories are combined when the film's needs in these areas are few, and the same crew is used for both departments. This is the case with the *Swingers* budget (see Figure 6–2) and the four sample budgets (see Figures 6–4 to 6–7).

Items 750-00: Properties

Props are any items that are handled or used by an actor within a scene. For instance, if the scene requires an actor to drink from a coffee cup, the cup would be considered a prop and would be the responsibility and cost of the prop department.

The prop master (line item 750-01) will secure the necessary props by either renting or purchasing them (line items 750-08 and 750-09) from prop supply houses or specialized stores. (Do not forget to apply sales tax to any purchased props under line item 750-09.)

Examine the day-out-of-days sheet for the film's props. Be sure to account for all of them. On *Swingers*, had we not been able to shoot in actual bars we would have needed to budget more money in this line item, to make any stage we used look like an actual bar (with alcohol bottles, ashtrays, bar stools, and so on). In *Swingers* (as with most scripts), certain props were needed at each location. For example, the scenes shot in Mike's apartment called for a telephone, an answering machine, an alarm clock, a Varga girl wall calendar, and a refrigerator. These props were rented, purchased, or borrowed and brought to the location we used to serve as Mike's apartment.

Item 750-04: Picture Vehicle, Labor and Maintenance

Budget in this line item for any labor, maintenance, or repairs that may arise on any purchased or rented picture vehicles that will be used in the film.

Item 750-05: Picture Vehicle Rentals

Budget for any vehicles that will be needed in the film. To keep costs down on *Swingers*, we used Jon Favreau's personal car as the character Trent's car, and other cars owned by the cast and crew were used as other scripted picture vehicles (see Figure 6–2). In sample budget 3 (see Figure 6–6), an older-model Cadillac Coupe Deville was needed, which was more cost efficient to purchase and repair than to rent. Call around to determine which is the cheaper alternative for your film. Be as creative as possible when securing vehicles. Check with old movie supply houses, garages, and auto shops that may have the vehicle you need. Use the schedules and vehicle day-out-of-days sheet to help determine when and for how many days each vehicle will work. You will also need to budget for fuel for the picture vehicles.

Item 750-06: Animals and Livestock

Should your script require animals, assess realistically what the true needs are. For example, do you need a household dog that lies around and it could be your or a friend's dog, or will the dog need to be trained in a specific way? Does your film require rare or exotic animals that can be obtained only through special trainers or farms? If the latter is true, check in your local film guides under "livestock and animals" and make preliminary calls to ascertain what the price may be. Most of the film guides now have Web sites through which you have the most up-to-date information at your fingertips. If you are not sure if your film guide has a Web site or need web addresses, type the name of the film guide for your city into a search engine such as Google or Yahoo. Should you have livestock, you will most likely be required to have wranglers or other animal coordinators.

Contact the Humane Society to file the proper paperwork. This is important because in order for you to run the clause at the end your film stating that no animals were harmed during the shooting of your film, which may be required by distributors, you must have the necessary paperwork from the Humane Society. They will send a representative to your set during filming.

Item 750-08: Prop Rentals
Budget here for all props that will be rented over the course of the show.

Items 755-00: Wardrobe

Wardrobe is the clothing worn by each of the characters and extras in the script. The wardrobe communicates the essence of each character and often conveys the period of the film. It helps to establish the overall look and feel of the film and to tell the story. For *Swingers*, it was essential that the actors look like throwbacks to the early fifties generation, complete with pocket chains, cuff links, wing-tipped shoes, wide-collared shirts, muscle tees, and zoot suits. The costume designer (line item 755-04) will create a breakdown of the wardrobe necessary for each character. Budget at least one assistant (line item 755-03), even if the cast is small, to help the designer with dressing actors, fittings, sewing, steaming, and picking up and returning clothes. Depending on the size of the cast and the wardrobe required for the film, more than one costume assistant may be needed. On heavier cast days, budget for several assistants to be sure that the cast is properly attended to and that the show remains on schedule.

Often, a second set of a given wardrobe is required. For example, if the clothing worn by an actor will be damaged, riddled with bullet holes, or stained, it may be easiest to have multiple sets on hand in order to film the scene again or for reshoots later. Do not forget that extras will need to be outfitted. If you ask extras to provide their own wardrobe, SAG requires that they be compensated. (Check with SAG for the current rate paid to actors for personal wardrobe use.) Budget a kit rental fee for the costume designer (line item 755-10), and remember to add sales tax into the budget for any purchased wardrobe items (line item 755-09). Line items such as alterations (755-06) and cleaning and dyeing (755-07) are other costs you will have to budget for in this category.

Items 760-00: Makeup and Hairstylists

The amount you will need to budget in this category will depend on your film. For instance, on *Swingers*, the principal cast consisted of five males who did not need any special makeup or wigs. Therefore, for the majority of the shoot we needed only one makeup artist, who also served as the hairstylist. On larger cast days (for example, those days we were shooting at The Derby) we had special hair and makeup needs for the female dancers and brought on another makeup artist/hairstylist. (See line items 760-01 and 760-02 in the *Swingers* budget shown in Figure 6–2).

The makeup artist/hairstylist for *Swingers* needed only half a day of prep to meet with the five principal males and ascertain their makeup needs. You may need to budget more prep time for your makeup and hair artists if cast members' hair must be cut or dyed before a show, wigs fit and cut, tattoos applied, contacts fit, or bruises, wounds, or other special makeup tested.

Special effects makeup, such as blood and other incidentals, are budgeted for in this category. You will also need makeup lights and chairs and should allocate money for them. Makeup and hair expendables can also be budgeted for in line item 775-07. Usually, makeup artists and hairstylists provide their own supplies, which they rent to the production as a kit rental (line item 760-10). Remember to add sales tax to purchases.

Items 765-00: Production Sound

The cleaner and less noisy the production sound track is, the less you will need to fix in post-production, and hence the less money it will cost. The sound mixer will know what type of microphones to use to best pick up an actor's lines. The decision depends on the shot, the space, and the amount of background noise.

Items 765-01 and 765-02: Sound Mixer, Boom Man
Budget for the sound mixer and the boom operator in these line items, based on the rate negotiated with each. Remember to apply the proper fringes and any kit rentals.

Item 765-05: Playback Operator

Discuss the film's needs with the sound department to determine whether you need to budget any money in this line item. The *Swingers* budget (see Figure 6–2) includes money for a playback operator and playback equipment. We needed to play back the song the band performed live in The Derby for the dancers in that scene.

Item 765-06: Sound Equipment Rentals

The sound mixer you hire may already own the basic sound package, which includes a mix board, recorder, cable, and microphones. Sound mixers often have batteries, walkie-talkies, a slate, and wireless microphones (called lavaliere microphones) as well. If not, you will need to rent these items from a production sound house. On *Swingers*, our sound mixer had almost all of this equipment, and we were able to negotiate a flat rate with him. This saved us money.

Item 765-11: Miscellaneous Expenses

This category is a perfect place to modestly pad your budget for things that may unexpectedly arise. It is also an appropriate line item to place anything that is specific to your script that does not obviously fit in anywhere else. In the *Swingers* budget (see Figure 6–2), we allocated money for beepers in this line item.

Items 770-00: Transportation

This category may account for one of the largest portions of the budget unless you are shooting your film entirely on a stage and will not have to transport equipment and materials from location to location each day. How you budget this category depends on whether the production is union or nonunion and whether you need a transportation captain and other drivers who are Teamsters and are paid union rates.

The sample budgets (Figures 6–4 to 6–7) are based on nonunion shows. Nonunion rates were budgeted for drivers on *Swingers* (see Figure 6–2) and in sample budgets 1 and 3. Sample budget 2 reflects a deal made with the Teamsters, requiring that we hire two union drivers for three days. (The film was shot on location where the union is very strict. We were safer to make a deal up front than to risk difficulties during the shoot.) On nonunion shows, have your crew members drive the vehicles whenever possible (that is, production assistants and members of any department who need to transport their materials and equipment by way of cube van or production truck). If the show is nonunion, you may experience some trouble with the local Teamsters. It is best to inform the local transportation union of your show's whereabouts and the budget. They may picket in front of sets and visit frequently, making filming difficult, if you do not.

If your show is union, you will have to hire Teamsters and budget properly for union rates in line items 770-02, 770-03, 770-08, and 770-09. Be sure to budget for overtime and per diem as well. Teamsters are usually paid a set rate for a 10-hour workday, and anything over 10 hours is considered overtime and is paid as such. (Contact the local transportation union for current rates.) Make sure to apply the appropriate union fringes. The blank budget form (see Figure 6–1) includes all of the line items that might be needed in this category. You may use only a few of them for your film.

Item 770-01: Messenger Service

Whether for delivering scripts or picking up packages, your production may incur messenger costs. To save money, have production assistants handle most pickups and deliveries. Budgeting a small amount of money in this line item will keep you on the safe side. Alternatively, you can budget for any messenger costs in the Administrative category (910-00).

Item 770-05: Mileage Allowance

If you will be reimbursing your crew for mileage to report to location, budget the cost in this line item. Often, mileage is not paid on low-budget independent films, and you will need to inform the cast and crew of this fact at the outset. (See also "Item 770-06: Fuel.") If you are shooting within the studio zone, you are not required to pay mileage to crew members for reporting to location. (Check with the city's film commission for studio zone limits.) Regardless, we recommend that you do budget some money for this line item. If the budget can afford it, pay mileage to those crew members who use their own cars to run errands for the production. Find out what the standard cost is per mile at the time you intend to begin pre-production.

Item 770-06: Fuel

In this line item account for fuel costs for all production vehicles, picture vehicles, grip/electric trucks, rental cars, and any other cars used to run errands or handle pickups and deliveries for the production. Be sure to budget sufficient money in this category, especially if you will be covering gas receipts rather than paying mileage to the crew. It is often more cost effective to cover gas receipts than to pay mileage. Budget for this line item on an allow or a weekly basis, as in the sample budgets (see Figures 6–4 to 6–7).

Item 770-10: Location Vehicles/Production Trucks/Equipment

Use this line item to budget for any cars or trucks needed to transport materials and equipment for the production. Budget for motor homes or honey wagons, rental cars, production trucks, cube vans, passenger vans, and any makeup and wardrobe trailers you will need. (Motor homes and honey wagons are often budgeted under line item 725-24, Dressing Room Rentals.) Most low-budget pictures cannot afford motor homes or honey wagons, but a location sometimes requires that you rent a motor home that can serve as an office, bathroom, and makeup/wardrobe space.

On *Swingers*, we budgeted a rental car for the production, which also served as the character Mike's car in the film. We had a production cube truck we used to transport production expendables, craft service items, and wardrobe. Because the production was small and the shoot was relatively short, this was feasible and cost effective. We rented a passenger van to take the crew to Las Vegas and budgeted it for four days. It was more cost effective than flying and kept the crew together, ensuring that everyone arrived at the location at the same time. You will not always lump these vehicles into one line item as we did. You can budget for each department's vehicle separately, as in the sample budgets (see Figures 6–4 to 6–7). Be sure to add sales and city taxes for rental vehicles if necessary.

Ideally, hire a key grip or gaffer who has his or her own truck and equipment, and make a flat deal for both so that you do not have to rent a grip and/or electric truck separately. (On larger-budget shows you would most likely budget for the trucks and the equipment separately.) On *Swingers*, we made an all-in grip/electric deal with a gaffer who had a truck with both grip and electrical equipment. This saved us a great deal of money. Our sound department had its own van to transport sound equipment.

You may need to budget for a camera truck that has a darkroom on board to download the film. (See the sample budgets shown in Figures 6–4 and 6–6.) On *Swingers*, we had a small camera that took 400-foot loads of film only, and we were constantly changing film magazines. We needed to be able to download and reload magazines quickly and did so in a camera bag, rather than in a camera van, which would have cost us a rental fee, mileage, fuel, and taxes.

Items 775-00: Location Expenses

This category will account for another large portion of the overall budget unless you are shooting entirely on a stage or in just one or two locations. Most films are shot at many different locations and often in different cities or states. *Swingers*, for example, was shot on location in and around Los Angeles and we traveled to Las Vegas. Sample budget 2 (see Figure 6–5) is for a film shot on location in New York State and Atlantic City, and sample budget 3 (see Figure 6–6) is for a film shot at a casino in Las Vegas or Reno. None of these films required shooting on a stage.

Locations can be very expensive to secure. Be sure to scout several potential locations to find the one that will best serve your film and your budget. Be creative when scouting for locations, and seek out locations that require minimal set dressing and props. This will keep costs down. If the rental and permit fees of a location where you want to film are too costly, investigate shooting on a stage, which may be more affordable, even with set dressing costs. Try to find locations near one another. This may reduce costs for permits. (See "Item 775-03: Site Rentals/Permits/Licenses.") Some of the line items that you may need to consider in this category are gratuities for restaurants or hotels (line item 775-17) and shipping (line item 775-20) film or dailies to the lab or editor.

Item 775-01: Survey Expense/Scouting

Include money in this line item for location scouting costs your show will incur during pre-production. Include money for gas, food, still film, and rental cars or vans, and add sales tax to purchases. You can also budget in this line item for any travel and lodging you require while scouting. Scouting trips are scheduled for one or several days, depending on the number of locations, their proximity to one another, how quickly the locations are locked, and the availability of the necessary crew members.

We budgeted for two location scouts in sample budget 3 (see Figure 6–6). The first was a small preliminary scout for the director, producers, and location manager. For the second scout we budgeted for the director, producers, location manager, DP, AD, production designer, gaffer, and key grip. We budgeted for costs we would incur while scouting (see sample budgets). The second scout was more cost effective and time efficient than the first because we had already scouted the area and were more certain of the amount of time needed, where our locations were, where to eat, and where to stay. A second trip is not always necessary; it will depend on the film, the budget, and the locations you have in mind.

Item 775-02: Location Staff

Budget for the location manager and, if necessary and affordable, an assistant or two in this line item. There is a significant amount of paperwork, arrangements, and organizing related to shooting on location (such as posting notices, obtaining releases, scouting, securing permits, taking photos, and negotiating agreements and contracts). The number of scripted locations will determine how much prep time the location manager needs. Use your schedules to help you when budgeting this line item. Keep in mind that locations take time to find and secure and that they often fall through. Allow sufficient time for the location manager to secure (or replace) locations.

Item 775-03: Site Rentals/Permits/Licenses

List each location by name in the budget, and include the cost of renting the locations in this line item. Refer to your schedule to ensure that you account for all of the locations and the amount of time (days or weeks) needed at each, and that you properly budget for the costs.

Also include permit fees in this line item. Permits must be secured in order to film at many locations. Do not steal locations! Secure permits! You will need a permit if you have a generator on the set, if the space in which you are filming is open to the public, if equipment will be set up outside, or if the location is a public place or is used as a public thoroughfare. If you fail to secure the proper filming permits your show could be shut down, which will cost more money in the long run. The location manager should contact the appropriate city filming office to determine which locations require permits and to ascertain the fees involved. He or she should also file the necessary paperwork.

The costs of the site and the permit fees will depend on the location and the city in which you are filming. Often, you can secure a blanket permit for all of your locations if they are near one another, rather than permitting each location separately. A blanket permit will save you money. Some cities issue permits free of cost (e.g., New York City), but acquiring the permits is just as time consuming and paperwork intensive as Los Angeles. In any case, have your proof of insurance and permits on the set at all times. (Securing locations and permits is discussed in Chapter 7.)

On *Kissing Jessica Stein*, several of the key locations were either donated by friends and family or the price was significantly lower due to the fact that friends and family were the renters. Therefore, this line item came in much lower than its original budget.

Item 775-04: Hotel and Lodging

Account here for the cost of all below-the-line crew lodging when filming at a distant location. Use your schedule to help you determine the number of days and the number of crew members for whom you will need to budget hotel costs. Budget per diem for crew when filming at a distant location. No fringes are added to per diems. The per diem minimum varies from city to city. Contact the local film commission for the rates. Apply sales tax to any hotel costs, and be prepared to pay gratuities.

Item 775-05: Catering Services

Do not skimp here! Most likely, your crew will work long hours at a reduced rate. Feeding crew members a hot, well-balanced meal is incredibly important for both morale and stamina. The schedule will help you determine how many days you will need to cater the shoot for and the number of people to be fed each day. Remember that any visitors and extras on the set will also need to eat. Err on the side of providing more meals rather than fewer. Call several catering companies to secure the best deal possible. If the catering company bids are too high, come up with a creative way to cater the shoot to keep costs down. (See Chapter 7.) Add sales tax on any food purchases. Refer to the sample budgets shown in Figures 6–4 to 6–6 to see how the catering costs were broken out.

Item 775-06: Meal Allowances/Extra Meals

SAG and union rules require that the cast and crew be fed every six hours. Regardless of whether the cast is SAG and the crew is union, you should follow these union rules. Meal penalties are paid on both cast and crew members if lunch or dinner is not served within the six-hour interval. Second meals are often walkaway or wrap-out meals (though they can be sit-down meals also) that are served if a shoot day will go into overtime and it has been six hours since lunch was served. The craft service person should keep a list of affordable restaurants located near each location in case a second meal must be served. The first AD should alert both the line producer and the craft service person approximately three hours before the second meal must be served, so that food can be ordered, delivered or picked up, and served on time.

Meals for the extras who will be filming on the set can be either box lunches or dinners ordered from restaurants, or extra meals ordered from the caterer. Often, if there are many extras it is cheaper to order box meals than to have the caterer prepare more food.

Item 775-07: Production Expendables

Budget this line item as an allowance. Include money for such items as a wardrobe steamer, wardrobe racks, cones, bullhorns, tables, chairs, desks, director's chairs, rope, bungee cord, coffee urns, coolers, craft service equipment, tablecloths, handcarts for carrying equipment, hangers, and makeup tables. Pad this line item a bit. You will want to be covered when unanticipated costs arise. Production expendables are often charged on a three-day week (you pay for three days' worth of rental to secure the equipment for an entire week), and many of the items needed will be inexpensive. Remember to add sales tax if you plan to purchase any of these items.

Item 775-11: Fire and Police

When permits are secured, the location manager, in conjunction with the permit office, will arrange for the proper fire and police personnel to be present at the necessary locations. If you plan to run a generator at your location or you will be shooting on a sidewalk or a public thoroughfare, the film commission may require that a firefighter or police officer be present. If you are filming at a location while it is open to the public, a police officer must be present. The city may check on the production and will shut it down if the proper officials are not present and the proper paperwork is not on hand. Firefighters and police officers are paid an hourly fee that is established by the city you are filming in, and there is usually a four-hour minimum, even if the official is needed for only one hour. Check local film guides, such as LA 411 or NYPG (New York Production Guide), or call the local permit office for the rates specific to the city in which you will be filming. Add the appropriate fringes to the rates.

Item 775-18: Office Rent/Furniture

In this line item budget for office rent and overhead over the course of the show and for office furniture or equipment you will need to rent. Alternatively, you may include office rent and furniture costs in the Administrative Expenses category under line item 910-17. Setting up a production office can be costly, so be as creative as possible. On *Swingers*, we ran the production out of our house. We budgeted a small amount for utilities and supplies in this line item, but not for rent. Find an inexpensive office with plenty of space, electrical outlets, and phone jacks.

You might also check out apartments for rent in a convenient and safe area. See if you can rent an apartment on a month-to-month basis. This is often cheaper than renting space that is specifically zoned for offices or businesses. Of course, if you have to install extra phone lines, outlets, and lights; rent a parking lot because there is not enough parking available on the street; walk up and down many stairs with equipment; or risk disturbing the neighbors, it may not be worth it to rent an apartment instead of an office. Investigate and weigh your options carefully.

Item 775-21: Location Security

Have security present to ensure the safety of equipment that is left overnight, during the filming of any scenes with many cast members and extras, to guard production vehicles with equipment on them, and when shooting in a dangerous neighborhood. Budget a small amount of money in this line item even if you do not anticipate hiring security personnel. If the money allocated here goes unused, you will have a pad to cover unexpected costs that arise.

Item 775-22: Parking Lots

This line item is for parking lots that have to be rented for office or set parking for the cast and crew. If you have to rent a secure lot for the overnight parking of production vehicles or housing expensive rented equipment, include the cost here.

Items 780-00: Process Photography

Budget in this category for shots you plan to create in a process studio. Suppose, for example, that you need a shot of an actor standing in front of a river but you do not want to travel to a river for that one shot. You can create the shot you need by projecting stock footage of a river onto a screen and positioning the actor in front of it. When you sync up the shot it will appear as if the actor is standing in front of the river. Today, blue screens are often used instead of process photography, and the images are combined in post-production.

Item 785-00: Production Dailies

This category covers developing the film, printing the dailies, transferring the sound, coding the dailies, and transferring the film to videotape. Call several for quotes to determine if they are able to accommodate your film's needs. If one of your crew members is a student, you can often obtain a discount on these costs.

Item 785-01: Negative Raw Stock

Discuss with the director and the DP the type of film stock (35-mm, 16-mm, super 8, super 16), the speed, and the quantity they will need. Then check with film supply houses for current prices. Raw stock is priced by the foot. Remember to add sales tax to any purchase. (Refer to the sample budgets shown in Figures 6–4 to 6–7 to see how we broke out our costs.) Instead of factory-unopened raw stock, you can purchase "recans" or short ends, which are less expensive. A recan is film that was loaded into a magazine but never shot, and then literally recanned. The disadvantage of using recanned film is that occasionally the film has been exposed or is bad, and you lose whatever footage you have shot. Test the film first. You can also purchase short ends at a reduced rate. These are partial rolls of film left over from someone else's shoot. Be aware that short ends are (by definition!) short and you will therefore be constantly reloading the camera, which can be time consuming and can prohibit long takes. The DP and director may want to film only with factory-unopened film, which is much more costly.

Film prices vary according to the type of stock, so budget carefully here. If your intention is to secure a distributor, we recommend that you budget and shoot with 35-mm film. If you secure distribution for a picture shot on 16-mm film, it will cost about the same amount in the long run if you have to blow the film up to 35 mm.

You can expect to shoot on average about 4,000 feet of 35-mm film per day. On *Swingers*, however, because it was mostly a dialogue piece, the actors were well rehearsed, and the cast and crew were small, we shot many pages each day and averaged approximately 7,000 feet per day. In total, we shot just over 90,000 feet of film, which we could never have afforded had we not used recans and short ends.

Item 785-02: Developing
Try to make a deal with a lab for developing, syncing, coding, and processing dailies. Costs are usually given per foot. Alert your lab if the film should be prepped for video transfer or if a work print will be struck. Should you be shooting in a digital format, you will not be budgeting for developing costs.

Item 785-03: Print Dailies
This line item covers the print the editor will work from when assembling the picture on a flatbed. Ideally, make a package deal with a lab that includes development and a work print, both costs assessed on a per-foot basis. Even if you are editing on an Avid, it is essential to print some of your film (especially at the beginning of a shoot) to make sure that there are no problems that cannot be seen in a video transfer. While it may seem that you do not have the money to print any dailies, we cannot stress the importance of this enough. It will ultimately cost you a great deal more if there turns out to be focus or ground glass problems that only show up in a print. We recommend printing at least 200 feet of film on each roll you shoot the first few days of production.

Item 785-05: Transfer Sound Dailies
Budget in this line item for syncing the production sound to the picture. The sound is matched to the exact place in the film where it has been slated, and code numbers are used. This process is also called syncing dailies.

Item 785-07: Coding Dailies
You will need to code dailies (key codes) only if you will be striking a work print. For the editor to maintain the synchronization of the picture and sound while cutting the film, he or she will need to refer to the key codes on the dailies. Check with a lab for the costs involved.

Item 785-09: Videotape Transfers
If the film will be edited digitally, it must be processed, prepped, and then transferred to video (telecine). Transfers are done in order to download the footage into the nonlinear digital editor and assemble the film. Should you be shooting in a digital format, you will not need to make video transfers.

Item 785-10: Tape Stock
Purchase tape stock from film and video houses rather than have the lab supply it. This is less expensive. If some goes unused, sell it back to the supply house where it was purchased at a reduced rate. It is also possible to purchase videotape that has been used. This is not a good idea for video masters but is a fine money saver for making copies for the music supervisor, music composer, and sound editor.

Items 790-00: Living Expenses

If you are shooting at a distant location and transporting your crew to the set, you will need to provide crew members with both housing and per diems. It may be more cost effective to rent apartments than to put the crew up in a hotel for a long period of time. If you rent apartments, be sure to budget for utility costs. If you are putting the crew up in a hotel, apply sales tax, and budget for gratuities. Ask crew members if they mind sharing rooms. Similarly, if you plan to hire any nonlocal crew members to work on the shoot, you will need to provide and budget for their living accommodations.

Items 795-00: Fringes

This category is for any government taxes that will be paid for below-the-line personnel. (Fringes applied to the cast are included in categories 630-00 and 640-00.) Taxes such as FICA, FUI, SUI, and SDI and other contributions are included here. The crew will fill out W4 and Start/I-9 forms in order to file their tax status, so that you or your payroll company will be able to account for each crew member's deductions properly.

In the sample budgets (see Figures 6–4 to 6–6) we chose to account for fringes within each category rather than as a separate line item, so that we could see each of the fringes paid. We find this to be more useful, and the fringes are automatically totaled into the overall budget. Contact SAG and the employment bureau in your area to confirm that your fringes are accurate.

We created a nonunion fringe in the Movie Magic Budgeting fringe setup box and set it at 18 percent. This fringe includes government taxes such as FICA, FUI, and SUI. This way, we only had to click on the nonunion fringe we created to account for all employee taxes. Do not apply fringes to cast or crew per diems or to loan-outs. (See "Budgeting Terms and Concepts" earlier in the chapter and categories 610-00, 620-00, and 630-00 for more on fringes and loan-outs.)

Items 797-00: Tests

Tests are done primarily for technical reasons. We usually budget this category on an allow basis, keeping in mind the elements and equipment we will need to secure. You will need the camera for a day or two, as well as the film stock, the DP, the director, the first camera assistant, the gaffer, and possibly the AD. You are testing not only the film stock but the camera and the lenses, to be sure that they are in proper working order and that it is the equipment you need. You may want to test the film stock you are using under certain lighting conditions, and maybe test an actor for aesthetic purposes. In sample budgets 2 and 3 (see Figures 6–5 and 6–6), we allocated money for tests. Do not forget that the film will need to be processed, which is another cost you will have to budget for. Categories 700-00 through 798-00 cover the production period costs.

Items 800-00: Editing

This category will account for another large portion of your overall budget. Included here are the cost of the editor, assistant and apprentice editors, music and sound effects editing, projection, negative cutting, the editing suite, and the equipment on which the film will be edited. Do not rush the editing process; be sure to budget enough time and money! (See Chapter 9 for more on editing.)

Items 800-01, 800-18, and 800-19: Film Editor, Assistant Editor, Apprentice Editor

Film editors' rates can vary significantly according to their experience, what type of show it is, how quickly the film needs to be put together, and what type of system (linear or nonlinear) the film will be cut on. You may find an editor who is willing to reduce his or her rate because the feature credit makes it worthwhile or because the material is great. The editor will usually come on board and begin cutting during the first week of production.

Film editors often prefer to work with a particular assistant. Many shows need more than one assistant and often a couple of apprentice editors. Budget for the assistant editor or editors in line item 800-18 and for the apprentices in line item 800-19.

Item 800-02: Sound Effects Editing

Sound effects are cut into the film digitally, most often after the picture has been locked. You will need to have a sound effects editor, or your editor may be willing to edit sound effects himself or herself. Check your budget to determine what you can afford. Call around for quotes and discuss the film's needs with the director, the editor, and the post-production supervisor.

Item 800-03: Music Editing

If you are unable to afford a music editor, your film editor may be able to do some of the music editing, especially if cutting on an Avid editor. The music editor will sync the recorded music to the picture and add the source music or score. With the Avid system, the music can be synced up to the picture on a time-coded digital audiotape (DAT), which will save some money. It is like a temp-mix. The music can be professionally mixed later to adjust the sound levels and cues.

Item 800-04: Negative Cutting

The cost for negative cutting, or conforming the negative, is approximately $600 per 35-mm reel. A reel of film is usually about 10 minutes long, so if the film is 100 minutes approximately 10 reels of negative will be cut, and conforming costs will be about $6,000. Through negotiation, it is possible to reduce each reel's cost a bit. You may need more than 10 reels cut, so be sure to budget ample money in this line item. The sample budgets (see Figures 6–4 to 6–6) are for 35-mm film stock. Rates will be different if you are shooting with 16-mm film stock. Keep in mind that if you secure distribution for a film shot on 16-mm film you will most likely need to blow it up to 35-mm for theatrical distribution, and this is costly. If you have shot your film in a digital format, you will not need a negative cutter. When and if you decide to transfer your digital picture to 35-mm film, you may need a negative cutter, but the work he or she does will be relatively minimal.

Item 800-06 Projection

Viewing the picture at the rough-cut stage is important during the editing process. The director, editor, and producer will want to view the picture, checking for rough spots, missing sound or effects, music cues, narrative continuity, and any needed ADR. It is essential to budget ample funds here. Once the picture has been locked, it may be screened for distribution purposes, for the cast and crew, and for other reasons.

Item 800-11: Editorial Facilities

This line item covers the cost of the cutting room itself (tables, bins, racks, hard drives, VCRs, televisions, and so on) and the equipment the film will be cut on (flatbed, Avid, D-Vision). Be sure to know exactly what the editor needs and what the facility has. You may need to rent editing equipment from an outside facility if it is not available where you are cutting. Try to make a package deal for the room and the equipment per week. If possible, limit the weeks of cutting without compromising the film and putting too much of a strain on the editor and the director. However, do not rush, and do not underestimate the time needed. If you budget for too little time and money on the editing suite and your equipment, you may not be able to extend your stay at the facility. Having to change to a different cutting room can be costly and time consuming.

Item 800-12: Editorial Supplies

Budget in this line item for editing expendables, such as pens, paper, notebooks, splicing tape, and 1/2-inch and 3/4-inch videotape (or whatever format you may use for your masters, such as D2, Beta SP, and so on). Be sure to budget food costs also. Keep in mind the length of time the editors will be cutting when budgeting for supplies and food. Include sales tax on these items.

Item 800-14: Post-production Supervisor

If the budget cannot afford a post-production supervisor for the entire post-production period, it is advisable to hire one for a short time to help organize the film's post-production needs. Post-production is costly, and it pays to have someone on board who is familiar with the process, can secure the best deals, understands the timing of each of the processes, and will oversee all of the film's needs (such as sound mix, sound effects, ADR, looping, music, main and end titles, opticals, and color timing). Post-production is time consuming, and if you are the producer you will be dealing with many other things during this period. (For more on post-production, see Chapter 9.)

Item 800-17: Other Costs

Budget a reasonable amount of money for this line item, even if just for padding. Unanticipated costs may arise during the editing process, and you will want to be covered.

Items 810-00: Music

In this category you will budget for all of the film's music needs, including the composer, musicians, and a supervisor. In the sample budgets (see Figures 6–4 to 6–7) we allocated money for many of the line items in this category as an allowance because we were uncertain what the actual costs would be.

Music can be source music or score. Music that appears to be coming from a radio, television, jukebox, and so on in the background of a given scene is source music. Score is any music that does not come from any visible source and that helps communicate the story or set the mood. Music can be composed specifically for the film, or the rights to existing songs can be licensed.

On a low-budget independent film, you may not be able to budget enough money in this category to cover all of the actual music costs. It will depend on how extensive your film's music needs are and how costly the music is. We usually budget this category as a package or an allowance that includes any festival music rights, some licensing, a composer, and a supervisor. Rarely, however, does the budgeted amount cover all costs. If you secure distribution, the distributor may either assume the costs, split them with you, or require that the music be changed to something more affordable. Music rights, composing, facilities, and licensing are very expensive, and deals are hard to come by. It is important to budget enough for a composer, a music supervisor, and any necessary rights, such as festival rights at the very least. (See Chapter 9 for more on music.)

Item 810-08: Composer

If you hire a composer to score the film, he or she will come on board during the editing process. Composers' rates vary, but for now, budget either a weekly rate for most of post-production or an allowance. Give the composer and the music supervisor video transfers of the film along the way, so that they can determine where music will be placed. The composer and the music supervisor (with the director, editor, and producer) will choose the music that best communicates the mood of the film and helps tell the story.

Items 810-09 Through 810-23

These line items are for different types of musicians. On larger-budget shows, most of these line items will be budgeted.

Item 810-25: Music Supervisor

Bring the music supervisor on board in late production or early post-production. The music supervisor will spot the film with the director and producer for music cues and will suggest either source music or score for specific areas in the film. He or she will help secure the necessary rights and licenses for scripted songs or music, determine master use and sync licensing fees, and negotiate with the publishing company or the record company for the use of songs. The music supervisor will secure festival rights if needed and will work closely with the composer (if one has been hired), arranging for any facilities or musicians needed. The music supervisor will help determine the film's needs and what they will cost.

Items 810-28 and 810-29: Master Use Licenses, Music Publishing Licenses

The licensing fees involved with these two line items often cost more than the entire budget of *Swingers*. Depending on the songs chosen and how many of them there are, these licenses can be very costly. In sample budget 2 (see Figure 6–5), the producers specifically requested that $8,000 be allocated in the music category. They needed to keep the budget under $1 million, so they chose to allocate a small sum of money in this category, knowing that they would have to figure out how to pay for rights and licenses later. Securing these rights is very important, and it may be difficult to obtain the songs you want for the money you have.

Items 820-00: Post-production Sound

In this line item budget for sound mixing, recording, rerecording, music, sound effects, dialogue, ADR, and foley. You can keep costs down in this category by making package deals at a sound facility and premixing some of the sound on an Avid if you are cutting on one. Sound package prices depend on the medium being used to mix the sound, the elements needed, and how many hours or days you will need to complete the mix. If there is a lot of usable dialogue on the production track, the film will require less ADR.

Item 820-01: Dialogue Recording (ADR)

Budget in this line item for the cost of renting an ADR facility. The cast will report to the facility during post-production to rerecord any lost lines they delivered during production or to record any additional lines. You should budget the actors' fees for recording ADR in the Cast category (630-00). (See Chapter 9 for information on low-budget ADR.)

Item 820-02: Narration Recording

If the film requires narration or voiceover, budget for it in this line item. Narration and voiceover can be recorded on a stage, usually after the picture is shot and then synced to the picture later. It usually makes sense to record voiceover during post-production because it can be used to alter or enhance the film's narrative.

Item 820-03: Sound Effects (Foley)

Budget here for foley artists and the sound stage they will use to add in any sound effects. Foley artists use props to create sounds that need to be added to a film to best communicate the full effect of a scene or for sounds that need to be replaced because they were not clean in the production track. They record sounds such as kissing, rain, and footsteps on a sound stage, matching each sound to the picture.

Item 820-06: Dubbing Session

In the dubbing session, or mix, the various sound elements (dialogue, music, and effects) are mixed on a dubbing stage while the film is projected. Try to make a flat deal with the dubbing facility. Be sure to dub on the largest stage you can afford. It makes a difference in the quality of the sound.

Most films are mixed into four analog channels (left, center, right, and surround). This is referred to as matrix stereo. For a fee, the mix can be supervised by Dolby Laboratories or Ultra-stereo. Both companies require the use of their names in advertising the film. Dolby SR (or its generic equivalent) is the best analog format around. Recently, three digital formats have been introduced: Digital Theater Sound (DTS), Dolby Digital, and Sony Digital Dynamic Sound (SDDS). In these formats, the film is mixed to five or more channels (left, center, right, left surround, and right surround). Most mixes are recorded onto 35-mm full coat, although you can save money by recording onto digital tape, such as DAT or D88.

Item 820-07: Sound Transfers

Budget in this line item for transferring sound (dialogue, music, and effects) to magnetic stripe film, creating the magnetic master composite mix. This magnetic soundtrack will be conformed to the answer print. Usually, the cost for transferring the sound is billed by the hour. Try to make an all-in package deal for the magnetic tape and the transfer. Have the sound editor arrange for the film's needs.

Item 820-09: Purchased Sound Effects

Budget for any prerecorded sound effects you will need to purchase to add to the film during the mix. Check with your editor and director.

Item 820-12: Magnetic Tape for Edit

Budget this line item for magnetic stripe film. (The cost is quoted per foot.) The soundtrack of the film will be transferred to a 35-mm magnetic master tape consisting of three stripes, which contain the music, the sound effects, and the dialogue of the film. Try to make a package deal on the magnetic tape and the transfer. Add sales tax to any purchases.

Items 830-00: Stock Shots

If you need a shot of an Egyptian tomb, for example, rather than building a replica of one or traveling to Egypt for the shot you may want to purchase footage from a stock footage library. Stock footage can be expensive. Be careful to purchase stock that matches the type of film you are using in order that the film looks and feels uniform. Call around for quotes.

Items 840-00: Titles

Budget here for the main and end titles (line items 840-01, 840-02, and 840-03) of the film. Main titles typically run at the beginning of the film, and the end titles at the end. We usually budget this category as an allowance until we determine the style of the titles and the total number of cards we will have to run. Be accurate in your allowance by calling for some preliminary quotes. You can be as creative as you like when determining how to run the film's titles. The more intricate title cards you have and the more stylized they are, the more expensive they will be. Be sure to adhere to size requirements when crediting the cast and crew. These requirements are usually prenegotiated in the cast and crew contracts along with the placement of the credit in the film.

Items 850-00: Opticals, Mattes, and Inserts

Most likely, you will have to budget an allowance for optical effects (line item 850-01) until you can determine accurately how many opticals you will need, and you will only know this once you begin to assemble the film. You may find that you have to correct or reposition shots optically or that you have to add elements that were not actually in the shot, such as creatures, volcanoes, windstorms, laser beams, and shooting stars. On *Swingers*, we found some shots that were slightly out of focus and others that needed to be repositioned because the ground glass in the viewfinder of our camera was not positioned correctly on one of our filming days.

Also budget here for any inserts, fade-ins, or dissolves you may need. These types of shots are done optically and can be costly, but visually they may serve the film best. Arrange for both title and optical work at the same facility so that the negative is not being shipped around to different title houses.

Items 860-00: Laboratory Processing

This category includes the costs for the post-production lab and related items.

Item 860-01: Reprinting and Developing

Often, through simple wear and tear on the film, certain shots will have to be reprinted and developed. Budget this line item as an allowance, because initially you will not be able to determine what the film will need. This line item applies only if the film is being cut on a flatbed.

You may need prints of the locked picture so that the music and sound editors can be sure that the music and sound are properly synced to the picture. The most cost-effective way to do this is to strike "dirty dupes," which are black-and-white prints of the locked picture made from the cut.

Item 860-02: First Trial Composite Print/Answer Print

This print reflects the first color timing pass combined with any opticals and the soundtrack. A color timer, together with the director and often the editor and the DP, makes color corrections to the film so that the color values of the film are the same throughout and the color for each scene is correct. The first trial print allows you to view first-round color corrections and to find any spots within the film that need further correction. This is also the first time you will see the film projected from a print that marries image and sound, allowing you to check for sync problems. You may need to strike several prints before the color is correct. The corrected composite is called your answer print. For sample budgets 1 and 2 (see Figures 6–4 and 6–5), the producers planned to strike only an answer print they would screen in hopes of securing distribution.

Item 860-07: Interpositive/Internegative

If you secure distribution you will need to strike both an interpositive print (IP) and an internegative print (IN). An IP is a timed print created directly from the original negative. It is used to create duplicate INs, which are used for striking additional release prints to prevent wear and tear on the original IN. Most low-budget films do not budget for an IP or an IN, and answer prints can be struck without them. The sample budgets (see Figures 6–4 to 6–7) do not allocate money for either an IP or an IN but do include an answer print. Categories 810-00 through 870-00 cover the post-production period costs.

Items 910-00: Administrative Expenses

Budget here for all of the film's administrative costs, including start-up costs, accounting supplies, office costs, party costs, and miscellaneous items or gifts. In the sample budgets (see Figures 6–4 to 6–6), we created our own line items to account for certain costs in this category. Many of the line items were not included in the blank budget forms that come with Movie Magic Budgeting.

Item 910-01: Accounting and Terminal Fees

Any accounting software, supplies, or forms you will purchase should be budgeted in this line item. If you will be preparing cast and crew payroll yourself rather than hiring an accountant or using a payroll company, budget for checks and any software programs you will use. If you are using an accountant, budget for checks and software costs here, but not for the accountant.

Item 910-02: MPAA Certificate

The Motion Picture Association of America (MPAA) will view your finished film and assign it a rating. A rating is required if the film is to be released. The certificate certifies that the film has been rated by the MPAA and that its production adhered to the MPAA's regulations and standards. The cost of the certificate will be based on the budget of the film.

Item 910-03: Postage, Shipping, and FedEx

Budget an allowance for this line item. Try to estimate what your shipping needs will be and where items will be shipped to. Budget enough money for all three stages of the film: pre-production, production, and post-production.

Item 910-04: Photocopying

Either rent a photocopier, purchase one, or find one you can borrow. You will need to make many copies every day, including call sheets, Exhibit Gs, contracts, production reports, and the script supervisor's notes. If you do not obtain your own photocopier, ask someone you know who has access to one to run script copies or set up an account at a local print shop and try to make a deal with them. Renting a copier is not very costly and will prove to be well worth the expense.

Item 910-05: Legal Expenses and Fees

You may not be able to afford an attorney, but with enough research you will be able to navigate through your contracts and paperwork. On *Swingers*, we did not have an attorney until after we sold the film and could afford one. Our attorney helped us with delivery paperwork for the distribution company. If you can afford an attorney, it will be money well spent. Usually, attorneys' fees are about 2 percent of the budget of the film, or the attorney will bill on an hourly basis. He or she will help with any financing and partnership contracts, production insurance, errors-and-omissions (E&O) insurance, and other paperwork. If you cannot afford an attorney, seek advice regarding any contracts, music licenses, or paperwork you need help with. You can refer to books about contracts, film guides, and organizations such as California Lawyers for the Arts. (See Appendix A: Resource Guide.) On *Kissing Jessica Stein*, we were able to arrange a flat fee with our attorney, plus give him a share in the film. Not only did this work out favorably for us, as we had a myriad of contracts and questions he helped us with, but it also turned out well for him (as he made money as an investor in the film).

Item 910-06: Telephone/Facsimile

When budgeting this line item, keep in mind where you will be calling. If you are on location, you may be making many long-distance calls and sending long-distance faxes. The crew will be making long-distance calls also. Do not skimp on this line item. A large part of your job will be done on the phone, and the cost of calls adds up. Make sure you get the best rate from the local phone company and long-distance carrier, and that your office has a sufficient number of phone lines.

Item 910-12: Preview Expense/Distribution Screening

If your film is not accepted at any festivals, you may want to set up your own distribution screening. Budget for the cost of a theater or screening room, press kits, invitations and flyers, and whatever else you need to make sure distributors attend the screening. The cost of renting a projection room is rarely less than $250. Sometimes, universities and film archives will screen a film inexpensively. (Chapter 10 explains how we organized the distribution screening for *Swingers*.) You may want to include in this line item costs for research screenings, preview screenings, cast and crew screenings, and any press or agent screenings you plan in order to get feedback or to generate buzz about the film.

Item 910-15: Cellular Phones

As the line producer, you must be reachable at all times, even when you are away from the office and the set. Generally, crew tend to use their personal cell phones on shoots and ask to be reimbursed. The caveat here is to be certain that no crew member has a plan that offers them very few minutes a month with an exorbitant per-minute charge when you exceed the said number of minutes. We have had crew approach us in tears with cell bills that are hundreds of dollars, hoping we will agree to pay it. It is important to let crew know when you hire them what your reimbursement policy is for cell phone usage. You may also want to caution them that if they need to increase the number of monthly minutes in their plan they should do it at the outset of the job.

Item 910-16: Festival Expenses

We created this line item in sample budgets 1 and 3 (see Figures 6–4 and 6–6). Often, festival costs, application fees, transferring the film to video, and shipping costs are overlooked when compiling a budget for a film. If the film is being submitted to any festivals, be sure to budget for all of these costs. Assume that each festival will require an application fee, still photographs, and at least a video dub of the film. If you are planning to apply to festivals overseas, budget for international shipping costs.

Item 910-18: Research Report/E&O Report

A research report is a safeguard that verifies that there are no illegal usages in the script. The researcher makes sure the script does not portray a living person or use actual phone numbers and that the names of all characters and locations are fictitious. A research report will identify any potential problems. The researcher will also verify whether the title of the film has been used before, and if it has where it originated and whether it is advisable that it be changed. Research reports can cost anywhere from $1,000 to $2,000. Call around for quotes. If you have absolutely no money for this report, a distribution company may file for a research report when it picks up the film.

Distributors also require E&O insurance on the film. They may assume the cost if you cannot afford it and have not secured it before distribution. This, however, is not ideal. E&O insurance protects the production company or distributor from liability lawsuits for slander, unauthorized use of the film's title, use of living people's names, and copyright infringement. To secure E&O coverage you must provide the carrier with a copy of the research report, described previously.

Item 910-20: Corporate Filing

Create a corporate entity that will be used for the sole purpose of making the film. The bank account for the funds used to make the film will be set up in this name, as will all vendor accounts. The entity may be structured in a variety of ways, including an S-corporation or a limited liability partnership. Discuss with your partners and investors how they want to structure the company. Forming a corporation or a limited liability partnership limits the liability of all investors. It can be expensive to do this through an attorney, and there are yearly and state fees involved. When making *Swingers*, we filed for our corporate status over the Internet, which was far cheaper (approximately $300) than using an attorney. The state and federal fees for corporations remained the same, and we had an accountant sort out the taxes the corporation needed to pay. If you are inexperienced in this area, speak with an attorney or an accountant to make sure you cover all the bases.

Item 910-21: Polaroid and B/W Still Film

Budget for both Polaroid film and black-and-white and color film for still photos. The art, set dressing, prop, wardrobe, location, and makeup and hair departments, as well as the script supervisor, will want to take photos as records (the photos will be placed in continuity notebooks) to ensure the continuity of the film in case scenes have to be recreated and reshot.

Item 910-22: Payroll Company

Hire a payroll company to pay the cast and crew. Payroll companies usually charge a small percentage of the total payroll or a small fee per check issued. The payroll company will compute and deduct the appropriate government taxes from each employee's check and will report withholdings to the proper government agencies. On *Swingers*, we hired a payroll company to pay the cast only. We totaled each cast member's hours each week, including any overtime or meal penalties, and sent the calculations to the payroll company. (We also sent the calculations to SAG at the end of each week.)

Item 910-23: Storage Facility

We created this line item because when a show is wrapped (or during production) items sometimes have to be stored. Some borrowed or rented items will be used again, and the production will own other things when the show is over. When budgeting this line item, consider such things as props, wardrobe, gels, expendables, and craft service equipment. We allowed $500 for this line item in sample budgets 1 and 3 (see Figures 6–4 and 6–6).

Item 910-35: Wrap Party

We created this line item in sample budgets 1 and 3 (see Figures 6–4 and 6–6). It is safe to assume that even if you cannot afford to have a wrap party you will want to do something to thank the cast and crew and to celebrate having completed the film. We recommend that you budget even a small amount of money for a wrap party of some kind.

Items 920-00: Publicity

Unit publicity on a film is very important. Ideally, the film will attract a distributor and generate buzz. Whether you hire a unit publicist or generate buzz about the film in other ways, it is important that you promote your film to the public. Publicity is often overlooked on low-budget films. Do not make this mistake. At the very least, have still photographs taken during production, and ask a friend to videotape some behind-the-scenes footage of the film. Then, when the time comes to put the film out to the world you will have the materials you need to promote it (refer to the Mark Pogachevsky interview on the companion CD-ROM). We could not afford a publicist on *Swingers* until after we sold the film, but we did have several talent agency contacts to whom we showed the film before securing a distributor. These contacts helped create a positive buzz about the film within the industry. Call around to publicists to determine the costs involved in hiring their services. See if you can put up a small retainer or work out a deferral arrangement.

Item 920-02: Still Photographer

Budget here for a still photographer for after the picture is completed and during any publicity or marketing of the film. Create a press kit of photos of the cast and core team of filmmakers to help create buzz about the film and attract a distributor.

Item 920-03: Still Film and Processing

Budget in this line item for supplies and processing for the still photographer. Call around to photo labs for costs. If you plan to purchase and process the film at the same place, it may save you money. If the still photographer has a relationship with a particular lab, see if he or she can secure a reduced rate on processing.

Items 950-00: Finance Charges

You may have to create this category to account for finance charges on a loan taken by the company. The production team foresee charges prior to knowing how your film will be financed.

Items 970-00: Delivery Expenses

In sample budget 2 (see Figure 6–5), this category was created for any paperwork, approvals, reports, prints, and so on that would have to be delivered if film distribution was secured. On low-budget films, financial problems often arise when distribution is secured but certain delivery items cannot be paid for because there is no money left in the budget. With some of the requirements that studios have on their delivery lists (such as HD transfers), it is recommended to budget approximately $200,000 for delivery items.

Insurance

Insurance was applied to the sample budgets (see Figures 6–4 to 6–6) at 2 percent. Typically, insurance is calculated at 2 to 3.5 percent of the budget. As stated previously, all independent films must be insured in order to secure equipment, locations, transportation, props, wardrobe, cast, crew, and so on, and the policy must be paid for before the production period officially begins.

The insurance cost is applied to the total above- and below-the-line costs, not to the grand total of the budget. Sample budget 3 (see Figure 6–6), for instance, has an insurance cost of $26,125, which is 2 percent of the above- and below-the-line total of $1,306,237. If you are using Movie Magic Budgeting, it will automatically apply the percentage you allocate to the above- and below-the-line total. You will want to insure the production for up to $1 million, which is the standard liability limit. This is the amount usually required to rent equipment and expendables and to secure locations.

WHEN YOUR BUDGET ESTIMATE IS TOO HIGH

If your budget calculation is accurate but higher than you had anticipated, you will have to go back and make changes. However, do not go through your budget and randomly slash numbers! If you do, you will have a final number that meets your needs, but you will not have a budget that reflects how much money you actually require to make the movie. The following are some things to reconsider if your budget is too high. (They do not appear in order of priority.)

- *Format:* Using digital or possibly 16-mm film instead of 35-mm film will keep your costs down, allowing you to get your movie in the can. If you shoot on 16-mm film stock, however, will you limit the possibilities for the movie and its release? You may have to have the film blown up to 35-mm film for its release, which is expensive, but 16-mm may save you money in the short term. Shooting on mini digital video (mini-DV), 24p, Beta SP IMX have all become real options (refer to the Gary Winick interview on the companion CD-ROM). Shooting on DV may reduce your production costs by half. If you purchase the equipment needed to shoot and edit your film, you will be able to make many movies and have your own edit facility. It is common now that folks will go out and purchase a mini-DV camera and a Final Cut Pro editing system, allowing them to make not only the film they set out to finish at the moment but many films down the line. (See Appendix A: Resource Guide for more information on digital filmmaking.) Soon after finishing *Swingers* we set out to make another film with Jon Favreau, a period western he had written. When we needed to bring the budget down as low as we possibly could, we thought about shooting it on digital. When we ran the numbers, we realized that what was making this film expensive was *really* the period costumes, the horses, and the special effects and pyrotechnics. Shooting digitally did not reduce the overall budget enough to justify shooting in a medium that aesthetically was not our first choice. You have to understand what story you are trying to tell and what about it makes it expensive. For any straightforward contemporary story, shooting on mini-DV is going to significantly reduce your production costs. Your tape stock is cheap in comparison to film, and you do not have processing and transfer costs. Conversely, however, post-production can be more costly and complicated, particularly in this time when exhibitors have not switched over to digital projection. If you are lucky enough to get theatrical distribution, you will have to transfer your project from video to film, which is expensive.

- *Crew rates*: Have you budgeted too much for your crew? Perhaps you can reduce everyone's weekly pay by $100.
- *Non-SAG actors*: Can you make the movie you want with non-SAG actors? If so, it will significantly reduce your cast expenses. On every independent film we have been involved with, the SAG cast members were the highest paid of anyone on the set. Keep in mind that this may not be the place to save money, because you do not want to make significant compromises insofar as the talent level of the cast is concerned.
- *Casting agent*: Can you get by without a casting agent? Perhaps you can find an able person who needs a first shot at casting and is willing to work at a reduced rate.
- *Catering*: Catering companies are expensive. Do you know anyone who would be willing to cook or donate meals for the production? Can you make a deal with several restaurants in town at $5 per person in exchange for a production credit? (See Chapter 7 for more catering ideas.)
- *Locations*: The right locations are important to the look of the movie and should not be compromised, but you might find an innovative way to deal with locations. Can you get a different bar, a different house, or a different store that will be cheaper? Can you use a friend's or a relative's house? Can you find locations that are near one another so that you are eligible for a blanket permit? (See Chapter 7 for more on permits.)
- *Recans versus factory-unopened raw stock*: Recans are much less expensive than factory-unopened film. Discuss your options carefully with the DP and the director.
- *Kit rentals*: Can you eliminate kit rentals from your budget, or can you negotiate lower fees? Make sure to still be fair and considerate of your crew.
- *Travel*: Can you eliminate travel expenses by rethinking a given location? Look for something within driving distance that can serve the same purpose.
- *Equipment Rentals*: Can you limit the number of weeks or days you rent equipment? Can you trim down your camera and lighting packages? Ask the DP and the gaffer what they can do without. (Do they really need that Steadi-Cam or that crane?)
- *Editing process*: Can you shorten post-production by several weeks without rushing too much? (Refer to the interview on the companion CD-ROM.) Alternatively, can you rent an Avid and have the editor cut in your apartment or in an inexpensive facility?
- *Transportation*: Reduce the number of production vehicles or at least the number of days you need some of them. Try to rent a cube truck that will accommodate several, or even all, of the departments. Can you borrow picture vehicles rather than rent them?

BUDGETING WITHOUT USING MOVIE MAGIC

Movie Magic Budgeting makes life a lot easier, but there are other ways to deal with budgeting an independent film. The $62,000 budget reproduced in Figure 6–8 was originally done by hand. You can use any spreadsheet program that tallies numbers for you, or you can use a pencil and a calculator. If you do not have the Movie Magic Scheduling program you will need to be careful to include all of the necessary elements specific to your script when you break it down and schedule it. Refer to your schedule as you budget.

The $62,000 film was shot on 16-mm film. It was a feature-length, dialogue-driven piece, shot in seven different interior locations and as many exterior locations. The shoot was 18 days long (three six-day weeks). Neither the non-SAG cast nor the 15-person crew received any pay. Instead, we signed deferral contracts with the cast and crew. Unfortunately, we were never able to pay out the deferral contracts.

We had student status at the time, which allowed for significant cost reductions at the lab, the permit office, and some of our equipment rental houses. Student status usually requires that a key member of your crew be enrolled full-time in a film school. Generally, a letter from the film department and a valid student identification will allow you access to student rates. Despite the corners we cut, we did have production insurance and permits, and we fed the cast and crew real meals.

We did not have Movie Magic Budgeting at the time, and we could not have afforded it. To budget, we used a calculator and entered the numbers into a word processor. Ideally, you should purchase a simple spreadsheet program so that you do not have to continually retally your numbers. This film was financed through a combination of personal savings, credit cards, and a private investor. The film traveled the festival circuit and was picked up for distribution by Turbulent Arts, a now defunct San Francisco-based art house distributor.

The crew, although unpaid, had varying degrees of experience. Each wanted an opportunity to work on a feature film. In many instances, crew members had had a lesser credit on previous films and wanted a key credit. Some of the crew had never worked on a film before but had some other qualifying experience. For example, our makeup artist had worked at a makeup counter in a department store and was eager to break into film work.

Some of the locations were secured at no cost, and several were rented for a nominal fee. For almost every interior location we had to pay repair fees for items that were broken or damaged during the production. For one location, a local cafe, we agreed to pay any electrical charges that were above and beyond the restaurant's usual electrical bill (we gave them a deposit as a guarantee), and we agreed to reimburse the cafe for the difference between what they usually earned during a morning shift and what they earned while we were shooting. The cafe fell short of its regular earnings by approximately $50.

The cost through the production period was $26,215, post-production came in at $36,410, and the grand total was $62,625. Pre-production was four weeks long, and the production period was three weeks. You will see when referring to the budget that we made most of our equipment deals based on a two-day week. This is not standard, but it can be done with a great deal of persuasion and patience. Crew members who used their cars extensively during pre-production and production were reimbursed for their gas receipts. We turned our apartment into the production office, so we had no added rental expense. We installed two extra phone lines, purchased office supplies, and bought a large table that served as multiple workstations.

Our lighting, grip, camera, and sound equipment packages were modest. We shot a combination of factory unopened 16-mm film stock and recans.

Most of the meals were prepared by the craft service per son in our kitchen. We also purchased meals from restaurants on several occasions for convenience and variety. For breakfast, we solicited donations of bagels and cream cheese and morning pastries from several cafés and were given a weekly donation of coffee in exchange for a thank-you in the film's credits.

We cut the film on a flatbed over a period of three months. We rented the flatbed from an ad we found in the back of the monthly publication of the Film Arts Foundation, a film-support organization based in San Francisco. A cutting room with the essential equipment was rented at the Saul Zaentz Film Center.

BLANK BUDGET (PARAMOUNT FORM)

PRODUCTION NUMBER:
PRODUCER:
DIRECTOR:
SCRIPT DATE:
START DATE:
FINISH DATE:

DATE:
LOCATIONS:
DAYS:
WEEKS:

NOTE:

Acct#	Category Title	Page	Total
600-00	STORY	1	$0
610-00	PRODUCER	1	$0
620-00	DIRECTOR	1	$0
630-00	CAST	1	$0
640-00	FRINGES	2	$0
650-00	TRAVEL & LIVING	2	$0
	Total Above-The-Line		**$0**
700-00	EXTRA TALENT	2	$0
705-00	PRODUCTION STAFF	2	$0
710-00	CAMERA	2	$0
715-00	SET DESIGN	3	$0
720-00	SET CONSTRUCTION	3	$0
721-00	SET STRIKING	3	$0
722-00	MINIATURES	3	$0
725-00	SET OPERATIONS	3	$0
730-00	ELECTRICAL	4	$0
735-00	SPECIAL EFFECTS	4	$0
740-00	SPECIAL SHOOTING UNITS	4	$0
745-00	SET DRESSING	4	$0
750-00	PROPERTIES	5	$0
755-00	WARDROBE	5	$0
760-00	MAKEUP & HAIRSTYLISTS	6	$0
765-00	PRODUCTION SOUND	6	$0
770-00	TRANSPORTATION	6	$0
775-00	LOCATION EXPENSE	7	$0
780-00	PROCESS PHOTOGRAPHY	7	$0
785-00	PRODUCTION DAILIES	7	$0
790-00	LIVING EXPENSE	8	$0
795-00	FRINGES	8	$0
797-00	TESTS	8	$0
798-00	FACILITIES FEES	8	$0
	Total Production		**$0**
800-00	EDITING	8	$0
810-00	MUSIC	9	$0
820-00	POSTPRODUCTION SOUND	9	$0
830-00	STOCK SHOTS	10	$0
840-00	TITLES	10	$0
850-00	OPTICALS, MATTES, INSERTS	10	$0

Figure 6–1 Movie Magic Budgeting sofware's Paramount budget form

Acct#	Category Title	Page	Total
860-00	LABORATORY PROCESSING	10	$0
870-00	FRINGES	10	$0
	Total Post Production		**$0**
910-00	ADMINISTRATIVE EXPENSES	10	$0
912-00	PPC INTERNAL	11	$0
920-00	PUBLICITY	11	$0
	Total Other		**$0**
	TOTAL ABOVE-THE-LINE		**$0**
	TOTAL BELOW-THE-LINE		**$0**
	TOTAL ABOVE & BELOW-THE-LINE		**$0**
	GRAND TOTAL		**$0**

(continued)

Figure 6–1 Movie Magic Budgeting sofware's Paramount budget form (continued)

BLANK BUDGET (PARAMOUNT FORM)

PRODUCTION NUMBER:
PRODUCER:
DIRECTOR:
SCRIPT DATE:
START DATE:
FINISH DATE:

DATE:
LOCATIONS:
DAYS:
WEEKS:

NOTE:

Acct#	Description	Amount	Units	X	Rate	Subtotal	Total
600-00	**STORY**						
600-01	RIGHTS PURCHASED						$0
600-03	WRITERS						$0
600-04	SCREENPLAY PURCHASE						$0
600-05	RESEARCH						$0
600-06	SECRETARIAL						$0
600-11	SCRIPT COPYING						$0
						Total For 600-00	**$0**
610-00	**PRODUCER**						
610-01	EXECUTIVE PRODUCER						$0
610-02	PRODUCER						$0
610-06	PRODUCER'S ASSISTANT						$0
						Total For 610-00	**$0**
620-00	**DIRECTOR**						
620-01	DIRECTOR						$0
620-02	STORYBOARD ARTIST						$0
620-03	TECHNICAL ADVISOR						$0
620-04	RESEARCH CONSULTANT						$0
620-05	CASTING DIRECTOR						$0
620-08	CASTING EXPENSES/FEES						$0
						Total For 620-00	**$0**
630-00	**CAST**						
630-01	PRINCIPAL PLAYERS						$0
630-02	DAY PLAYERS						$0
630-03	REHEARSAL						$0
630-04	STUNT PERFORMERS						$0
630-05	SAG RESIDUALS						$0
630-06	LOOPING/ADR						$0
630-07	MEAL PENALTIES						$0
630-08	OVERTIME						$0
630-09	MEDICAL EXAMS						$0
630-10	CHILDREN'S TUTOR						$0
						Total For 630-00	**$0**

Figure 6–1 Movie Magic Budgeting sofware's Paramount budget form (continued)

Acct#	Description	Amount	Units	X	Rate	Subtotal	Total
640-00	**FRINGES**						
						Total For 640-00	**$0**
650-00	**TRAVEL & LIVING**						
650-01	PRODUCERS						$0
650-02	DIRECTOR						$0
650-03	WRITER						$0
650-04	FOCUS PULLER						$0
650-05	STORYBOARD ARTIST						$0
650-06	CAST TRAVEL, LIVING & P...						$0
650-07	CHAPERONES						$0
						Total For 650-00	**$0**
	Total Above-The-Line						**$0**
700-00	**EXTRA TALENT**						
700-01	SIDELINE MUSICIANS						$0
700-02	EXTRAS AND STAND-INS						$0
700-03	WELFARE WORKERS						$0
700-04	PAYROLL FRINGES						$0
700-05	EXTRAS CASTING						$0
						Total For 700-00	**$0**
705-00	**PRODUCTION STAFF**						
705-01	LINE PRODUCER/UPM						$0
705-02	PRODUCTION COORDINAT...						$0
705-03	1ST ASSISTANT DIRECTOR						$0
705-04	2ND ASSISTANT DIRECTOR						$0
705-05	3RD ASSISTANT DIRECTOR						$0
705-06	SCRIPT SUPERVISOR						$0
705-08	PRODUCTION ACCOUNTANT						$0
705-09	ASST. DIRECTOR TRAINEE						$0
705-10	PRODUCTION ASSISTANTS						$0
705-11	PREPRODUCTION EXPEN...						$0
						Total For 705-00	**$0**
710-00	**CAMERA**						
710-01	DIRECTOR OF PHOTOGRA...						$0
710-02	OPERATOR						$0
710-03	1ST ASSISTANT CAMERA...						$0
710-04	2ND ASSISTANT CAMERA...						$0
710-05	FILM LOADERS						$0
710-06	STILL PHOTOGRAPHER						$0
710-08	CAMERA RENTALS						$0
710-09	CAMERA SUPPLIES						$0
710-11	CAMERA ACCES./VIDEO E...						$0

(continued)

Figure 6–1 Movie Magic Budgeting sofware's Paramount budget form (continued)

Acct#	Description	Amount	Units	X	Rate	Subtotal	Total
710-00	**CAMERA (CONT'D)**						
710-20	LOSS, DAMAGE, AND REP...						$0
							Total For 710-00 $0
715-00	**SET DESIGN**						
715-01	PRODUCTION DESIGNER						$0
715-02	ART DIRECTOR						$0
715-03	SET DESIGNER/LEADMAN						$0
715-04	SWING GANG						$0
715-05	ART RENTALS						$0
715-06	PURCHASES/SUPPLIES						$0
715-07	RESEARCH						$0
715-10	BOX RENTAL						$0
							Total For 715-00 $0
720-00	**SET CONSTRUCTION**						
720-01	CONSTRUCTION LABOR						$0
720-02	CONSTRUCTION MATERIALS						$0
							Total For 720-00 $0
721-00	**SET STRIKING**						
							Total For 721-00 $0
722-00	**MINIATURES**						
							Total For 722-00 $0
725-00	**SET OPERATIONS**						
725-01	KEY GRIP						$0
725-02	BEST BOY GRIP						$0
725-03	CRANE/DOLLY GRIP						$0
725-04	EXTRA GRIPS/COMPANY ...						$0
725-05	CAMERA DOLLIES						$0
725-06	CAMERA CRANES						$0
725-07	TARPING AND DIFFUSION						$0
725-08	GRIP EQUIPMENT RENTALS						$0
725-09	GRIP EQUIPMENT PURCH...						$0
725-10	GRIP BOX RENTALS						$0
725-11	CRAFT SERVICEMAN						$0
725-12	CLEANUP AND TRASH						$0
725-13	STANDBY NURSERYMEN						$0
725-14	STANDBY PAINTERS						$0
725-15	STANDBY SECURITY						$0
725-19	FIRST AID						$0
725-21	ELECTRICAL HOOKUPS						$0
725-22	HEATING/AIR CONDITIONING						$0
725-23	DRESSING RM. INSTALL						$0
725-24	DRESSING ROOM RENTALS						$0

Figure 6–1 Movie Magic Budgeting sofware's Paramount budget form (continued)

(continued)

Acct#	Description	Amount	Units	X	Rate	Subtotal	Total
725-00	**SET OPERATIONS (CONT'D)**						
725-25	MISCELLANEOUS EXPENSE						$0
725-30	LOCATION LOAD AND UNL...						$0
						Total For 725-00	**$0**
730-00	**ELECTRICAL**						
730-01	GAFFER						$0
730-02	BEST BOY						$0
730-03	LAMP OPERATORS/ELECT...						$0
730-04	LOCATION RIGGING/STRIKE						$0
730-05	GLOBES/CARBONS/SUPP...						$0
730-06	POWER						$0
730-07	GENERATOR RENTAL						$0
730-08	ELEC. EQUIP. RENTAL						$0
730-09	ELEC. EQUIP. PURCHASE						$0
730-10	BOX RENTAL						$0
730-11	STUDIO GENERATOR OPE...						$0
730-12	LOCATION GENERATOR OP.						$0
730-13	MISC. EXPENSE						$0
730-15	LOC. ELEC. MAINTENENCE						$0
730-20	LOSS, DAMAGE, AND REP...						$0
						Total For 730-00	**$0**
735-00	**SPECIAL EFFECTS**						
735-01	CO. SPECIAL EFFECTS MAN						$0
735-02	ASST SPECIAL EFFECTS...						$0
735-03	MANUFACTURING - SHOP...						$0
735-04	STANDBY PROPMAKERS						$0
735-08	SPEC. EFFECTS EQUIP RE...						$0
735-09	SPEC. EFFECTS PURCHAS...						$0
735-10	SPECIAL EFFECTS BOX R...						$0
735-11	ADDED SPECIAL EFFECTS						$0
						Total For 735-00	**$0**
740-00	**SPECIAL SHOOTING UNITS**						
740-01	UNIT #1						$0
740-02	UNIT #2						$0
740-03	UNIT #3						$0
740-04	UNIT #4						$0
740-05	UNIT #5						$0
						Total For 740-00	**$0**
745-00	**SET DRESSING**						
745-01	SET DECORATOR						$0
745-02	LEADMAN						$0
745-02	SWING GANG						$0
745-03	SET DRESSING - ALTER/M...						$0

(continued)

Figure 6–1 Movie Magic Budgeting sofware's Paramount budget form (continued)

Acct#	Description	Amount	Units	X	Rate	Subtotal	Total
745-00	**SET DRESSING (CONT'D)**						
745-04	SET DRESSING PURCHASED						$0
745-05	SET DRESSING RENTALS						$0
745-07	SET DRESSING CLEAN & ...						$0
745-08	DRAPERY RENTALS						$0
745-09	DRAPERY PURCHASES						$0
745-11	DRAPERY INSTALL & STRI...						$0
745-12	DRAPERY MANUFACTURE						$0
745-13	DRAPERY CLEAN & DYE						$0
745-14	CARPET-INSTALL-STRIKE						$0
745-16	CARPET PURCHASES						$0
745-20	LOSS, DAMAGE & REPAIR						$0
745-25	MISCELLANEOUS EXPENSE						$0
						Total For 745-00	**$0**
750-00	**PROPERTIES**						
750-01	PROPERTY MASTER						$0
750-02	ASSISTANT PROPERTY M...						$0
750-03	EXTRA PROP MEN						$0
750-04	PICTURE VEHICLE - L&M						$0
750-05	PICTURE VEHICLE RENTALS						$0
750-06	ANIMALS & LIVESTOCK						$0
750-07	HANDLERS/WRANGLERS						$0
750-08	PROP RENTALS						$0
750-09	PROP PURCHASES						$0
750-10	PROP BOX RENTALS						$0
750-11	ANIMAL FEED & STABLING						$0
750-12	EXPENDABLES						$0
750-19	PICTURE VEHICLE PURCH...						$0
750-20	LOSS, DAMAGE & REPAIRS						$0
						Total For 750-00	**$0**
755-00	**WARDROBE**						
755-02	ASSISTANT WARDROBE						$0
755-03	ASSISTING WARDROBE						$0
755-04	COSTUME DESIGNER						$0
755-05	WARDROBE MANUF - L&M						$0
755-06	ALTERATIONS - L&M						$0
755-07	CLEANING & DYEING						$0
755-08	WARDROBE RENTALS						$0
755-09	WARDROBE PURCHASES						$0
755-10	HAND BOX RENTALS						$0
755-20	LOSS, DAMAGE & REPAIRS						$0
						Total For 755-00	**$0**

(continued)

Figure 6–1 Movie Magic Budgeting sofware's Paramount budget form (continued)

Acct#	Description	Amount	Units	X	Rate	Subtotal	Total
760-00	**MAKEUP & HAIRSTYLISTS**						
760-01	MAKE-UP ARTISTS						$0
760-02	EXTRA MAKE-UP ARTISTS						$0
760-03	BODY MAKE-UP ARTISTS						$0
760-04	KEY HAIR STYLIST						$0
760-05	EXTRA HAIR STYLISTS						$0
760-06	WIG & HAIR PURCHASE						$0
760-07	WIG & HAIR RENTAL						$0
760-09	MAKEUP SUPPLIES/APPLI...						$0
760-10	MAKE-UP/HAIR KIT RENTA...						$0
						Total For 760-00	**$0**
765-00	**PRODUCTION SOUND**						
765-01	SOUND MIXER						$0
765-02	BOOM MAN						$0
765-03	SOUND RECORDER						$0
765-04	CABLE MEN						$0
765-05	PLAYBACK OPERATOR (A...						$0
765-06	SOUND EQUIP RENTALS						$0
765-07	PLAYBACK EQUIP RENTAL						$0
765-11	MISCELLANEOUS EXPENSE						$0
						Total For 765-00	**$0**
770-00	**TRANSPORTATION**						
770-01	MESSENGER SERVICE						$0
770-02	TRANSPORTATION COORD.						$0
770-02	DRIVER CAPTAIN						$0
770-03	STANDBY DRIVERS						$0
770-04	STANDBY VEHICLES						$0
770-05	MILEAGE ALLOWANCE						$0
770-06	FUEL						$0
770-07	PICTURE CAR DRIVERS						$0
770-08	LOCATION DRIVERS						$0
770-09	LOCAL HIRE DRIVERS						$0
770-10	LOC. VEHICLES/TRUCKS						$0
770-11	CAMERA DEPARTMENT						$0
770-12	CONSTRUCTION DEPART...						$0
770-13	DRAPERY DEPARTMENT						$0
770-14	SOUND DEPARTMENT						$0
770-15	ELECTRICAL DEPARTMENT						$0
770-16	GRIP DEPARTMENT						$0
770-17	LABOR DEPARTMENT						$0
770-18	PAINT DEPARTMENT						$0
770-19	PRODUCERS OFFICE						$0
770-20	LOSS, DAMAGE, REPAIRS						$0
770-21	PRODUCTION DEPARTMENT						$0
770-22	PROPERTY DEPARTMENT						$0

(continued)

Figure 6–1 Movie Magic Budgeting sofware's Paramount budget form (continued)

Acct#	Description	Amount	Units	X	Rate	Subtotal	Total
770-00	**TRANSPORTATION (CONT'D)**						
770-23	PUBLICITY DEPARTMENT						$0
770-24	SOUND DEPARTMENT						$0
770-25	SPECIAL EFFECTS DEPT						$0
770-26	WARDROBE DEPARTMENT						$0
770-27	ALL OTHER DEPARTMENTS						$0
770-28	ALL OTHER TRANSPORTA...						$0
770-35	STUDIO RENTAL CHARGES						$0
						Total For 770-00	**$0**
775-00	**LOCATION EXPENSE**						
775-01	SURVEY EXPENSE						$0
775-02	LOCATION STAFF						$0
775-03	SITE RENTALS/PERMITS/L...						$0
775-04	HOTEL & LODGING						$0
775-05	CATERING SERVICES						$0
775-06	MEAL ALLOWANCES/EXT...						$0
775-07	PRODUCTION EXPENDABL...						$0
775-08	TRASH FEES/CARTAGE						$0
775-11	FIREMAN/POLICE						$0
775-14	AIRPORT PICK UP/DELIVE...						$0
775-15	LOCATION LOAD & UNLOAD						$0
775-16	MISCELLANEOUS TRANSP...						$0
775-17	GRATUITIES						$0
775-18	OFFICE-RENT/FURNITURE						$0
775-19	LOCATION MEDICAL EXPE...						$0
775-20	SHIPPING						$0
775-21	LOCATION SECURITY						$0
775-22	PARKING LOTS						$0
						Total For 775-00	**$0**
780-00	**PROCESS PHOTOGRAPHY**						
780-01	INSTALL/HOOKUP EQUIP						$0
780-02	PROCESS CAMERAMAN						$0
780-03	VIDEO DESIGN & PLAYBACK						$0
780-04	OTHER PROCESS LABOR						$0
780-05	PROCESS BACKGROUND ...						$0
780-08	PROCESS EQUIPMENT RE...						$0
780-09	RENT/PURCHASE/MFG. PL...						$0
						Total For 780-00	**$0**
785-00	**PRODUCTION DAILIES**						
785-01	NEGATIVE RAW STOCK						$0
785-02	DEVELOPING						$0
785-03	PRINT DAILIES						$0
785-04	SOUND RECORDING TAPE						$0
785-05	TRANSFER SOUND DAILIES						$0

(continued)

Figure 6–1 Movie Magic Budgeting sofware's Paramount budget form (continued)

Acct#	Description	Amount	Units	X	Rate	Subtotal	Total
785-00	**PRODUCTION DAILIES (CONT'D)**						
785-07	CODING DAILIES						$0
785-08	SCREEN DAILIES						$0
785-09	VIDEO TAPE TRANSFERS						$0
785-10	TAPE STOCK						$0
						Total For 785-00	**$0**
790-00	**LIVING EXPENSES**						
790-01	LIVING EXPENSES-CONTR...						$0
790-02	OTHER LIVING EXPENSES						$0
790-03	FARES-OTHER THAN TO L...						$0
						Total For 790-00	**$0**
795-00	**FRINGES**						
						Total For 795-00	**$0**
797-00	**TESTS**						
797-01	TEST #1						$0
797-02	TEST #2						$0
797-03	TEST #3						$0
797-04	TEST #4						$0
						Total For 797-00	**$0**
798-00	**FACILITIES FEES**						
798-01	STAGE CONSTRUCTION						$0
798-02	STAGE SHOOTING						$0
798-03	STAGE HOLDING						$0
798-04	OFFICE SPACE						$0
798-05	TESTS/INSERTS/PROMOS						$0
						Total For 798-00	**$0**
	Total Production						**$0**
800-00	**EDITING**						
800-01	FILM EDITOR						$0
800-02	SOUND EFFECTS EDITING						$0
800-03	MUSIC EDITING						$0
800-04	NEGATIVE CUTTING						$0
800-06	PROJECTION						$0
800-07	CONTINUITY SCRIPTS						$0
800-11	EDITORIAL FACILITIES						$0
800-12	EDITORIAL SUPPLIES						$0
800-14	POSTPROD. SUPERVISION						$0
800-17	OTHER COSTS						$0
800-18	ASSISTANT EDITOR						$0

(continued)

Figure 6–1 Movie Magic Budgeting sofware's Paramount budget form (continued)

Acct#	Description	Amount	Units	X	Rate	Subtotal	Total
800-00	**EDITING (CONT'D)**						
800-19	APPRENTICE EDITOR						$0
							Total For 800-00 $0
810-00	**MUSIC**						
810-08	COMPOSER						$0
810-09	CONDUCTOR						$0
810-10	SONGWRITER						$0
810-11	LYRICIST						$0
810-21	RECORDING MUSICIANS						$0
810-22	SINGERS & VOCAL COAC...						$0
810-23	ORCHESTRATORS & ARRA...						$0
810-24	COPYISTS & PROOFREAD...						$0
810-25	MUSIC SUPERVISOR						$0
810-26	MUSIC CLEARANCE SALA...						$0
810-27	MUSIC CLERICAL						$0
810-28	MASTER USE LICENSES						$0
810-29	MUSIC PUBLISHING LICEN...						$0
810-30	PRESCORE						$0
810-31	REHEARSAL MUSICIANS						$0
810-32	DEMO COSTS						$0
810-33	SCORE (FACILITIES)						$0
810-34	STUDIO EQUIPMENT RENT...						$0
810-35	MUSIC INSTRUMENT RENT...						$0
810-36	MUSIC INSTRUMENT CART...						$0
810-37	MUSIC TRANSFERS						$0
810-38	NEW USE/REUSE (MUSICI...						$0
810-39	NEW USE/REUSE (SINGERS)						$0
810-40	TRAVEL & PER DIEM						$0
810-41	PAYROLL TAXES/FRINGES						$0
810-42	PHONO						$0
810-43	MUSIC RESEARCH REPOR...						$0
							Total For 810-00 $0
820-00	**POSTPRODUCTION SOUND**						
820-01	DIALOGUE RECORDING (A...						$0
820-02	NARRATION RECORDING						$0
820-03	SOUND EFFECTS (FOLEY)						$0
820-06	DUBBING SESSION						$0
820-07	SOUND TRANSFERS						$0
820-09	PURCHASED SOUND EFFE...						$0
820-11	SOUND TRANSFER 35 & 3...						$0
820-12	MAGNETIC TAPE FOR EDIT						$0
820-13	OPTICAL NEG 35 & 35/32						$0
820-14	PREVIEW EXPENSES						$0
							Total For 820-00 $0

(continued)

Figure 6–1 Movie Magic Budgeting sofware's Paramount budget form (continued)

Acct#	Description	Amount	Units	X	Rate	Subtotal	Total
830-00	**STOCK SHOTS**						
830-01	LIBRARY EXPENSE						$0
830-03	LABORATORY PROCESSING						$0
830-09	RENTAL & PURCHASE						$0
						Total For 830-00	**$0**
840-00	**TITLES**						
840-01	TITLES (MAIN & END)						$0
840-02	MAIN TITLES						$0
840-03	END TITLES						$0
840-04	MISCELLANEOUS TITLES						$0
840-05	LABORATORY PROCESSING						$0
						Total For 840-00	**$0**
850-00	**OPTICALS, MATTES, INSERTS**						
850-01	OPTICAL EFFECTS/DUPE...						$0
850-02	MASTER POSITIVES						$0
850-03	LABORATORY PROCESSING						$0
850-04	SPECIAL PHOTO EFFECTS						$0
850-05	INSERTS						$0
850-11	PURCHASES						$0
						Total For 850-00	**$0**
860-00	**LABORATORY PROCESSING**						
860-01	REPRINTING & DEVELOPING						$0
860-02	1ST TRIAL COMPOSITE P...						$0
860-03	MASTER POSITIVE PRINT						$0
860-04	DUPLICATE NEGATIVES						$0
860-06	DEVELOP SOUND NEGATI...						$0
860-07	ANSWER PRINT						$0
860-17	LEADER & MISCELLANEOUS						$0
						Total For 860-00	**$0**
870-00	**FRINGES**						
						Total For 870-00	**$0**
	Total Post Production						**$0**
910-00	**ADMINISTRATIVE EXPENSES**						
910-01	ACCOUNTING & TERMINAL...						$0
910-02	MPAA CERTIFICATE						$0
910-03	POSTAGE & STATIONERY						$0
910-04	PHOTOCOPYING (No Scripts)						$0
910-05	LEGAL EXPENSE & FEES						$0
910-06	TELEPHONE/FACSIMILE						$0
910-09	MATERIAL MGMT PURCHA...						$0
910-12	PREVIEW EXPENSE						$0

(continued)

Figure 6–1 Movie Magic Budgeting sofware's Paramount budget form (continued)

Acct#	Description	Amount	Units	X	Rate	Subtotal	Total
910-00	**ADMINISTRATIVE EXPENSES (CONT'D)**						
910-14	PARKING LOT EXPENSES						$0
910-15	CELLULAR PHONES						$0
910-17	OFFICE RENT & OTH EXPE...						$0
						Total For 910-00	**$0**
912-00	**PPC INTERNAL**						
912-02	RENT-STUDIO OFFICES						$0
912-03	PARKING FEES-STUDIO						$0
						Total For 912-00	**$0**
920-00	**PUBLICITY**						
920-01	UNIT PUBLICIST						$0
920-02	SPEC. STILL PHOTOGRAP...						$0
920-03	STILL FILM & PROCESSING						$0
920-05	PUBLICITY STAFF - T&E						$0
920-09	SPACE MEDIA						$0
920-11	OUTSIDE SERVICES						$0
						Total For 920-00	**$0**
	Total Other						**$0**
	TOTAL ABOVE-THE-LINE						**$0**
	TOTAL BELOW-THE-LINE						**$0**
	TOTAL ABOVE & BELOW-THE-LINE						**$0**
	GRAND TOTAL						**$0**

Figure 6–1 Movie Magic Budgeting sofware's Paramount budget form (continued)

"SWINGERS" BUDGET

PRODUCTION NO.:
PRODUCER:
DIRECTOR:
SCRIPT DATE:
START DATE: 8/31/95
FINISH DATE: 9/22/95

DATE: AUGUST 31, 1995
LOCATIONS: HLYWD/VEGAS
BASED ON: 3 WEEK SHOOT
6 DAY WEEK
SAG

NOT A FINAL SHOOTING BUDGET

Acct#	Category Title	Page	Total
600-00	STORY	1	$1,000
610-00	PRODUCER	1	$5,792
620-00	DIRECTOR	1	$3,200
630-00	CAST	1	$33,128
650-00	TRAVEL & LIVING	2	$2,053
	TOTAL ABOVE-THE-LINE		**$45,173**
700-00	EXTRA TALENT	3	$5,589
705-00	PRODUCTION STAFF	3	$18,360
710-00	CAMERA	4	$12,819
715-00	ART/SET DESIGN (MATERIALS IN PROPS)	5	$3,600
725-00	SET OPERATIONS	5	$16,180
730-00	ELECTRICAL	6	$13,201
745-00	SET DRESSING	6	$0
750-00	PROPERTIES	6	$5,965
755-00	WARDROBE	7	$9,937
760-00	MAKEUP & HAIRSTYLISTS	7	$1,780
765-00	PRODUCTION SOUND	8	$9,160
770-00	TRANSPORTATION	8	$4,977
775-00	LOCATION EXPENSE	8	$28,282
785-00	PRODUCTION DAILIES	10	$17,753
	TOTAL SHOOTING PERIOD		**$147,603**
800-00	EDITING	10	$26,148
810-00	MUSIC	11	$3,000
820-00	POSTPRODUCTION SOUND	11	$8,300
840-00	TITLES	11	$1,000
850-00	OPTICALS, MATTES, INSERTS	11	$1,000
860-00	LABORATORY PROCESSING	11	$11,350
	TOTAL COMPLETION PERIOD		**$50,798**
910-00	ADMINISTRATIVE EXPENSES	11	$6,608
920-00	PUBLICITY	12	$0
	TOTAL OTHER		**$6,608**
	Completion Bond: 0.00%		$0
	Contingency: 10.00%		$25,018
	Overhead: 0.00%		$0
	Insurance: 1.75%		$4,378

(continued)

Figure 6–2 Preliminary budget for Swingers

Acct#	Category Title	Page	Total
	TOTAL ABOVE-THE-LINE		$45,173
	TOTAL BELOW-THE-LINE		$205,008
	TOTAL ABOVE & BELOW-THE-LINE		$250,181
	GRAND TOTAL		$279,577

(continued)

Figure 6–2 Preliminary budget for Swingers *(continued)*

"SWINGERS" BUDGET

PRODUCTION NO.:
PRODUCER:
DIRECTOR:
SCRIPT DATE:
START DATE: 8/31/95
FINISH DATE: 9/22/95

DATE: AUGUST 31, 1995
LOCATIONS: HLYWD/VEGAS
BASED ON: 3 WEEK SHOOT
6 DAY WEEK
SAG

NOT A FINAL SHOOTING BUDGET

Acct#	Description	Amount	Units	X	Rate	Subtotal	Total
600-00	**STORY**						
600-01	RIGHTS PURCHASED						
	Writer		ALLOW		1,000	1,000	$1,000
600-03	WRITERS						$0
600-04	SCREENPLAY PURCHASE						$0
						Total For 600-00	**$1,000**
610-00	**PRODUCER**						
610-01	EXECUTIVE PRODUCER						$0
610-02	PRODUCER						
	PRODUCER	15	WEEKS		300	4,500	$4,500
610-03	ASSOCIATE PRODUCER						$0
610-07	PRODUCER'S ENT.						
	Producer's Entertainment		ALLOW		209	209	$209
610-08	PREPRODUCTION EXPEN...						
	Ent./food/film/supplies		ALLOW		1,000	1,000	
	SALES TAX	8.25%			1,000	83	$1,083
						Total For 610-00	**$5,792**
620-00	**DIRECTOR**						
620-01	DIRECTOR						
	DIRECTOR	1	FLAT		1,000	1,000	$1,000
620-05	CASTING DIRECTOR						
	CASTING FEES/EXPENSE...	1	FLAT		2,000	2,000	$2,000
620-08	CASTING EXPENSES						
	CASTING EXPENSES		ALLOW		200	200	$200
						Total For 620-00	**$3,200**
630-00	**CAST**						
630-01	PRINCIPAL PLAYERS						
	SUE	1	WEEK		1,558	1,558	
	Pro-rata	3	DAYS		343	1,029	
	MIKE	3	WEEKS		1,558	4,674	
	TRENT	2	WEEKS		1,558	3,116	
	Pro-rata	3	DAYS		343	1,029	
	ROB	8	DAYS		448	3,584	

(continued)

Figure 6–2 Preliminary budget for Swingers *(continued)*

Acct#	Description	Amount	Units	X	Rate	Subtotal	Total
630-00	**CAST (CONT'D)**						
630-01	PRINCIPAL PLAYERS (CONT'D)						
	CHARLES	1	WEEK		1,558	1,558	
	Pro-rata	1	DAY		343	343	
	SAG CORP	12.8%			16,891	2,162	
	FICA #1	6.2%			16,891	1,047	
	FICA #2	1.45%			16,891	245	
	SUI	5.4%			7,000	378	
	FUI	0.8%			7,000	56	
	AGENCY COMMISS.	10.0%			16,891	1,689	$22,468
630-02	DAY PLAYERS						
	BLUE HAIR	1	DAY		448	448	
	DEALER	1	DAY		448	448	
	PIT BOSS						
	CASINO WAITRESS	1	DAY		50	50	
	PARTY BLONDE						
	GIRL IN HAT	1	DAY		448	448	
	LISA	2	DAYS		448	896	
	CHRISTY	3	DAYS		448	1,344	
	NIKKI	1	DAY		448	448	
	LORRAINE	3	DAYS		448	1,344	
	BALD GUY	1	DAY		448	448	
	SAG CORP	12.8%			5,874	752	
	FICA #1	6.2%			5,874	364	
	FICA #2	1.45%			5,874	85	
	SUI	5.4%			5,874	317	
	FUI	0.8%			5,874	47	
	AGENCY COMMISS.	10.0%			5,874	587	$8,027
630-06	LOOPING/ADR (INCL. 1 DA...						$0
630-08	OVERTIME						
	OVERTIME		ALLOW		500	500	
	SAG CORP	12.8%			500	64	
	FICA #1	6.2%			500	31	
	FICA #2	1.45%			500	7	
	SUI	5.4%			500	27	
	FUI	0.8%			500	4	$633
630-09	MEDICAL EXAMS						
	Medical Exams		ALLOW	5	100	500	$500
630-20	SIDE DEALS						
	SIDE DEALS		ALLOW		1,500	1,500	$1,500
						Total For 630-00	**$33,128**
650-00	**TRAVEL & LIVING**						
650-03	WRITER'S TRAVEL						$0
650-03	WRITER'S LIVING						$0
650-01	PRODUCER'S TRAVEL						$0

(continued)

Figure 6–2 Preliminary budget for Swingers *(continued)*

Acct#	Description	Amount	Units	X	Rate	Subtotal	Total
650-00	**TRAVEL & LIVING (CONT'D)**						
650-01	PRODUCER'S LIVING						
	PRODUCER'S LIVING	3	NIGHTS		25	75	
	PER DIEM	3	DAYS		25	75	
	SALES TAX	8.25%			75	6	$156
650-02	DIRECTOR'S TRAVEL						$0
650-02	DIRECTOR'S LIVING						
	DIRECTOR'S LIVING	3	NIGHTS		25	75	
	PER DIEM	3	DAYS		25	75	
	SALES TAX	8.25%			75	6	$156
650-06	CAST TRAVEL1						
	CAST TRAVEL- FLIGHTS		ALLOW	3	70	210	$210
650-06	CAST LIVING						
	CAST LIVING	3	NIGHTS	5	25	375	
	PER DIEM	3	DAYS	5	75	1,125	
	SALES TAX	8.25%			375	31	$1,531
						Total For 650-00	**$2,053**
	TOTAL ABOVE-THE-LINE						**$45,173**
700-00	**EXTRA TALENT**						
700-02	EXTRAS AND STAND-INS						
	THREE-YEAR-OLD	1	DAY		73	73	
	VALET	1	DAY		73	73	
	CASHIER	1	DAY		73	73	
	BACKGROUND CASINO CO...	1	DAY	2	73	146	
	PINK DOT	1	DAY		73	73	
	HWD. DINER DINERS	1	DAY	4	73	292	
	TRENDY GIRLS	1	DAY	2	73	146	
	DRESDEN BARTENDER	1	DAY		73	73	
	DRESDEN BKG.	1	DAY	12	73	876	
	SCHOOL GIRLS		ALLOW	2	73	146	
	DERBY DANCERS		ALLOW	14	73	1,022	
	HOLLYWOOD DINER WAIT...	1	DAY		73	73	
	BIKER	1	DAY		73	73	
	COUPLE AT TABLE	1	DAY	2	73	146	
	DINER WAITRESS 2	1	DAY		73	73	
	SAG CORP	12.8%			3,358	430	
	FICA #1	6.2%			3,358	208	
	FICA #2	1.45%			3,358	49	
	SUI	5.4%			3,358	181	
	FUI	0.8%			3,358	27	
	AGENCY COMMISS.	10.0%			3,358	336	$4,589
700-05	EXTRAS CASTING						
	EXTRA'S CASTING		ALLOW		1,000	1,000	$1,000
						Total For 700-00	**$5,589**

(continued)

Figure 6–2 Preliminary budget for Swingers *(continued)*

Acct#	Description	Amount	Units	X	Rate	Subtotal	Total
705-00	**PRODUCTION STAFF**						
705-01	LINE PRODUCER						
	LINE PRODUCER-PRE-PRO...	4	WEEKS		300	1,200	
	PRODUCTION	3	WEEKS		300	900	
	POST PRODUCTION	6	WEEKS		300	1,800	$3,900
705-02	PROD. MGR.						
	PREP	3	WEEKS		300	900	
	SHOOT	3	WEEKS		300	900	
	WRAP	1	WEEK		300	300	$2,100
705-03	FIRST ASSISTANT DIRECT...						
	PREP	3	WEEKS		300	900	
	SHOOT	3	WEEKS		300	900	
	WRAP	0.6	WEEKS		300	180	$1,980
705-04	SECOND ASSISTANT DIRE...						
	PREP	2	WEEKS		300	600	
	SHOOT	3	WEEKS		300	900	$1,500
705-06	SCRIPT SUPERVISOR						
	PREP	0.6	WEEKS		300	180	
	SHOOT	3	WEEKS		300	900	
	WRAP	0.6	WEEKS		0	0	$1,080
705-08	PROD. ACCOUNTANT						$0
705-10	PRODUCTION ASSISTANTS						
	PA ONE-PREP	3	WEEKS		300	900	
	SHOOT	3	WEEKS		300	900	
	WRAP	1	WEEK		300	300	
	PA TWO-PREP	2	WEEKS		300	600	
	SHOOT	3	WEEKS		300	900	
	WRAP	1	WEEK		300	300	
	PA THREE-PREP						
	SHOOT	3	WEEKS		300	900	
	PA FOUR-PREP						
	SHOOT	3	WEEKS		300	900	
	PA-PROD. OFFICE - PREP	2	WEEKS		300	600	
	SHOOT	3	WEEKS		300	900	
	WRAP	2	WEEKS		300	600	$7,800
						Total For 705-00	**$18,360**
710-00	**CAMERA**						
710-01	DIRECTOR OF PHOTOGRA...						
	DIRECTOR OF PHOTOGRA...						$0
710-03	1ST ASST CAMERAMAN						
	PREP	0.6	WEEKS		300	180	
	SHOOT	3	WEEKS		300	900	$1,080
710-04	2ND ASST CAMERAMAN /...						
	PREP	0.6	WEEKS		300	180	
	SHOOT	3	WEEKS		300	900	$1,080
710-06	STILL PHOTOGRAPHER						

(continued)

Figure 6–2 Preliminary budget for Swingers *(continued)*

Acct#	Description	Amount	Units	X	Rate	Subtotal	Total
710-00	**CAMERA (CONT'D)**						
710-06	STILL PHOTOGRAPHER (CONT'D)						
	STILL PHOTOGRAPHER	5	DAYS		100	500	
	SUPPLIES/DEVELOPING		ALLOW		500	500	$1,000
710-08	CAMERA RENTALS						
	Camera Package	4	WEEKS		2,000	8,000	$8,000
710-09	CAMERA SUPPLIES						
	Camera Expendables		ALLOW		350	350	
	SALES TAX	8.25%			350	29	$379
710-11	CAM ACCESSORIES/VIDE...						
	Camera Accessories		ALLOW		280	280	$280
710-20	LOSS, DAMAGE & REPAIR						
	Loss and damage		ALLOW		1,000	1,000	$1,000
						Total For 710-00	**$12,819**
715-00	**ART/SET DESIGN (MATERIALS IN PROPS)**						
715-01	PRODUCTION DESIGNER						
	Prod. Designer - PREP	3	WEEKS		300	900	
	SHOOT	3	WEEKS		300	900	
	WRAP	1	WEEK		300	300	$2,100
715-02	ART/SET DIRECTOR						
	PREP	2	WEEKS		300	600	
	SHOOT	3	WEEKS		300	900	$1,500
715-03	SET DESIGNERS						$0
						Total For 715-00	**$3,600**
725-00	**SET OPERATIONS**						
725-01	1ST COMPANY GRIP/KEY ...						
	PREP	0.6	WEEKS		300	180	
	SHOOT	3	WEEKS		300	900	$1,080
725-02	BEST BOY GRIP						
	PREP	0.6	WEEKS		300	180	
	SHOOT	3	WEEKS	2	300	1,800	$1,980
725-03	CRANE/DOLLY GRIPS						
	CRANE/DOLLY GRIP	1	WEEK		1,000	1,000	$1,000
725-04	EXTRA GRIPS/COMPANY ...						
	EXTRA GRIP	1	WEEK		300	300	$300
725-05	CAMERA DOLLIES						
	Dolly W/ TRACK	3	DAYS		150	450	$450
725-06	CAMERA CRANES						$0
725-08	GRIP EQUIPMENT RENTALS						
	GRIP EQUIPMENT (TRUCK I...	3	WEEKS		2,000	6,000	
	CAR MOUNTS	3	DAYS		50	150	
	EXPENDABLES	3	WEEKS		200	600	$6,750
725-09	GRIP EQUIPMENT PURCH...						
	Grip Purchases		ALLOW		500	500	
	SALES TAX	8.25%			500	41	$541

(continued)

Figure 6–2 Preliminary budget for Swingers *(continued)*

Acct#	Description	Amount	Units	X	Rate	Subtotal	Total
725-00	**SET OPERATIONS (CONT'D)**						
725-10	GRIP BOX RENTALS						$0
725-11	CRAFT SERVICE/SERVICE...						
	CRAFT SERVICEMAN-PREP	0.6	WEEKS		300	180	
	SHOOT	3	WEEKS		300	900	
	CRAFT SERVICE FOOD	3	WEEKS		400	1,200	
	SALES TAX	8.25%			1,200	99	$2,379
725-12	SET CLEANUP & TRASH DI...						
	SET CLEANUP & TRASH DI...		ALLOW		200	200	$200
725-19	FIRST AID						
	First Aid		ALLOW		500	500	$500
725-20	LOSS & DAMAGE						
	L&D		ALLOW		1,000	1,000	$1,000
725-24	DRESSING ROOM RENTALS						$0
725-30	LOCATION LOAD AND UNL...						$0
						Total For 725-00	**$16,180**
730-00	**ELECTRICAL**						
730-01	GAFFER						
	PREP	0.6	WEEKS		300	180	
	SHOOT	3	WEEKS		300	900	$1,080
730-02	BEST BOY						
	PREP	0.6	WEEKS		300	180	
	SHOOT	3	WEEKS	2	300	1,800	$1,980
730-05	GLOBES/CARBONS/SUPP...						
	GLOBES/CARBONS/SUPP...		ALLOW		200	200	$200
730-07	GENERATOR RENTAL						
	Generator	3	WEEKS		600	1,800	
	Gas and oil	3	WEEKS		200	600	$2,400
730-08	ELEC. EQUIP. RENTALS						
	ELECTRICAL PACKAGE	3	WEEKS		1,700	5,100	
	KINO FLOWS/PRACTICALS	3	WEEKS		300	900	
	TRUCK INCLUDED						$6,000
730-09	ELEC. EQUIP. PURCHASE						
	ELEC. PURCHASE/EXPEN...		ALLOW		500	500	
	SALES TAX	8.25%			500	41	$541
730-10	BOX RENTAL						$0
730-20	LOSS, DAMAGE, & REPAIR						
	LOSS & DAMAGE		ALLOW		1,000	1,000	$1,000
						Total For 730-00	**$13,201**
745-00	**SET DRESSING**						
						Total For 745-00	**$0**
750-00	**PROPERTIES**						
750-01	PROPERTY MASTER (SEE...						$0
750-04	PICTURE VEHICLES LABO...						

Figure 6–2 Preliminary budget for Swingers *(continued)*

Acct#	Description	Amount	Units	X	Rate	Subtotal	Total
750-00	**PROPERTIES (CONT'D)**						
750-04	PICTURE VEHICLES LABOR/MAINT. (CONT'D)						
	REPAIRS		ALLOW		1,000	1,000	$1,000
750-05	PICTURE VEHICLE RENTALS						
	TRENT CAR	3	WEEKS		0	0	
	SUE CAR	1	DAY		100	100	
	EL CAMINOS	1	DAY	2	50	100	
	ROB CAR						
	ALEX CAR						$200
750-08	PROP RENTALS						
	PROP RENTALS		ALLOW		2,000	2,000	$2,000
750-09	PROP PURCHASES						
	PROP PURCHASES		ALLOW		2,000	2,000	
	SALES TAX	8.25%			2,000	165	$2,165
750-10	PROP BOX RENTALS						
	PROP BOX RENTALS		ALLOW		100	100	$100
750-20	LOSS & DAMAGE						
	LOSS & DAMAGE		ALLOW		500	500	$500
						Total For 750-00	**$5,965**
755-00	**WARDROBE**						
755-04	COSTUME DESIGNER						
	PREP	3	WEEKS		300	900	
	SHOOT	3	WEEKS		300	900	
	WRAP	1	WEEK		300	300	$2,100
755-03	ASST. WARDROBE						
	Wardrobe Assistant-PREP	2	WEEKS		300	600	
	SHOOT	3	WEEKS		300	900	
	WRAP	1	WEEK		300	300	$1,800
755-06	ALTERATIONS - L&M						
	ALTERATIONS		ALLOW		100	100	$100
755-07	CLEANING & DYEING						
	CLEAN & DYE		ALLOW		213	213	$213
755-08	WARDROBE RENTALS						
	WARDROBE RENTALS		ALLOW		3,500	3,500	$3,500
755-09	WARDROBE PURCHASES						
	WARDROBE PURCHASES		ALLOW		1,500	1,500	
	SALES TAX	8.25%			1,500	124	$1,624
755-10	HAND BOX RENTALS						
	KIT RENTAL		ALLOW		100	100	$100
755-20	LOSS, DAMAGE & REPAIRS						
	L&D		ALLOW		500	500	$500
						Total For 755-00	**$9,937**

(continued)

Figure 6–2 Preliminary budget for Swingers *(continued)*

Acct#	Description	Amount	Units	X	Rate	Subtotal	Total
760-00	**MAKEUP & HAIRSTYLISTS**						
760-01	MAKEUP AND HAIR ARTIST						
	MAKEUP ARTIST (HAIR)	0.6	WEEKS		300	180	
	SHOOT	3	WEEKS		300	900	$1,080
760-02	EXTRA MAKEUP AND HAIR ...						
	EXTRA MAKEUP ARTIST	1	WEEK		300	300	$300
760-06	WIG & HAIR PURCHASE						
	HAIR PURCHASE		ALLOW		100	100	$100
760-09	MAKEUP SUPPLIES/APPLI...						
	MAKEUP SUPPLIES		ALLOW		200	200	$200
760-10	KIT RENTALS		ALLOW		100	100	$100
						Total For 760-00	**$1,780**
765-00	**PRODUCTION SOUND**						
765-01	SOUND MIXER						
	SOUND MIXER - PREP	0.2	WEEKS		300	60	
	SHOOT	3	WEEKS		300	900	$960
765-02	BOOM MAN						
	BOOMMAN-PREP	0.2	WEEKS		300	60	
	SHOOT	3	WEEKS		300	900	$960
765-05	PLAYBACK OPERATOR						
	PLAYBACK OPERATOR	1	DAY		500	500	
	(W/EQUIPMENT)	1	DAY		500	500	$1,000
765-06	SOUND EQUIP RENTALS						
	SOUND PACKAGE (w/nagra...	3	WEEKS		1,200	3,600	
	walkie/slate included)						$3,600
765-11	EXPENDABLES						
	MAG STOCK		ALLOW		1,000	1,000	
	BATTERIES	3	WEEKS	3	100	900	
	BEEPERS	6	WEEKS	5	8	240	$2,140
765-20	LOSS & DAMAGE						
	Loss & damage		ALLOW		500	500	$500
						Total For 765-00	**$9,160**
770-00	**TRANSPORTATION**						
770-01	MESSENGER SERVICE						
	MESSENGER SERVICE		ALLOW		200	200	$200
770-02	TRANSPORTATION COORD.						$0
770-05	MILEAGE ALLOWANCE						$0
770-06	FUEL						
	FUEL		ALLOW		800	800	$800
770-10	LOC. VEHICLES/TRUCKS						
	MIKE'S CAR (RENTAL CAR)	6	WEEKS		150	900	
	CUBE VANS ART (KEY HA...						
	WARDROB/PROD. VAN	5	WEEKS		300	1,500	
	SOUND VAN (MIXER HAS...						
	15 PASS VAN (FOR TRAVE...	1	WEEK		300	300	

Figure 6–2 Preliminary budget for Swingers *(continued)*

Acct#	Description	Amount	Units	X	Rate	Subtotal	Total
770-00	**TRANSPORTATION (CONT'D)**						
770-10	LOC.VEHICLES/TRUCKS (CONT'D)						
	SALES TAX	8.25%			2,700	223	
	CITY TAX	6.0%			900	54	$2,977
770-11	CAMERA DEPARTMENT						$0
770-20	LOSS, DAMAGE, REPAIRS						
	LOSS & DAMAGE		ALLOW		1,000	1,000	$1,000
						Total For 770-00	**$4,977**
775-00	**LOCATION EXPENSE**						
775-01	SURVEY EXPENSE						
	SCOUTING - FUEL		ALLOW		200	200	
	FOOD	15	DAYS		10	150	
	POLAROID		ALLOW		100	100	
	CALLS/TIPS/SUPPLIES		ALLOW		200	200	
	SALES TAX	8.25%			650	54	$704
775-02	LOCATION STAFF						
	LOCATION MANAGER - PR...	3	WEEKS		300	900	
	SHOOT	3	WEEKS		300	900	$1,800
775-03	SITE RENTALS/PERMITS/L...						
	Hollywood Hills Diner	1	DAY		1,000	1,000	
	Mike's Apt. (pay rent 1 month)		ALLOW		790	790	
	Casino	3	DAYS		0	0	
	Casino Coffee Shop						
	Lounge (local shoot)	1	NIGHT		500	500	
	Kristi's Trailer	1	DAY		500	500	
	Pitch and Putt (fees only)	1	DAY		150	150	
	Sue's Apartment		ALLOW		80	80	
	Dark Alley (power only)	1	DAY		50	50	
	The Room (3 of clubs)						
	Chateau Bungalow (party fo...	1	DAY		500	500	
	Hollywood streets (Car Train)						
	Dresden Room	1	DAY		1,000	1,000	
	Parking Lot (behind Dresden)		ALLOW		200	200	
	The Derby (3 nights)	3	NIGHTS		1,000	3,000	
	Permits		ALLOW		500	500	$8,270
775-04	HOTEL & LODGING						
	CREW HOTEL & LODGING	10	ROOMS	3	25	750	
	PER DIEM	3	NIGHTS	12	25	900	
	SALES TAX	8.25%			750	62	$1,712
775-05	CATERING SERVICES						
	RITA FLORA (3 DAYS)	3	DAYS		300	900	
	GAUCHO GRILL (3 DAYS)	3	DAYS		300	900	
	EAST INDIA GRILL (3 DAYS)	2	DAYS		250	500	
	LOUISES (3 DAYS)	2	DAYS		200	400	
	JACOPOS (3 DAYS)	2	DAYS		150	450	
	LA BOTTEGA	2	DAYS		300	600	

(continued)

Figure 6–2 Preliminary budget for Swingers *(continued)*

Acct#	Description	Amount	Units	X	Rate	Subtotal	Total
775-00	**LOCATION EXPENSE (CONT'D)**						
775-05	CATERING SERVICES (CONT'D)						
	1ST DAY EAT OUT DAY		ALLOW		200	200	$3,950
775-06	2ND MEALS/EXTRA MEALS						
	2ND MEALS		ALLOW		2,000	2,000	
	SALES TAX	8.25%			2,000	165	$2,165
775-07	PRODUCTION EXPENDABL...						
	PRODUCTION EXPENDALB...		ALLOW		552	552	
	INCLUDING CRAFT SERVIC...						
	SALES TAX	8.25%			552	46	$598
775-11	FIRE/POLICE						
	FIRE/POLICE-FOR GENER...	8	HOURS	7	48	2,688	
	FICA #1	6.2%			2,688	167	
	FICA #2	1.45%			2,688	39	
	SUI	5.4%			2,688	145	
	FUI	0.8%			2,688	22	$3,060
775-14	AIRPORT PICKUP/DELIVERY						$0
775-15	LOCATION LOCK & UNLOAD						$0
775-17	GRATUITIES						
	TIPS		ALLOW		200	200	$200
775-18	OFFICE RENT/FURNITURE/...						
	OFFICE RENT/OVERHEAD		ALLOW		1,000	1,000	
	SUPPLIES		ALLOW		1,500	1,500	
	SALES TAX	8.25%			1,500	124	$2,624
775-20	LOSS & DAMAGE						
	LOSS & DAMAGE		ALLOW		1,000	1,000	$1,000
775-21	LOCATION SECURITY						
	LOCATION SECURITY (FO...		ALLOW		1,500	1,500	$1,500
775-22	PARKING LOTS (FOR CRE...						
	TRUCK PARKING		ALLOW		700	700	$700
						Total For 775-00	**$28,282**
785-00	**PRODUCTION DAILIES**						
785-01	NEGATIVE RAWSTOCK						
	RAWSTOCK (5298 RECAN...	65,000	FEET		0.20	13,000	
	RAWSTOCK (5248 RECAN...	20,000	FEET		0.14	2,800	
	SALES TAX	8.25%			15,800	1,304	$17,104
785-04	SOUND RECORDING TAPE						$0
785-09	VIDEOTAPE TRANSFERS						
	1 LIGHT TRANSFER (DEFE...						
	3/4" TAPES	40	TAPES		15	600	
	SALES TAX	8.25%			600	50	$650
						Total For 785-00	**$17,753**
	TOTAL SHOOTING PERIOD						**$147,603**

Figure 6–2 Preliminary budget for Swingers *(continued)*

Acct#	Description	Amount	Units	X	Rate	Subtotal	Total
800-00	**EDITING**						
800-01	FILM EDITOR						
	FILM EDITOR	10	WEEKS		300	3,000	$3,000
800-02	SOUND EFFECTS EDITING						$0
800-03	MUSIC EDITING						$0
800-04	NEGATIVE CUTTING						
	NEGATIVE CUTTING	10	REELS		500	5,000	$5,000
800-06	PROJECTION						
	PROJECTION		ALLOW		500	500	$500
800-11	EDITORIAL FACILITIES						
	EDIT BAY	1	FLAT		12,000	12,000	$12,000
800-12	EDITORIAL SUPPLIES						
	SUPPLIES/FOOD	15	WEEKS		200	3,000	
	SALES TAX	8.25%			3,000	248	$3,248
800-14	POSTPROD. SUPERVISION						$0
800-18	ASSISTANT EDITOR						
	ASSISTANT EDITOR	8	WEEKS		300	2,400	$2,400
800-19	APPRENTICE EDITOR (INT...						$0
							Total For 800-00 $26,148
810-00	**MUSIC**						
810-08	COMPOSER						
	COMPOSER	5	WEEKS		300	1,500	$1,500
810-25	MUSIC SUPERVISOR						
	MUSIC SUPERVISOR	5	WEEKS		300	1,500	$1,500
810-26	MUSIC CLEARANCE SALA...						$0
810-27	MUSIC CLERICAL						$0
810-28	MASTER USE LICENSES						$0
810-29	MUSIC PUBLISHING LICEN...						$0
810-30	PRESCORE						$0
810-31	REHEARSAL MUSICIANS						$0
810-32	DEMO COSTS						$0
810-33	SCORE (FACILITIES)						$0
810-34	STUDIO EQUIPMENT RENT...						$0
810-35	MUSIC INSTRUMENT RENT...						$0
810-37	MUSIC TRANSFERS						$0
							Total For 810-00 $3,000
820-00	**POSTPRODUCTION SOUND**						
820-01	DIALOGUE RECORDING/ADR						
	ADR FACILITY/FOOD		ALLOW		300	300	$300
820-02	NARRATION RECORDING						$0
820-03	SOUND EFFECTS (FOLEY)						
	FOLEY	1	FLAT		1,000	1,000	$1,000
820-06	DUBBING SESSION						
	SOUND MIX	1	FLAT		5,000	5,000	$5,000
820-07	SOUND TRANSFERS						
	SOUND TRANSFERS		ALLOW		2,000	2,000	$2,000
							Total For 820-00 $8,300

(continued)

Figure 6–2 Preliminary budget for Swingers *(continued)*

Acct#	Description	Amount	Units	X	Rate	Subtotal	Total
840-00	**TITLES**						
840-01	TITLES (MAIN & END)						
	MAIN AND END TITLES	1	FLAT		1,000	1,000	$1,000
840-02	MAIN TITLES						$0
840-03	END TITLES						$0
840-04	MISCELLANEOUS TITLES						$0
840-05	LABORATORY PROCESSING						$0
						Total For 840-00	**$1,000**
850-00	**OPTICALS, MATTES, INSERTS**						
850-01	OPTICAL EFFECTS/DUPE...						
	OPTICALS		ALLOW		1,000	1,000	$1,000
850-02	MASTER POSITIVES						$0
850-03	LABORATORY PROCESSING						$0
850-04	SPECIAL PHOTO EFFECTS						$0
850-11	PURCHASES						$0
						Total For 850-00	**$1,000**
860-00	**LABORATORY PROCESSING**						
860-01	REPRINTING & DEVELOPING						$0
860-02	1ST TRIAL COMOSITE P...						
	WORK PRINT		ALLOW		2,000	2,000	$2,000
860-03	MASTER POSITIVE PRINT						$0
860-06	DEVELOP SOUND NEGATI...						$0
860-07	ANSWER PRINT						
	Answer Print	8,500	FEET		1.1	9,350	$9,350
						Total For 860-00	**$11,350**
	TOTAL COMPLETION PERIOD						**$50,798**
910-00	**ADMINISTRATIVE EXPENSES**						
910-01	ACCOUNTING & TERMINAL...						
	ACCOUNTING PACKAGE		ALLOW		100	100	
910-02	MPAA CERTIFICATE						
	MPAA CERTIFICATE		ALLOW		900	900	
910-03	POSTAGE & SHIPPING & F...						
	POSTAGE & SHIPPING & F...		ALLOW		300	300	
910-04	PHOTOCOPYING (NO SCRI...						
	PHOTOCOPYING		ALLOW		400	400	
910-05	LEGAL EXPENSES & FEES						
	LEGAL FEES & EXPENSES		ALLOW	0	5,000	0	
910-00	**ADMINISTRATIVE EXPENSES (CONT'D)**						
910-06	TELEPHONE/FACSIMILE						
	TELEPHONE & FAX		ALLOW		1,200	1,200	$1,200
910-12	PREVIEW EXPENSE/DIST. ...						
	PREVIEW		ALLOW		2,000	2,000	$2,000
910-18	RESEARCH REPORT/TITLE...						
	RESEARCH REPORT		ALLOW		1,000	1,000	$1,000
910-19	PRODUCTION EXPENDABL...						
910-20	CORPORATE FILING						
	Filing over Internet	1			300	300	
910-21	POLAROID & B/W STILL FI...						
	POLAROID & STILL FILM		ALLOW		300	300	
910-22	PAYROLL CO.						
	PAYROLL COMPANY	3	WEEKS	12	3	108	
						Total For 910-00	**$6,608**

	TOTAL OTHER			**$6,608**
	Completion Bond: 0.00%			
	Contingency: 10.00%			$25,018
	Overhead: 0.00%			
	Insurance: 1.75%			$4,378
	TOTAL ABOVE-THE-LINE			**$45,173**
	TOTAL BELOW-THE-LINE			**$205,008**
	TOTAL ABOVE- & BELOW-THE-LINE			**$250,181**
	GRAND TOTAL			**$279,577**

Figure 6–2 Preliminary budget for Swingers *(continued)*

"SWINGERS"

ACTUALIZED BUDGET
PRODUCTION NO.:
PRODUCER:
DIRECTOR:
SCRIPT DATE:
START DATE:8/31/95
FINISH DATE:9/22/95

DATE: AUGUST 31, 1995
LOCATIONS: HLYWD/VEGAS
BASED ON: 3 WEEK SHOOT
6 DAY WEEK
SAG

NOT FINAL SHOOTING BUDGET

Acct #	Category Title	Page	Original	Total	Variance
600-00	STORY	1	$1,000	$1,000	$0
610-00	PRODUCER	1	$5,983	$5,792	($191)
620-00	DIRECTOR	1	$3,200	$3,200	$0
630-00	CAST	1	$33,708	$33,128	($580)
650-00	TRAVEL & LIVING	2	$1,891	$2,053	$162
	TOTAL ABOVE-THE-LINE		**$45,781**	**$45,173**	**($608)**
700-00	EXTRA TALENT	3	$4,253	$5,589	$1,336
705-00	PRODUCTION STAFF	4	$20,940	$18,360	($2,580)
710-00	CAMERA	4	$12,711	$12,819	$108
715-00	ART/SET DESIGN (MATERIALS IN PROPS)	5	$3,600	$3,600	$0
725-00	SET OPERATIONS	5	$15,580	$16,180	$600
730-00	ELECTRICAL	6	$12,701	$13,201	$500
750-00	PROPERTIES	6	$6,665	$5,965	($700)
755-00	WARDROBE	7	$8,637	$9,937	$1,300
760-00	MAKEUP & HAIRSTYLISTS	8	$1,680	$1,780	$100
765-00	PRODUCTION SOUND	8	$9,333	$9,160	($173)
770-00	TRANSPORTATION	8	$6,430	$4,977	($1,453)
775-00	LOCATION EXPENSE	9	$26,094	$28,282	$2,188
785-00	PRODUCTION DAILIES	10	$21,836	$17,753	($4,083)
	TOTAL SHOOTING PERIOD		**$150,460**	**$147,603**	**($2,857)**
800-00	EDITING	11	$21,983	$26,148	$4,165
810-00	MUSIC	11	$3,000	$3,000	$0
820-00	POST PRODUCTION SOUND	11	$8,000	$8,300	$300
840-00	TITLES	11	$1,500	$1,000	($500)
850-00	OPTICALS, MATTES, INSERTS	12	$1,000	$1,000	$0
860-00	LABORATORY PROCESSING	12	$11,350	$11,350	$0
	TOTAL COMPLETION PERIOD		**$46,833**	**$50,798**	**$3,965**
910-00	ADMINISTRATIVE EXPENSES	12	$7,257	$6,608	($649)
	TOTAL OTHER		**$7,257**	**$6,608**	**($649)**
	Completion Bond: 0.00%		$0	$0	$0
	Contingency: 10.00%		$25,033	$25,018	($15)
	Overhead: 0.00%		$0	$0	$0
	Insurance: 1.75%		$4,381	$4,378	($3)

(continued)

Figure 6–3 Top sheet of actualized budget for Swingers

SWINGERS

Acct #	Category Title	Page	Original	Total	Variance
	TOTAL ABOVE-THE-LINE		$45,781	$45,173	($608)
	TOTAL BELOW-THE-LINE		$204,549	$205,008	$459
	TOTAL ABOVE- & BELOW-THE-LINE		$250,331	$250,181	($149)
	GRAND TOTAL		$279,745	$279,577	($168)

Figure 6–3 Top sheet of actualized budget for Swingers *(continued)*

SAMPLE BUDGET 1

PRODUCTION NO.:
PRODUCER:
DIRECTOR:
SCRIPT DATE:
START DATE:
FINISH DATE:

DATE:
LOCATION: LOCAL SHOOT
BASED ON: 5 WEEK PREPRODUCTION
3 WEEK SHOOT- 6 DAY WEEK
SAG - UNDER $2 MILLION AGRMT.
LOCAL/NONUNION CREW/FLAT
NOT A FINAL SHOOTING BUDGET

Acct#	Category Title	Page	Total
600-00	STORY	1	$2,500
610-00	PRODUCER	1	$12,165
620-00	DIRECTOR	1	$12,541
630-00	CAST	1	$84,541
650-00	TRAVEL & LIVING	3	$0
	TOTAL ABOVE-THE-LINE		**$111,747**
700-00	EXTRA TALENT/STUNTS	3	$9,240
705-00	PRODUCTION STAFF	4	$40,922
710-00	CAMERA	5	$26,587
715-00	ART/SET DESIGN	6	$27,535
725-00	SET OPERATIONS	6	$23,257
730-00	ELECTRICAL	7	$19,262
745-00	SET DRESSING (see PROPS/ART)	8	$0
750-00	PROPERTIES	8	$21,069
755-00	WARDROBE	9	$22,881
760-00	MAKEUP & HAIR	9	$8,714
765-00	PRODUCTION SOUND	10	$11,044
770-00	TRANSPORTATION	10	$25,350
775-00	LOCATION EXPENSES	11	$75,720
785-00	PRODUCTION DAILIES	12	$85,633
	TOTAL SHOOTING PERIOD		**$397,213**
800-00	EDITING	13	$62,036
810-00	MUSIC	13	$22,694
820-00	POSTPRODUCTION SOUND	13	$19,403
840-00	TITLES	14	$2,500
850-00	OPTICALS, MATTES, INSERTS	14	$3,000
860-00	LABORATORY PROCESSING	14	$16,723
	TOTAL COMPLETION PERIOD		**$126,355**
910-00	ADMINISTRATIVE EXPENSES	14	$26,328
920-00	PUBLICITY	15	$0
	TOTAL OTHER		**$26,328**
	Completion Bond: 0.00%		$0
	Contingency: 10.00%		$66,164
	Overhead: 0.00%		$0
	Insurance: 2.00%		$13,233

(continued)

Figure 6–4 Sample budget 1, developed for a character-driven piece (continued)

Acct#	Category Title	Page	Total
	TOTAL ABOVE-THE-LINE		$111,747
	TOTAL BELOW-THE-LINE		$549,896
	TOTAL ABOVE- & BELOW-THE-LINE		$661,643
	GRAND TOTAL		$741,040

(continued)

Figure 6–4 Sample budget 1, developed for a character-driven piece (continued)

SAMPLE BUDGET 1

PRODUCTION NO.:
PRODUCER:
DIRECTOR:
SCRIPT DATE:
START DATE:
FINISH DATE:

DATE:
LOCATION: LOCAL SHOOT
BASED ON: 5 WEEK PREPRODUCTION
3 WEEK SHOOT- 6 DAY WEEK
SAG - UNDER $2 MILLION AGRMT.
LOCAL/NONUNION CREW/FLAT
NOT A FINAL SHOOTING BUDGET

Acct #	Description	Amount	Units	X	Rate	Subtotal	Total
600-00	**STORY**						
600-01	RIGHTS PURCHASED						
	OPTION PRICE	1	FLAT		500	500	$500
600-03	WRITERS						$0
600-04	SCREENPLAY PURCHASE						
	SCREENPLAY PURCHASE	1	FLAT		2,000	2,000	$2,000
						Total For 600-00	**$2,500**
610-00	**PRODUCER**						
610-01	EXECUTIVE PRODUCER						$0
610-02	PRODUCER						
	PRODUCERS - LOAN-OUT	1	FLAT	2	5,000	10,000	$10,000
610-03	ASSOCIATE PRODUCER						$0
610-07	PRODUCER'S ENT.						$0
610-08	PREPRODUCTION EXPEN...						
	ENT./FOOD/FILM/SUPPLIES		ALLOW		2,000	2,000	
	SALES TAX	8.25%			2,000	165	$2,165
						Total For 610-00	**$12,165**
620-00	**DIRECTOR**						
620-01	DIRECTOR						
	DIRECTOR - LOAN-OUT	1	FLAT		7,500	7,500	$7,500
620-05	CASTING DIRECTOR						
	CASTING FEES (loan-out)	3	WEEKS		1,500	4,500	$4,500
620-08	CASTING EXPENSES						
	CASTING EXPENSES		ALLOW		500	500	
	SALES TAX	8.25%			500	41	$541
						Total For 620-00	**$12,541**
630-00	**CAST**						
630-01	PRINCIPAL PLAYERS						
	DAVE	3	WEEKS		1,620	4,860	
	JANE	3	WEEKS		1,620	4,860	
	SCOTT	2	WEEKS		1,620	3,240	
	MATT	1	WEEK		1,620	1,620	
	JONATHAN	1	WEEK		1,620	1,620	

(continued)

Figure 6–4 Sample budget 1, developed for a character-driven piece (continued)

Acct #	Description	Amount	Units	X	Rate	Subtotal	Total
630-00	**CAST (CONT'D)**						
630-01	PRINCIPAL PLAYERS (CONT'D)						
	MARK	1	WEEK		1,620	1,620	
	BROOKE	2	WEEKS		1,620	3,240	
	MARCI	2	WEEKS		1,620	3,240	
	OVERTIME	20%			24,300	4,860	
	SAG CORP	13.3%			24,300	3,232	
	FICA #1	6.2%			24,300	1,507	
	FICA #2	1.45%			24,300	352	
	SUI	5.4%			7,000	378	
	FUI	0.8%			7,000	56	
	AGENCY COMMISS.	10.0%			24,300	2,430	$37,115
630-02	DAY PLAYERS						
	MR. TULLY	3	DAYS		466	1,398	
	JENSEN	3	DAYS		466	1,398	
	BOBBY MARTEL	2	DAYS		466	932	
	JOSH	1	DAY		466	466	
	STEPHANIE	1	DAY		466	466	
	CARRIE	1	DAY		466	466	
	MRS. JOHNSON	2	DAYS		466	932	
	TUSTIN GREEN	1	DAY		466	466	
	HARRY	1	DAY		466	466	
	JUSTINE	2	DAYS		466	932	
	DANCERS	2	DAYS	4	466	3,728	
	VALETS	1	DAY	3	466	1,398	
	ELIZABETH	1	DAY		466	466	
	CHRISTOPHER	1	DAY		466	466	
	KYLE	2	DAYS		466	932	
	BARTENDERS	3	2	3	466	4,194	
	AMANDA	1	DAY		466	466	
	OVERTIME	20%			19,572	3,914	
	SAG CORP	13.3%			19,572	2,603	
	FICA #1	6.2%			19,572	1,213	
	FICA #2	1.45%			19,572	284	
	SUI	5.4%			14,922	806	
	FUI	0.8%			14,922	119	
	AGENCY COMMISS.	10.0%			19,572	1,957	$30,469
630-03	REHEARSAL						
	DAVE	3	DAYS		466	1,398	
	JANE	3	DAYS		466	1,398	
	SCOTT	2	DAYS		466	932	
	BROOKE	2	DAYS		466	932	
	MARCI	2	DAYS		466	932	
	OVERTIME	20%			5,592	1,118	
	SAG CORP	13.3%			5,592	744	
	FICA #1	6.2%			5,592	347	
	FICA #2	1.45%			5,592	81	

(continued)

Figure 6–4 Sample budget 1, developed for a character-driven piece (continued)

Acct #	Description	Amount	Units	X	Rate	Subtotal	Total
630-00	**CAST (CONT'D)**						
630-03	REHEARSAL (CONT'D)						
	SUI	5.4%			5,592	302	
	FUI	0.8%			5,592	45	
	AGENCY COMMISS.	10.0%			5,592	559	$8,788
630-04	WELFARE WORKER						$0
630-06	LOOPING/ADR (INCL. 1 DA...						
	DAVE	1	DAY		466	466	
	JANE	1	DAY		466	466	
	SCOTT	1	DAY		466	466	
	BROOKE	1	DAY		466	466	
	MARCI	1	DAY		466	466	
	MR. TULLY	1	DAY		466	466	
	JENSEN	1	DAY		466	466	
	OVERTIME	20%			3,262	652	
	SAG CORP	13.3%			3,262	434	
	FICA #1	6.2%			3,262	202	
	FICA #2	1.45%			3,262	47	
	SUI	5.4%			3,262	176	
	FUI	0.8%			3,262	26	
	AGENCY COMMISS.	10.0%			3,262	326	$5,126
630-07	MEAL PENALTIES						
	MEAL PENALTIES-CAST		ALLOW		2,000	2,000	
	SAG CORP	13.3%			2,000	266	
	FICA #1	6.2%			2,000	124	
	FICA #2	1.45%			2,000	29	
	SUI	5.4%			2,000	108	
	FUI	0.8%			2,000	16	$2,543
630-09	MEDICAL EXAMS						
	Medical Exams		ALLOW	5	100	500	$500
630-20	SIDE DEALS						$0
						Total For 630-00	**$84,541**
650-00	**TRAVEL & LIVING**						
650-03	WRITER'S TRAVEL						
							$0
650-03	WRITER'S LIVING						$0
650-01	PRODUCER'S TRAVEL						$0
650-01	PRODUCER'S LIVING						$0
650-02	DIRECTOR'S TRAVEL						$0
650-02	DIRECTOR'S LIVING						$0
650-06	CAST TRAVEL						$0
650-06	CAST LIVING						$0
						Total For 650-00	**$0**
	TOTAL ABOVE-THE-LINE						**$111,747**

(continued)

Figure 6–4 Sample budget 1, developed for a character-driven piece (continued)

Acct #	Description	Amount	Units	X	Rate	Subtotal	Total
700-00	**EXTRA TALENT/STUNTS**						
700-02	EXTRAS & STAND-INS						
	EXTRAS - STREET EXTRAS	2	DAYS	5	90	900	
	BAR (WHILE OPEN)	3	DAYS	15	90	4,050	
	DINER (SHOOT WHILE OP...						
	CLUB (WHILE OPEN)						
	NEIGHBORS	2	DAYS	5	90	900	
	ICE CREAM PARLOR (WHI...						
	SAG CORP	13.3%			5,850	778	
	FICA #1	6.2%			5,850	363	
	FICA #2	1.45%			5,850	85	
	SUI	5.4%			5,850	316	
	FUI	0.8%			5,850	47	
	AGENCY COMMISS.	10.0%			5,850	585	$8,023
700-05	EXTRAS CASTING						
	EXTRAS CASTING	1	WEEK		1,000	1,000	
	EXTRAS CASTING EXPEN...	1	FLAT		200	200	
	SALES TAX	8.25%			200	17	$1,217
						Total For 700-00	**$9,240**
705-00	**PRODUCTION STAFF**						
705-01	LINE PRODUCER/UPM						
	LINE PRODUCER-PREPRO	5	WEEKS		600	3,000	
	PRODUCTION	3	WEEKS		600	1,800	
	WARP	2	WEEKS		600	1,200	
	NON-UNION	18%			6,000	1,080	$7,080
705-02	PROD. COORD.						
	PREP	4	WEEKS		500	2,000	
	SHOOT	3	WEEKS		500	1,500	
	WRAP	1	WEEKS		500	500	
	NON-UNION	18%			4,000	720	$4,720
705-03	FIRST ASSISTANT DIRECT...						
	PREP	3	WEEKS		600	1,800	
	SHOOT	3	WEEKS		600	1,800	
	WRAP	0.6	WEEKS		600	360	
	NON-UNION	18%			3,960	713	$4,673
705-04	SECOND ASSISTANT DIRE...						
	PREP	2	WEEKS		500	1,000	
	SHOOT	3	WEEKS		500	1,500	
	WRAP	0.6	WEEKS		500	300	
	NON-UNION	18%			2,800	504	$3,304
705-05	SECOND SECOND ASST. D...						
	SECOND SECOND DIRECT...	2	WEEKS		400	800	
	NON-UNION	18%			800	144	$944
705-06	SCRIPT SUPERVISOR						
	PREP	0.6	WEEKS		600	360	
	SHOOT	3	WEEKS		600	1,800	

(continued)

Figure 6–4 Sample budget 1, developed for a character-driven piece (continued)

Acct #	Description	Amount	Units	X	Rate	Subtotal	Total
705-00	**PRODUCTION STAFF (CONT'D)**						
705-06	SCRIPT SUPERVISOR (CONT'D)						
	WRAP	0.6	WEEKS		600	360	
	NON-UNION	18%			2,520	454	$2,974
705-08	ESTIMATOR/PROD. ACCO...						
	ACCOUNTANT-PREP	4	WEEKS		600	2,400	
	SHOOT	3	WEEKS		600	1,800	
	WRAP	2	WEEKS		600	1,200	
	NON-UNION	18%			5,400	972	$6,372
705-10	PRODUCTION ASSISTANTS						
	PA ONE-PREP	4	WEEKS		400	1,600	
	SHOOT	3	WEEKS		400	1,200	
	WRAP	1	WEEK		400	400	
	PA TWO-PREP	2	WEEKS		400	800	
	SHOOT	3	WEEKS		400	1,200	
	WRAP	1	WEEK		400	400	
	PA THREE - SHOOT	3	WEEKS		400	1,200	
	PA-PROD. OFFICE - PREP	2	WEEKS		400	800	
	SHOOT	3	WEEKS		400	1,200	
	WRAP	1	WEEK		400	400	
	NON-UNION	18%			9,200	1,656	$10,856
						Total For 705-00	**$40,922**
710-00	**CAMERA**						
710-01	DIRECTOR OF PHOTOGRA...						
	DIRECTOR OF PHOTOGRA...	1	FLAT		5,000	5,000	$5,000
710-03	1ST ASST CAMERAMAN						
	PREP	0.6	WEEKS		600	360	
	SHOOT	3	WEEKS		600	1,800	
	NON-UNION	18%			2,160	389	$2,549
710-04	2ND ASST CAMERAMAN / ...						
	PREP	0.6	WEEKS		500	300	
	SHOOT	3	WEEKS		500	1,500	
	NON-UNION	18%			1,800	324	$2,124
710-06	STILL PHOTOGRAPHER						
	STILL PHOTOGRAPHER	5	DAYS		100	500	
	SUPPLIES/DEVELOPING		ALLOW		500	500	
	NON-UNION	18%			500	90	
	SALES TAX	8.25%			500	41	$1,131
710-08	CAMERA RENTALS						
	CAMERA PACKAGE W/AC...	3	WEEKS		2,000	6,000	$6,000
710-09	CAMERA SUPPLIES						
	Camera Expendables		ALLOW		350	350	
	SALES TAX	8.25%			350	29	$379
710-10	STEADI-CAM						
	STEADI-CAM	1	WEEK		1,500	1,500	
	STEADI-CAM OPERATOR	1	WEEK		1,000	1,000	

(continued)

Figure 6–4 Sample budget 1, developed for a character-driven piece (continued)

Acct #	Description	Amount	Units	X	Rate	Subtotal	Total
710-10	**CAMERA (CONT'D)**						
710-10	STEADI-CAM (CONT'D)						
	NON-UNION	18%			1,000	180	$2,680
710-11	VIDEO EQUIPMENT						
	MONITOR	3	WEEKS		1,200	3,600	
	VIDEO ASST. OPERATOR	3	WEEKS		600	1,800	
	NON-UNION	18%			1,800	324	$5,724
710-20	LOSS, DAMAGE & REPAIR						
	Loss and damage		ALLOW		1,000	1,000	$1,000
						Total For 710-00	**$26,587**
715-00	**ART/SET DESIGN**						
715-01	PRODUCTION DESIGNER						
	Prod. Designer - PREP	5	WEEKS		600	3,000	
	SHOOT	3	WEEKS		600	1,800	
	WRAP	1	WEEK		600	600	
	NON-UNION	18%			5,400	972	$6,372
715-02	ART/SET DIRECTOR						
	REP	4	WEEKS		600	2,400	
	SHOOT	3	WEEKS		600	1,800	
	WRAP	1	WEEKS		600	600	
	NON-UNION	18%			4,800	864	$5,664
715-03	SET DESIGNER/LEADMAN						
	ART SWING - PREP	3	WEEKS		500	1,500	
	SHOOT	3	WEEKS		500	1,500	
	WRAP	1	WEEK		500	500	
	NON-UNION	18%			3,500	630	$4,130
715-04	SWING GANG						
	ART SWING - PREP	1	WEEK		400	400	
	SHOOT	3	WEEKS		400	1,200	
	WRAP	0.6	WEEKS		400	240	
	NON-UNION	18%			1,840	331	$2,171
715-05	ART RENTAL						
	ART RENTALS	3	WEEKS		1,500	4,500	$4,500
715-06	ART PURCHASE						
	ART PURCHASE	1	FLAT		3,000	3,000	
	SALES TAX	8.25%			3,000	248	$3,248
715-10	BOX RENTAL						
	KIT RENTALS	3	WEEKS	2	75	450	$450
715-20	LOSS & DAMAGE						
	LOSS & DAMAGE		ALLOW		1,000	1,000	$1,000
						Total For 715-00	**$27,535**
725-00	**SET OPERATIONS**						
725-01	1ST COMPANY GRIP/KEY...						
	PREP	1	WEEK		600	600	
	SHOOT	3	WEEKS		600	1,800	

(continued)

Figure 6–4 Sample budget 1, developed for a character-driven piece (continued)

Acct #	Description	Amount	Units	X	Rate	Subtotal	Total
725-00	**SET OPERATIONS (CONT'D)**						
725-01	1ST COMPANY GRIP/KEY GRIP (CONT'D)						
	NON-UNION	18%			2,400	432	$2,832
725-02	BEST BOY GRIP						
	PREP	0.6	WEEKS		500	300	
	SHOOT	3	WEEKS		500	1,500	
	NON-UNION	18%			1,800	324	$2,124
725-03	DOLLY GRIPS						
	CRANE/DOLLY GRIP-SHOOT	3	WEEKS		500	1,500	
	NON-UNION	18%			1,500	270	$1,770
725-04	EXTRA GRIPS/COMPANY ...						
	COMPANY GRIP - SHOOT	3	WEEKS		500	1,500	
	NON-UNION	18%			1,500	270	$1,770
725-05	CAMERA DOLLIES						
	Dolly W/ TRACK	3	WEEKS		800	2,400	
	SALES TAX	8.25%			2,400	198	$2,598
725-07	CRANES & OP						$0
725-08	GRIP EQUIPMENT RENTALS						
	GRIP EQUIPMENT	3	WEEKS		1,500	4,500	
	ADDL. EQUIP	3	WEEKS		300	900	
	SALES TAX	8.25%			900	74	$5,474
725-09	GRIP PURCHASES						
	Grip Purchases		ALLOW		500	500	
	SALES TAX	8.25%			500	41	$541
725-10	GRIP BOX RENTALS						
	BOX RENTALS	3	WEEKS		75	225	$225
725-11	CRAFT SERVICE/SERVICE...						
	CRAFT SERVICEMAN-PREP	0.6	WEEKS		500	300	
	SHOOT	3	WEEKS		500	1,500	
	CRAFT SERVICE FOOD	3	WEEKS		600	1,800	
	CRAFT SERVICE EXPEND...	3	WEEKS		200	600	
	NON-UNION	18%			1,800	324	
	SALES TAX	8.25%			2,400	198	$4,722
725-12	SET CLEANUP & TRASH DI...						
	SET CLEANUP & TRASH DI...		ALLOW		200	200	$200
725-20	LOSS & DAMAGE						
	L&D		ALLOW		1,000	1,000	$1,000
725-24	DRESSING ROOM RENTALS						$0
725-30	LOCATION LOAD AND UNL...						$0
						Total For 725-00	**$23,257**
730-00	**ELECTRICAL**						
730-01	GAFFER						
	PREP	1	WEEK		600	600	
	SHOOT	3	WEEKS		600	1,800	
	NON-UNION	18%			2,400	432	$2,832
730-02	BEST BOY						

(continued)

Figure 6–4 Sample budget 1, developed for a character-driven piece (continued)

Acct #	Description	Amount	Units	X	Rate	Subtotal	Total
730-00	**ELECTRICAL (CONT'D)**						
730-02	BEST BOY (CONT'D)						
	PREP	0.6	WEEKS		500	300	
	SHOOT	3	WEEKS		500	1,500	
	NON-UNION	18%			1,800	324	$2,124
730-03	ELECTRICIANS						
	ELECTRICIANS - SHOOT	3	WEEKS		500	1,500	
	NON-UNION	18%			1,500	270	$1,770
730-05	GLOBES/CARBONS/SUPP...						
	GLOBES/CARBONS/SUPP...		ALLOW		300	300	
	SALES TAX	8.25%			300	25	$325
730-07	GENERATOR RENTAL/FUEL						
	GENERATOR	3	WEEKS		1,000	3,000	
	FUEL	3	WEEKS		250	750	
	SALES TAX	8.25%			750	62	$3,812
730-08	ELECTRICAL EQUIP RENT...						
	ELECTRICAL PACKAGE	3	WEEKS		2,000	6,000	$6,000
730-09	ELECTRICAL EQUIP PURC...						
	ELEC. PURCHASE/EXPEN...	3	WEEKS		300	900	
	SALES TAX	8.25%			900	74	$974
730-10	BOX RENTAL						
	BOX RENTAL	3	WEEKS		75	225	$225
730-11	POWER/TIE-IN						
	POWER-TIE-IN		ALLOW		200	200	$200
730-20	LOSS, DAMAGE, & REPAIR						
	LOSS & DAMAGE		ALLOW		1,000	1,000	$1,000
						Total For 730-00	**$19,262**
745-00	**SET DRESSING (see PROPS/ART)**						
							$0
						Total For 745-00	**$0**
750-00	**PROPERTIES**						
750-01	PROPERTY MASTER						
	PROP MASTER	3	WEEKS		600	1,800	
	SHOOT	3	WEEKS		600	1,800	
	WRAP	1	WEEK		600	600	
	NON-UNION	18%			4,200	756	$4,956
750-02	ASST. PROPS						
	ASST. PROPS - PREP	2	WEEKS		500	1,000	
	SHOOT	3	WEEKS		500	1,500	
	WRAP	1	WEEK		500	500	
	NON-UNION	18%			3,000	540	$3,540
750-04	PICTURE VEHICLES LABO...						
	REPAIRS		ALLOW		500	500	
	FUEL		ALLOW		500	500	
	SALES TAX	8.25%			1,000	83	$1,083

(continued)

Figure 6–4 Sample budget 1, developed for a character-driven piece (continued)

Acct #	Description	Amount	Units	X	Rate	Subtotal	Total
750-00	**PROPERTIES (CONT'D)**						
750-05	PICTURE VEHICLE RENTALS						
	X	3	WEEKS		1,000	3,000	
	X	2	WEEKS		500	1,000	
	X	1	WEEK		500	500	$4,500
750-08	PROP RENTALS						
	PROP RENTALS	3	WEEKS		1,200	3,600	$3,600
750-09	PROP PURCHASES						
	PROP PURCHASES		ALLOW		2,000	2,000	
	SALES TAX	8.25%			2,000	165	$2,165
750-10	PROP BOX RENTALS						
	PROP BOX RENTALS	3	WEEKS		75	225	$225
750-20	LOSS & DAMAGE						
	LOSS & DAMAGE		ALLOW		1,000	1,000	$1,000
						Total For 750-00	**$21,069**
755-00	**WARDROBE**						
755-04	COSTUME DESIGNER						
	PREP	4	WEEKS		600	2,400	
	SHOOT	3	WEEKS		600	1,800	
	WRAP	1	WEEK		600	600	
	NON-UNION	18%			4,800	864	$5,664
755-03	ASST. WARDROBE						
	WARDROBE ASST. - PREP	2	WEEKS		500	1,000	
	SHOOT	3	WEEKS		500	1,500	
	WARDROBE ASST. - SHOOT	2	WEEKS		500	1,000	
	WRAP	1	WEEK		500	500	
	NON-UNION	18%			4,000	720	$4,720
755-06	ALTERATIONS - L&M						
	ALTERATIONS		ALLOW		200	200	$200
755-07	CLEANING & DYEING						
	CLEAN & DYE		ALLOW		300	300	
	SALES TAX	8.25%			300	25	$325
755-08	WARDROBE RENTALS						
	WARDROBE RENTALS	3	WEEKS		2,500	7,500	$7,500
755-09	WARDROBE PURCHASES						
	WARDROBE PURCHASES		ALLOW		3,000	3,000	
	SALES TAX	8.25%			3,000	248	$3,248
755-10	HAND BOX RENTALS						
	KIT RENTAL	3	WEEKS		75	225	$225
755-20	LOSS, DAMAGE & REPAIRS						
	L&D		ALLOW		1,000	1,000	$1,000
						Total For 755-00	**$22,881**

(continued)

Figure 6–4 Sample budget 1, developed for a character-driven piece (continued)

Acct #	Description	Amount	Units	X	Rate	Subtotal	Total
760-00	**MAKEUP & HAIR**						
760-01	MAKEUP ARTIST						
	MAKEUP ARTIST(HAIR)-P...	0.6	WEEKS		600	360	
	SHOOT	3	WEEKS		600	1,800	
	NON-UNION	18%			2,160	389	$2,549
760-02	HAIR ARTIST						
	HAIR ARTIST - PREP	0.6	WEEKS		600	360	
	HAIR ARTIST - SHOOT	3	WEEKS		600	1,800	
	NON-UNION	18%			1,800	324	$2,484
760-03	ASST. MAKEUP/HAIR ART...						
	HAIR/MAKEUP ARTIST SH...	3	WEEKS		500	1,500	
	NON-UNION	18%			1,500	270	$1,770
760-06	WIG & HAIR PURCHASE						
	HAIR PURCHASE	3	WEEKS		200	600	
	SALES TAX	8.25%			600	50	$650
760-09	MAKEUP SUPPLIES/APPL...						
	MAKEUP SUPPLIES	3	WEEKS		250	750	
	SALES TAX	8.25%			750	62	$812
760-10	KIT RENTALS						
	KIT RENTALS	3	WEEKS	2	75	450	$450
						Total For 760-00	**$8,714**
765-00	**PRODUCTION SOUND**						
765-01	SOUND MIXER						
	SOUND MIXER - PREP	0.2	WEEKS		600	120	
	SHOOT	3	WEEKS		600	1,800	
	NON-UNION	18%			1,920	346	$2,266
765-02	BOOMMAN						
	SHOOT	3	WEEKS		500	1,500	
	NON-UNION	18%			1,500	270	$1,770
756-05	PLAYBACK OPERATOR						
765-06	SOUND EQUIP RENTALS						
	SOUND PACKAGE (w/nagra...	3	WEEKS		1,200	3,600	
	walkie/slate included)						$3,600
765-10	KIT RENTALS						
	KIT RENTAL	3	WEEKS		75	225	$225
765-11	MISCELLANEOUS/EXPEN...						
	MAG STOCK		ALLOW		1,000	1,000	
	BATTERIES		ALLOW		500	500	
	BEEPERS	7	WEEKS	8	10	560	
	SALES TAX	8.25%			1,500	124	$2,184
765-20	LOSS & DAMAGE						
	Loss & damage		ALLOW		1,000	1,000	$1,000
						Total For 765-00	**$11,044**

(continued)

Figure 6–4 Sample budget 1, developed for a character-driven piece (continued)

Acct #	Description	Amount	Units	X	Rate	Subtotal	Total
770-00	**TRANSPORTATION**						
770-01	MESSENGER SERVICE						
	MESSENGER SERVICE		ALLOW		300	300	$300
770-02	TRANSPORTATION COORD.						$0
770-05	MILEAGE ALLOWANCE						$0
770-06	FUEL						
	FUEL/CARS/TRUCKS	8	WEEKS	10	50	4,000	
	SALES TAX	8.25%			4,000	330	$4,330
770-09	EXTRA DRIVERS						
	DRIVERS	5	WEEKS	2	400	4,000	
	DRIVERS	3	WEEKS	2	400	2,400	
	NON-UNION	18%			6,400	1,152	$7,55 2
770-10	LOC. VEHICLES/PROD. TR...						
	CUBE VANS (SCOUT/P/U'S)	6	WEEKS		300	1,800	
	CAMERA/SOUND	3	WEEKS		400	1,200	
	PRODUCTION CUBE	5	WEEKS		350	1,750	
	WARDROBE CUBE	5	WEEKS		350	1,750	
	PROP/ART CUBE	5	WEEKS		350	1,750	
	GRIP/ELECTRIC TRUCK	3	WEEKS		800	2,400	
	SALES TAX	8.25%			10,650	879	
	CITY TAX	6.0%			10,650	639	$12,168
770-20	LOSS, DAMAGE, REPAIRS						
	LOSS & DAMAGE		ALLOW		1,000	1,000	$1,000
						Total For 770-00	**$25,350**
775-00	**LOCATION EXPENSES**						
775-01	SURVEY EXPENSE						
	LOCATION MGR. SCOUT -F...	20	DAYS		15	300	
	GAS	5	WEEKS		100	500	
	TIPS		ALLOW		100	100	
	FILM/PROCESS/SUPPLIES	5	WEEKS		200	1,000	
	PHONE/CELL	5	WEEKS		100	500	
	SCOUTING WITH CREW						
	FOOD	3	DAYS	10	12	360	
	POLAROID FILM		ALLOW		200	200	
	CELLULAR	3	DAYS		50	150	
	FUEL		ALLOW		150	150	
	sales tax	8.25%			2,510	207	$3,467
775-02	LOCATION STAFF						
	LOCATION MANAGER - PR...	5	WEEKS		600	3,000	
	SHOOT	3	WEEKS		600	1,800	
	WRAP	1	WEEK		600	600	
	NON-UNION	18%			5,400	972	$6,372
775-03	SITE RENTALS/PERMITS/L...						
	HOUSE	3	DAYS		750	2,250	
	MAIN STREET (PERMIT RO...		ALLOW		200	200	

(continued)

Figure 6–4 Sample budget 1, developed for a character-driven piece (continued)

Acct #	Description	Amount	Units	X	Rate	Subtotal	Total
775-00	**LOCATION EXPENSES (CONT'D)**						
775-03	SITE RENTALS/PERMITS/LIC. (CONT'D)						
	HOUSE	3	DAYS		500	1,500	
	BAR	5	DAYS		1,000	5,000	
	PARK (PERMIT ONLY)		ALLOW		150	150	
	DINER	1	DAY		500	500	
	CLUB + (PARK LOT)	3	DAYS		1,500	4,500	
	STORE	2	DAYS		300	600	
	ICE CREAM PARLOR	1	DAY		300	300	
	PERMITS/SITE RENTALS		ALLOW		750	750	$15,750
775-04	CREW TRAVEL & LODGING						$0
775-05	CATERING SERVICES						
	CATERING-B'FAST	18	DAYS	60	5	5,400	
	LUNCH (INCL. EXTRAS)	18	DAYS	75	10	13,500	
	SALES TAX	8.25%			18,900	1,559	$20,459
775-06	2ND MEALS/EXTRA MEALS						
	2ND MEALS	8	MEALS	50	8	3,200	
	SALES TAX	8.25%			3,200	264	$3,464
775-07	PRODUCTION EXPENDABL...						
	EXPENDABLES	3	WEEKS		500	1,500	
	SALES TAX	8.25%			1,500	124	$1,624
775-11	FIRE/POLICE						
	FIREMAN	80	HOURS		52	4,160	
	POLICE OFFICER	60	HOURS		48	2,880	
	IA	33.0%			7,040	2,323	
	FICA #1	6.2%			4,160	258	
	FICA #2	1.45%			4,160	60	
	SUI	5.4%			4,160	225	
	FUI	0.8%			4,160	33	$9,939
775-13	A/C & HEAT FEES						
	A/C HEAT FEES (OFFICE)	8	WEEKS		100	800	$800
775-14	AIRPORT PICKUP/DELIVE...						$0
775-15	LOCATION LOCK & UNLOAD						$0
775-17	GRATUITIES						
	TIPS		ALLOW		200	200	$200
775-18	OFFICE RENT/FURNITURE/...						
	OFFICE RENT/OVERHEAD/...	2	MONTHS		1,000	2,000	
	SUPPLIES		ALLOW		2,000	2,000	
	SALES TAX	8.25%			2,000	165	$4,165
775-20	LOSS & DAMAGE						
	LOSS & DAMAGE		ALLOW		1,000	1,000	$1,000
775-21	LOCATION SECURITY						
	LOCATION SECURITY (BAR...	2	WEEKS		3,000	6,000	
	NON-UNION	18%			6,000	1,080	$7,080
775-22	PARKING LOTS (FOR CREW)						
	PARKING LOT FOR CREW/...	2	WEEKS		700	1,400	$1,400

(continued)

Figure 6–4 Sample budget 1, developed for a character-driven piece (continued)

Acct #	Description	Amount	Units	X	Rate	Subtotal	Total
775-00	**LOCATION EXPENSES (CONT'D)**						
							$0
						Total For 775-00	**$75,720**
785-00	**PRODUCTION DAILIES**						
785-01	NEGATIVE RAW STOCK						
	RAW STOCK (5298 RE-CAN...	90,000	FEET		0.40	36,000	
	SALES TAX	8.25%			36,000	2,970	$38,970
785-02	DEVELOPING						
	80,000 FT DEVELOP	90,000	FEET		0.12	10,800	
	PREP @ 80,000 FEET	90,000	FEET		0.07	6,300	$17,100
785-03	TRANSFER DAILIES						
	TRANSFER TO VIDEO - 3/4"	90,000	FEET		0.24	21,600	$21,600
785-05	TRANSFER SOUND DAILIES						
	TRANSFER SOUND DAILIES		ALLOW		5,000	5,000	$5,000
785-08	SCREEN DAILIES						
	SCREEN DAILIES		ALLOW		500	500	$500
785-10	TAPE STOCK						
	TAPE STOCK - BETA 3/4" -...	25	TAPES		24	600	
	BETA SP TAPES	25	TAPES		41	1,025	
	VHS TAPES	50	TAPES		13	650	
	Sales tax	8.25%			2,275	188	$2,463
						Total For 785-00	**$85,633**
	TOTAL SHOOTING PERIOD						**$397,213**
800-00	**EDITING**						
800-01	FILM EDITOR						
	FILM EDITOR	16	WEEKS		600	9,600	
	NON-UNION	18%			9,600	1,728	$11,328
800-02	SOUND EFFECTS/MUSIC E...						
	SOUND EFFECTS EDIT		ALLOW		5,000	5,000	$5,000
800-03	MUSIC EDITING						$0
800-04	NEGATIVE CUTTING						
	NEGATIVE CUTTING	10	REELS		500	5,000	$5,000
800-06	PROJECTION						
	PROJECTION		ALLOW		500	500	$500
800-11	EDITORIAL FACILITIES/AVID						
	EDIT BAY	16	WEEKS		1,500	24,000	$24,000
800-12	EDITORIAL SUPPLIES						
	SUPPLIES/FOOD	16	WEEKS		200	3,200	
	SALES TAX	8.25%			3,200	264	$3,464
800-14	POST PROD. SUPERVISION						
	POST. SUPER	8	WEEKS		600	4,800	
	NON-UNION	18%			4,800	864	$5,664
800-18	ASSISTANT EDITOR						
	ASSISTANT EDITOR	12	WEEKS		500	6,000	

(continued)

Figure 6–4 Sample budget 1, developed for a character-driven piece (continued)

Acct #	Description	Amount	Units	X	Rate	Subtotal	Total
800-00	**EDITING (CONT'D)**						
800-18	ASSISTANT EDITOR (CONT'D)						
	NON-UNION	18%			6,000	1,080	$7,080
800-19	APPRENTICE EDITOR (INT...						$0
						Total For 800-00	**$62,036**
810-00	**MUSIC**						
810-08	COMPOSER						
	COMPOSER	8	WEEKS		600	4,800	
	NON-UNION	18%			4,800	864	$5,664
810-25	MUSIC SUPERVISOR						
	MUSIC SUPERVISOR	10	WEEKS		600	6,000	
	NON-UNION	18%			6,000	1,080	$7,080
810-26	MUSIC CLEARANCE SALA...						$0
810-27	MUSIC CLERICAL						$0
810-28	MASTER USE LICENSES/F...						
	FESTIVAL LICENSES		ALLOW		1,000	1,000	$1,000
810-29	MUSIC PUBLISHING LICEN...						$0
810-30	PRESCORE						$0
810-31	REHEARSAL MUSICIANS						
	MUSICIANS	5	PEOP...		500	2,500	
	NON-UNION	18%			2,500	450	$2,950
810-32	DEMO COSTS						$0
810-33	SCORE (FACILITIES)						
	SCORE FACILITIES	2	DAYS		1,500	3,000	$3,000
810-34	STUDIO EQUIPMENT RENT...						$0
810-35	MUSIC INSTRUMENT RENT...						$0
810-37	MUSIC TRANSFERS						
	MUSIC TRANSFERS		ALLOW		3,000	3,000	$3,000
						Total For 810-00	**$22,694**
820-00	**POSTPRODUCTION SOUND**						
820-01	DIALOGUE RECORDING (A...						
	ADR FACILITY		ALLOW		2,500	2,500	$2,500
820-03	SOUND EFFECTS (FOLEY)						
	SOUND EFFECTS/FOLEY		ALLOW		3,000	3,000	$3,000
820-06	DUBBING SESSION						
	SOUND MIX-TEMP AND FI...		ALLOW		10,000	10,000	$10,000
820-09	PURCHASED SOUND EFFE...						
	PURCHASED SOUND EFFE...		ALLOW		1,500	1,500	$1,500
820-12	MAGNETIC TAPE FOR EDIT						
	Mag Tape		ALLOW		1,000	1,000	
	Sales tax	8.25%			1,000	83	$1,083
820-13	OPTICAL NEG 35 & 35/32						
	DEVELOP OPTICAL NEG...	12,000	FEET		0.11	1,320	$1,320

(continued)

Figure 6–4 Sample budget 1, developed for a character-driven piece (continued)

Acct #	Description	Amount	Units	X	Rate	Subtotal	Total
820-00	**POSTPRODUCTION SOUND (CONT'D)**						
							$0
							Total For 820-00 $19,403
840-00	**TITLES**						
840-01	TITLES (MAIN & END)						
	MAIN AND END TITLES		ALLOW		1,500	1,500	$1,500
840-02	MAIN TITLES						$0
840-03	END TITLES						$0
840-04	MISCELLANEOUS TITLES						$0
840-05	LABORATORY PROCESSING						
	TITLE PROCESSING FILM		ALLOW		1,000	1,000	$1,000
							Total For 840-00 $2,500
850-00	**OPTICALS, MATTES, INSERTS**						
850-01	OPTICAL EFFECTS/DUPE ...						
	OPTICALS		ALLOW		3,000	3,000	$3,000
850-02	MASTER POSITIVES						$0
850-03	LABORATORY PROCESSING						$0
850-04	SPECIAL PHOTO EFFECTS						$0
850-11	PURCHASES						$0
							Total For 850-00 $3,000
860-00	**LABORATORY PROCESSING**						
860-01	REPRINTING & DEVELOPING						
	REPRINT & DEVELOP	3,000	FEET		0.22	660	$660
860-02	1ST TRIAL COMPOSITE P...						$0
860-07	ANSWER PRINT/COLOR TI...						
	ANSWER PRINT	10,000	FEET		0.86	8,600	$8,600
860-08	SYNC REEL CHARGE						
	SYNC REEL CHARGE	10	REELS		38	380	$380
860-09	TELECINE						
	TELECINE	30	HOURS		200	6,000	$6,000
860-17	LEADER & MISCELLANEOUS						
	LEADER & TAPE		ALLOW		1,000	1,000	
	Sales tax	8.25%			1,000	83	$1,083
							Total For 860-00 $16,723
	TOTAL COMPLETION PERIOD						**$126,355**
910-00	**ADMINISTRATIVE EXPENSES**						
910-01	ACCOUNTING & TERMINAL...						
	ACCOUNTING PACKAGE		ALLOW		200	200	$200
910-02	MPAA CERTIFICATE						
	MPAA CERTIFICATE		ALLOW		1,000	1,000	$1,000
910-03	POSTAGE & SHIPPING & F...						
	POSTAGE & SHIPPING		ALLOW		1,000	1,000	$1,000

(continued)

Figure 6–4 Sample budget 1, developed for a character-driven piece (continued)

Acct #	Description	Amount	Units	X	Rate	Subtotal	Total
910-00	**ADMINISTRATIVE EXPENSES (CONT'D)**						
910-04	PHOTOCOPYING (NO SCRI...						
	XEROX & FAX RENTAL	20	WEEKS	2	150	6,000	$6,000
910-05	LEGAL EXPENSES & FEES						
	LEGAL FEES & EXPENSES		ALLOW		5,000	5,000	$5,000
910-06	TELEPHONE/FACSIMILE						
	TELEPHONE & FAX	20	WEEKS		300	6,000	
	SALES TAX	8.25%			6,000	495	$6,495
910-10	SCRIPT COPYRIGHT						
	SCRIPT COPYRIGHT		ALLOW		50	50	$50
910-12	PREVIEW EXPENSE/DIST....						
	PREVIEW SCREEN & MAT...		ALLOW		1,500	1,500	$1,500
910-16	FESTIVAL EXPENSES						
	FESTIVAL EXPENSES		ALLOW		200	200	$200
910-18	RESEARCH REPORT/TITLE...						$0
910-20	CORPORATE FILING						
	Filing over Internet	1			300	300	$300
910-21	POLAROID & B/W STILL FI...						
	POLAROID & STILL FILM		ALLOW		1,000	1,000	
	SALES TAX	8.25%			1,000	83	$1,083
910-22	PAYROLL COMPANY						
	PAYROLL COMPANY	1	FLAT		2,000	2,000	$2,000
910-23	STORAGE						
	STORAGE FACILITY		ALLOW		500	500	$500
910-35	WRAP PARTY						
	WRAP PARTY		ALLOW		1,000	1,000	$1,000
						Total For 910-00	**$26,328**
	TOTAL OTHER						**$26,328**
	Completion Bond: 0.00%						**$0**
	Contingency: 10.00%						$66,164
	Overhead: 0.00%						$0
	Insurance: 2.00%						$13,233
	TOTAL ABOVE-THE-LINE						**$111,747**
	TOTAL BELOW-THE-LINE						**$549,896**
	TOTAL ABOVE- & BELOW-THE-LINE						**$661,643**
	GRAND TOTAL						**$741,040**

(continued)

Figure 6–4 Sample budget 1, developed for a character-driven piece (continued)

SAMPLE BUDGET 2

PRODUCTION NO.:
PRODUCER:
DIRECTOR:
SCRIPT DATE:
START DATE:
FINISH DATE:

DATE:
LOCATIONS: N. Y. State/Atlantic City
Based on 23-day shoot
5 weeks prep
SAG/NON-UNION CREW
FAVORED NATIONS
NOTE:

Acct#	Category Title	Page	Total
600-00	STORY	1	$52,934
610-00	PRODUCER	1	$5,500
620-00	DIRECTOR	1	$10,000
630-00	CAST	1	$96,739
650-00	TRAVEL & LIVING	2	$21,340
	TOTAL ABOVE-THE-LINE		**$186,513**
700-00	EXTRA TALENT	3	$20,796
705-00	PRODUCTION STAFF	4	$52,842
710-00	CAMERA	5	$43,331
715-00	SET DESIGN/DRESSING	5	$38,867
725-00	SET OPERATIONS	6	$26,957
730-00	ELECTRICAL	7	$30,640
750-00	PROPERTIES	7	$11,647
755-00	WARDROBE	8	$18,355
760-00	MAKEUP & HAIRSTYLISTS	8	$9,594
765-00	PRODUCTION SOUND	9	$15,110
770-00	TRANSPORTATION	9	$33,622
775-00	LOCATION EXPENSES	10	$107,891
785-00	PRODUCTION DAILIES	12	$80,677
797-00	TESTS	12	$350
	TOTAL SHOOTING PERIOD		**$490,679**
800-00	EDITING	13	$41,168
810-00	MUSIC	13	$8,000
820-00	POSTPRODUCTION SOUND	13	$25,000
840-00	TITLES	14	$3,600
850-00	OPTICALS, MATTES, & INSERTS	14	$1,900
860-00	LABORATORY PROCESSING	14	$10,799
	TOTAL COMPLETION PERIOD		**$90,467**
910-00	ADMINISTRATIVE EXPENSES	14	$64,970
920-00	PUBLICITY	15	$2,802
970-00	DELIVERY EXPENSES	15	$47,579
	TOTAL OTHER		**$115,351**
	Completion Bond: 3.00%		$26,490
	Contingency: 10.00%		$88,301
	Overhead: 0.00%		$0

(continued)

Figure 6–5 Sample budget 2, developed for a nonunion crew at a daily rate

Acct#	Category Title	Page	Total
	TOTAL ABOVE-THE-LINE		$186,513
	TOTAL BELOW-THE-LINE		$696,496
	TOTAL ABOVE- & BELOW-THE-LINE		$883,009
	GRAND TOTAL		$997,800

(continued)

Figure 6–5 Sample budget 2, developed for a nonunion crew at a daily rate (continued)

SAMPLE BUDGET 2

PRODUCTION NO.:
PRODUCER:
DIRECTOR:
SCRIPT DATE:
START DATE:
FINISH DATE:

DATE:
LOCATIONS: N.Y. State/Atlantic City
Based on 23-day shoot
5 weeks prep
SAG/NON-UNION CREW
FAVORED NATIONS
NOTE:

Acct #	Description	Amount	Units	X	Rate	Subtotal	Total
600-00	**STORY**						
600-01	RIGHTS PURCHASED						
	Purchase Price	1			50,000	50,000	$50,000
600-04	SCREENPLAY PURCHASE						
	Screenplay purchase	1			2,500	2,500	$2,500
600-11	SCRIPT COPYING						
	Script copies	100	SCRI...		4	400	$400
600	Total Fringes						
	Sales Tax	8.5%			400	34	$34
							Total For 600-00 $52,934
610-00	**PRODUCER**						
610-01	EXECUTIVE PRODUCER						
	EXEC PROD		ALLOW		500	500	$500
610-02	PRODUCER						
	PRODUCER FEE #1		ALLOW		2,500	2,500	
	PRODUCER FEE #2		ALLOW		2,500	2,500	$5,000
							Total For 610-00 $5,500
620-00	**DIRECTOR**						
620-01	DIRECTOR						
	DIRECTOR'S FEE		ALLOW		2,500	2,500	$2,500
620-04	RESEARCH CONSULTANT						
	Choreographer Expenses	1	DAY		200	200	$200
620-05	CASTING DIRECTOR						
	Casting Director		ALLOW		7,000	7,000	$7,000
620-08	CASTING EXPENSES		ALLOW		300	300	$300
							Total For 620-00 $10,000
630-00	**CAST**						
630-01	PRINCIPAL PLAYERS						
	HILDA NURSE	4	WEEKS		1,890	7,560	
	EDWIN NURSE	1	WEEK		1,890	1,890	
	KARL	2.4	WEEKS		1,890	4,536	
	JILL	1.2	WEEKS		1,890	2,268	
	MARY	1	WEEK		1,890	1,890	

(continued)

Figure 6–5 Sample budget 2, developed for a nonunion crew at a daily rate (continued)

Acct #	Description	Amount	Units	X	Rate	Subtotal	Total
630-00	**CAST (CONT'D)**						
630-01	PRINCIPAL PLAYERS (CONT'D)						
	LISA	1	WEEK		1,890	1,890	
	MARGARET	1	DAY		466	466	
	TOMMY	1	WEEK		1,890	1,890	
	URSULA NURSE	1	WEEK		1,890	1,890	
	XAVIER NURSE	3	WEEKS		1,890	5,670	
	MIKE QUACK JR	1	WEEK		1,890	1,890	
	MIKE QUACK SR	1	WEEK		1,890	1,890	
	OFFICER DRUID	5	DAYS		466	2,330	
	HOMELESS WOMAN	1	WEEK		1,890	1,890	
	Overtime	1	%	20	37,950	7,590	
	LOOPING ALLOWANCE	5	DAYS		466	2,330	
	TRAVELING ALLOWANCE	13	DAYS		466	6,058	$53,928
630-02	DAY PLAYERS						
	TICKET MAN	2	DAYS		466	932	
	FAT WOMAN	1	DAY		466	466	
	OLD MAN	1	DAY		466	466	
	CHARLIE	2	DAYS		466	932	
	DEALER	2	DAYS		466	932	
	SCOTT CARLSON	2	DAYS		466	932	
	NICK	1	DAY		466	466	
	BUFFY TOMSON	1	DAY		466	466	
	DR. CLARKE	1	DAY		466	466	
	Overtime	1	%	20	6,058	1,212	
	TRAVELING ALLOWANCE	2	DAYS		466	932	$8,202
630-03	REHEARSAL						
	Rehearsal, principal players	3	DAYS	5	466	6,990	$6,990
630-06	SAG PER DIEM						
	See 650 Account						$0
630-07	MEAL PENALTIES						
	MEAL PENALTIES		ALLOW		500	500	$500
630-09	MEDICAL EXAMS						
	Med exams		ALLOW		300	300	$300
630-10	TUTOR/WELFARE WORKER						$0
630	Total Fringes						
	SAG CORP	13.3%			69,120	9,193	
	NONUNION	15.5%			69,120	10,714	
	Agency Fee	10.0%			69,120	6,912	$26,819
						Total For 630-00	**$96,739**
650-00	**TRAVEL & LIVING**						
650-01	PRODUCER'S TRAVEL						
	Roundtrip airfare LA-NYC	4	FLIGHTS		400	1,600	$1,600
650-03	WRITER'S TRAVEL						$0
650-03	WRITER'S LIVING						$0
650-04	PRODUCER'S LIVING						

(continued)

Figure 6–5 Sample budget 2, developed for a nonunion crew at a daily rate (continued)

Acct #	Description	Amount	Units	X	Rate	Subtotal	Total
650-00	**TRAVEL & LIVING (CONT'D)**						
650-04	PRODUCER'S LIVING (CONT'D)						
	PRODUCER'S LIVING-ASB...	26	DAYS	2	16	832	
	NEW JERSEY	3	DAYS	2	30	180	$1,012
650-06	CAST TRAVEL/PER DIEM						
	LA-NY/first class	3	FARES		800	2,400	
	LA-NY/first class	1	FLAT		2,500	2,500	
	HILDA NURSE	24	DAYS		53	1,272	
	EDWIN NURSE	20	DAYS		53	1,060	
	KARL	13	DAYS		53	689	
	JILL	8	DAYS		53	424	
	MARY	6	DAYS		53	318	
	MARGARET	7	DAYS		53	371	
	TOMMY	6	DAYS		53	318	
	URSULA NURSE	6	DAYS		53	318	
	XAVIER NURSE	7	DAYS		53	371	
	MIKE QUACK JR	6	DAYS		53	318	
	MIKE QUACK SR	6	DAYS		53	318	
	OFFICER DRUID	6	DAYS		53	318	
	HOMELESS WOMAN	6	DAYS		53	318	
	TICKET MAN	3	DAYS		53	159	
	FAT WOMAN	3	DAYS		53	159	
	OLD MAN	1	DAY		53	53	
	CHARLIE	1	DAY		53	53	
	DEALER	2	DAYS		53	106	
	SCOTT CARLSON	2	DAYS		53	106	
	NICK	1	DAY		53	53	
	BUFFY TOMSON	1	DAY		53	53	
	DR. CLARKE	1	DAY		53	53	$12,108
650-08	CAST TRAVEL						
	Cast to set Train/Car	30	TRIPS		70	2,100	$2,100
650-09	CAST LIVING						
	Cast living	1	DAY	145	16	2,320	
	New Jersey	3	DAYS	5	30	450	
	Cast Living New York	5	DAYS		150	750	
	Star Cast Living	7	DAYS		100	700	$4,220
650	Total Fringes						
	N.J. sales tax	6.0%			2,950	177	
	Sales tax	8.5%			1,450	123	
	A.P. sales tax	0%			1,012	0	$300
						Total For 650-00	**$21,340**
	TOTAL ABOVE-THE-LINE						**$186,513**

(continued)

Figure 6–5 Sample budget 2, developed for a nonunion crew at a daily rate (continued)

Acct #	Description	Amount	Units	X	Rate	Subtotal	Total
700-00	**EXTRA TALENT**						
700-02	EXTRAS & STAND-INS						
	SAG EXTRAS	1	DAY	40	102	4,080	
	DAY PLAY EXTRAS Man D...	1	DAY	20	25	500	
	CONTINUITY EXTRAS	1	DAY	130	40	5,200	
	Travel Time/Expenses	10	ALLOW		70	700	$10,480
700-03	WELFARE WORKER						
	TUTOR/WELFARE WORKER	17	DAYS		200	3,400	$3,400
700-05	EXTRAS CASTING						
	Extras Casting Agent	8	WEEKS		250	2,000	
	Extras Advertisement	2	ADS		135	270	$2,270
700-08	ALLOWANCES-CAR						
	Miles/report to location		ALLOW		200	200	$200
700-09	STUNT COORDINATOR						
	STUNT COORDINATOR	2	DAYS		871	1,742	$1,742
700	Total Fringes						
	SAG CORP	13.3%			5,822	774	
	NONUNION	15.5%			11,222	1,739	
	N.J. sales tax	6.0%			270	16	
	Agency fee	10.0%			1,742	174	$2,704
						Total For 700-00	**$20,796**
705-00	**PRODUCTION STAFF**						
705-01	LINE PRODUCER/UPM						
	LINE PRODUCER/UPM	9	WEEKS		1,000	9,000	
	Kit rental		ALLOW		75	75	$9,075
705-02	PRODUCTION COORDINAT...						
	COORDINATOR	44	DAYS		125	5,500	$5,500
705-03	1ST ASSISTANT DIRECTOR						
	AD	42	DAYS		125	5,250	$5,250
705-04	2ND ASSISTANT DIRECTOR						
	2nd AD	28	DAYS		100	2,800	$2,800
705-05	2ND 2ND ASSISTANT DIR						
	2nd 2nd AD	25	DAYS		80	2,000	$2,000
705-06	SCRIPT SUPERVISOR						
	Script supervisor	29	DAYS		125	3,625	$3,625
705-07	APOC						
	Coordinator #2	41	DAYS		80	3,280	$3,280
705-08	PRODUCT PLACEMENT						
	PRODUCT PLACEMENT	ALLOW			200	200	$200
705-10	PRODUCTION ASSISTANTS						
	Key Set PA	28	DAYS		80	2,240	
	Set PA	26	DAYS		50	1,300	
	Set PA	26	DAYS		50	1,300	
	Set PA	10	DAYS		50	500	
	PA/Talent Driver	23	DAYS		50	1,150	
	Office PA	15	DAYS		70	1,050	

(continued)

Figure 6–5 Sample budget 2, developed for a nonunion crew at a daily rate (continued)

Acct #	Description	Amount	Units	X	Rate	Subtotal	Total
705-00	**PRODUCTION STAFF (CONT'D)**						
705-10	PRODUCTION ASSISTANTS (CONT'D)						
	Office PA	50	DAYS		50	2,500	
	Car Rental Allowance	4	WEEKS	2	50	400	$10,440
705-11	PREPRODUCTION EXPEN...						
	Meals		ALLOW		1,400	1,400	
	Office Supplies		ALLOW		1,400	1,400	$2,800
705	Total Fringes						
	Crew Overtime	15.0%			19,175	2,876	
	NONUNION	15.5%			30,695	4,758	
	Sales Tax	8.5%			2,800	238	$7,872
						Total For 705-00	**$52,842**
710-00	**CAMERA**						
710-01	DIRECTOR OF PHOTOGRA...						
	Prep	19	DAYS		150	2,850	
	Shoot	24	DAYS		300	7,200	
	Kit Rental	4	WEEKS		100	400	$10,450
710-03	1ST ASST CAMERAMAN						
	1ST AC	27	DAYS		125	3,375	$3,375
710-04	2ND ASST CAMERAMAN						
	2ND AC	27	DAYS		100	2,700	$2,700
710-05	FILM LOADER						
	LOADER	23	DAYS		80	1,840	$1,840
710-06	STILL PHOTOGRAPHER						
	PHOTOGRAPHER		ALLOW		500	500	
	EXPENDABLES/SUPPLIES		ALLOW		700	700	$1,200
710-08	CAMERA RENTALS						
	Camera Package (vid tap inc)	4	WEEKS		4,500	18,000	$18,000
710-09	CAMERA SUPPLIES						
	Camera SUPPLIES		ALLOW		500	500	$500
710-11	CAM ACCESORIES/VIDEO...						
	other toys		ALLOW		250	250	$250
710-20	LOSS, DAMAGE & REPAIR		ALLOW		1,200	1,200	$1,200
710	Total Fringes						
	Crew Overtime	15.0%			6,075	911	
	NONUNION	15.5%			18,465	2,862	
	Sales Tax	8.5%			500	43	$3,816
						Total For 710-00	**$43,331**
715-00	**SET DESIGN/DRESSING**						
715-01	PRODUCTION DESIGNER						
	PROD. DESIGNER	54	DAYS		125	6,750	$6,750
715-02	ART DIRECTOR						
	ART DIRECTOR	40	DAYS		125	5,000	$5,000
715-03	SET DESIGNER/LEAD MAN						
	LEAD MAN	23	DAYS		100	2,300	$2,300

(continued)

Figure 6–5 Sample budget 2, developed for a nonunion crew at a daily rate (continued)

Acct #	Description	Amount	Units	X	Rate	Subtotal	Total
715-00	**SET DESIGN/DRESSING (CONT'D)**						
715-04	SET DRESSER						
	DRESSER	54	DAYS		80	4,320	
	Carpenters/local hire	26	DAYS		80	2,080	
	Additional Carpenter	5	DAYS		80	400	
	Painters/local hire	20	DAYS		80	1,600	$8,400
715-05	RENTALS						
	Rentals/non-taxed		ALLOW		2,000	2,000	$2,000
715-06	SUPPLIES						
	Materials		ALLOW		4,500	4,500	
	Purchases		ALLOW		2,500	2,500	$7,000
715-10	KIT RENTAL		ALLOW		975	975	$975
715-11	ART PAs						
	PA	28	DAYS		50	1,400	$1,400
715	Total Fringes						
	Crew Overtime	15.0%			5,000	750	
	NONUNION	15.5%			23,850	3,697	
	Sales Tax	8.5%			7,000	595	$5,042
						Total For 715-00	**$38,867**
725-00	**SET OPERATIONS**						
725-01	1ST COMPANY GRIP						
	Key grip	28	DAYS		125	3,500	$3,500
725-02	BEST BOY GRIP						
	GRIP	26	DAYS		100	2,600	
	COMPANY GRIP	26	DAYS	0	80	0	$2,600
725-03	GRIPS						
	GRIP	23	DAYS		80	1,840	
	ADDITIONAL LABOR	10	DAYS		80	800	$2,640
725-05	CAMERA DOLLIES						
	DOLLY/W/ALL ACCES.	4	WEEKS	0	1,200	0	$0
725-08	GRIP EQUIPMENT RENTALS						
	GRIP RENTALS		ALLOW		8,500	8,500	$8,500
725-09	GRIP PURCHASES						
	PURCHASES		ALLOW		500	500	
	TRUCK BUILD		ALLOW		500	500	$1,000
725-10	KIT RENTAL						
	KIT RENTAL		ALLOW		400	400	$400
725-11	CRAFT SERVICE						
	CRAFT PERSON	24	DAYS		50	1,200	
	CRAFT FOOD	5	WEEKS		600	3,000	$4,200
725-25	MISCELLANEOUS EXPENSE						
	Miscellaneous		ALLOW		250	250	$250
725-20	LOSS, DAMAGE & REPAIR		ALLOW		750	750	$750
725	Total Fringes						
	Crew Overtime	15.0%			8,740	1,311	
	NONUNION	15.5%			9,940	1,541	

(continued)

Figure 6–5 Sample budget 2, developed for a nonunion crew at a daily rate (continued)

Acct #	Description	Amount	Units	X	Rate	Subtotal	Total
725-00	**SET OPERATIONS (CONT'D)**						
725	Total Fringes (CONT'D)						
	N.J. sales tax	6.0%			3,000	180	
	Sales tax	8.5%			1,000	85	$3,117
						Total For 725-00	**$26,957**
730-00	**ELECTRICAL**						
730-01	GAFFER						
	Gaffer	28	DAYS		125	3,500	$3,500
730-02	BEST BOY						
	Best Boy	23	DAYS		100	2,300	$2,300
730-03	ELECTRICIANS						
	ELECTRIC	23	DAYS		80	1,840	
	SWING/DRIVER	25	DAYS		80	2,000	$3,840
730-04	LOCATION REGGING/STRIKE		ALLOW		250	250	$250
730-05	GLOBES/CARBONS/SUPP...		ALLOW		2,000	2,000	$2,000
730-06	POWER						
	POWER		ALLOW		1,000	1,000	$1,000
730-07	GENERATOR RENTAL						
	Rental	4	WEEKS		1,000	4,000	$4,000
730-08	ELECTRICAL EQUIP RENT...		ALLOW		8,500	8,500	$8,500
730-10	KIT RENTAL						
	KIT RENTAL		ALLOW		400	400	$400
730-13	MISCELLANEOUS EXPENSE						
	MISC.		ALLOW		250	250	$250
730-20	LOSS, DAMAGE, & REPAIR		ALLOW		1,200	1,200	$1,200
730	Total Fringes						
	Crew Overtime	15.0%			9,640	1,446	
	NONUNION	15.5%			9,640	1,494	
	N.J. sales tax	6.0%			2,000	120	
	Sales tax	8.5%			4,000	340	$3,400
						Total For 730-00	**$30,640**
750-00	**PROPERTIES**						
750-01	PROPERTY MASTER						
	Prop Master	12	DAYS		125	1,500	
	Prop Master	26	DAYS		80	2,080	$3,580
750-02	ASSISTANT PROPERTY M...						
	PROP PA	32	DAYS		50	1,600	$1,600
750-05	PICTURE VEHICLE RENTALS						
	Ambulance (Product Placed)						
	Police Car (Product Placed)						
	Academy Bus (Product Plac...						
	Old Cadillac		ALLOW		150	150	
	Lincoln Continental		ALLOW		150	150	
	'77 Gray Cadillac		ALLOW		150	150	
	'79 Gr Chevy Nova		ALLOW		150	150	
	'86 White Caddy Seville		ALLOW		150	150	$750

(continued)

Figure 6–5 Sample budget 2, developed for a nonunion crew at a daily rate (continued)

Acct #	Description	Amount	Units	X	Rate	Subtotal	Total
750-00	**PROPERTIES (CONT'D)**						
750-08	PROP RENTALS						
	RENTALS		ALLOW		1,500	1,500	$1,500
750-09	PROP PURCHASES						
	PURCHASES		ALLOW		1,500	1,500	$1,500
750-10	KIT RENTALS						
	KIT RENTALS		ALLOW	0	150	0	$0
750-12	EXPENDABLES		ALLOW		500	500	$500
750-20	LOSS, DAMAGE & REPAIRS		ALLOW		750	750	$750
750	Total Fringes						
	Crew Overtime	15.0%			3,580	537	
	NONUNION	15.5%			5,180	803	
	Sales Tax	8.5%			1,500	128	$1,467
						Total For 750-00	**$11,647**
755-00	**WARDROBE**						
755-04	COSTUME DESIGNER						
	COSTUME DESIGNER	41	ALLOW		125	5,125	$5,125
755-03	ASSISTING WARDROBE P...						
	WARD. ASST.	35	DAYS		100	3,500	
	WARDROBE PA/SWING	21	DAYS		50	1,050	$4,550
755-06	ALTERATIONS - L&M		ALLOW		100	100	$100
755-07	CLEANING & DYEING		ALLOW		500	500	$500
755-08	WARDROBE RENTALS		ALLOW		2,200	2,200	$2,200
755-09	WARDROBE PURCHASES						
	PURCHASES		ALLOW		2,200	2,200	$2,200
755-10	KIT RENTAL						
	KIT RENTALS		ALLOW		200	200	$200
755-20	LOSS, DAMAGE & REPAIRS						
	L&D		ALLOW		500	500	$500
755	Total Fringes						
	Crew Overtime	15.0%			8,625	1,294	
	NONUNION	15.5%			9,675	1,500	
	Sales Tax	8.5%			2,200	187	$2,980
						Total For 755-00	**$18,355**
760-00	**MAKEUP & HAIRSTYLISTS**						
760-01	MAKEUP & HAIR ARTIST						
	M/U/HAIRSTYLIST	27	DAYS		125	3,375	$3,375
760-02	ASSISTANT MAKEUP/HAI...						
	ASST. HAIR AND M/U	24	DAYS		100	2,400	$2,400
760-03	MAKEUP/HAIR PA						
	Makeup/Hair PA Bus Station	5	DAYS		100	500	$500
760-06	WIG & HAIR PURCHASE						
	WIG/HAIR PURCHASE		ALLOW		350	350	$350
760-09	MAKEUP SUPPLIES/APPLI...						
	MAKEUP SUPPLIES		ALLOW		700	700	$700

(continued)

Figure 6–5 Sample budget 2, developed for a nonunion crew at a daily rate (continued)

Acct #	Description	Amount	Units	X	Rate	Subtotal	Total
760-00	**MAKEUP&HAIRTSTYLISTS (CONT'D)**						
760-10	MAKEUP/HAIR KIT RENTALS						
	KIT RENTAL	4	WEEKS	2	50	400	$400
760-11	BLOOD/GORE		ALLOW	0	1,200	0	$0
760	Total Fringes						
	Crew Overtime	15.0%			5,775	866	
	NONUNION	15.5%			6,275	973	
	Sales Tax	8.5%			350	30	$1,869
						Total For 760-00	**$9,594**
765-00	**PRODUCTION SOUND**						
765-01	SOUND MIXER						
	SOUND MIXER	24	DAYS		125	3,000	$3,000
765-02	BOOM MAN						
	BOOM MAN	23	DAYS		100	2,300	$2,300
765-06	SOUND EQUIP RENTALS						
	FULL PACKAGE	23	DAYS		175	4,025	
	SPECIAL RENTALS		ALLOW		400	400	
	Walkie Talkies	4	WEEKS		410	1,640	$6,065
765-11	PURCHASES						
	408 Ampex Rolls	23	DAYS	3	7	483	
	DAT Tapes	10	TAPES		10	100	
	BATTERIES AND MISC	23	DAYS		15	345	$928
765-20	LOSS & DAMAGE						
	L&D		ALLOW		1,200	1,200	$1,200
765	Total Fringes						
	Crew Overtime	15.0%			5,300	795	
	NONUNION	15.5%			5,300	822	$1,617
						Total For 765-00	**$15,110**
770-00	**TRANSPORTATION**						
770-01	MESSENGER SERVICE						
	MESSENGER SERVICE		ALLOW		275	275	$275
770-02	TEAMSTERS						
	Teamsters	3	DAYS	2	500	3,000	
	Teamster Per Diem	3	ALLOW	2	25	150	$3,150
770-06	FUEL & TOLLS						
	FUEL		ALLOW		5,000	5,000	
	TOLLS		ALLOW		500	500	$5,500
770-10	PRODUCTION VEHICLES						
	PRODUCTION CUBE	6	WEEKS		275	1,650	
	ART CUBE	8	WEEKS		275	2,200	
	G/E TRUCK	4.5	WEEKS	0	275	0	
	CAMERA TRUCK	4.5	WEEKS		275	1,238	
	PROPS CARGO	6	WEEKS		250	1,500	
	WARDROBE TRUCK	4.5	WEEKS		275	1,238	
	Lumber & Labor - Truck Guts		ALLOW		500	500	

(continued)

Figure 6–5 Sample budget 2, developed for a nonunion crew at a daily rate (continued)

Acct #	Description	Amount	Units	X	Rate	Subtotal	Total
770-00	**TRANSPORTATION (CONT'D)**						
770-10	PRODUCTION VEHICLES (CONT'D)						
	Production Car	8	WEEKS		170	1,360	
	Production 15-pass.	5	WEEKS		270	1,350	
	Production 15-pass.	5	WEEKS		270	1,350	
	Location Car	8	WEEKS		170	1,360	
	Production Minivan	4	WEEKS		250	1,000	
	Producer's Car	4.5	WEEKS		170	765	
	Executive Producer Car	5	WEEKS		170	850	
	3 Vehicle Weekly Allowance	8	WEEKS	4	50	1,600	
	Additional Car	2.5	WEEKS		170	425	$18,386
770-20	LOSS, DAMAGE, REPAIRS		ALLOW		1,500	1,500	$1,500
770-28	ALL OTHER TRANSPORTA...						
	Cab Allowance		ALLOW		500	500	$500
770-30	PREPRO/NONLOCAL CRE...						
	PrePro Crew Travel time	50			25	1,250	
	Crew Travel time (N.J.)	50			25	1,250	$2,500
770	Total Fringes						
	Teamster Fringes	29.0%			3,150	914	
	Crew Overtime	15.0%			3,150	473	
	Sales Tax	8.5%			5,000	425	$1,811
						Total For 770-00	**$33,622**
775-00	**LOCATION EXPENSES**						
775-01	SURVEY EXPENSE						
	Tech Scout/Expenses		ALLOW		1,200	1,200	$1,200
775-02	LOCATION STAFF						
	LOCATION MANAGER	48	DAYS		125	6,000	
	LOCATION PA	38	DAYS		50	1,900	$7,900
775-03	SITE RENTALS/PERMITS/L...						
	Newman House		ALLOW		1,500	1,500	
	Holding & Lunch Site Newman		ALLOW		1,000	1,000	
	Quib House		ALLOW		1,500	1,500	
	Holding & Lunch Site Quib...		ALLOW		900	900	
	Jackie & Mary's Rm - Holida...		ALLOW		500	500	
	Holding & Lunch Site Hotel		ALLOW		200	200	
	Bob's TV Store		ALLOW		50	50	
	City Boardwalk		ALLOW	0	400	0	
	Bus Station		ALLOW		4,000	4,000	
	Bus Station - Women's Bath...		ALLOW		300	300	
	Holding & Lunch Site Bathro...		ALLOW		200	200	
	Casino - Interiors		ALLOW		500	500	
	Church (Incl. Holding)		ALLOW		400	400	
	Cocktail Lounge		ALLOW		150	150	
	Pawn Shop		ALLOW	0	400	0	
	Holding & Lunch Site Pawn		ALLOW		200	200	
	Donut Shop		ALLOW		500	500	

(continued)

Figure 6–5 Sample budget 2, developed for a nonunion crew at a daily rate (continued)

Acct #	Description	Amount	Units	X	Rate	Subtotal	Total
775-00	**LOCATION EXPENSE (CONT'D)**						
775-03	SITE RENTALS/PERMITS/LIC. (CONT'D)						
	Hospital		ALLOW		250	250	
	Exterior Liquor Store		ALLOW		300	300	
	High School		ALLOW	0	500	0	
	Holding & Lunch Site High S...		ALLOW		200	200	
	Movie Theater		ALLOW		300	300	
	Holding & Lunch Site Theater		ALLOW		200	200	
	Holding Bus Station	12	DAYS		50	600	
	PERMITS		ALLOW	0	500	0	
	Electricity & Water		ALLOW		800	800	
	Dumpster		ALLOW		600	600	
	Location Supplies		ALLOW		500	500	$15,650
775-04	HOTEL & LODGING						
	CREW LIVING NJ PART PR...	20	NIGHTS	10	16	3,200	
	CREW LIVING NJ PARK PR...	27	NIGHTS	38	16	16,416	
	CREW LIVING NJ PARK-W...	7	NIGHTS	7	16	784	
	CREW LIVING-other NJ	3	NIGHTS	30	30	2,700	
	ADDITIONAL HOUSING		ALLOW		500	500	$23,600
775-05	CATERING SERVICES						
	CATERING - 60 @ $12/DAY	23	DAYS	60	12	16,560	
	EXTRAS CATERING Man D...	200	DAYS		6	1,200	$17,760
775-06	MEAL ALLOWANCES/2ND...						
	Prepro Per Diem	24	DAYS	7	10	1,680	
	PerDiem - Weekend crew m...	5	DAYS	40	15	3,000	
	Per Diem Shoot	23	DAYS	50	10	11,500	
	SECOND MEALS	10	DAYS	40	10	4,000	
	EVENING CRAFT SERVICES		ALLOW		800	800	$20,980
775-07	PRODUCTION EXPENDABL...		ALLOW		1,200	1,200	$1,200
775-11	FIRE/POLICE						
	FIREMAN/POLICE		ALLOW		2,100	2,100	$2,100
775-21	LOCATION SECURITY						
	Prepro	12	NIGHTS		192	2,304	
	Shoot	28	NIGHTS		100	2,800	
	Additional Man Days	10	NIGHTS		120	1,200	
	Hotel Security	26	NIGHTS		100	2,600	$8,904
775-14	AIRPORT PICKUP/DELIVERY						
	CREW/CAST	10	ALLOW		95	950	$950
775-17	GRATUITIES		ALLOW		300	300	$300
775-18	OFFICE FURNITURE		ALLOW		250	250	$250
775-19	LOCATION MEDICAL EXPE...		ALLOW		100	100	$100
775-23	PHOTO SHOOT		ALLOW		1,200	1,200	$1,200
775-25	SHIPPING		ALLOW		250	250	$250
775-20	LOSS & DAMAGE						
	L&D		ALLOW		500	500	$500
775	Total Fringes						
	Teamster Fringes	29.0%			2,100	609	

(continued)

Figure 6–5 Sample budget 2, developed for a nonunion crew at a daily rate (continued)

Acct #	Description	Amount	Units	X	Rate	Subtotal	Total
775-00	**LOCATION EXPENSES (CONT'D)**						
775	Total Fringes (CONT'D)						
	NONUNION	15.5%			7,900	1,225	
	N.J. sales tax	6.0%			28,400	1,704	
	Sales Tax	8.5%			17,760	1,510	$5,047
						Total For 775-00	**$107,891**
785-00	**PRODUCTION DAILIES**						
785-01	NEGATIVE RAW STOCK						
	5293 KODAK STOCK	25,875	FEET		0.46	11,903	
	5279 FACTORY SEALED	77,625	FEET		0.48	37,260	
	SHIPPING FILM TO LOCAT...		ALLOW		750	750	$49,913
785-02	DEVELOPING						
	PROCESS NORMAL/PREP	103,500	FEET		0.105	10,868	
	Shipping Film To Lab	23	DAYS		75	1,725	$12,593
785-03	TRANSFER DAILIES						
	TRANSFER TO BETA (64 H...	103,500	FEET	0.85	0.1284	11,296	
	PREP FOR TRANSFER		ALLOW	0	375	0	$11,296
785-05	TRANSFER SOUND DAILIES						
	NO COSTS PER LAB						$0
785-08	SCREEN DAILIES						
	PROJECTED DAILIES (8,00...	8,000	FEET		0.186	1,488	
	SCREENING		ALLOW		500	500	
	DATA DISK	30	DISK		10	300	$2,288
785-09	VIDEOTAPE TRANSFERS						
	Dub 3 VHS Tapes from Beta	23	DAYS	3	15	1,035	
	Shipping Dailies from L/A	23		2	50	2,300	$3,335
785-10	TAPE STOCK						
	BETA SP TAPES	25	TAPES		32.47	812	
	DAT TAPES	25	TAPES		10.83	271	$1,083
785	Total Fringes						
	Sales Tax	8.5%			1,988	169	$169
						Total For 785-00	**$80,677**
797-00	**TESTS**						
797-01	TEST #1						
	TEST		ALLOW		350	350	$350
						Total For 797-00	**$350**
	TOTAL SHOOTING PERIOD						**$490,679**
800-00	**EDITING**						
800-01	FILM EDITOR						
	Editor	14	WEEKS		700	9,800	$9,800
800-18	ASSISTANT EDITOR						
	Assistant Editor	6	WEEKS		500	3,000	$3,000
800-03	MUSIC EDITING						$0
800-04	NEGATIVE CUTTING						

(continued)

Figure 6–5 Sample budget 2, developed for a nonunion crew at a daily rate (continued)

Acct #	Description	Amount	Units	X	Rate	Subtotal	Total
800-00	**EDITING (CONT'D)**						
800-04	NEGATIVE CUTTING (CONT'D)						
	NEGATIVE CUTTING		ALLOW		5,500	5,500	$5,500
800-05	DIALOGUE EDITING						
	DIALOGUE EDITING		ALLOW		1,750	1,750	$1,750
800-11	EDITORIAL FACILITIES						
	EDIT SUITE	3.5	MON...		378	1,323	
	EDIT SYSTEM	14	WEEKS		1,000	14,000	
	SET UP CHARGE		ALLOW		350	350	
	DIGITAL DECK	5	WEEKS	0	150	0	
	PARKING		ALLOW		100	100	
	MEAL ALLOWANCE	12	WEEKS		75	900	$16,673
800-12	EDITORIAL SUPPLIES						
	Supplies		ALLOW		750	750	$750
800-17	VIDEOTAPES/MISC.						
	Videotapes		ALLOW		1,200	1,200	
	Messenger	23	DAYS		15	345	$1,545
800	Total Fringes						
	NONUNION	15.5%			12,800	1,984	
	Sales Tax	8.5%			1,950	166	$2,150
						Total For 800-00	**$41,168**
810-00	**MUSIC**						
810-00	MUSIC						
	MUSIC		ALLOW		8,000	8,000	$8,000
						Total For 810-00	**$8,000**
820-00	**POSTPRODUCTION SOUND**						
820-01	DIALOGUE RECORDING (A...						
	ADR		ALLOW		4,000	4,000	$4,000
820-02	NARRATION RECORDING						
	NARRATION RECORDING		ALLOW		1,000	1,000	$1,000
820-03	SOUND EFFECTS (FOLEY)		ALLOW		4,000	4,000	$4,000
820-06	DUBBING SESSION						
	DUBBING/MIX		ALLOW		8,000	8,000	$8,000
820-07	SOUND TRANSFER 35 & 3...						
	SOUND TRANSFER		ALLOW		5,000	5,000	$5,000
820-09	PURCHASED SOUND EFFE...						
	PURCHASED SOUND EFFE...		ALLOW		1,500	1,500	$1,500
820-13	PRINT MASTER TO DA88		ALLOW		1,000	1,000	$1,000
820-14	PREVIEW EXPENSES		ALLOW		500	500	$500
						Total For 820-00	**$25,000**
840-00	**TITLES**						
840-01	TITLES (MAIN & END)						
	16 Cards White over Black		ALLOW		1,120	1,120	
	3 Minute End Crawl (Title Ho...		ALLOW		1,480	1,480	$2,600

(continued)

Figure 6–5 Sample budget 2, developed for a nonunion crew at a daily rate (continued)

Acct #	Description	Amount	Units	X	Rate	Subtotal	Total
840-00	**TITLES (CONT'D)**						
840-02	MISCELLANEOUS TITLES		ALLOW		200	200	$200
840-05	LABORATORY PROCESSING						
	LAB PROCESSING		ALLOW		800	800	$800
						Total For 840-00	**$3,600**
850-00	**OPTICALS, MATTES, & INSERTS**						
850-01	OPTICAL EFFECTS/DUPE...						
	5 Dissolves (Title House Bid)		ALLOW		1,400	1,400	$1,400
850-03	LABORATORY PROCESSING		ALLOW		500	500	$500
						Total For 850-00	**$1,900**
860-00	**LABORATORY PROCESSING**						
860-01	REPRINTING & DEVELOPING						
	REPRINTING & DEVELOPING		ALLOW		1,000	1,000	$1,000
860-07	ANSWER PRINT						
	Answer print	9,700	FEET		0.842	8,167	
	2 Ck Prints/No Cost Per Fot...						$8,167
860-08	SYNC REEL CHARGE						
	Sync reel charge	11	REEL		38	418	$418
860-09	DYNAMIC LIGHT CONTROL...						
	DYNAMIC LIGHT CONTROL...		ALLOW		400	400	$400
860-17	LEADER & MISCELLANEOUS						
	Videotape/other		ALLOW		750	750	$750
860	Total Fringes						
	Sales Tax	8.5%			750	64	$64
						Total For 860-00	**$10,799**
	TOTAL COMPLETION PERIOD						**$90,467**
910-00	**ADMINISTRATIVE EXPENSES**						
910-01	ACCOUNTING & TERMINAL...						
	ACCOUNTANT (PRODUCTI...	9	WEEKS		800	7,200	
	ACCOUNTANT (POST-1 day...	15	WEEKS		175	2,625	
	COMPUTER RENTAL	2.5	MONTHS	0	100	0	$9,825
910-02	MPAA CERTIFICATE						$0
910-03	POSTAGE/STATIONERY/S...						
	SHIPPING		ALLOW		2,000	2,000	$2,000
910-04	PHOTOCOPYING (No Scripts)						
	PHOTOCOPYING (Production)		ALLOW		1,500	1,500	$1,500
910-05	LEGAL EXPENSE & FEES						
	Legal Fee		ALLOW		15,000	15,000	
	Vetting screenplay		ALLOW		400	400	
	Clearance Research		ALLOW		1,000	1,000	
	Clearance Checks		ALLOW		1,000	1,000	$17,400
910-06	TELEPHONE/FACSIMILE/T...						
	TELEPHONE/FAX		ALLOW		7,250	7,250	

(continued)

Figure 6–5 Sample budget 2, developed for a nonunion crew at a daily rate (continued)

Acct #	Description	Amount	Units	X	Rate	Subtotal	Total
910-00	**ADMINISTRATIVE EXPENSES (CONT'D)**						
910-06	TELEPHONE/FACSIMILE/TELEX (CONT'D)						
	PAGERS	5	PAGERS		60	300	$7,550
910-08	INSURANCE						
	Bid (Including E&O)		ALLOW		18,792	18,792	$18,792
910-14	PARKING LOT EXPENSES						
	PARKING		ALLOW		1,500	1,500	$1,500
910-17	OFFICE RENT & OTH EXPE...						
	OFFICE RENT (NEW JERS...	30	DAYS		16	480	
	Office Rent (New York)	2	MON...		500	1,000	
	Office Supplies		ALLOW		750	750	
	Polaroid		ALLOW		800	800	
	Temporary Office Expenses		ALLOW		300	300	
	PRODUCTION SOFTWARE		ALLOW		630	630	$3,960
910-22	PAYROLL EXPENSE						
	Payroll Expense (incl fringe		ALLOW		500	500	
	Additional Payroll Exp (P&W...	1		60	7	420	$920
910	Total Fringes						
	NONUNION	15.5%			9,825	1,523	$1,523
						Total For 910-00	**$64,970**
920-00	**PUBLICITY**						
920-01	UNIT PUBLICIST						
	Unit Publicist		ALLOW		1,000	1,000	$1,000
920-02	SPECIAL STILL PHOTOGR...						
	Special Publicity Still Photog	1	FLAT		500	500	$500
920-03	STILL FILM & PROCESSING						
	Publicity Materials		ALLOW		1,200	1,200	$1,200
920	Total Fringes						
	Sales Tax	8.5%			1,200	102	$102
						Total For 920-00	**$2,802**
970-00	**DELIVERY EXPENSES**						
970-00	Film and Audio Elements						
	35mm Interpostive	9,700	ALLOW		0.964	9,351	
	35mm Internegative	9,700	ALLOW		0.842	8,167	
	Textless interpo/titles						
	Check Print	9,700	ALLOW		0.202	1,959	
	35mm Release Print	9,700	ALLOW		0.105	1,019	
	35mm Optical Sound track	9,700	ALLOW		0.39	3,783	
	M&E (on DAT)		ALLOW		5,000	5,000	
	3-track mono D-M-E on DA88		ALLOW		400	400	
	Video transfer (film to tape w		ALLOW		12,500	12,500	
	D1 NTSC Video master		ALLOW		900	900	
	D1 PAL Master		ALLOW		1,800	1,800	
	Stereo (Dolby) License		ALLOW		2,500	2,500	
	VHS Screeners		ALLOW		200	200	$47,579

(continued)

Figure 6–5 Sample budget 2, developed for a nonunion crew at a daily rate (continued)

Acct #	Description	Amount	Units	X	Rate	Subtotal	Total
970-00	**DELIVERY EXPENSES(CONT'D)**						
970-50	Advertising and Pub Materials						
	20 Color Slide Dupes	20	SLIDES	2	0	0	
	Black & White Copy Negs/Pr...	20	NEGS	2	0	0	$0
							Total For 970-00 $47,579
	TOTAL OTHER						**$115,351**
	Completion Bond: 3.00%						$26,490
	Contingency: 10.00%						$88,301
	Overhead: 0.00%						$0
	TOTAL ABOVE-THE-LINE						**$186,513**
	TOTAL BELOW-THE-LINE						**$696,496**
	TOTAL ABOVE- & BELOW-THE-LINE						**$883,009**
	GRAND TOTAL						**$997,800**

Figure 6–5 Sample budget 2, developed for a nonunion crew at a daily rate (continued)

SAMPLE BUDGET 3

PRODUCTION NO.:
PRODUCERS:
DIRECTOR:
SCRIPT DATE:
START DATE:
FINISH DATE:

DATE:
LOCATION: LOS ANGELES
5 WEEKS SHOOT - 5 DAY WEEK
LOCAL NONUNION CREW
SAG LOW-BUDGET AGRMT.

NOT FINAL SHOOTING BUDGET

Acct#	Category Title	Page	Total
600-00	STORY	1	$5,000
610-00	PRODUCER	1	$52,452
620-00	DIRECTOR	1	$34,083
630-00	CAST	1	$135,165
650-00	TRAVEL & LIVING	3	$17,258
	Total Above-The-Line		**$243,957**
700-00	EXTRA TALENT	5	$41,076
705-00	PRODUCTION STAFF	5	$79,578
710-00	CAMERA	6	$60,712
715-00	SET DESIGN	7	$48,835
720-00	SET CONSTRUCTION	8	$14,019
725-00	SET OPERATIONS	8	$59,521
730-00	ELECTRICAL	9	$51,138
735-00	SPECIAL EFFECTS	10	$7,500
740-00	SPECIAL SHOOTING UNITS	10	$16,846
745-00	SET DRESSING (included in 715)	11	$0
750-00	PROPERTIES	11	$37,635
755-00	WARDROBE	12	$39,035
760-00	MAKEUP & HAIRSTYLISTS	12	$31,180
765-00	PRODUCTION SOUND	13	$22,075
770-00	TRANSPORTATION	13	$37,613
775-00	LOCATION EXPENSE	14	$162,155
785-00	PRODUCTION DAILIES	16	$74,513
797-00	TESTS	17	$500
	Total Production		**$783,931**
800-00	EDITING	17	$115,226
810-00	MUSIC	18	$35,200
820-00	POSTPRODUCTION SOUND	18	$41,383
840-00	TITLES	19	$7,000
850-00	OPTICALS, MATTES, INSERTS	19	$10,000
860-00	LABORATORY PROCESSING	19	$20,103
	Total PostProduction		**$228,911**
910-00	ADMINISTRATIVE EXPENSES	19	$43,439
920-00	PUBLICITY	20	$6,000
	Total Other		**$49,439**
	Completion Bond: 3.00%		$39,187

(continued)

Figure 6–6 Sample budget 3, developed for a nonunion crew at a flat weekly rate

Acct#	Category Title	Page	Total
	Contingency: 10.00%		$130,624
	Overhead: 1.00%		$13,062
	Insurance: 2.00%		$26,125
	TOTAL ABOVE-THE-LINE		**$243,957**
	TOTAL BELOW-THE-LINE		**$1,062,280**
	TOTAL ABOVE- & BELOW-THE-LINE		**$1,306,237**
	GRAND TOTAL		**$1,515,235**

(continued)

Figure 6–6 Sample budget 3, developed for a nonunion crew at a flat weekly rate (continued)

SAMPLE BUDGET 3

PRODUCTION NO.:
PRODUCERS:
DIRECTOR:
SCRIPT DATE:
START DATE:
FINISH DATE:

DATE:
LOCATION: LOS ANGELES
5 WEEK SHOOT - 5 DAY WEEK
LOCAL NONUNION CREW
SAG LOW-BUDGET AGRMT.

NOT FINAL SHOOTING BUDGET

Acct #	Description	Amount	Units	X	Rate	Subtotal	Total
600-00	**STORY**						
600-01	RIGHTS/OPTION PURCHAS...						$0
600-03	WRITERS						$0
600-04	SCREENPLAY PURCHASE						
	SCREENPLAY PURCHASE	1	FLAT		5,000	5,000	$5,000
600- 05	RESEARCH						$0
600-11	SCRIPT COPY						$0
						Total For 600-00	**$5,000**
610-00	**PRODUCER**						
610-01	EXECUTIVE PRODUCER						$0
610-02	PRODUCER						
	PRODUCERS - LOAN -OUT	1	FLAT	2	20,000	40,000	$40,000
610-06	PRODUCER'S ASST.						
	PRODUCER'S ASSISTANT-...	5	WEEKS		600	3,000	
	SHOOT	5	WEEKS		600	3,000	
	WRAP	3	WEEKS		600	1,800	
	NONUNION	18.0%			7,800	1,404	$9,204
610-08	PREPRO EXPENSES/ENT.						
	PRE-PRO EXPENSES	6	WEEKS		500	3,000	
	Sales tax	8.25%			3,000	248	$3,248
						Total For 610-00	**$52,452**
620-00	**DIRECTOR**						
620-01	DIRECTOR						
	DIRECTOR (per contract) - L...	1	FLAT		25,000	25,000	$25,000
620-02	STORYBOARD ARTIST						$0
620-04	RESEARCH CONSULTANT						$0
620-05	CASTING DIRECTOR						
	CASTING DIRECTOR - LOA...	4	WEEKS		2,000	8,000	$8,000
620-08	CASTING EXPENSES						
	CASTING FEES/FACILITY/F...		ALLOW		1,000	1,000	
	Sales tax	8.25%			1,000	83	$1,083
						Total For 620-00	**$34,083**

(continued)

Figure 6–6 Sample budget 3, developed for a nonunion crew at a flat weekly rate (continued)

Acct #	Description	Amount	Units	X	Rate	Subtotal	Total
630-00	**CAST**						
630-01	PRINCIPAL PLAYERS (OT...						
	JOHNSON	6	WEEKS		1,620	9,720	
	TRAVIS	6	WEEKS		1,620	9,720	
	L.D.	3	WEEKS		1,620	4,860	
	GEOFFREY	3	WEEKS		1,620	4,860	
	CALLIE	4	WEEKS		1,620	6,480	
	ROXANNE	1	WEEKS		1,620	1,620	
	MARCUS	1.6	WEEKS		1,620	2,592	
	OREN	1.6	WEEKS		1,620	2,592	
	LEO	1	WEEK		1,620	1,620	
	ERIC	1	WEEK		1,620	1,620	
	JERRY	1	WEEK		1,620	1,620	
	URSULA	1	WEEK		1,620	1,620	
	FLOOR BOSS	1	WEEK		1,620	1,620	
	PIT BOSS	2	WEEKS		1,620	3,240	
	ROSS	2	WEEKS		1,620	3,240	
	FUI	1.0%			57,024	570	
	Overtime	20%			57,024	11,405	
	AGENCY FEE	10.0%			57,024	5,702	
	SAG CORP	13.3%			57,024	7,584	
	FICA	6.2%			57,024	3,535	
	FICA 2	1.45%			57,024	827	
	SUI	5.4%			57,024	3,079	$89,727
630-02	DAY PLAYERS						
	STERNS	2	DAYS		466	932	
	ELSON	2	DAYS		466	932	
	CAR MAN	2	DAYS		466	932	
	CAR WOMAN	2	DAYS		466	932	
	CAR KID	2	DAYS		466	932	
	ROBERT H.	2	DAYS		466	932	
	HARRY	2	DAYS		466	932	
	MOTO COP	2	DAYS		466	932	
	VALETS	2	DAYS	3	466	2,796	
	CONCIERGE	1	DAY		466	466	
	HUSBAND	2	DAYS		466	932	
	WIFE	2	DAYS		466	932	
	SECURITY GUARDS	3	DAYS	2	466	2,796	
	BARTENDER	1	DAY		466	466	
	FLOOR BOSS	4	DAYS		466	1,864	
	ARCHIE	2	DAYS		466	932	
	GAMING MANAGER	2	DAYS		466	932	
	MASON	1	DAYS		466	466	
	FUI	1.0%			20,038	200	
	Overtime	20%			20,038	4,008	
	AGENCY FEE	10.0%			20,038	2,004	
	SAG CORP	13.3%			20,038	2,665	

(continued)

Figure 6–6 Sample budget 3, developed for a nonunion crew at a flat weekly rate (continued)

Acct #	Description	Amount	Units	X	Rate	Subtotal	Total
630-00	**CAST (CONT'D)**						
630-02	DAY PLAYERS (CONT'D)						
	FICA	6.2%			20,038	1,242	
	FICA 2	1.45%			20,038	291	
	SUI	5.4%			20,038	1,082	$31,530
630-06	LOOPING/ADR						
	JOHNSON	2	DAYS		466	932	
	TRAVIS	2	DAYS		466	932	
	L.D.	1	DAY		466	466	
	GEOFFREY	1	DAY		466	466	
	CALLIE	1	DAY		466	466	
	OREN	1	DAY		466	466	
	LEO	1	DAY		466	466	
	URSULA	1	DAY		466	466	
	RAMONA	1	DAY		466	466	
	FUI	1.0%			5,126	51	
	AGENCY FEE	10.0%			5,126	513	
	SAG CORP	13.3%			5,126	682	
	FICA	6.2%			5,126	318	
	FICA 2	1.45%			5,126	74	
	SUI	5.4%			5,126	277	$7,041
630-07	MEAL PENALTIES						
	MEAL PENALTIES		ALLOW		5,000	5,000	
	FUI	1.0%			5,000	50	
	SAG CORP	13.3%			5,000	665	
	FICA	6.2%			5,000	310	
	FICA 2	1.45%			5,000	73	
	SUI	5.4%			5,000	270	$6,368
630-09	MEDICAL EXAMS						
	Key Cast Medical Exams	1	EXAMS	5	100	500	$500
						Total For 630-00	**$135,165**
650-00	**TRAVEL & LIVING**						
650-01	PRODUCERS						
	PRODUCERS - TRAVEL	2	FLIG...		170	340	
	LIVING	14	DAYS		60	840	
	Sales tax	8.25%			840	69	$1,249
650-02	DIRECTOR						
	DIRECTOR/LEAD ACTOR	1	FLIG...		170	170	
	HOTEL	14	DAYS		100	1,400	
	Sales tax	8.25%			1,400	116	$1,686
650-06	CAST TRAVEL/LIVING & P...						
	JOHNSON-FLIGHT (FROM...		ALLOW		550	550	
	HOTEL	14	NIGHTS		60	840	
	JOHNSON - PER DIEM	14	DAYS		53	742	
	TRAVIS - PER DIEM	14	DAYS		53	742	
	L.D. -FLIGHT		ALLOW		170	170	

(continued)

Figure 6–6 Sample budget 3, developed for a nonunion crew at a flat weekly rate (continued)

Acct #	Description	Amount	Units	X	Rate	Subtotal	Total
650-00	**TRAVEL & LIVING (CONT'D)**						
650-06	CAST TRAVEL/LIVING & PER DIEM (CONT'D)						
	HOTEL	8	NIGHTS		60	480	
	L.D. - PER DIEM	10	DAYS		53	530	
	GEOFFREY - FLIGHT		ALLOW		170	170	
	HOTEL	5	DAYS		60	300	
	GEOFFREY - PER DIEM	7	DAYS		53	371	
	CALLIE - FLIGHT		ALLOW		170	170	
	HOTEL	8	DAYS		60	480	
	CALLIE - PER DIEM	14	DAYS		53	742	
	ROXANNE - FLIGHT		ALLOW		170	170	
	HOTEL	3	DAYS		60	180	
	ROXANNE - PER DIEM	3	DAYS		53	159	
	OREN - FLIGHT		ALLOW		170	170	
	HOTEL	4	DAYS		60	240	
	OREN - PER DIEM	5	DAYS		53	265	
	MARCUS - FLIGHT		ALLOW		170	170	
	HOTEL	4	DAYS		60	240	
	MARCUS - PER DIEM	5	DAYS		53	265	
	LEO - FLIGHT		ALLOW		170	170	
	HOTEL	3	DAYS		60	180	
	LEO - PER DIEM	5	DAYS		53	265	
	ERIC - FLIGHT		ALLOW		170	170	
	HOTEL	4	DAYS		60	240	
	ERIC - PER DIEM	5	DAYS		53	265	
	JERRY - FLIGHT		ALLOW		170	170	
	HOTEL	4	DAYS		60	240	
	JERRY - PER DIEM	5	DAYS		53	265	
	URSULA - FLIGHT		ALLOW		170	170	
	HOTEL	5	DAYS		60	300	
	URSULA - PER DIEM	5	DAYS		53	265	
	GLADYS - FLIGHT		ALLOW		170	170	
	HOTEL	3	DAYS		60	180	
	GLADYS - PER DIEM	3	DAYS		53	159	
	STERNS - HOTEL	2	DAYS		60	120	
	STERNS - FLIGHT		ALLOW		170	170	
	STERNS - PER DIEM	2	DAYS		53	106	
	ELSON - HOTEL	2	DAYS		60	120	
	ELSON - FLIGHT		ALLOW		170	170	
	ELSON - PER DIEM	2	DAYS		53	106	
	CAR MAN - HOTEL	1	DAY		60	60	
	CAR MAN - FLIGHT		ALLOW		170	170	
	CAR MAN - PER DIEM	2	DAYS		53	106	
	CAR WOMAN - HOTEL	1	DAY		60	60	
	CAR WOMAN - FLIGHT		ALLOW		170	170	
	CAR WOMAN - PER DIEM	2	DAYS		53	106	
	CAR KID - HOTEL	1	DAY		60	60	

(continued)

Figure 6–6 Sample budget 3, developed for a nonunion crew at a flat weekly rate (continued)

Acct #	Description	Amount	Units	X	Rate	Subtotal	Total
650-00	**TRAVEL & LIVING (CONT'D)**						
650-06	CAST TRAVEL/LIVING & PER DIEM (CONT'D)						
	CAR KID - FLIGHT		ALLOW		170	170	
	CAR KID - PER DIEM	2	DAYS		53	106	
	MASON - HOTEL	2	DAYS		60	120	
	MASON - FLIGHT		ALLOW		170	170	
	MASON - PER DIEM	2	DAYS		53	106	
	ARCHIE - HOTEL	2	DAYS		60	120	
	ARCHIE - FLIGHT		ALLOW		170	170	
	ARCHIE - PER DIEM	2	DAYS		53	106	
	Sales tax	8.25%			4,560	376	$14,323
						Total For 650-00	**$17,258**
	Total Above-The-Line						**$243,957**
700-00	**EXTRA TALENT**						
700-02	ALL EXTRA TALENT & STA...						
	CASINO EXTRAS	7	DAYS	30	90	18,900	
	CASINO EXTRAS	5	DAYS	20	50	5,000	
	EXTRAS - DINER	2	DAYS	15	90	2,700	
	FUI	1.0%			26,600	266	
	AGENCY FEE	10.0%			26,600	2,660	
	SAG CORP	13.3%			26,600	3,538	
	FICA	6.2%			26,600	1,649	
	FICA 2	1.45%			26,600	386	
	SUI	5.4%			26,600	1,436	$36,535
700-05	EXTRAS CASTING						
	EXTRAS CASTING	2	WEEKS		2,000	4,000	
	EXTRAS CASTING EXPEN...	1	WEEK		500	500	
	Sales tax	8.25%			500	41	$4,541
						Total For 700-00	**$41,076**
705-00	**PRODUCTION STAFF**						
705-01	LINE PRODUCER/UPM						
	PREP	6	WEEKS		800	4,800	
	SHOOT	5	WEEKS		800	4,000	
	WRAP	2	WEEKS		800	1,600	
	NONUNION	18.0%			10,400	1,872	$12,272
705-02	PRODUCTION COORDINAT...						
	PREP	5	WEEKS		600	3,000	
	SHOOT	5	WEEKS		600	3,000	
	WRAP	1	WEEK		600	600	
	NONUNION	18.0%			6,600	1,188	
	Overtime	20%			3,000	600	$8,388
705-03	1ST ASSISTANT DIRECTOR						
	PREP	3	WEEKS		800	2,400	
	SHOOT	5	WEEKS		800	4,000	

(continued)

Figure 6–6 Sample budget 3, developed for a nonunion crew at a flat weekly rate (continued)

Acct #	Description	Amount	Units	X	Rate	Subtotal	Total
705-00	**PRODUCTION STAFF (CONT'D)**						
705-03	1ST ASSISTANT DIRECTOR (CONT'D)						
	WRAP	0.6	WEEKS		800	480	
	NONUNION	18.0%			6,880	1,238	
	Overtime	20%			4,000	800	$8,918
705-04	2ND ASSISTANT DIRECTOR						
	PREP	2	WEEKS		600	1,200	
	SHOOT	5	WEEKS		600	3,000	
	WRAP	0.6	WEEKS		600	360	
	NONUNION	18.0%			4,560	821	
	Overtime	20%			3,360	672	$6,053
705-05	2ND 2ND ASSISTANT DIRE...						
	2ND 2ND ASSISTANT DIREC...	5	WEEKS		500	2,500	
	NONUNION	18.0%			2,500	450	
	Overtime	20%			2,500	500	$3,450
705-06	SCRIPT SUPERVISOR						
	PREP	0.6	WEEKS		800	480	
	SHOOT	5	WEEKS		800	4,000	
	WRAP	0.6	WEEKS		800	480	
	NONUNION	18.0%			4,960	893	
	Overtime	20%			4,000	800	$6,653
705-08	PRODUCTION ACCOUNTANT						
	ACCOUNTANT-PREP	4	WEEKS		800	3,200	
	SHOOT	5	WEEKS		800	4,000	
	WRAP	2	WEEKS		800	1,600	
	NONUNION	18.0%			8,800	1,584	$10,384
705-10	PRODUCTION ASSISTANTS						
	PA 1 (OFFICE PA) - PREP	5	WEEKS		500	2,500	
	SHOOT	5	WEEKS		500	2,500	
	WRAP	1	WEEK		500	500	
	PA 2 - PREP	3	WEEKS		500	1,500	
	SHOOT	5	WEEKS		500	2,500	
	WRAP	1	WEEK		500	500	
	PA 3 - PREP	2	WEEKS		500	1,000	
	SHOOT	5	WEEKS		500	2,500	
	WRAP	1	WEEK		500	500	
	PA 4 - PREP	1	WEEK		500	500	
	SHOOT	5	WEEKS		500	2,500	
	NONUNION	18.0%			17,000	3,060	
	Overtime	20%			17,000	3,400	$23,460
						Total For 705-00	**$79,578**
710-00	**CAMERA**						
710-01	DIRECTOR OF PHOTOGRA...						
	DP-LOAN OUT	6	WEEKS		2,500	15,000	$15,000
710-03	1ST AC						
	PREP	0.6	WEEKS		800	480	

(continued)

Figure 6–6 Sample budget 3, developed for a nonunion crew at a flat weekly rate (continued)

Acct #	Description	Amount	Units	X	Rate	Subtotal	Total
710-00	**CAMERA (CONT'D)**						
710-03	1ST AC (CONT'D)						
	SHOOT	5	WEEKS		800	4,000	
	NONUNION	18.0%			4,480	806	
	Overtime	20%			4,000	800	$6,086
710-04	2ND CAMERA ASST./LOAD...						
	PREP	0.6	WEEKS		600	360	
	SHOOT	5	WEEKS		600	3,000	
	NONUNION	18.0%			3,360	605	
	Overtime	20%			3,000	600	$4,565
710-06	STILL PHOTOGRAPHER						
	STILL PHOTOGRAPHER	1	FLAT		2,000	2,000	
	NONUNION	18.0%			2,000	360	$2,360
710-08	CAMERA RENTALS						
	All Camera Package	5	WEEKS		2,500	12,500	$12,500
710-09	CAMERA SUPPLIES						
	CAMERA PURCHASES		ALLOW		500	500	
	Sales tax	8.25%			500	41	$541
710-11	CAMERA ACCESORIES						
	MONITOR	5	WEEKS		1,200	6,000	
	MONITOR OPERATOR	5	WEEKS		800	4,000	
	STEADI-CAM	2	WEEKS		1,500	3,000	
	STEADI-CAM OPERATOR	2	WEEKS		1,500	3,000	
	NONUNION	18.0%			7,000	1,260	
	Overtime	20%			7,000	1,400	$18,660
710-20	LOSS & DAMAGE						
	LOSS & DAMAGE		ALLOW		1,000	1,000	$1,000
						Total For 710-00	**$60,712**
715-00	**SET DESIGN**						
715-01	PRODUCTION DESIGNER						
	PROD. DESIGNER - PREP	4	WEEKS		800	3,200	
	SHOOT	5	WEEKS		800	4,000	
	WRAP	0.6	WEEKS		800	480	
	NONUNION	18.0%			7,680	1,382	
	Overtime	20%			4,000	800	$9,862
715-02	ART DIRECTOR						
	ART DIRECTOR - PREP	3	WEEKS		800	2,400	
	SHOOT	5	WEEKS		800	4,000	
	WRAP	0.6	WEEKS		800	480	
	NONUNION	18.0%			6,880	1,238	
	Overtime	20%			4,000	800	$8,918
715-03	SET DESIGNER/LEADMAN						
	PREP	3	WEEKS		600	1,800	
	SHOOT	5	WEEKS		600	3,000	
	WRAP	1	WEEK		600	600	
	NONUNION	18.0%			5,400	972	

(continued)

Figure 6–6 Sample budget 3, developed for a nonunion crew at a flat weekly rate (continued)

Acct #	Description	Amount	Units	X	Rate	Subtotal	Total
715-00	**SET DESIGN (CONT'D)**						
715-03	SET DESIGNER/LEAD MAN (CONT'D)						
	Overtime	20%			3,000	600	$6,972
715-04	SWING GANG						
	PREP	1	WEEK	2	500	1,000	
	SHOOT	5	WEEKS	2	500	5,000	
	WRAP	1	WEEK		500	500	
	NONUNION	18.0%			6,500	1,170	
	Overtime	20%			5,000	1,000	$8,670
715-05	ART RENTALS						
	RENTALS	5	WEEKS		1,500	7,500	$7,500
715-06	PURCHASE SUPPLIES						
	ART PURCHASE		ALLOW		5,000	5,000	
	Sales tax	8.25%			5,000	413	$5,413
715-10	KIT RENTAL						
	KIT RENTAL	5	WEEKS	2	50	500	$500
715-20	LOSS & DAMAGE						
	ART DEPT L&D		ALLOW		1,000	1,000	$1,000
						Total For 715-00	**$48,835**
720-00	**SET CONSTRUCTION**						
720-01	CONSTRUCTION LABOR						
	CONSTRUCTION LABOR		ALLOW		5,000	5,000	
	NONUNION	18.0%			5,000	900	$5,900
720-02	CONSTRUCTION MATERIA...						
	MATERIALS/PURCHASES		ALLOW		7,500	7,500	
	Sales tax	8.25%			7,500	619	$8,119
						Total For 720-00	**$14,019**
725-00	**SET OPERATIONS**						
725-01	KEY GRIP						
	PREP	1	WEEK		800	800	
	SHOOT	5	WEEKS		800	4,000	
	NONUNION	18.0%			4,800	864	
	Overtime	20%			4,000	800	$6,464
725-02	BEST BOY GRIP						
	PREP	0.4	DAYS		600	240	
	SHOOT	5	WEEKS		600	3,000	
	NONUNION	18.0%			3,240	583	
	Overtime	20%			3,000	600	$4,423
725-03	CRANE/DOLLY GRIPS						
	Dolly Grip	4	WEEKS		600	2,400	
	NONUNION	18.0%			2,400	432	
	Overtime	20%			2,400	480	$3,312
725-04	EXTRA COMPANY GRIPS						
	COMPANY GRIPS	5	WEEKS	2	500	5,000	
	NONUNION	18.0%			5,000	900	

(continued)

Figure 6–6 Sample budget 3, developed for a nonunion crew at a flat weekly rate (continued)

Acct #	Description	Amount	Units	X	Rate	Subtotal	Total
725-00	**SET OPERATIONS (CONT'D)**						
725-04	EXTRA COMPANY GRIPS (CONT'D)						
	Overtime	20%			5,000	1,000	$6,900
725-05	CAMERA DOLLY						
	DOLLY W/ACCESSORIES/...	4	WEEKS		1,200	4,800	$4,800
725-06	CAMERA CRANE						
	CRANE	2	DAYS		1,500	3,000	
	CRANE OPERATOR	2	DAYS		200	400	
	NONUNION	18.0%			400	72	$3,472
725-08	GRIP EQUIPMENT RENTALS						
	RENTALS	5	WEEKS		1,500	7,500	
	Car Mounts	2	WEEKS		300	600	$8,100
725-09	GRIP PURCHASES						
	EXPENDABLES/GELS/BUB...	5	WEEKS		1,000	5,000	
	Sales tax	8.25%			5,000	413	$5,413
725-10	KIT RENTALS						
	KEY GRIP KIT RENTAL	5	WEEKS		50	250	$250
725-11	CRAFT SERVICE/SERVICE...						
	Craft Service Person - PREP	1	WEEK		600	600	
	SHOOT	5	WEEKS		600	3,000	
	PURCHASES	5	WEEKS		750	3,750	
	Rentals	5	WEEKS		250	1,250	
	KIT RENTAL	5	WEEKS		50	250	
	Sales tax	8.25%			3,750	309	
	NONUNION	18.0%			3,600	648	
	Overtime	20%			3,000	600	$10,407
725-10	KIT RENTAL						$0
725-20	LOSS & DAMAGE						
	ALL L&D		ALLOW		1,000	1,000	$1,000
725-25	MISCELLANEOUS						
	WALKIES	5	WEEKS	12	50	3,000	
	BEEPERS	10	WEEKS	6	8	480	$3,480
725-30	LOCATION LOAD & UNLOAD						
	LOCATION LOAD & UNLOAD	2	WEEKS		750	1,500	$1,500
						Total For 725-00	**$59,521**
730-00	**ELECTRICAL**						
730-01	GAFFER						
	KEY ELEC. - PREP	1	WEEK		800	800	
	SHOOT	5	WEEKS		800	4,000	
	NONUNION	18.0%			4,800	864	
	Overtime	20%			4,000	800	$6,464
730-02	BEST BOY						
	BEST BOY - SHOOT	5	WEEKS		600	3,000	
	NONUNION	18.0%			3,000	540	
	Overtime	20%			3,000	600	$4,140
730-03	ELECTRICS						

(continued)

Figure 6–6 Sample budget 3, developed for a nonunion crew at a flat weekly rate (continued)

Acct #	Description	Amount	Units	X	Rate	Subtotal	Total
730-00	**ELECTRICAL (CONT'D)**						
730-03	ELECTRICS (CONT'D)						
	ELECTRICIANS	5	WEEKS	2	600	6,000	
	NONUNION	18.0%			6,000	1,080	
	Overtime	20%			6,000	1,200	$8,280
730-05	GLOBES/CARBONS						
	GLOBES & CARBONS	5	WEEKS		100	500	
	Sales tax	8.25%			500	41	$541
730-06	POWER						
	POWER/TIE-IN	3	WEEKS		100	300	$300
730-07	GENERATOR RENTAL						
	GENERATOR	5	WEEKS		1,200	6,000	
	FUEL FOR GENERATOR	5	WEEKS		300	1,500	$7,500
730-08	ELECTRICAL RENTAL PACK						
	ELEC. PACK RENTAL	5	WEEKS		3,000	15,000	$15,000
730-09	ELECTRICAL PURCHASES						
	ELECTRICAL PURCHASES	5	WEEKS		1,000	5,000	
	Sales tax	8.25%			5,000	413	$5,413
730-10	KIT RENTAL						
	KIT RENTAL	5	WEEKS		500	2,500	$2,500
730-20	LOSS & DAMAGE						
	All L&D	1			1,000	1,000	$1,000
						Total For 730-00	**$51,138**
735-00	**SPECIAL EFFECTS**						
735-01	SPECIAL EFFECTS						
	SPECIAL EFFECTS (CGI)		ALLOW		7,500	7,500	$7,500
						Total For 735-00	**$7,500**
740-00	**SPECIAL SHOOTING UNITS**						
740-01	UNIT #1/PICKUPS INSERTS						
	2ND UNIT EXTERIORS- CR...						
	DP	0.6	WEEKS		2,500	1,500	
	AD	0.6	WEEKS		800	480	
	2ND AD	0.6	DAYS		600	360	
	KEY GRIP	0.6	WEEKS		800	480	
	BEST BOY	0.6	WEEKS		600	360	
	GAFFER	0.6	WEEKS		800	480	
	ELECTRICIAN	0.6	DAYS		600	360	
	1ST AC	0.6	WEEKS		800	480	
	2ND AC/LOADER	0.6	WEEKS		500	300	
	SCRIPT SUPERVISOR	0.6	WEEKS		800	480	
	PA	0.6	WEEKS	2	500	600	
	LOCATION MANAGER	0.6	WEEKS		800	480	
	LEAD MAN	0.6	WEEKS		600	360	
	EQUIPMENT & MATERIALS	3	DAYS		2,000	6,000	
	MEALS - BREAKFAST	3	DAYS	16	5	240	

(continued)

Figure 6–6 Sample budget 3, developed for a nonunion crew at a flat weekly rate (continued)

Acct #	Description	Amount	Units	X	Rate	Subtotal	Total
740-00	**SPECIAL SHOOTING UNITS (CONT'D)**						
740-01	UNIT #1/PICKUPS INSERTS (CONT'D)						
	MEALS - DINNER	3	DAYS	16	10	480	
	HOTELS (SHARE)	10	ROOMS	3	40	1,200	
	15 PASS VAN	1	WEEK		300	300	
	City tax	6.0%			300	18	
	Sales tax	8.25%			8,220	678	
	NONUNION	18.0%			6,720	1,210	$16,846
						Total For 740-00	**$16,846**
745-00	**SET DRESSING (included in 715)**						
745-01	SET DECORATOR						$0
745-02	LEAD MAN						$0
745-02	SWING GANG						$0
745-04	SET DRESSING PURCHASED						$0
745-05	SET DRESSING RENTALS						$0
745-07	SET DRESSING CLEAN & ...						$0
745-08	DRAPERY RENTALS						$0
745-09	DRAPERY PURCHASES						$0
745-20	LOSS, DAMAGE & REPAIR						$0
745-25	MISCELLANEOUS EXPENSE						$0
						Total For 745-00	**$0**
750-00	**PROPERTIES**						
750-01	PROPERTY MASTER						
	PROP MASTERS-PREP	3	WEEKS		800	2,400	
	SHOOT	5	WEEKS		800	4,000	
	WRAP	0.6	WEEKS		800	480	
	NONUNION	18.0%			6,880	1,238	
	Overtime	20%			4,000	800	$8,918
750-02	ASST. PROP MASTER						
	ASST. PROP MASTER - PR...	2	WEEKS		600	1,200	
	SHOOT	5	WEEKS		600	3,000	
	WRAP	1	WEEK		600	600	
	NONUNION	18.0%			4,800	864	
	Overtime	20%			3,000	600	$6,264
750-05	PICTURE VEHICLES						
	NEW LEXUS	1	DAY		200	200	
	PICK-UP TRUCK	1	DAY	2	300	600	
	INDIAN MOTORCYCLE	1	DAY		500	500	
	JEEP	3	DAYS		100	300	
	POLICE BIKE	1	DAY		1,000	1,000	
	CADILLAC	1	FLAT		7,500	7,500	
	City tax	6.0%			500	30	
	Sales tax	8.25%			8,000	660	$10,790
750-08	PROP RENTALS						
	PROP RENTALS	5	WEEKS		1,000	5,000	$5,000

(continued)

Figure 6–6 Sample budget 3, developed for a nonunion crew at a flat weekly rate (continued)

Acct #	Description	Amount	Units	X	Rate	Subtotal	Total
750-00	**PROPERTIES (CONT'D)**						
750-09	PROP PURCHASES						
	PROP PURCHASES	5	WEEKS		1,000	5,000	
	Sales tax	8.25%			5,000	413	$5,413
750-10	PROP BOX RENTALS						
	PROP KIT RENTALS	5	WEEKS		50	250	$250
750-20	LOSS, DAMAGE & REPAIRS						
	L&D		ALLOW		1,000	1,000	$1,000
						Total For 750-00	**$37,635**
755-00	**WARDROBE**						
755-04	COSTUME DESIGNER						
	PREP	4	WEEKS		800	3,200	
	SHOOT	5	WEEKS		800	4,000	
	WRAP	1	WEEK		800	800	
	NONUNION	18.0%			8,000	1,440	
	Overtime	20%			4,000	800	$10,240
755-03	ASSISTANT WARDROBE						
	PREP	4	WEEKS		600	2,400	
	SHOOT	5	WEEKS		600	3,000	
	WRAP	0.6	WEEKS		600	360	
	EXTRA WARDROBE ASSIS...	5	WEEKS		600	3,000	
	NONUNION	18.0%			8,760	1,577	
	Overtime	20%			6,000	1,200	$11,537
755-06	COSTUME ALTERATION						
	ALTER		ALLOW		300	300	
	Sales tax	8.25%			300	25	$325
755-07	COSTUME CLEANING						
	CLEANING		ALLOW		250	250	
	Sales tax	8.25%			250	21	$271
755-08	COSTUME RENTAL						
	All Rental	5	WEEKS		2,000	10,000	$10,000
755-09	COSTUME PURCHASE						
	WARDROBE PURCHASES		ALLOW		5,000	5,000	
	Sales tax	8.25%			5,000	413	$5,413
755-10	KIT RENTAL						
	KIT RENTAL	5	WEEKS		50	250	$250
755-20	LOSS & DAMAGE						
	L&D		ALLOW		1,000	1,000	$1,000
						Total For 755-00	**$39,035**
760-00	**MAKEUP & HAIRSTYLISTS**						
760-01	KEY MAKE-UP ARTIST						
	PREP	1	WEEK		800	800	
	SHOOT	5	WEEKS		800	4,000	
	NONUNION	18.0%			4,800	864	
	Overtime	20%			4,000	800	$6,464

(continued)

Figure 6–6 Sample budget 3, developed for a nonunion crew at a flat weekly rate (continued)

Acct #	Description	Amount	Units	X	Rate	Subtotal	Total
760-00	**MAKEUP & HAIRSTYLISTS (CONT'D)**						
760-02	ASST. MAKEUP ARTISTS						
	SHOOT	5	WEEKS		600	3,000	
	NONUNION	18.0%			3,000	540	
	Overtime	20%			3,000	600	$4,140
760-04	KEY HAIR STYLIST						
	KEY HAIR - PREP	1	WEEK		800	800	
	SHOOT	5	WEEKS		800	4,000	
	NONUNION	18.0%			4,800	864	
	Overtime	20%			4,000	800	$6,464
760-05	ASST. HAIR						
	ASST. HAIR	5	WEEKS		600	3,000	
	NONUNION	18.0%			3,000	540	
	Overtime	20%			3,000	600	$4,140
760-06	HAIR SUPPLY						
	HAIR SUPPLY	5	WEEKS		1,000	5,000	
	Sales tax	8.25%			5,000	413	$5,413
760-09	MAKE-UP SUPPLIES/APPL...						
	MAKE-UP SUPPLIES	5	WEEKS		750	3,750	
	Sales tax	8.25%			3,750	309	$4,059
760-10	KIT RENTAL						
	KIT RENTAL	5	WEEKS	2	50	500	$500
						Total For 760-00	**$31,180**
765-00	**PRODUCTION SOUND**						
765-01	SOUND MIXER						
	SHOOT	5	WEEKS		800	4,000	
	NONUNION	18.0%			4,000	720	
	Overtime	20%			4,000	800	$5,520
765-02	BOOM MAN						
	SHOOT	5	WEEKS		600	3,000	
	NONUNION	18.0%			3,000	540	
	Overtime	20%			3,000	600	$4,140
765-04	CABLE MAN						
	CABLEMAN	4	WEEKS		600	2,400	
	NONUNION	18.0%			2,400	432	
	Overtime	20%			2,400	480	$3,312
765-05	PLAYBACK OPERATOR (A...						$0
765-06	SOUND EQUIP RENTALS						
	All Equipment Rental	5	WEEKS		1,300	6,500	$6,500
765-11	MISC.						
	PURCHASES&EXPENDAB...	5	WEEKS		250	1,250	
	Sales tax	8.25%			1,250	103	$1,353
765-10	KIT RENTALS						
	KIT RENTAL	5	WEEKS		50	250	$250
765-20	LOSS & DAMAGE						

(continued)

Figure 6–6 Sample budget 3, developed for a nonunion crew at a flat weekly rate (continued)

Acct #	Description	Amount	Units	X	Rate	Subtotal	Total
765-00	**PRODUCTION SOUND (CONT'D)**						
765-20	LOSS & DAMAGE (CONT'D)						
	All L&D	1			1,000	1,000	$1,000
						Total For 765-00	**$22,075**
770-00	**TRANSPORTATION**						
770-01	MESSENGER SERVICE/FE...						
	MESSENGER & FEDEX	12	WEEKS		150	1,800	$1,800
770-02	DRIVER CAPTAIN						$0
770-05	MILEAGE ALLOWANCE						
	MILEAGE	5,000	MILES		0.31	1,550	$1,550
770-06	FUEL						
	FUEL - CARS/TRUCKS	8	WEEKS		700	5,600	
	Sales tax	8.25%			5,600	462	$6,062
770-10	LOC. VEHICLES/TRUCKS						
	PRODUCTION MOTORHOME	2	WEEKS		1,500	3,000	
	TENTING	1	WEEK		500	500	
	CAMERA TRUCK W/ GUTS	5	WEEKS		600	3,000	
	ART/PROP TRUCK	8	WEEKS		400	3,200	
	15 PASS. VAN	5	WEEKS	2	350	3,500	
	CUBE	7	WEEKS		400	2,800	
	WARDROBE DEPT. CUBE	7	WEEKS		400	2,800	
	GRIP/ELEC. TRUCK	5	WEEKS		400	2,000	
	RENTAL CARS	3	WEEKS	4	350	4,200	
	City tax	6.0%			3,000	180	
	Sales tax	8.25%			24,500	2,021	$27,201
770-20	LOSS, DAMAGE, & REPAIRS						
	L&D		ALLOW		1,000	1,000	$1,000
						Total For 770-00	**$37,613**
775-00	**LOCATION EXPENSE**						
775-01	SURVEY EXPENSE						
	FOOD	22	DAYS		15	330	
	FILM	5	WEEKS		75	375	
	GAS	5	WEEKS		75	375	
	PHONE/TIPS		ALLOW		200	200	
	SCOUT #1-DESERT						
	FOOD	3	DAYS	4	20	240	
	FILM	1	FLAT		150	150	
	RENTAL CAR	3	DAYS		50	150	
	GAS	1	FLAT		100	100	
	PHONES/CELLULAR/TIPS		ALLOW		150	150	
	SCOUT #2-DESERT						
	FOOD	2	DAYS	9	20	360	
	RENTAL CAR	2	DAYS	3	60	360	

(continued)

Figure 6–6 Sample budget 3, developed for a nonunion crew at a flat weekly rate (continued)

Acct #	Description	Amount	Units	X	Rate	Subtotal	Total
775-00	**LOCATION EXPENSE (CONT'D)**						
775-01	SURVEY EXPENSE (CONT'D)						
	GAS	2	DAYS	3	20	120	
	PHONES/CELLULAR/TIPS		ALLOW		250	250	
	City tax	6.0%			510	31	
	Sales tax	8.25%			2,560	211	$3,402
775-02	LOCATION STAFF						
	LOCATION MANAGER-PREP	5	WEEKS		800	4,000	
	SHOOT	5	WEEKS		800	4,000	
	LOCATION PA - PREP	3	WEEKS		600	1,800	
	LOCATION PA-SHOOT	4	WEEKS		600	2,400	
	NONUNION	18.0%			12,200	2,196	
	Overtime	20%			6,400	1,280	$15,676
775-03	SITE RENTALS/PERMITS						
	BRECKENSTEIN'S ARCO	2	DAYS		750	1,500	
	DESERT DAHLIA	3	DAYS		1,000	3,000	
	KOUNTRY KITCHEN	2	DAYS		1,000	2,000	
	SITE/PERMIT FEES		ALLOW		5,000	5,000	
	TRAILER	2	DAYS		1,000	2,000	
	CASINO(ALL ROOMS, GAR...	2	WEEKS		10,000	20,000	
	SUITES, VALET ST., ELEV.,...						
	SLOTS, TABLES)						$33,500
775-04	HOTEL & LODGING						
	DP HOTEL	14	DAYS		40	560	
	DP PER DIEM	14	DAYS		30	420	
	1ST AC-HOTEL	12	DAYS		40	480	
	1ST AC PER DIEM	10	DAYS		30	300	
	2ND AC/LOADER - HOTEL	12	DAYS		40	480	
	2ND AC/LOADER-PER DIEM	10	DAYS		30	300	
	1ST AD HOTEL	14	DAYS		40	560	
	1ST AD PER DIEM	14	DAYS		30	420	
	2ND AD HOTEL	12	DAYS		40	480	
	2ND AD PER DIEM	12	DAYS		30	360	
	WARDROBE HOTEL	10	DAYS	2	40	800	
	WARDROBE PER DIEM	10	DAYS	2	30	600	
	MAKEUP HOTEL	10	DAYS	2	40	800	
	MAKEUP PER DIEM	10	DAYS	2	30	600	
	SOUND HOTEL	10	DAYS	2	40	800	
	SOUND PER DIEM	10	DAYS	2	30	600	
	GAFFER HOTEL	10	DAYS	2	40	800	
	GAFFER PER DIEM	10	DAYS	2	30	600	
	GRIP HOTEL	10	DAYS	2	40	800	
	GRIP DEPT. PER DIEM	10	DAYS	2	30	600	
	PROD.'S ASST. HOTEL	14	WEEKS		40	560	
	PROD.'S ASST. PER DIEM	14	DAYS		30	420	
	SCRIPT SUPERVISOR HOT...	10	DAYS		40	400	
	PER DIEM	10	DAYS		30	300	

(continued)

Figure 6–6 Sample budget 3, developed for a nonunion crew at a flat weekly rate (continued)

Acct #	Description	Amount	Units	X	Rate	Subtotal	Total
775-00	**LOCATION EXPENSE (CONT'D)**						
775-04	HOTEL & LODGING (CONT'D)						
	PROD. DESIGN HOTEL	14	DAYS		40	560	
	PROD. DESIGN PER DIEM	14	DAYS		30	420	
	ART. DIR. HOTEL	10	DAYS	2	40	800	
	ART. DIR. PER DIEM	10	DAYS	2	30	600	
	PROP. HOTEL	10	DAYS	2	40	800	
	PROP. PER DIEM	10	DAYS	2	30	600	
	LOCATION HOTEL	14	DAYS		40	560	
	LOCATION PER DIEM	14	DAYS		30	420	
	PA HOTEL	14	DAYS	2	40	1,120	
	PA PER DIEM	14	DAYS	3	30	1,260	
	Sales tax	8.25%			11,360	937	$21,117
775-05	CATERING SERVICES						
	BREAKFAST @ $5/HEAD	25	DAYS	60	5	7,500	
	LUNCH $11/HEAD	25	DAYS	60	11	16,500	
	Sales tax	8.25%			24,000	1,980	$25,980
775-06	EXTRA MEALS/SECOND M...						
	2ND MEAL	10	DAYS	60	10	6,000	
	EXTRA MEALS	10	DAYS		300	3,000	
	Sales tax	8.25%			9,000	743	$9,743
775-07	PRODUCTION EXPENDABL...						
	PRODUCTION EXPENDABL...	5	WEEKS		400	2,000	
	Sales tax	8.25%			2,000	165	$2,165
775-08	CARTAGE						
	TRASH FEES		ALLOW		500	500	$500
775-11	FIREMAN/POLICE						
	FIREMAN	10	HOURS	20	52	10,400	
	POLICE	8	HOURS	15	52	6,240	
	TEAMSTERS	30%			16,640	4,992	$21,632
775-12	PARKING LOTS						
	PARKING LOTS	2	WEEKS		700	1,400	$1,400
775-13	A/C/HEAT FEES						
	A/C/HEAT FEES		ALLOW		500	500	$500
775-17	GRATUITIES						
	GRATUITIES - TIPS		ALLOW		300	300	$300
775-18	OFFICE						
	Office Rental & Furniture	20	WEEKS		500	10,000	
	OFFICE SUPPLIES		ALLOW		3,000	3,000	
	PHOTOCOPY/FAX RENTAL	20	WEEKS		200	4,000	
	Sales tax	8.25%			7,000	578	$17,578
775-19	LOCATION MEDICAL EXPE...						
	ALLOCATION		ALLOW		500	500	$500
775-20	SHIPPING						
	FILM SHIPPING		ALLOW		1,000	1,000	
	Sales tax	8.25%			1,000	83	$1,083
775-21	LOCATION SECURITY						

(continued)

Figure 6–6 Sample budget 3, developed for a nonunion crew at a flat weekly rate (continued)

Acct #	Description	Amount	Units	X	Rate	Subtotal	Total
775-00	**LOCATION EXPENSE (CONT'D)**						
775-21	LOCATION SECURITY (CONT'D)						
	LOCATION SECURITY	15	DAYS		300	4,500	
	NIGHT WATCHMAN	5	NIGHTS		300	1,500	
	NONUNION	18.0%			6,000	1,080	$7,080
						Total For 775-00	**$162,155**
785-00	**PRODUCTION DAILIES**						
785-01	NEGATIVE RAW STOCK						
	RAW STOCK (5298 - UNOP...	35,000	FEET		0.52	18,200	
	RAW STOCK (5298 - RECAN	25,000	FEET		0.3	7,500	
	RAW STOCK (5248 - RECAN))	20,000	FEET		0.20	4,000	
	Sales tax	8.25%			29,700	2,450	$32,150
785-02	DEVELOPING						
	80,000 FT DEVELOP	80,000	FEET		0.12	9,600	
	PREP @ 80,000 FEET	80,000	FEET		0.07	5,600	$15,200
785-03	TRANSFER DAILIES						
	TRANSFER TO VIDEO - 3/4″	80,000	FEET		0.24	19,200	$19,200
785-04	TAPE STOCK						
	TAPE STOCK - BETA 3/4″	25	TAPES		24	600	
	BETA SP TAPES	25	TAPES		41	1,025	
	VHS TAPES	50	TAPES		13	650	
	Sales tax	8.25%			2,275	188	$2,463
785-05	TRANSFER SOUND DAILIES						
	TRANSFER SOUND DAILIES		ALLOW		5,000	5,000	$5,000
785-08	SCREEN DAILIES						
	SCREEN DAILIES		ALLOW		500	500	$500
						Total For 785-00	**$74,513**
797-00	**TESTS**						
797-02	TEST #1/FILM STOCK/CAM...						
	TEST		ALLOW		500	500	$500
						Total For 797-00	**$500**
	Total Production						**$783,931**
800-00	**EDITING**						
800-01	FILM EDITOR						
	Editor	20	WEEKS		800	16,000	
	NONUNION	18.0%			16,000	2,880	$18,880
800-02	SOUND EFFECTS EDITING						
	SOUND EFFECTS EDITING		ALLOW		3,000	3,000	$3,000
800-03	MUSIC EDITING						
	Allocation		ALLOW		3,000	3,000	$3,000
800-04	NEGATIVE CUTTING						
	Allocation		ALLOW		5,000	5,000	$5,000
800-05	DIALOGUE EDITING						

(continued)

Figure 6–6 Sample budget 3, developed for a nonunion crew at a flat weekly rate (continued)

Acct#	Description	Amount	Units	X	Rate	Subtotal	Total
800-00	**EDITING (CONT'D)**						
800-05	DIALOGUE EDITING (CONT'D)						
	DIALOGUE EDITING		ALLOW		5,000	5,000	$5,000
800-06	PROJECTION						
	PROJECTION		ALLOW		500	500	$500
800-07	CONTINUITY SCRIPTS						
	Continuity Scripts		ALLOW		500	500	$500
800-11	EDITORIAL FACILITIES						
	EDIT SUITE (INCL. PARKING)	20	WEEKS		1,000	20,000	
	AVID SYSTEM	20	WEEKS		1,200	24,000	
	HARD DRIVES/DECKS	20	WEEKS		300	6,000	$50,000
800-12	EDITORIAL SUPPLIES/FOOD						
	SUPPLIES	20	WEEKS		150	3,000	
	FOOD	20	WEEKS		200	4,000	
	Sales tax	8.25%			7,000	578	$7,578
800-14	POST PROD. SUPERVISION						
	POSTPRO SUPERVISION	10	WEEKS		800	8,000	
	NONUNION	18.0%			8,000	1,440	$9,440
800-17	OTHER COSTS						
	MISCELLANEOUS ITEMS		ALLOW		1,000	1,000	$1,000
800-18	ASSISTANT EDITOR						
	ASSISTANT EDITOR	16	WEEKS		600	9,600	
	NONUNION	18.0%			9,600	1,728	$11,328
800-19	APPRENTICE EDITOR (INT...						
	APPRENTICE EDITOR (INT...						$0
						Total For 800-00	$115,226
810-00	**MUSIC**						
810-08	COMPOSER						
	COMPOSER	1	FLAT		7,500	7,500	
	NONUNION	18.0%			7,500	1,350	$8,850
810-10	SONGWRITER						$0
810-21	RECORDING MUSICIANS						$0
810-22	SINGERS & VOCAL COAC...						$0
810-25	MUSIC SUPERVISOR						
	MUSIC SUPERVISOR	1	FLAT		7,500	7,500	
	NONUNION	18.0%			7,500	1,350	$8,850
810-26	MUSIC CLEARANCE SALA...						$0
810-27	MUSIC CLERICAL						$0
810-28	MASTER USE LICENSES						
	FESTIVAL LICENSES		ALLOW		2,500	2,500	$2,500
810-29	MUSIC PUBLISHING LICEN...						
	MUSIC PUBLISHING LICEN...		ALLOW		10,000	10,000	$10,000
810-33	SCORE (FACILITIES)						
	Score facilities		ALLOW		5,000	5,000	$5,000
810-34	STUDIO EQUIPMENT RENT...						$0
810-35	MUSIC INSTRUMENT RENT...						$0

(continued)

Figure 6–6 Sample budget 3, developed for a nonunion crew at a flat weekly rate (continued)

Acct #	Description	Amount	Units	X	Rate	Subtotal	Total
810-00	**MUSIC (CONT'D)**						
810-36	MUSIC INSTRUMENT CART...						$0
810-41	PAYROLL TAXES/FRINGES						$0
810-42	PHONO						$0
810-43	MUSIC RESEARCH REPOR...						$0
						Total For 810-00	**$35,200**
820-00	**POSTPRODUCTION SOUND**						
820-01	DIALOGUE RECORDING (A...						
	ADR FACILITY		ALLOW		5,000	5,000	$5,000
820-03	SOUND EFFECTS (FOLEY)						
	SOUND EFFECTS/FOLEY		ALLOW		5,000	5,000	$5,000
820-06	DUBBINGV SESSION						
	SOUND MIX-TEMP AND FI...		ALLOW		15,000	15,000	$15,000
820-07	SOUND TRANSFERS						
	SOUND TRANSFERS		ALLOW		5,000	5,000	$5,000
820-09	PURCHASED SOUND EFFE...						
	PURCHASED SOUND EFFE...		ALLOW		1,500	1,500	$1,500
820-12	MAGNETIC TAPE FOR EDIT						
	Mag Tape		ALLOW		1,000	1,000	
	Sales tax	8.25%			1,000	83	$1,083
820-13	OPTICAL NEG 35 & 35/32						
	DEVELOP OPTICAL NEG. ...	80,000	FEET		0.11	8,800	$8,800
						Total For 820-00	**$41,383**
840-00	**TITLES**						
840-01	TITLES (MAIN & END)						
	MAIN TITLE CARDS		ALLOW		3,000	3,000	
	END CREDIT CARDS/CRAWL		ALLOW		2,000	2,000	$5,000
840-02	MAIN TITLES						$0
840-03	END TITLES						$0
840-04	MISCELLANEOUS TITLES						$0
840-05	LABORATORY PROCESSING						
	LAB PROCESS FEE FOR TI...		ALLOW		2,000	2,000	$2,000
						Total For 840-00	**$7,000**
850-00	**OPTICALS, MATTES, INSERTS**						
850-01	OPTICAL EFFECTS/DUPE...						
	OPTICAL EFFECTS		ALLOW		10,000	10,000	$10,000
850-02	MASTER POSITIVES						$0
850-03	LABORATORY PROCESSING						$0
850-04	SPECIAL PHOTO EFFECTS						$0
850-05	INSERTS						$0
850-11	PURCHASES						$0
						Total For 850-00	**$10,000**

(continued)

Figure 6–6 Sample budget 3, developed for a nonunion crew at a flat weekly rate (continued)

Acct #	Description	Amount	Units	X	Rate	Subtotal	Total
860-00	**LABORATORY PROCESSING**						
860-01	REPRINTING & DEVELOPING						
	RE-PRINT & DEVELOP	5,000	FEET		0.22	1,100	$1,100
860-02	1ST TRIAL COMPOSITE P...						
	1ST TRIAL PRINT	9,000	FEET		0.20	1,800	$1,800
860-07	ANSWER PRINT/COLOR TI...						
	ANSWER PRINT	9,000	FEET		0.86	7,740	$7,740
860-08	SYNC REEL CHARGE						
	SYNC REEL CHARGE	10	REELS		38	380	$380
860-09	TELECINE						
	TELECINE	40	HOURS		200	8,000	$8,000
860-17	LEADER & MISCELLANEOUS						
	LEADER & TAPE		ALLOW		1,000	1,000	
	Sales tax	8.25%			1,000	83	$1,083
						Total For 860-00	**$20,103**
	Total Postproduction						**$228,911**
910-00	**ADMINISTRATIVE EXPENSES**						
910-01	ACCOUNTING & TERMINAL...						
	SUPPLIES		ALLOW		500	500	$500
910-02	MPAA CERTIFICATE						
	MPAA CERTIFICATE		ALLOW		1,500	1,500	$1,500
910-03	POSTAGE & STATIONERY						
	Allocation		ALLOW		1,000	1,000	$1,000
910-05	LEGAL EXPENSE & FEES						
	LEGAL FEES		ALLOW		5,000	5,000	
	CORP. REGISTER/FILES/F...		ALLOW		1,000	1,000	$6,000
910-06	TELEPHONE/FACSIMILE						
	PHONE/FAX	20	WEEKS		500	10,000	
	CELLULARS	20	WEEKS	3	200	12,000	
	Sales tax	8.25%			22,000	1,815	$23,815
910-12	DISTRIBUTION SCREENING						
	DISTRIBUTION SCREENING		ALLOW		2,000	2,000	$2,000
910-14	PARKING LOT EXPENSES						$0
910-16	FESTIVAL EXPENSES						
	FESTIVAL EXPENSES		ALLOW		500	500	$500
910-18	TITLE/CLEARANCE RPT.						
	TITLE & CLEARANCE REP ...		ALLOW		1,000	1,000	$1,000
910-21	POLAROID/STILL FILM						
	POLAROID FILM		ALLOW		500	500	
	STILL FILM/DEVELOP		ALLOW		1,000	1,000	
	Sales tax	8.25%			1,500	124	$1,624
910-22	PAYROLL CO.						
	PAYROLL CO.		ALLOW		3,000	3,000	$3,000
910-23	STORAGE						
	STORAGE FACILITY		ALLOW		500	500	$500

(continued)

Figure 6–6 Sample budget 3, developed for a nonunion crew at a flat weekly rate (continued)

Acct #	Description	Amount	Units	X	Rate	Subtotal	Total
910-00	**ADMINISTRATIVE EXPENSES (CONT'D)**						
910-35	WRAP PARTY						
	WRAP PARTY		ALLOW		2,000	2,000	$2,000
						Total For 910-00	**$43,439**
920-00	**PUBLICITY**						
920-01	UNIT PUBLICIST						
	PUBLICIST	1	MONTH		3,000	3,000	$3,000
920-02	STILL PHOTOGRAPHER						
	STILL PHOTOGRAPHER	1	FLAT		2,000	2,000	$2,000
920-03	STILL FILM & PROCESSING						
	Still supplies & expendables		ALLOW		1,000	1,000	$1,000
						Total For 920-00	**$6,000**
	Total Other						**$49,439**
	Completion Bond: 3.00%						$39,187
	Contingency: 10.00%						$130,624
	Overhead: 1.00%						$13,062
	Insurance: 2.00%						$26,125
	TOTAL ABOVE-THE-LINE						**$243,957**
	TOTAL BELOW-THE-LINE						**$1,062,280**
	TOTAL ABOVE- & BELOW-THE-LINE						**$1,306,237**
	GRAND TOTAL						**$1,515,235**

Figure 6–6 Sample budget 3, developed for a nonunion crew at a flat weekly rate (continued)

Acct No	Description	Amount	Units	X	Curr	Rate	Subtotal	Total
60-00	**STORY**							
						Account Total for 60-00		**0**
60-00	**DEVELOPMENT COSTS DUE**							
						Account Total for 60-00		**55,500**
61-00	**PRODUCER**							
61-00	PRODUCER							
	Wurmfeld - Prep/Shoot	9	WEEKS	1		575	5,175	
	Wurmfeld- Prep/Shoot -kit	9	WEEKS	1		125	1,125	
	Wurmfeld- Post	3	WEEKS	1		2,100	6,300	
	Wurmfeld- Prep/Shoot -kit	3	MONTHS	1		400	1,200	
	Co-Producer -prep	1	WEEK	1		575	575	
	Co-Producer Kit	1	WEEK	1		125	125	
	Co-Producer - Prep	1	WEEK	1		575	575	
	Co-Producer - Prep - Kit	1	WEEK	1		125	125	
	Total							
	Other Fringes	16.5%				12,630.3	2,084	17,284
61-00	GIFTS/FLOWERS, etc	1	ALLOW	1		2,000	2,000	2,000
						Account Total for 61-00		**19,284**
62-00	**DIRECTOR**							
62-00	DIRECTOR							
	pre	5	WEEKS	1		575	2,875	
	kit	5		1		125	625	
	production	4	WEEKS	1		575	2,300	
	kit	4		1		125	500	
	post	12	WEEKS	1		575	6,900	
	kit	12		1		125	1,500	
	Total							
	Other Fringes	16.5%				12,078.79	1,993	16,693
62-00	CASTING DIRECTOR							
	Casting Director	1	ALLOW	1		7,500	7,500	
	Casting Expenses	1	ALLOW	1		1,500	1,500	
	Total							
	Sales Tax	8.25%				1,503.03	124	9,124
						Account Total for 62-00		**25,817**
63-00	**CAST**							
63-00	PRINCIPAL PERFORMERS							
	Jessica	4	WEEKS	1		1,620	6,480	
		3	DAYS	1		486	1,458	
	Helen	4	WEEKS	1		1,620	6,480	
		3	DAYS	1		486	1,458	
	Josh	3	WEEKS	1		1,620	4,860	
	Judy	2.5	WEEKS	1		1,620	4,050	
	Joan	2	WEEKS	1		1,620	3,240	
	Martin	1	WEEK	1		1,620	1,620	
	Sebastian	1	WEEK	1		1,620	1,620	
	Dan	1	WEEK	1		1,620	1,620	
	Stephen	1	WEEK	1		1,620	1,620	
	Damien	1	WEEK	1		1,620	1,620	
	Total							
	Other Fringes	16.5%				36,121.21	5,960	
	SAG	13.15%				36,129.28	4,751	
	Agency Fee	10%				36,130	3,613	

(continued)

Figure 6–7 Sample budget 4, developed for Kissing Jessica Stein

Acct No	Description	Amount	Units	X	Curr	Rate	Subtotal	Total
	Overtime	15%				20,253.33	3,038	53,488
63-00	ACTORS							
	Sydney	1	WEEK	1		1,620	1,620	
	Hannah	1	WEEK	1		1,620	1,620	
	Grandma Esther	2	DAYS	1		466	932	
	Greg	2	DAYS	1		466	932	
	Stanley	1	DAY	1		466	466	
	Guy	1	DAY	1		466	466	
	Charles	1	DAY	1		466	466	
	Diana	1	DAY	1		466	466	
	Rod	1	DAY	1		466	466	
	Howard	1	DAY	1		466	466	
	Marnie	1	DAY	1		466	466	
	Rabbi	1	DAY	1		466	466	
	Hugh	1	DAY	1		466	466	
	Trent	1	DAY	1		466	466	
	Writer	2	DAYS	1		466	932	
	Matthew	1	DAY	1		466	466	
	New Age Guy	1	DAY	1		466	466	
	Aunt Sophie	1	DAY	1		466	466	
	Effeminate Guy	1	DAY	1		466	466	
	Guy WHo THinks he's Slick	1	DAY	1		466	466	
	Messenger	1	DAY	1		466	466	
	Ned	1	DAY	1		466	466	
	Clerk	1	DAY	1		466	466	
	Cashier	1	DAY	1		466	466	
	Woman	1	DAY	1		466	466	
	Rachel	1	DAY	1		466	466	
	Blonde	1	DAY	1		466	466	
	Pathetic Woman	1	DAY	1		466	466	
	Butchy Woman	1	DAY	1		466	466	
	Roy	1	DAY	1		466	466	
	Jim	1	DAY	1		466	466	
	Total							
	Other Fringes	16.5%				18,169.7	2,998	
	SAG	13.15%				18,106.47	2,381	
	Agency Fee	10%				18,250	1,825	
	Overtime	15%				18,173.33	2,726	28,082
63-00	REHEARSALS							
	Food for rehearsals	1	ALLOW	1		200	200	
	Total							200
63-00	LOOPING	2	DAYS	2		466	1,864	
	SAG	13.15%				1,863.12	245	
	Agency Fee	10%				1,860	186	2,295
							Account Total for 63-00	**84,065**
65-00	**TRAVEL & LIVING**							
							Account Total for 65-00	**0**
	Total Above-The-Line							**184,666**
70-50	**PRODUCTION STAFF**							
70-50	1ST ASSISTANT DIRECTOR							
	prep	2	WEEKS	1		700	1,400	
	shoot	4	WEEKS	1		700	2,800	
	Total							
	Other Fringes	16.5%				4,200	693	4,893
70-50	2ND ASSISTANT DIRECTOR							

(continued)

Figure 6–7 Sample budget 4, developed for Kissing Jessica Stein *(continued)*

Acct No	Description	Amount	Units	X	Curr	Rate	Subtotal	Total
	prep	1	WEEK	1		600	600	
	shoot	4	WEEKS	1		600	2,400	
	wrap	2	DAYS	1		117	234	
	Total							
	Other Fringes	16.5%				3,236.36	534	3,768
70-50	KEY SET PA							
	prep	2	DAYS	1		100.0	200	
	shoot	4	WEEKS	1		400	1,600	
	wrap	1	DAY	1		100.0	100	
	Total							
	Other Fringes	16.5%				1,903.03	314	2,214
70-50	SCRIPT SUPERVISOR							
	prep	1	WEEK	1		700	700	
	shoot	4	WEEKS	1		700	2,800	
	Total							
	Other Fringes	16.5%				3,503.03	578	4,078
70-50	PRODUCTION MANAGER							
	prep	5	WEEKS	1		700	3,500	
	shoot	4	WEEKS	1		700	2,800	
	wrap	2	WEEKS	1		700	1,400	
	Total							
	Other Fringes	16.5%				7,703.03	1,271	8,971
70-50	POC							
	prep	4	WEEKS	1		600	2,400	
	shoot	4	WEEKS	1		600	2,400	
	wrap	2	WEEKS	1		600	1,200	
	Total							
	Other Fringes	16.5%				6,000	990	6,990
70-51	PA #1							
	prep	1	WEEK	5		400	2,000	
	shoot	1	WEEK	4		400	1,600	
	wrap	1	WEEK	2		400	800	
	Total							
	Other Fringes	16.5%				4,400	726	5,126
70-51	KITS/COMPUTERS/MILEAGE							
	3 bodies	8	WEEKS	3		50.0	1,200	
	Total							1,200
70-51	OFFICE MEALS							
	Pre-pro Office MEals (12 heads @$8 e	5	WEEKS	1		480	2,400	
	shoot (5 head @ $8)	4	WEEKS	1		40.0	160	
	wrap	2	Weeks	1		480	960	
	Total							
	Sales Tax	8.25%				3,515.15	290	3,810
							Account Total for 70-50	52,234
70-70	**EXTRAS/STAND-INS**							
70-70	Extras							
	non SAG Extras	24	DAYS	10		40.0	9,600	
	SAG Extras	18	DAYS	10		108	19,440	
	Total							
	Other Fringes	16.5%				29,042.42	4,792	
	SAG	13.15%				19,437.26	2,556	
	Overtime	15%				19,440	2,916	39,304
70-70	Extras Casting							
	Casting Fee	1	ALLOW	1		2,000	2,000	
	Total							2,000
70-70	Wardrobe Allowance							
	WARDOBE ALLOWANCE	1	ALLOW	1		500	500	

Figure 6–7 Sample budget 4, developed for Kissing Jessica Stein *(continued)*

Acct No	Description	Amount	Units	X	Curr	Rate	Subtotal	Total
	Total							500
							Account Total for 70-70	41,804
71-00	**CAMERA**							
71-00	dop							
	prep	3	WEEKS	1		700	2,100	
	shoot	4	WEEKS	1		700	2,800	
	Consulting Fee	1	ALLOW	1		2,000	2,000	
	Total							
	Other Fringes	16.5%				6,903.03	1,139	8,039
71-00	1st AC							
	prep	0.5	WEEKS	1		600	300	
	shoot	1	WEEK	4		600	2,400	
	wrap	1	DAY	1		100.0	100	
	Total							
	Other Fringes	16.5%				2,806.06	463	3,263
71-00	2nd AC							
	prep	0.5	WEEKS	1		500	250	
	shoot	4	Weeks	1		500	2,000	
	wrap	1	DAY	1		85.0	85	
	Total							
	Other Fringes	16.5%				2,333.33	385	2,720
71-01	Camera Package							
	Camera Package	4	WEEKS	1		3,000	12,000	
	Total							12,000
71-01	Video Assist							
	Equipment	1	ALLOW	1		600	600	
	Total							600
71-01	Still Photography							
	Still Film	1	ALLOW	1		600	600	
	Still Process	1	ALLOW	1		1,000	1,000	
	Total							
	Sales Tax	8.25%				1,612.12	133	1,733
71-02	Loss and Damage	1	ALLOW	1		1,000	1,000	1,000
							Account Total for 71-00	29,355
71-50	**SET DESIGN**							
71-50	PRODUCTION DESIGNER							
	prep	4	WEEKS	1		700	2,800	
	shoot	4	WEEKS	1		700	2,800	
	Total							
	Other Fringes	16.5%				5,600	924	6,524
71-50	ART DIRECTOR							
	prep	3	WEEKS	1		600	1,800	
	shoot	4	WEEKS	1		600	2,400	
	wrap	0.5	WEEKS	1		600	300	
	Total							
	Other Fringes	16.5%				4,503.03	743	5,243
71-50	ART PA							
	prep	1	WEEK	1		400	400	
	shoot	4	WEEKS	1		400	1,600	
	wrap	0.5	WEEKS	1		400	200	
	Total							
	Other Fringes	16.5%				2,200	363	2,563
71-50	ART DEPT RUNNER							
	prep	4	WEEKS	1		400	1,600	
	shoot	4	WEEKS	1		400	1,600	

(continued)

Figure 6–7 Sample budget 4, developed for Kissing Jessica Stein *(continued)*

Acct No	Description	Amount	Units	X	Curr	Rate	Subtotal	Total
	wrap	1	WEEK	1		400	400	
	Total							
	Other Fringes	16.5%				3,600	594	4,194
71-50	ART DEPT PURCHASES	1	ALLOW	1		7,000	7,000	
	Sales Tax	8.25%				7,006.06	578	7,578
71-50	ART DEPT RENTALS	1	ALLOW	1		5,000	5,000	5,000
71-50	BOX RENTALS/MILEAGE							
	5 KITS	9	WEEKS	4		25.0	900	
	Car Allowance/Transpo	9	WEEKS	4		25.0	900	
	Total							1,800
71-51	ART DEPT MISC							
	Copies, polaroid film	1	ALLOW	1		1,000	1,000	
	Total							
	Sales Tax	8.25%				1,006.06	83	1,083
						Account Total for 71-50		33,985
72-50	**SET OPERATIONS**							
72-50	KEY GRIP							
	Prep	0.5	WEEKS	1		700	350	
	shoot	4	WEEKS	1		700	2,800	
		1		1		0.0	0	
	1st Co Grip	4	WEEKS	1		700	2,800	
	Total							
	Other Fringes	16.5%				5,951.51	982	6,932
72-50	CRANE/DOLLY GRIP							
	Dolly Grip	4	WEEKS	1		700	2,800	
	Total							
	Other Fringes	16.5%				2,800	462	3,262
72-50	GRIP/ELECTRIC EQUIIPMENT							
	Super Pee Wee Dolly	4	WEEKS	1		1,500	6,000	
	Grip Package & Truck	4	WEEKS	1		3,500	14,000	
	Total							20,000
72-50	CRAFT SERVICE PURCHASE							
	Food Purchase	4	WEEKS	1		800	3,200	
	Total							
	Sales Tax	8.25%				3,200	264	3,464
72-50	CRAFT SERVICE LABOR							
	Craft Service person	4.5	WEEKS	1		500	2,250	
	Total							
	Other Fringes	16.5%				2,248.48	371	2,621
72-51	SET STRIKING							
	Labor	1	ALLOW	1		800	800	
	Materials/REntals	1	ALLOW	1		250	250	
	Total							
	Other Fringes	16.5%				800	132	1,182
72-51	PRODUCTION EXPENDABLES							
	chairs, tables, crafty serve, ext cords	4	WEEKS	1		1,000	4,000	
	Total							4,000
72-51	SECOND MEAL							
	Second meal based on 40 people	1	ALLOW	1		3,000	3,000	
	Total							
	Sales Tax	8.25%				3,006.06	248	3,248
						Account Total for 72-50		44,709
73-00	**ELECTRICAL**							
73-00	GAFFER							
	Prep	0.5	WEEKS	1		700	350	

Figure 6–7 Sample budget 4, developed for Kissing Jessica Stein *(continued)*

Acct No	Description	Amount	Units	X	Curr	Rate	Subtotal	Total
	shoot	4	WEEKS	1		700	2,800	
	Total							
	Other Fringes	16.5%				3,151.52	520	3,670
73-00	BEST BOY ELECTRIC							
	prep (5 day flat wkly rate)	0.5	WEEKS	1		600	300	
	shoot	4	WEEKS	1		600	2,400	
	wrap	1	WEEK	1		600	600	
	Total							
	Other Fringes	16.5%				3,303.03	545	3,845
73-00	ELECTRIC							
	shoot	4	WEEKS	1		600	2,400	
	Total							
	Other Fringes	16.5%				2,400	396	2,796
73-00	EQUIPMENT PURCHASE/EXPENDABLE							
	Other purchase	1	ALLOW	1		2,000	2,000	
	Expendable Purchase	1	ALLOW	1		1,000	1,000	
	Total							
	Sales Tax	8.25%				3,006.06	248	3,248
73-00	KITS	4	WEEKS	4		25.0	400	400
							Account Total for 73-00	**13,959**
75-00	**PROPERTIES**							
75-00	PROPERTY MASTER							
	prep	3	WEEKS	1		700	2,100	
	shoot	4	WEEKS	1		700	2,800	
	Total							
	Other Fringes	16.5%				4,903.03	809	5,709
75-00	ASSISTANT PROPERTY MASTER							
	prep	2	WEEKS	1		600	1,200	
	shoot	4	WEEKS	1		600	2,400	
	wrap	0.5	WEEKS	1		600	300	
	Total							
	Other Fringes	16.5%				3,903.03	644	4,544
75-00	PICTURE VEHICLE - L&M	1	ALLOW	1		500	500	500
75-00	PICTURE VEHICLE RENTALS							
	Cabs, atmosphere	1	ALLOW	1		2,000	2,000	
	Total							2,000
75-00	PROP RENTALS	1	ALLOW	1		3,500	3,500	3,500
75-00	PROP PURCHASES	1	ALLOW	1		4,500	4,500	
	Sales Tax	8.25%				4,496.97	371	4,871
75-01	PROP BOX RENTALS	8	WEEKS	2		50.0	800	800
75-01	EXPENDABLES	1	ALLOW	1		500	500	500
75-02	LOSS, DAMAGE & REPAIRS	1	ALLOW	1		500	500	500
							Account Total for 75-00	**22,924**
75-50	**WARDROBE**							
75-50	ASSISTING COSTUME DESIGNER							
	ASst Costume Designer - prep	4	WEEKS	1		600	2,400	
	shoot	4	WEEKS	1		600	2,400	
	wrap	0.5	WEEKS	1		600	300	
	Total							
	Other Fringes	16.5%				5,103.03	842	5,942
75-50	COSTUME DESIGNER							
	prep	4	WEEKS	1		700	2,800	
	shoot	4	WEEKS	1		700	2,800	
	wrap	0.5	WEEKS	1		700	350	
	Total							

(continued)

Figure 6–7 Sample budget 4, developed for Kissing Jessica Stein *(continued)*

Acct No	Description	Amount	Units	X	Curr	Rate	Subtotal	Total
	Other Fringes	16.5%				5,951.51	982	6,932
75-50	ALTERATIONS - L&M	1	ALLOW	1		250	250	250
75-50	CLEANING & DYEING	1	ALLOW	1		500	500	500
75-50	WARDROBE RENTALS	1	ALLOW	1		4,500	4,500	4,500
75-50	WARDROBE PURCHASES	1	ALLOW	1		5,000	5,000	
	Sales Tax	8.25%				5,006.06	413	5,413
75-51	HAND BOX RENTALS	9	WEEKS	1		50.0	450	450
75-52	LOSS, DAMAGE & REPAIRS	1		1		250	250	250
							Account Total for 75-50	**24,237**
76-00	**MAKEUP & HAIRSTYLISTS**							
76-00	MAKE-UP ARTISTS							
	Dept Head -	0.5	WEEKS	1		700	350	
	shoot	4	WEEKS	1		700	2,800	
	wrap	0.5	WEEKS	1		700	350	
		1		1		0.0	0	
	Makeup Asst	4	WEEKS	1		500	2,000	
	Total							
	Other Fringes	16.5%				5,503.03	908	6,408
76-00	KEY HAIR STYLIST							
	PRep	0.5	WEEKS	1		700	350	
	Shoot	4	WEEKS	1		700	2,800	
	shoot	4	WEEKS	1		500	2,000	
	Total							
	Other Fringes	16.5%				5,151.51	850	6,000
76-00	EXTRA HAIR STYLISTS							
	Asst Hair Artist #1 -	2	WEEKS	1		600	1,200	
	Total							
	Other Fringes	16.5%				1,200	198	1,398
76-00	WIG & HAIR PURCHASE	1	ALLOW	1		400	400	
	Sales Tax	8.25%				400	33	433
76-00	MAKEUP SUPPLIES/APPLIANCE	1	ALLOW	1		450	450	
	Sales Tax	8.25%				448.48	37	487
76-01	MAKE-UP/HAIR KIT RENTALS	4	WEEKS	2		50.0	400	400
							Account Total for 76-00	**15,126**
76-50	**PRODUCTION SOUND**							
76-50	SOUND MIXER							
	shoot	4	WEEKS	1		700	2,800	
	Total							
	Other Fringes	16.5%				2,800	462	3,262
76-50	BOOMMAN							
	shoot - boom #1	4	WEEKS	1		600	2,400	
	Total							
	Other Fringes	16.5%				2,400	396	2,796
76-50	SOUND EQUIP RENTALS							
	Soundman's Equip	4	WEEKS	1		1,300	5,200	
	Total							5,200
76-50	WALKIE TALKIE RENTAL							
	$25 per week per walkie	4	WEEKS	25		25.0	2,500	
	Total							2,500
76-51	PURCHASES/MISCELLANEOUS EXPENS							
	DAT purchase, cables, batteries etc.	1	ALLOW	1		500	500	
	Total							
	Sales Tax	8.25%				496.97	41	541
							Account Total for 76-50	**14,299**

Figure 6–7 Sample budget 4, developed for Kissing Jessica Stein *(continued)*

Acct No	Description	Amount	Units	X	Curr	Rate	Subtotal	Total
77-00	**TRANSPORTATION**							
77-00	MESSENGER SERVICE							
	Messenger	1	ALLOW	1		500	500	
	Total							500
77-00	DRIVERS							
	Honeywagon - shoot	3	WEEKS	1		1,500	4,500	
	Total							
	Other Fringes	16.5%				4,503.03	743	
	TEAMSTERS	11.17%				4,504.14	503	5,746
77-00	VEHICLES							
	Art Dept Cube - prep	2	WEEKS	1		600	1,200	
	shoot	4	WEEKS	1		600	2,400	
	wrap	0.5	WEEKS	1		600	300	
		1		1		0.0	0	
		1		1		0.0	0	
	Honeywagon - shoot (8 room)	3	WEEKS	1		1,400	4,200	
		1		1		0.0	0	
	Other 14 Ft Cube	4.5	WEEKS	1		600	2,700	
		1		1		0.0	0	
	Production 14 Ft Cube	5	WEEKS	1		600	3,000	
	Total							
	Sales Tax	8.25%				13,818.18	1,140	14,940
77-00	FUEL							
	Fuel -prep	5	WEEKS	1		250	1,250	
	fuel - shoot	4	WEEKS	1		1,000	4,000	
	Total							5,250
77-00	PICTURE CARS/ DRIVERS							
	Taxi w. decals, etc	1	ALLOW	1		1,000	1,000	
	Total							
	Other Fringes	16.5%				1,000	165	
	Overtime	15%				1,000	150	
	TEAMSTERS	11.17%				1,002.91	112	1,427
77-02	LOSS, DAMAGE, REPAIRS							
	Loss and Damage	1	ALLOW	1		1,000	1,000	
	Total							1,000
						Account Total for 77-00		**28,863**
77-50	**LOCATION EXPENSE**							
77-50	SURVEY EXPENSE							
	Still Film	1	ALLOW	1		500	500	
	Develop	1	ALLOW	1		700	700	
	Food/Cell Phone	1	ALLOW	1		1,000	1,000	
	Total							2,200
77-50	LOCATION STAFF							
	LOCATION MGR -PREP	5	WEEKS	1		700	3,500	
	shoot	4	WEEKS	1		700	2,800	
	Asst. Loc Manager - prep	4	WEEKS	1		500	2,000	
	shoot	2	WEEKS	1		500	1,000	
	wrap	0.5	WEEKS	1		500	250	
	Total							
	Other Fringes	16.5%				9,551.51	1,576	11,126
77-50	SITE RENTALS/PERMITS/LIC.							
	Jessica's Apt	1		1		2,500	2,500	
	Helen's Apt	1		1		2,000	2,000	
	New York Times Office	1		1		2,000	2,000	
	Schuller Gallery	1		1		2,000	2,000	
	The CoffeeHouse	1		1		1,000	1,000	
	Starbucks	1		1		1,000	1,000	

(continued)

Figure 6–7 Sample budget 4, developed for Kissing Jessica Stein *(continued)*

Acct No	Description	Amount	Units	X	Curr	Rate	Subtotal	Total
	Trendy Restaurant	1		1		1,500	1,500	
	Bar	1		1		2,000	2,000	
	Another Restaurant	1		1		1,000	1,000	
	Martin & Sebastian	1		1		1,000	1,000	
	Joan & Matthew's Apt	1		1		1,000	1,000	
	Union Square Cafe Bar	1		1		2,000	2,000	
	Second Ave Estab	1		1		500	500	
	Indian Restaurant	1		1		1,000	1,000	
	DOJO Cafe	1		1		2,000	2,000	
	Gyno's Office	1		1		700	700	
	Barnes & Noble	1		1		1,500	1,500	
	Ext Times Square'	1		1		500	500	
	China Grill	1		1		1,200	1,200	
	Stein's Scarsdale Residence	1		1		1,000	1,000	
	24th St Flea Market	1		1		250	250	
	Mt. Sinai Hosp Room	1		1		1,000	1,000	
	Dept Store	1		1		2,000	2,000	
	Synagogue	1		1		1,000	1,000	
	Temple Beth Israel	1		1		0.0	0	
	Wedding Reception HAll	1		1		2,000	2,000	
	Josh Meyer's Apt	1		1		500	500	
	Supermarket	1		1		2,000	2,000	
	Royalton Hotel Lobby	1		1		2,000	2,000	
	Police Officers (40 hr week)	2	WEEKS	1		1,200	2,400	
	Permit Office Fee	1	ALLOW	1		250	250	
	Total							
	Other Fringes	16.5%				2,400	396	
	IATSE 891	18%				2,400	432	
	Overtime	15%				2,400	360	41,988
77-50	CATERING SERVICES							
	Catering - Breakfast - Lunch	55	HEADS	24		20.0	26,400	
	Labor Costs	1	ALLOW	1		2,000	2,000	
	Total							
	Other Fringes	16.5%				2,000	330	28,730
77-51	AIRPORT PICKUP/DELIVERY	1	ALLOW	1		250	250	250
77-51	LOCATION LOAD & UNLOAD	1	ALLOW	1		250	250	250
77-51	GRATUITIES	1	ALLOW	1		250	250	250
77-51	OTHER EXPENSE							
	miscellaneous	1	ALLOW	1		300	300	
	Total							300
77-52	SHIPPING	1	ALLOW	1		200	200	200
77-52	LOCATION SECURITY							
	24 Hour Security	4	DAYS	1		400	1,600	
	Security	10	DAYS	1		150	1,500	
	Total							
	Other Fringes	16.5%				3,103.03	512	3,612
							Account Total for 77-50	**88,906**
78-50	**PRODUCTION DAILIES**							
78-50	NEGATIVE RAW STOCK							
	Kodak Recans	120,000	FEET	1		0.38	45,600	
	Total							
	Sales Tax	8.25%				45,600	3,762	49,362
78-50	DEVELOPING							
	PROCESS Original Negative	120,000	FEET	1		0.12	14,400	
	PREP	120,000	FEET	1		0.04	4,800	
	Total							19,200
78-50	DAT TAPES							

Figure 6–7 Sample budget 4, developed for Kissing Jessica Stein *(continued)*

Acct No	Description	Amount	Units	X	Curr	Rate	Subtotal	Total
	DAT Purchase	1	ALLOW	1		800	800	
	Total							
	Sales Tax	8.25%				800	66	866
78-50	TRANSFER SOUND DAILIES	1	ALLOW	1		3,000	3,000	3,000
78-50	VIDEO TAPE TRANSFERS							
	Transfer 120000 (Vidfilm, quote)	1	ALLOW	1		15,000	15,000	
	Total							15,000
							Account Total for 78-50	**87,428**
	Total Production							**497,829**
80-00	**EDITING**							
80-00	FILM EDITOR							
	Post starting 2nd day production	1	ALLOW	1		12,000	12,000	
	Total							12,000
80-00	MUSIC EDITING	1	ALLOW	1		1,500	1,500	1,500
80-00	NEGATIVE CUTTING	1	ALLOW	1		6,000	6,000	6,000
80-00	PROJECTION							
	Preview and Test Screenings	2	SCREENS	1		500	1,000	
	Total							1,000
80-00	CONTINUITY SCRIPTS	1	ALLOW	1		1,000	1,000	1,000
80-00	TRANSFERS							
	Black & Code Tapes	16	WEEKS	2		100.0	3,200	
	Total							3,200
80-01	EDITORIAL SUPPLIES							
	Beta tapes, copies, sharpies, 1/2", etc	1	ALLOW	1		1,000	1,000	
	Total							
	Sales Tax	8.25%				1,006.06	83	1,083
							Account Total for 80-00	**25,783**
81-00	**MUSIC**							
81-02	MUSIC SUPERVISOR	1	ALLOW	1		3,500	3,500	
	Other Fringes	16.5%				3,503.03	578	4,078
81-02	MASTER USE LICENSES/FESTIVAL LIC							
	Festival Licenses only	1	ALLOW	1		5,000	5,000	
	Total							5,000
81-02	MUSIC PUBLISHING LICENSES	1	ALLOW	1		2,000	2,000	2,000
							Account Total for 81-00	**11,078**
82-00	**POST PRODUCTION SOUND**							
							Account Total for 82-00	**2,500**
84-00	**TITLES**							
84-00	TITLES (MAIN & END)							
	MAIN TITLES	15	TITLES	1		350	5,250	
	END CRAWL 5 MINUTES	1	ALLOW	1		2,000	2,000	
	Total							7,250
							Account Total for 84-00	**7,250**
85-00	**OPTICALS, MATTES, INSERTS**							
85-00	OPTICAL EFFECTS/DUPE NEG	1	ALLOW	1		6,500	6,500	6,500
							Account Total for 85-00	**6,500**
86-00	**LABORATORY PROCESSING**							
86-00	1ST TRIAL COMPOSITE PRINT	10,000	FEET	1		0.95	9,500	9,500
86-01	LEADER & MISCELLANEOUS	1	ALLOW	1		2,500	2,500	2,500

(continued)

Figure 6–7 Sample budget 4, developed for Kissing Jessica Stein *(continued)*

Acct No	Description	Amount	Units	X	Curr	Rate	Subtotal	Total
							Account Total for 86-00	**12,000**
	Total Post Production							**65,111**
91-00	**ADMINISTRATIVE EXPENSES**							
91-00	ACCOUNTING & TERMINAL FEE							
	Computers/programs, etc	1	ALLOW	1		500	500	
	Total							500
91-00	POSTAGE & STATIONERY							
	Postage	1	ALLOW	1		800	800	
	Messenger Service	1	ALLOW	1		350	350	
	FEDEX	1	ALLOW	1		450	450	
	Total							1,600
91-00	XEROX/MIMEO							
	COPY MACHINE RENTAL	4	MONTHS	1		600	2,400	
	Total							2,400
91-00	LEGAL EXPENSE & FEES							
	Production Legal/LLC Setup/Financial	1	ALLOW	1		13,500	13,500	
	Total							13,500
91-00	TELEPHONE/TELEGRAPH/TELEX							
	Phone Install	1	ALLOW	1		2,000	2,000	
	Phone & Fax	1	MONTH	6		500	3,000	
	Cell Phone Expenses	6	MONTHS	5		149.99	4,500	
	Total							9,500
91-00	WRAP PARTY							
	wrap gifts	75	GIFTS	1		10.0	750	
		1	ALLOW	1		500	500	
	Total							
	Sales Tax	8.25%				751.52	62	1,312
91-00	SCRIPT COPYRIGHT	1	ALLOW	1		40.0	40	40
91-00	OFFICE SUPPLIES							
	prep	4	WEEKS	1		100.0	400	
	shoot	4	WEEKS	1		150	600	
	post	16	WEEKS	1		100.0	1,600	
	Total							
	Sales Tax	8.25%				2,606.06	215	2,815
91-01	POLAROID & STILL FILM	1	ALLOW	1		2,000	2,000	
	Sales Tax	8.25%				2,000	165	2,165
91-01	STORAGE	6	MONTHS	1		150	900	900
91-01	BANK/FINACE CHARGES							
	BAnk Fees	12	MONTHS	1		30.0	360	
	Total							360
91-01	PARKING LOT EXPENSES/TICKETS							
	Total parking for all tranpo vehicles p	8	WEEKS	1		1,000	8,000	
	Tickets	1	ALLOW	1		750	750	
	Total							8,750
91-01	OFFICE RENT & OTH EXPENSE							
	Office REnt	3	MONTHS	1		2,500	7,500	
	furniture	9	WEEKS	1		100.0	900	
	Total							8,400
91-01	CLEARANCE & TITLE REPORT	1	ALLOW	1		2,000	2,000	2,000
							Account Total for 91-00	**54,242**
92-00	**PUBLICITY**							
							Account Total for 92-00	**1,000**
93-00	**FESTIVALS**							

Figure 6–7 Sample budget 4, developed for Kissing Jessica Stein *(continued)*

Acct No	Description	Amount	Units	X	Curr	Rate	Subtotal	Total
						Account Total for 93-00		350
	Total Other							**55,592**
	Insurance							6,000
	Total Above-The-Line							**184,666**
	Total Below-The-Line							**618,532**
	Total Above and Below-The-Line							**803,198**
	Grand Total							**809,198**

(continued)

Figure 6–7 Sample budget 4, developed for Kissing Jessica Stein *(continued)*

Acct No	Category Description	Page	Total
60-00	DEVELOPMENT COSTS DUE	1	55,500
61-00	PRODUCER	1	19,284
62-00	DIRECTOR	1	25,817
63-00	CAST	1	84,065
	Total Above-The-Line		**184,666**
70-50	PRODUCTION STAFF	2	52,234
70-70	EXTRAS/STAND-INS	3	41,804
71-00	CAMERA	4	29,355
71-50	SET DESIGN	4	33,985
72-50	SET OPERATIONS	5	44,709
73-00	ELECTRICAL	5	13,959
75-00	PROPERTIES	6	22,924
75-50	WARDROBE	6	24,237
76-00	MAKEUP & HAIRSTYLISTS	7	15,126
76-50	PRODUCTION SOUND	7	14,299
77-00	TRANSPORTATION	8	28,863
77-50	LOCATION EXPENSE	8	88,906
78-50	PRODUCTION DAILIES	9	87,428
	Total Production		**497,829**
80-00	EDITING	10	25,783
81-00	MUSIC	10	11,078
82-00	POST PRODUCTION SOUND	10	2,500
84-00	TITLES	10	7,250
85-00	OPTICALS, MATTES, INSERTS	10	6,500
86-00	LABORATORY PROCESSING	10	12,000
	Total Post Production		**65,111**
91-00	ADMINISTRATIVE EXPENSES	11	54,242
92-00	PUBLICITY	11	1,000
93-00	FESTIVALS	11	350
	Total Other		**55,592**
	Insurance		6,000
	Total Above-The-Line		**184,666**
	Total Below-The-Line		**618,532**
	Total Above and Below-The-Line		**803,198**
	Grand Total		**809,198**

Figure 6–7 Sample budget 4, developed for Kissing Jessica Stein *(continued)*

$62,000 Budget Production	
SCRIPT DEVELOPMENT	
Printing/photocopying	$500
Mailing	$250
Application fees (writing workshops, etc.)	$100
Phone	$250
TOTAL SCRIPT DEVELOPMENT	**$1,100**
PREPRODUCTION	
Graphics	$100
Script copies (x90)	$750
Audition space	$150
Rehearsal space	$300
Set construction	$1,000
Costumes	$1,000
Props	$500
Food	$200
TOTAL PREPRODUCTION	**$4,000**
PRODUCTION	
EQUIPMENT -	
Camera (@ 1000/day × 6 days, based on a 2-day week)	$6,000
Lights (@ 250/day × 6, based on a 2-day week)	$1,500
Sound (@ 100/day × 6, based on a 2-day week)	$600
Incidentals (tape, gels, bulbs, cleaners, etc.)	$400
Generator rental/tie-ins	$300
Truck rental	$900
Equipment Insurance	$1,100
TOTAL EQUIPMENT	**$10,800**
STOCK & PROCESSING -	
Film (400 mins=16,000 ft=40 cans)	$3,360
Processing (16,000 ft @ .15/ft)	$2,400
Nagra tape (14 30-min tapes @ $20 each)	$280
Videotape	$100
TOTAL STOCK & PROCESSING	**$6,140**
CREW	
Camera special	$600
Food	$2,100
TOTAL CREW	**$2,700**
LOCATIONS	
Permits	$50

(continued)

Figure 6–8 $62 K budget

Rental cafe	$150
Rental 110 Capp	$400
Reparation S. Van Ness	$300
Reparation Davis	$25
TOTAL LOCATIONS	**$925**
Administrative	
Phone	$250
Gas	$250
Photocopies (log sheets, etc.)	$50
TOTAL ADMINISTRATIVE	**$550**
TOTAL PRODUCTION	**$26,215**

(continued)

Figure 6–8 $62 K budget (continued)

$62,000 Budget Postproduction	
ADMINISTRATIVE	**COST**
Office supplies	$250
Phone/fax	$500
Photocopies	$200
Stills	$200
Mailing	$100
Gas	$250
Videotape	$50
Videocassettes	$30
TOTAL ADMINISTRATIVE	**$1,580**
ROUGH CUT	
Shipping	$100
Nagra transfer (16,000 ft @ .75 less 10%)	$1,080
Sync sound	$0
Edge coating (32,000 ft @ .02/ft)	$576
Flatbed rental ($700/mo)	$2,100
Editing expendables and equipment (bench, etc.)	$2,400
Editing room rental	$600
Editing special 1	$2,050
Editing special 2	$600
Tape/DAT to mag transfer	$500
Sound design	$250
Pickups shoot	$1,000
Rough cut screening room rental	$300
Hospitality/stewardship	$150
TOTAL ROUGH CUT	**$11,706**
FINE CUT	
Shipping	$300
Sound design/score expenses	$250
Conforming	$2,000
Answer print from AB roll (3,600 ft @ 1.05/ft)	$3,402
Mix sound (incl. Foley)	$10,000
Optical track negative (3,600 ft @ .20/ft)	$648
Release prints (3,600 ft @ .32/ft × 2) $1,037 × 2	$2,074
Titles	$1,000
Hospitality/stewardship	$150
TOTAL FINE CUT	**$19,824**
FESTIVALS	**COST**
Transfer to video (once, workprint/once, release print)	$1,200
Video copies	$150

(continued)

Figure 6–8 $62 K postproduction budget

Shipping	$200
Submission fees (6 festivals @ $50/ea)	$300
Publicist	$500
Press kits	$250
Press mailing	$250
Stills	$300
Hospitality/stewardship	$150
TOTAL FESTIVAL PHASE	**$3,300**
Total Postproduction	**$36,410**
Total Production	**$26,215**
Grand Total Production & Postproduction	**$62,625**

Figure 6–8 #62 K postproduction budget (continued)

7 PRE-PRODUCTION

"Well, if pre-production goes well, I am pretty much not very busy during production, and that is the ideal. Pre-production periods tend to be intensely geared toward organizing every single day as much as possible, all with an eye toward figuring if our days are that organized, we'll be able to have a little time left."

—*Christine Vachon, Killer Films*

For the line producer, the bulk of the work is during pre-production. Staying focused, organized, on schedule, and in constant communication with the crew (while trying to remain calm) will ensure a smooth run into production. There is a saying about producers: "If you've done your job right in pre-production, you'll have nothing to do during production." That, of course, is not exactly true. There will be plenty to do during production, but it will be less hectic if all goes smoothly during pre-production. Make sure the crew is on track and able to move forward. If you find you are idle for a time during any part of the day, help someone else. There is not enough time or money for oversights or inefficiency.

When you are ready for pre-production you might say to yourself, "Where do I begin?" From our experience with productions (and that same feeling), we have compiled a master list (the pre-production checklists) of everything we have needed to prepare, set up, organize, and account for when beginning each show. Following these checklists has helped ensure that our shows run smoothly and efficiently. Look at the scheduling section as well, because there is a gray zone that could be called pre-pre-production. If you have been with the project from the beginning (you may be the writer, director, producer, or all three!), usually there is someone who has ushered a project to the official pre-production stage. That person should be wary of what needs to be completed in the pre-pre-production phase so that pre-production can begin without the sense that you are already behind. The items on the pre-production checklist with asterisks next to them are those that might fall into a pre-pre-production phase.

Remember, each film is different and will have specific needs, but you will probably have to deal with each item on each checklist while prepping for almost any film. There may be additional items to add to your checklists, depending on your film's needs. Use the checklists that follow as guidelines.

GETTING THE BEST DEAL

Getting the best deal does not necessarily mean compromising the film or skimping on locations, crew, or equipment. Being creative and honest are the keys to making deals that are affordable. Be honest with vendors, location owners, and others about your budget, and explain the type of film you are making. You would be surprised how supportive and agreeable people can be.

Try to make flat-rate deals or weekly flat-rate deals rather than paying for equipment and expendables by the day. Whenever possible, secure equipment based on a three-day week. This means that if a vendor quotes you a price per day you will only be charged for three days over the course of one week. This is an important negotiating point. Sometimes, you can even negotiate a two-day week.

When calling vendors to discuss your equipment needs, availability, and prices, you will often put equipment you need to rent on hold. A hold ensures that the equipment you want will not be rented to another production during the dates you specify. Ask the vendor how long equipment can be held and what the hold guarantees. If you put equipment on hold at a particular rental house but find a better deal at a second place, or find that you no longer need the equipment, you should notify the first vendor. This courtesy is important in establishing a relationship with vendors. It also ensures that you are not tying up equipment unnecessarily and will not ultimately be charged for it. You might also ask the first rental house if they can match the best price you have been quoted.

Making the best deal may save you money for any unanticipated costs that may arise. Take another look at the equipment, supplies, locations, crew, catering services, and vehicles your film needs. Will a creative approach to any of these areas save money without compromising your film, cast, or crew? (See "When Your Budget Estimate Is Way Too High" in Chapter 6.)

THE FUNCTIONAL OFFICE

Before you enter the war zone of pre-production, equip and organize your office with the essentials. This may sound ridiculous, but if you do not properly set up and organize your office beforehand, a huge mess will ensue. During each day of pre-production, you will amass papers, contracts, purchase orders, and notes you will need to refer to later but might not be able to find unless you operate in an organized manner. (See Figure 7–1.)

Choose carefully the space you will be working in. Keep in mind that you will need bathrooms, air-conditioning or heat as the weather dictates, ample space, and windows. You will be keeping long hours, so be considerate of neighbors who will be disturbed by traffic.

Office furniture can be costly. Look for good deals on used furniture online in the classifieds (Craig's list or Ebay) or at swap meets. Do anything necessary to set up your office so that it is functional, comfortable, and spacious enough for crew.

You will need ample desk space and a good light for each person working in the office. Ideally, you will have extra desks for various department people who roam in and out of the office and need to do paperwork or make calls. Each workstation should be equipped with a decent chair, pens, notepads, and a phone.

Filing cabinets are essential to the functional office. Set up your filing system before you amass a pile of daunting paperwork. Go through the pre-production and production checklists, and create files for every item listed. Let the files hang there empty. When the need arises, you will be able to find or file each piece of paper.

Go to the office supply store and load up on pens, paper, paper clips, a stapler, staples, sticky notes, an address card file, corkboards, whiteboards, tacks, and other essentials. Purchase what you need to do your job correctly. Do not forget petty cash booklets, purchase order books, and other forms from the office supply or stationery store. You will thank yourself for having the necessary supplies handy when you have three phone lines holding and several department heads waiting for petty cash. You do not want your efficiency to be hindered by not having set up your office properly.

In addition to office supplies, you will need to consider such capital items as phones, T-1 line or other fast Internet access, a fax machine, computers, a copy machine, a refrigerator, and a microwave. These should be one-time expenses. Phone lines are the production office's lifeline. Install enough phone lines to sustain the office. It will be money well spent. A fax machine and e-mail are other office musts. Install a designated fax line.

Most key production personnel will have their own computers. If not, consider renting a few computers for key personnel or securing a product placement agreement with a computer manufacturer if there is a way to work it into your film. It is essential that you have one computer that functions as the brain of the production. It must have ample memory and the necessary software loaded, including word-processing software, a spreadsheet program, and perhaps Movie Magic Scheduling and Budgeting. Finally, if you can purchase, rent, or borrow a copy machine, do so. If not, befriend the proprietor of the local copy shop and set up an account there; you will need to make many copies each day. Having a small refrigerator and possibly a microwave is also important. It will increase the chances of healthy eating by production office staff.

Resource guides, maps, telephone books, production books (such as LA 411 or NYPG), and street atlases should be available on the production office bookshelf. You may need more than one copy of some of these books. Check if crew members own these before you spend the cash on multiple copies. All the production resource guides also have web sites. Some of the information they offer is free, and other areas of the sites require that you pay a fee. Check it out and see what is most cost effective for your purposes. A functional office, set up and organized before the crew comes on and pre-production officially begins, will be a sturdy leg to stand on when things get nuts—and they will.

PRE-PRODUCTION CHECKLISTS

Some of the tasks included in the pre-production checklists will carry over into the production period. The week in which you deal with many of these items will vary according to the needs of your film and how much

"TITLE"
PROCEDURES

PRODUCTION OFFICE

Production Company, Inc.
Address

Phone and Fax

OFFICE HOURS

During preproduction, office hours are *Monday thru Saturday,*_____ am to _____ pm. The last week of preproduction which is "dates", the office will stay open later, and on Saturday "date", if your department needs to be working. If it is an emergency, and you need to reach "Name", feel free to call at any time. If you need to come to the office after hours, make arrangements with "Name" first, or call before coming. Please do not just show up. During shooting, the office will have the same call time as the set, if not earlier. Please keep in mind that if you will be coming to the office and it is late at night or in the early morning hours, please be very quiet and respectful of the neighbors. You may park_____.

TIME CARDS

All time crew cards must be turned in by the first lunch/dinner break on Wednesdays. Payday is every Thursday.

PETTY CASH

All petty cash must be submitted on a weekly basis (if possible) in the envelope provided from the production office. Each receipt must be affixed to an 8 1/2" by 11" piece of paper, and must be numbered according to the number on the envelope. All receipts must be originals, not photocopies. This includes messenger charges, bills for photocopying, gas charges, or any other receipt which is to be reimbursed. "Name" is the only one who can distribute petty cash.

DEAL MEMOS

Please make sure you have completed a deal memo, W4, an I-9 form, and a start form. All payroll-related forms must be returned to "Names" *as soon as possible.*

HOUSE ACCOUNTS/VENDORS

All applications and/or inquiries for house accounts must be processed and approved by "Name". The name, address, telephone number, and tax ID number for each vendor must appear on the application. We will need to know who is authorized to sign on the account. We will notify you when the account has been opened.

PURCHASE ORDERS

Purchase orders or numbers and forms are available in the production office. Each time you rent or purchase an item(s) from a vendor, you must give them an official purchase order, and a copy to the production office. When placing an order, you are required to obtain the actual or estimated rental cost of the items. All purchase orders should be submitted to the production office for approval prior to placing an order or purchasing goods. However, purchase orders should never be held waiting for an amount or an invoice to match. The production office will handle those functions. No invoices will be paid without pre-approved purchase orders to back them up.

CHECK REQUESTS

Check requests are available in the production office. If you need a rush check, please mark it rush and indicate the date the check is needed clearly on the request and to whom it should be returned. Put all check requests in the check request box for approval.

Use a check request form if you have not received an invoice. However, we do need a paid invoice and a purchase order to back up any request when the check is distributed.

***If there is anything you need in way of forms, supplies, or vendor information, ask the office staff. Also, we may already have an account with certain vendors, have done business with them before, or want to use a specific vendor. Please inquire within the office first.**

CHECK CASHING AND BANK INFORMATION

Bank Address and Phone Number
Contact: "Name"

Figure 7–1 Office procedures sample

pre-production time you have. The checklists that follow are based on a four- to six-week pre-production period (see also the companion CD-ROM).

Legal, Financial, and Accounts Checklist

The following items should be taken care of during the first two weeks of pre-production.

- File the necessary paperwork to incorporate the production company.
- Hire an accountant.
- Engage a lawyer.
- Set up a bank account and order checks.
- Secure production insurance and certificates (week 2).
- Fill out and file SAG paperwork and post bond (week 1).
- Engage a payroll company.
- Set up a computerized accounting system and a check register.
- File contact information, driver's licenses, Social Security numbers, and credit card information for the producer, line producer, and director.
- Create a chart of accounts based on the budget.
- Always have petty cash on hand.
- Set up vendor accounts (week 2 and as department heads are hired).
- Start a list of deposits paid that you will need to recover from vendors.
- Negotiate your lab deal (week 2).
- Make product placement inquiries and prepare product placement letters (weeks 2 and 3).
- Have a research/title report done and clear usages in script for legal purposes (weeks 2 and 3).

Details of the Legal, Financial, and Accounts Checklist

Incorporation

The production company making the movie must be incorporated. File for your company's corporate status in the state in which it will conduct business. An accountant or an attorney can help you with this, or you can incorporate the company yourself over the Internet. You will need to pay filing fees and state corporation fees. Ideally, this will have been taken care of prior to the start of official pre-production (see Chapter 5). The reason for this is that much of what you will need to establish with some alacrity in the first days of official pre-production will require a Federal Identification number and your Operating Agreement or Letter of Incorporation.

Accountant

If you plan to hire an accountant who will cut checks to vendors, oversee the accounting of the show, and pay cast and crew payroll, he or she should start at the outset.

Hiring a Lawyer

If you can afford to do so, hire a lawyer to prepare your above-the-line contracts and set up the corporate structure of the production entity making the film. A lawyer will ensure that your contracts and paperwork are in order and can advise you with any legal issues pertaining to the script. If you cannot afford a lawyer, seek advice from organizations that provide free legal advice (such as California Lawyers for the Arts), from colleagues, and from legal contract books (see Appendix A: Resource Guide).

Bank Account

Set up a bank account immediately so that you can issue deposit or rent checks for your office space, purchase office supplies, retain an attorney, and establish credit with vendors. Set up the bank account in the name of the production company, and order checks for that account. (Ideally, this should be an interest-bearing account.) The bank will require documents of incorporation. The line producer should be able to sign these checks.

Production Insurance

Secure production insurance for the course of the show. You will need it to rent equipment, secure locations, hire the cast, and more. Your show must be insured against any loss, injury, or damage. Do this in week 1 of pre-production so that insurance certificates can be issued to vendors and locations. The standard liability limit on production insurance policies is $1 million. Check online film guides, and contact local film organizations, an attorney, or the film commission in the city in which you are filming if you need assistance finding a production insurance company.

SAG Paperwork

To employ SAG actors, your production company must become a signatory of the Guild. Contact SAG and let them know your budget level, and they will forward you the required paperwork. The Guild usually requires financial assurances in the form of a bond, a cash deposit, or a security agreement. Bonds are posted on a film for the protection of the performers employed by the production company. The bond amount is a percentage of the total wages for actors in your budget, not to exceed 40 percent. When you have paid the actors and filed the necessary payroll and completion paperwork, SAG will return the bond.

Request and begin filling out the SAG paperwork package immediately!

You should request the SAG paperwork from the Guild at least 30 days before production is scheduled to begin. You will be assigned a SAG representative (your "rep"), who will work with you throughout the show. The package is dense and will take some time to fill out. Much of the paperwork must be filed with the Guild early on. You will file other items at the end of the show. Instructions are included in the package. (See "Cast Checklist" in the material that follows for more on SAG paperwork.)

Payroll Company

Call around and compare the rates of payroll companies before you engage one. It is advisable to have a payroll company pay both cast and crew paychecks, especially if yours is a SAG show. Payroll companies usually require a setup fee and charge per check issued. It is well worth the money to hire a payroll company to account for deductions and fringes, which can be time consuming. Upon securing a payroll company, send copies of all cast and crew contracts, W-4 forms, I-9 forms, and weekly time cards. Often the payroll company will provide you with software, and sometimes with a computer for accounting.

Check Register/Accounting System

Set up a check register on your computer to account for all checks issued, deposits, transfers, and withdrawals. It is extremely important that you account for every transaction made within the production account, whether it be a payment or a deposit. This check register should indicate the date any transaction was made, the check number of each check issued, and the budget account code and item for which the purchase was made. This way, when you actualize your budget you have accounted for all checks and are able to know whether you are over- or underbudget.

Important Information to Keep on File

Often, you will need a credit card or other form of identification (such as a driver's license or Social Security number) to set up accounts or to make purchases. A credit card may be required as a deposit when renting equipment, and is invaluable in the event of an emergency. It is advisable to have the producer's or line producer's credit card information, Social Security number, and driver's license on file, just in case. Try to avoid using credit cards for purchases. Whenever possible purchase items and make deposits with checks instead. Have the bank account information and the film's employee identification number on file where they will be easy to find. (When you file to incorporate your production company, the state in which you file will assign the corporation an *employer identification number.*) This information may be required on credit applications and purchase orders.

Chart of Accounts

Create a chart of accounts (account codes that correspond to each line item in the budget). If you are using Movie Magic Budgeting, you have the option of printing out a chart of accounts based on the budget. Use these codes when actualizing the budget, writing checks, and coding petty cash envelopes. This will allow you to determine how much money is spent in each category and on which line item, helping you remain on budget. (See the *Swingers* chart of accounts reproduced in Figure 7–2.)

Petty Cash

Petty cash is used for small purchases, such as gas, tolls, tips, parking, office supplies, inexpensive props, and food. Always have petty cash on hand and have crew members properly account for the petty cash they receive and spend. Keep track of all petty cash given to crew members. Code each purchase listed on the completed petty cash envelopes according to the chart of accounts. You will need to account for petty cash purchases when actualizing the budget.

Vendor Accounts

Whenever possible, set up credit accounts with vendors to avoid having to pay for equipment and supplies upon receipt (unless, of course, you can make a better deal by paying up front). Often, department heads will have relationships with equipment houses, allowing you to secure the best possible deal from those vendors. Start organizing your needs and setting up accounts early on.

Deposits

Vendors will often require a deposit for equipment or materials you will be renting for the production. Keeping track of deposits made to vendors will help you remember who you will need to get money back from when the show has wrapped. You will need to be sure to account for any deposits that will be returned when actualizing your budget. Remember that until a deposit is returned it is money that is unavailable during production.

Lab/Video Transfers

Call around to determine which lab will accommodate the needs of your film for the best rates. Do this during week 2 of pre-production or when the editor is hired, so that the

SWINGERS

Chart Of Accounts

Acct#	Description	Acct#	Description	Acct#	Description
		600-00	**STORY**		
600-01	RIGHTS PURCHASED	600-03	WRITERS	600-04	SCREENPLAY PURCHASE
		610-00	**PRODUCER**		
610-01	EXECUTIVE PRODUCER	610-02	PRODUCER	610-03	ASSOCIATE PRODUCER
610-07	PRODUCER'S ENT.	610-08	PRE-PRODUCTION EXPENSES		
		620-00	**DIRECTOR**		
620-01	DIRECTOR	620-05	CASTING DIRECTOR	620-08	CASTING EXPENSES
		630-00	**CAST**		
630-01	PRINCIPAL PLAYERS	630-02	DAY PLAYERS	630-06	LOOPING/ADR (INCL. 1 DA...
630-08	OVERTIME	630-09	MEDICAL EXAMS	630-20	SIDE DEALS
		650-00	**TRAVEL & LIVING**		
650-03	WRITER'S TRAVEL	650-03	WRITER'S LIVING	650-01	PRODUCER'S TRAVEL
650-01	PRODUCER'S LIVING	650-02	DIRECTOR'S TRAVEL	650-02	DIRECTOR'S LIVING
650-06	CAST TRAVEL	650-06	CAST LIVING		
		700-00	**EXTRA TALENT**		
700-02	EXTRAS AND STAND-INS	700-05	EXTRAS CASTING		
		705-00	**PRODUCTION STAFF**		
705-01	LINE PRODUCER	705-02	PROD. MGR.	705-03	FIRST ASSISTANT DIRECT...
705-04	SECOND ASSISTANT DIREC...	705-06	SCRIPT SUPERVISOR	705-08	ESTIMATOR/PROD. ACCOU...
705-10	PRODUCTION ASSISTANTS				
		710-00	**CAMERA**		
710-01	DIRECTOR OF PHOTOGRAPHY	710-03	1ST ASST. CAMERAMAN	710-04	2ND ASST. CAMERAMAN /...
710-06	STILL CAMERAMAN	710-08	CAMERA RENTALS	710-09	CAMERA SUPPLIES
710-11	CAM ACCESSORIES/VIDEO...	710-20	LOSS, DAMAGE, & REPAIR		
		715-00	**ART/SET DESIGN (MATERIALS IN PROPS)**		
715-01	PRODUCTION DESIGNER	715-02	ART/SET DIRECTOR	715-03	SET DESIGNERS
		725-00	**SET OPERATIONS**		
725-01	1ST COMPANY GRIP/KEY...	725-02	BEST BOY GRIP	725-03	CRANE/DOLLY GRIPS
725-04	EXTRA GRIPS	725-05	CAMERA DOLLIES	725-06	CAMERA CRANES
725-08	GRIP EQUIPMENT RENTALS	725-09	GRIP PURCHASES	725-10	GRIP BOX RENTALS
725-11	CRAFT SERVICE/SERVICE...	725-12	SET CLEANUP & TRASH DI...	725-19	FIRST AID
725-20	LOSS & DAMAGE	725-24	DRESSING ROOM RENTALS	725-30	LOCATION LOAD AND UNLO...
		730-00	**ELECTRICAL**		
730-01	GAFFER	730-02	BEST BOY	730-05	GLOBES/CARBONS/SUPPL...
730-07	GENERATOR RENTAL	730-08	ELECTRICAL EQUIP RENTALS	730-09	ELECTRICAL EQUIP. PURCH...
730-10	BOX RENTAL	730-20	LOSS, DAMAGE, & REPAIR		
		745-00	**SET DRESSING**		
		750-00	**PROPERTIES**		
750-01	PROPERTY MASTER (SEE S...	750-04	PICTURE VEHICLES LABOR...	750-05	PICTURE VEHICLE RENTALS
750-08	PROP RENTALS	750-09	PROP PURCHASES	750-10	PROP BOX RENTALS
750-20	LOSS & DAMAGE				
		755-00	**WARDROBE**		
755-04	COSTUME DESIGNER	755-03	ASST. WARDROBE	755-06	ALTERATIONS - L&M
755-07	CLEANING & DYEING	755-08	WARDROBE RENTALS	755-09	WARDROBE PURCHASES
755-10	HAND BOX RENTALS	755-20	LOSS, DAMAGE, & REPAIRS		
		760-00	**MAKEUP & HAIRSTYLISTS**		
760-01	MAKEUP ARTIST (AND HAI...	760-02	EXTRA MAKEUP ARTIST (A...	760-06	WIG & HAIR PURCHASE
760-09	MAKEUP SUPPLIES/APPL...	760-10	KIT RENTALS		

(continued)

Figure 7–2 Swingers *chart of accounts*

Chart Of Accounts

Acct#	Description	Acct#	Description	Acct#	Description
		765-00	**PRODUCTION SOUND**		
765-01	SOUND MIXER	765-02	BOOMMAN	756-05	PLAYBACK OPERATOR
765-06	SOUND EQUIP. RENTALS	765-11	SUPPLIES AND EXPENDAB...	765-20	LOSS & DAMAGE
		770-00	**TRANSPORTATION**		
770-01	MESSENGER SERVICE	770-02	TRANSPORTATION COORD.	770-05	MILEAGE ALLOWANCE
770-06	FUEL	770-10	LOC. VEHICLES/PRODUCTI...	770-11	CAMERA DEPARTMENT
770-20	LOSS, DAMAGE, REPAIRS				
		775-00	**LOCATION EXPENSE**		
775-01	SURVEY EXPENSE	775-02	LOCATION STAFF	775-03	SITE RENTALS/PERMITS/...
775-04	HOTEL & LODGING	775-05	CATERING SERVICES	775-06	2ND MEALS/EXTRA MEALS
775-07	PRODUCTION EXPENDABLES	775-11	FIRE/POLICE	775-14	AIRPORT PICKUP/DELIVERY
775-15	LOCATION LOCK & UNLOAD	775-17	GRATUITIES	775-18	OFFICE RENT/FURNITURE/...
775-20	LOSS & DAMAGE	775-21	LOCATION SECURITY	775-22	PARKING LOTS (FOR CREW...
		785-00	**PRODUCTION DAILIES**		
785-01	NEGATIVE RAW STOCK	785-04	SOUND RECORDING TAPE	785-09	VIDEOTAPE TRANSFERS
		800-00	**EDITING**		
800-01	FILM EDITOR	800-02	SOUND EFFECTS EDITING	800-03	MUSIC EDITING
800-04	NEGATIVE CUTTING	800-06	PROJECTION	800-11	EDITORIAL FACILITIES
800-12	EDITORIAL SUPPLIES/FOOD	800-14	POST-PROD. SUPERVISION	800-18	ASSISTANT EDITOR
800-19	APPRENTICE EDITOR (INTE...				
		810-00	**MUSIC**		
810-08	COMPOSER	810-25	MUSIC SUPERVISOR	810-26	MUSIC CLEARANCE SALAR...
810-27	MUSIC CLERICAL	810-28	MASTER USE LICENSES	810-29	MUSIC PUBLISHING LICENS...
810-30	PRESCORE	810-31	REHEARSAL MUSICIANS	810-32	DEMO COSTS
810-33	SCORE (FACILITIES)	810-34	STUDIO EQUIPMENT RENT...	810-35	MUSIC INSTRUMENT RENT...
810-37	MUSIC TRANSFERS				
		820-00	**POST-PRODUCTION SOUND**		
820-01	DIALOGUE RECORDING/ADR	820-02	NARRATION RECORDING/V...	820-03	SOUND EFFECTS (FOLEY)
820-06	DUBBING SESSION	820-07	SOUND TRANSFERS	820-13	OPTICAL NEG 35 & 35/32
		840-00	**TITLES**		
840-01	TITLES (MAIN & END)	840-02	MAIN TITLES	840-03	END TITLES
840-04	MISCELLANEOUS TITLES	840-05	LABORATORY PROCESSING		
		850-00	**OPTICALS, MATTES, INSERTS**		
850-01	OPTICAL EFFECTS/DUPE N...	850-02	MASTER POSITIVES	850-03	LABORATORY PROCESSING
850-04	SPECIAL PHOTO EFFECTS	850-11	PURCHASES		
		860-00	**LABORATORY PROCESSING**		
860-01	REPRINTING & DEVELOPING	860-02	1ST TRIAL COMPOSITE PR...	860-03	MASTER POSITIVE PRINT
860-06	DEVELOP SOUND NEGATIVE	860-07	ANSWER PRINT		
		910-00	**ADMINISTRATIVE EXPENSES**		
910-01	ACCOUNTING & TERMINAL...	910-02	MPAA CERTIFICATE	910-03	POSTAGE & SHIPPING & F...
910-04	XEROX & MIMEO (NO SCRI...	910-05	LEGAL EXPENSES & FEES	910-06	TELEPHONE/FACSIMILE
910-12	PREVIEW EXPENSE/DIST. S...	910-18	RESEARCH REPORT/TITLE...	910-19	PRODUCTION EXPENDABLES
910-20	CORPORATE FILING	910-21	POLAROID & B/W STILL FI...	910-22	PAYROLL CO.
		920-00	**PUBLICITY**		
920-01	PUBLICITY - ALL COSTS	920-02	SPEC. STILL PHOTOGRAPH...	920-03	STILL FILM & PROCESSING
920-05	PUBLICITY STAFF - T&E	920-09	SPACE MEDIA	920-11	OUTSIDE SERVICES

Figure 7–2 Swingers *chart of accounts (continued)*

producer, director, and editor can discuss the film's needs. If possible, secure a package deal at a reduced rate with the lab. Many labs offer reduced rates for student films and nonprofit films. Be prepared to write the lab a deposit check. Discuss the turnaround time on dailies, and coordinate drop-off and pickup times. Establish a contact person at the lab in case a problem arises. If you are shooting on video, it is advisable to have dubs made of all tapes.

Product Placement/Legal Clearance

Go through the script to identify any brand-name products you plan to use in the film. Contact the manufacturer of each to request clearance and a product donation (see Figure 7–3). For example, if there is a particular brand of beverage you want to have in a shot, contact the manufacturer to obtain a signed letter clearing the use of the beverage in the film and to request that the manufacturer donate beverages to the production. The company may want to see the script and how you plan to use or refer to the product in the film. If you do not get permission to use specific brand-name items in the film, do not use them. You will run the risk of being sued, and the unauthorized use of brand names could hinder your ability to set up a distribution deal later.

Product placement means free advertising for the manufacturer, and it can also be a way to raise money toward the production budget. It may be worth your while to ask the beverage company for a financial donation, in that you will be promoting and advertising its product. If you have the means, you can hire a company to approach potential product sponsors for you. Product placement arrangements can save you money, and you may be surprised how many companies are willing to donate their products.

Research/Title Report

Research reports are done on a script in order to ensure all usages and references made in the script are kosher. This process is sometimes referred to as vetting the script. These reports are prepared to avoid illegal usages. For instance, if references are made to actual persons or places, the research report will indicate if and why a change to a particular reference is necessary. This is a safeguard against any lawsuits made against the production company or a distributor if and when the film secures distribution. A title report is done on the title of a film to alert you when and if other films, books, television shows, articles, and so on have been released under the same title, and whether it is necessary to make a title change. If the film secures distribution, these reports will be delivery items required by the distributor.

Office Setup Checklist

The following items should be taken care of during the first week of pre-production:

- Post the production office's rules and procedures; hand them out to crew members when hired.
- Purchase office supplies.
- Set up the production office.
- Rent or purchase furniture.
- Organize the filing system; create files for each item in the pre-production and production checklists.
- Purchase, rent, or borrow a computer; install software programs.
- Purchase local film guides, phone books, street atlases, form books, and other reference materials.
- Purchase petty cash sign-out books and purchase order books.
- Have extra keys made for the office.
- Hang a calendar or whiteboard, and a bulletin board for notes, memos, and dates.
- Set up a computerized check log; create a check-log/purchase-order notebook.
- Set up check request and petty cash request systems.
- Organize a contract book with divisions for the production company, writer, partnership, director, crew, cast, and so on.
- Organize your personal production binder with labeled dividers.
- Prepare two production notebooks.
- Enter phone numbers and other contact information into the address database or card file.
- Post the address, phone and fax numbers, name of contact person, hours of operation, and night drop times for the lab you will be using to process film each day.
- Prepare and gather production forms, SAG forms, and contracts.

Details of the Office Setup Checklist

Just as important as a comfortable and functional office is the internal setup of that office. It is worthwhile to spend time preparing forms, contracts, notebooks, and so on, to ensure the efficient operation of your office.

Check-Log/Purchase-Order Notebook

Organize a check-log/purchase-order notebook so that all accounts and paid checks are filed with the corresponding paperwork. If there is ever a dispute about payment, you can refer to your canceled checks. Refer to this notebook when actualizing your budget and preparing a daily cost overview. A check log is similar to the check register you

PRODUCT PLACEMENT RELEASE

PRODUCTION COMPANY, Inc.
ADDRESS

The undersigned agrees to provide the following product to PRODUCTION COMPANY, Inc. for use in the motion picture/movie now entitled *"TITLE"* (the "Picture"):

____

____

The company grants to you, your successors, licenses and assigns, the nonexclusive right, but not the obligation to use and include all or part of the trademark and/or logo associated with the above listed product in the Picture, without limitation as to time or number of runs, for reproduction, exhibition and exploitation, in any and all manner, methods, and media, whether now known or hereafter known or devised, and in the advertising, publicizing, promotion, trailers, and exploitation thereof.

The company warrants and represents that it is the owner of the product or direct provider of the services listed above or a representative of such and has the right to enter this agreement and grant the rights granted to PRODUCTION COMPANY, Inc. hereunder, with the understanding that PRODUCTION COMPANY, Inc. will not discredit the aforementioned product.

In full consideration of the Company providing the product to PRODUCTION COMPANY, Inc., PRODUCTION COMPANY, INC. agrees to accord "Company" screen credit in the end titles of the positive prints of the Picture in the following form:
"________________________furnished by__________."

The Company understands that any broadcast identification of its products, trademarks, trade names or the like which PRODUCTION COMPANY, Inc. may furnish, shall, in no event, be beyond that which is reasonably related to the program content.

I further represent that neither I nor the Company which I represent will directly or indirectly publicize, or otherwise exploit the use, exhibition or demonstration of the above product and/or services in the picture without the express written consent of PRODUCTION COMPANY.

Sincerely yours,

Agreed and Accepted by

____
(Authorized Signatory)

____
(Please Print Name)

By_______________

____
(Producer)

____
(Production Company
Address and Phone Number)

Figure 7–3 Product placement release

keep for your own checking account, except that attached to each printed-out check entry is the purchase order or invoice that belongs to it.

Check Request System
A check request system will keep you organized. Create a check request box for filled-out check request forms so that each day you or the accountant can prepare the necessary checks.

Personal Production Binder
Get a large three-ring binder with labeled dividers to keep as your personal production notebook during the course of the show. The following list is an example of what you may want to have in your personal notebook. (Some of the forms listed here are defined in the section "Details of the Legal, Financial, and Accounts Checklist." Other forms are explained later in this section.)

- Bank account information
- Budget
- Calendar
- Cast list
- Cell phone numbers
- Chart of accounts
- Crew list
- Copies of Exhibit G forms, Taft-Hartley forms, call sheets, and production reports
- Copy of the script and any page changes
- Daily cost overview sheets
- Daily raw stock log
- Emergency numbers, equipment maintenance numbers, and other phone numbers
- Insurance certificates
- Lab information
- List of locations and location contracts
- Petty cash tracking sheet for petty cash issued
- Permits issued by film commissions
- Schedules, day-out-of-days sheets, strip boards, and breakdowns
- Small SAG rule booklet
- Vendor list

Production Notebooks
Compile two production notebooks. Divide each of these large notebooks into numbered sections for each day of filming. For example, if you will be shooting for 30 days, you will need 30 dividers. File the call sheet, production report, Exhibit G forms, Taft-Hartley forms, script notes, camera reports, and sound reports for each shoot day in the numbered section for that day. The producer will keep one of the notebooks, and the other will remain with the production company after the show has been wrapped. The production notebook is an important delivery item should your film be acquired for distribution.

Production Forms, SAG Forms, and Contracts
Gather and prepare the production forms, SAG forms, and contracts you will need for pre-production and production. Create a file for each. You may want to store some forms in manila envelopes on the wall or on a table in the office so that they are easily accessible to the crew. Check requests, vendor/cast/crew packs, petty cash envelopes, and mileage sheets, for example, should be easily accessible. The sections that follow describe the forms you should have on hand.

Call Sheets. Call sheets, which provide vital information for each shoot day, are issued to the cast and crew daily during production. The front of the call sheet lists the director, producer, location, weather, interior or exterior scene, cast, and special equipment information. The back of the call sheet lists each cast and crew member and his or her call time for that day. A map or directions to the location should be attached to the call sheet. A copy of each day's call sheet should be filed in the appropriate notebooks and office files. Figure 7–4 shows an example of a call sheet.

Production Reports. During production, the assistant director will fill out a production report each day and turn it in to the office the next day. The reports should be filed in the appropriate office file, your production binder, and the production notebook with that day's call sheet, Exhibit G forms, and other paperwork. The production report, an example of which is shown in Figure 7–5, will indicate when each cast member reported to set and was released from makeup, what time he or she began filming, when he or she was released from the set, and what time he or she broke for meals. Crew call times, crew meal times, camera call times, first shot, the amount of footage shot, which scenes were shot that day, and which shots were retakes are also recorded on the production report. The back of the production report is the same as the back of the call sheet. Production reports also list information about faulty equipment, meal penalties, and on-set injuries. Copies are sent to SAG and the payroll company each week, and the original is filed in the production notebook.

Exhibit G Forms. The Exhibit G form, an example of which is shown in Figure 7–6, is provided and required by SAG. The AD will fill it out each day on the set. The call time, makeup time, and meal break times for each cast member who worked that day are reported on the form, which the cast member must sign. The Exhibit G must be

CALL SHEET

DATE 7/2/95
DIRECTOR Doug Liman
PRODUCER Simpkins/LaLoggia
LOCATION Mike's Apartment 5870 Franklin
SUNRISE 6:27 am SUNSET 7:15 pm
ANTICIPATED WEATHER Hot & sun 70/101

PRODUCTION COMPANY Double Down
SHOW SWINGERS
SERIES EPISODE
PROD# DAY # 3 OUT OF 20

IS TODAY A DESIGNATED DAY OFF? ☐ YES ☐ NO
CREW CALL 4:30 pm
LEAVING CALL
SHOOTING CALL 5:30 pm

☐ Weather Permitting
☒ Report to Location
☒ See Attached Map
☐ Bus to Location

Set Description	Scene Nos.	Cast	D/N	Pages	Location
INT. Mike's Apartment DAY	pu 53	1	D		Mike's Apt.
-Mike against wall					
INT. Mike's Apartment NIGHT	3	1	N	4	
-answering machine/Trent on phone					
INT. Mike's Apartment NIGHT	64	1	N	3/8	
-Mike considers calling Lorraine					

Cast	Part Of	Leave	Makeup	Set Call	Remarks
Jon Favreau	MIKE	5:00 pm		5:30 pm	

Atmosphere & Stand-ins	

NOTE: No forced calls without previous approval of unit production manager or assistant director. All calls subject to change.

Advance Schedule Or Changes

7/5/95 Set #3

CHRISTY'S TRAILER
Valley Village Mobile Home Park 8250 Lankershim, N. Hollywood
Scene #19-25

Assistant Director ______ Production Manager ______

(continued)

Figure 7–4 Call sheet (front) (Reprinted by permission of ________)

PRODUCTION REQUIREMENTS

PICTURE: NO. DATE

NO.	ITEM	TIME	NO.	ITEM	TIME	NO.	ITEM	TIME
	PRODUCTION			SOUND			MEALS	
	DIRECTOR			MIXER			BREAKFASTS	
	UNIT MANAGER			RECORDER			BOX LUNCHES	
	ASST. DIRECTORS			MIKE BOOM			HOT LUNCHES	
	SCRIPT SUPERVISOR			CABLE UTIL.			DINNERS	
	DIALOGUE COACH							
	STUDIO TEACHER			PLAYBACK OPERATOR			TRANSPORTATION	
	CHILD WELFARE WORKER			PLAYBACK MACHINE			DRIVER CAPTAIN	
							DRIVERS	
	CAMERA			PROPERTY				
	DIRECTOR OF PHOTO.			PROPERTY MASTER				
	CAMERA OPERATOR			ASST. PROP. MASTER			CAMERA INSERT CAR	
	1ST. ASSISTANT						CAMERA TRUCK	
	2ND. ASSISTANT						PICTURE CARS	
	EXTRA OPERATOR			SET DECORATOR				
	STEADICAM			LEADMAN				
	ASST.			SWING GANG			MISC CARS	
	EXTRA OPERATOR							
	EXTRA ASSISTANT							
	STILL CAMERA						STANDBY CARS	
	OPERATIONS			MAKE-UP				
	ART DIRECTOR			MAKEUP ARTIST				
	CONST. COORD.						STRETCHOUT	
	KEY GRIP							
	2ND. CO. GRIP			HAIR STYLIST			BUSSES	
	DOLLY GRIP							
	EXTRA GRIPS							
				BODY MAKEUP WOMAN			GOOSE WITH SOUND	
	CRAB DOLLY						SOUND TRUCK	
	CRANE						ELECTRICAL TRUCK	
	HYSTER FOR HIGH SPOT			BODY MAKEUP MAN			PROP TRUCK	
							WARD. TRUCK	
				COSTUME			GRIP TRUCK	
	CRAFT SERVICE			COSTUMER (MEN)			HORSE WAGON TRUCK	
							WATER TRUCK	
	GREENSMAN						HONEY WAGON	
				COSTUMER (WOMEN)			DRESSING ROOM TRAIL.	
	PAINTER							
	SPECIAL EFFECTS							
				MUSIC				
				MUSIC REP.				
	PORT. DRESSING RMS.			SIDELINE MUSCIANS			ANIMAL TRAINER	
				SINGERS			ANIMAL HANDLER	
							DOGS	
	SCHOOL ROOMS			PROCESS			CATS	
				PROCESS PROJECT.			HORSES	
	ELECTRICAL			PROCESS GRIPS				
	GAFFER			PROCESS EQUIP.			OTHER ANIMALS	
	BEST BOY							
	GENERATOR OPERATOR						ANIMAL WELFARE (A.H.S.)	
	LAMP OPERATORS			POLICE/FIREMED.				
				STUDIO POLICE				
				WHISTLEMAN				
	GENERATOR			MOTORCYCLE POLICE				
	WIND MACHINE			FIRE WARDEN				
				FIREMAN				
				FLAGMAN				
				WATCHMAN				
				FIRST AID				

DEPARTMENT	SPECIAL INSTRUCTIONS

ASST. DIR. ____________ UNIT PROD. MGR. ____________

Figure 7–4 Call sheet (back) (Reprinted by permission of ________) (continued)

DAILY PRODUCTION REPORT

No. of Days on Picture Including Today

REH.	TRAVEL	HOLIDAYS	IDLE	RETAKES & ADDED SCENES	WORK	TOTAL	AHEAD	
							BEHIND	

DIRECTOR ______ DATE ______
WORKING TITLE ______ DATE STARTED ______
PRODUCTION NO. ______ ESTIMATED FINISH DATE ______
SET ______
SET NO. ______ LOCATION ______
CALL ______ LEAVE ______ ARR. LOCATION ______ 1st SHOT ______ AM ______ PM ______ WRAP ______ ARR. STUDIO/HOTELS ______
CREW LUNCH ______ TO ______ CREW SUPPER ______ TO ______ 1st SHOT ______
CAMERA CALL ______ CAMERA WHIP ______ SOUND CALL ______ SOUND WRAP ______

SCRIPT	SCENES	PAGES	MINUTES	SETUPS	ADDED SCENES	RETAKES	Scenes Completed Today
Scenes in Script							
Taken Previously							
Taken Today							
Yet to be Taken							
FILM USE/STOCK							
Good							
Waste							
N.G.							
Total Today							
Total-to-Date							

CAST	W H S F R TR	MAKEUP WDBE.	WORKTIME		MEALS		TRAVEL TIME			
			ON SET	DIS. STUDIO	1ST MEAL IN	1ST MEAL OUT	LEAVE FOR LOCATION	ARRIVE LOCATION	DIS. LOC.	ARRIVE STUDIO

EXTRA TALENT-MUSICIANS, ETC.

NO.	RATE	ADJ. TO	O.T.	T.T.	WARD.	MPV		NO.	RATE	ADJ. TO	O.T.	T.T.	WARD.	MPV

Figure 7–5 Daily production report

Screen Actors Guild Performers Production Time Report

Exhibit G

Picture Title SWINGERS Prod. No. 1 Date 9-5-95 Contact NICOLE LALOGGIA Phone No. (213) 555-1239
Shooting Location CHRISTY'S TRAILER Is Today a Designated Day Off? * Yes___ No ✓
Please Complete in Ink Using 24 Hour Clock (ex. 4:00 pm = 16:00):

WORK - W, START - S, REHEARSAL - R, HOLD - H, FITTING - FT, TEST - T, TRAVEL - TR, FINISH - F

CAST	MINOR	CHARACTER	W H S F R T TR FT	Report Makeup Wdbe.	Work Time: Report on set	Work Time: Dismiss on set	Dismiss Makeup Wardrobe	In / Out: ND Meal	Meals: 1st Meal Start	Meals: 1st Meal Finish	Meals: 2nd Meal Start	Meals: 2nd Meal Finish	Travel Time: Leave for Location	Travel Time: Arrive on Location	Travel Time: Leave Location	Travel Time: Arrive at Studio	Stunt Adj.	Minors Tutoring Time	Wardrobe: No. of Outfits Provided	Forced Call / MPVs	PERFORMER'S SIGNATURE
JON FAVREAU		MIKE	W	6:00 A	8:00 A	2:00 A	2:30 P		12:00 P	12:30 P											[illegible]
VINCE VAUGHN		TRENT	SW	7:45 A	9:30 A	3:45 P	4:00 P		12:00 P	12:30 P											[illegible]
DEENA MARTIN		CHRISTY	SW	7:30 A	9:30 A	3:30 P	4:15 P		12:00 P	12:30 P											[illegible]
KATHRINE KENDAL		LISA	SW	6:45 A	8:00 A	2:45 P	3:15 P		12:00 P	12:30 P											[illegible]

Figure 7–6 Exibit G form

sent to the payroll company and to SAG each week, and should be filed in the office notebooks and files each day.

Taft-Hartley Forms. The Taft-Hartley is another SAG form the AD will fill out on the set if necessary. Under the provisions of the Taft-Hartley agreement, a non-Guild member is permitted to work on a SAG show for a 30-day period. After the initial 30 days, the actor must join the Guild to continue working on the SAG set. The production company must fill out and submit a Taft-Hartley form to SAG within 15 days of the actor's first day of work, or the production company will be fined. There is a cost involved when you "Taft-Hartley" an actor, and it is typically paid by the production company. Taft-Hartley forms are also sent to the payroll company and should be kept in the office files. Examples of SAG Taft-Hartley reports are shown in Figures 7–7 and 7–8.

Mileage Sheets. Mileage sheets should be available to all crew members who use their personal vehicles to run errands for the production. If you are paying mileage rather than gas, the driver must fill out a mileage sheet. Submit these forms to your production accountant or payroll company. An example of a mileage log is shown in Figure 7–9.

Check Requests. A check request is exactly what it sounds like: a request for a check. Any item or piece of equipment that has to be paid for up front requires a check request. (Remember to keep a list of all checks issued as deposits so that you can get them back at the end of the show.) The check request should indicate what the check is for (you will need to account for it by account code later, when you actualize the budget), to whom it should be made out, and the amount. If the check must be mailed, the request should also indicate to whom the check should be sent, the address, and the date it is needed. If the check is issued to a vendor or another company, make sure the crew member filling out the request form, an example of which is shown in 7–10, fills in the vendor's employee identification number in the space provided.

Petty Cash Requests. The same information found on a check request should be indicated on a petty cash request. Set up the same system for petty cash requests as you do for check requests.

Petty Cash Envelopes. When crew members are given petty cash, they must take a petty cash envelope and record each item purchased and its cost on the envelope. Petty cash envelopes, an example of which is shown in Figure 7–11, can be turned in each week or when the crew member has spent all of the petty cash. He or she should take a new envelope when more petty cash is doled out. When petty cash envelopes are turned in to the office, code each purchase on the envelope according to your chart of accounts. Use these envelopes when actualizing the budget and when preparing your daily cost overview.

Daily Raw Stock Logs. Daily raw stock logs are forms you either purchase or create to keep track of the amount of film shot, wasted, and unused each day. Figures 7–12 a and b show, respectively, an example of a raw stock inventory form and a daily raw stock log.

Walkie-talkie Sign-out Sheets. Have walkie-talkie sign-out sheets available on the set daily. Borrowed walkie-talkies should be returned at the end of each day. In the event one is missing, the sign-out sheet will be of use in tracking it down. An example of a walkie-talkie sign-out sheet is shown in Figure 7–13.

Stationery and Fax Cover Sheets. Create letterhead and fax cover sheets for the production company. Make copies, and keep them in the office for all outgoing correspondence.

Location, Cast, and Crew Contracts. You can purchase standard contract forms from a production supply house or create them yourself. Keep enough copies of each on hand. The film's needs may be such that special paragraphs have to be included in the standard contracts. Having them on a computer makes them easy to amend. Such forms include a location agreement (see Figure 7–14), neighboring location agreement (see Figure 7–15), crew deal memo (see Figure 7–16), crew deal memo and W-4 form (see Figure 7–17), and cast deal memo (see Figure 7–18).

Purchase Orders. Use a purchase order (PO), an example of which is shown in Figure 7–19, when renting vehicles or equipment or when purchasing materials or expendables. File POs in the check log with the corresponding invoices and checks. Even if you are not reporting to the accounting office of a production company (which would require POs), filling out a PO each time you put equipment or materials on hold will be helpful in keeping track of what has been ordered from which rental house, as well as the cost and date. The rental house may refer to your order by PO number rather than by item or production company name.

Petty Cash Sign-out Books. When crew members receive petty cash, they should sign the petty cash book or sign-out sheet. This system will help you keep track of who was issued petty cash and how much.

Location/Filming Notices. Filming notices are posted at a location to alert patrons or passersby that filming is taking place on the premises. The AD should have notices available on the set, and the location manager will post

SCREEN ACTORS GUILD
TAFT/HARTLEY REPORT

ATTENTION: ______________________ ATTACHED ?: ☐ RESUME* ☐ PHOTO

EMPLOYEE INFORMATION

NAME ______________________ SS# ______________

ADDRESS ______________________ AGE (IF MINOR) ______________

CITY/STATE ______________ ZIP ________ PHONE (____) ______________

EMPLOYER INFORMATION

NAME ______________________ Check one: ☐ AD AGENCY
☐ STUDIO
ADDRESS ______________________ ☐ PRODUCTION COMPANY

CITY/STATE ______________ ZIP ________ PHONE (____) ______________

EMPLOYMENT INFORMATION

Check one: CONTRACT: ☐ DAILY ☐ 3-DAY ☐ WEEKLY CATEGORY: ☐ ACTOR ☐ SINGER ☐ STUNT ☐ OTHER

WORK DATE(S) ______________________ SALARY ______________

PRODUCTION TITLE ______________________ PROD'N/COM'L # ______________

SHOOTING LOCATION (City & State) ______________________

REASON FOR HIRE (be specific) ______________________

____

____

____

____

____

Employer is aware of General Provision, Section 14 of the Basic Agreement that applies to Theatrical and Television production, and Schedule B of the Commercials Contract, wherein Preference of Employment shall be given to qualified professional actors (except as otherwise stated). Employer will pay to the Guild as liquidated damages, the sums indicated for each breach by the Employer of any provision of those sections.

SIGNATURE ______________________ DATE ______________
Producer or Casting Director – Indicate which

PRINT NAME ______________________ PHONE (____) ______________

*PLEASE BE CERTAIN RESUME LISTS ALL TRAINING AND/OR EXPERIENCE IN THE ENTERTAINMENT INDUSTRY.

Figure 7–7 SAG Taft-Hartley report

SAG EXTRA

TAFT/HARTLEY REPORT

ATTENTION: ______________________ ATTACHED ?: ☐ RESUME ☐ PHOTO

EMPLOYEE INFORMATION

NAME ______________________ SS# ______________________

ADDRESS ______________________ AGE (IF MINOR) ______________________

CITY/STATE ______________ ZIP ________ PHONE (____) ______________

EMPLOYER INFORMATION

NAME ______________________ Check one: ☐ CASTING OFFICE
☐ STUDIO
ADDRESS ______________________ ☐ PRODUCTION COMPANY

CITY/STATE ______________ ZIP ________ PHONE (____) ______________

EMPLOYMENT INFORMATION

CHECK ONE: General Extra ☐ Special Ability Extra ☐ Dancer ☐

WORK DATE(S) ______________________ SALARY ______________________

PRODUCTION TITLE ____

SHOOTING LOCATION (City & State) ______________________________

REASON FOR HIRE (be specific) ______________________________

____

____

____

____

____

Employer is aware of General Provision, Section 14.G of the Screen Actors Guild Codified Basic Agreement of 1989 for Independent Producers as amended that applies to Theatrical and Television production, wherein Preference of Employment shall be given to qualified professional extras (except as otherwise stated). Employer will pay to the Guild as liquidated damages, a sum which shall be determined by binding arbitration for each breach by the Employer of any provision of those sections.

SIGNATURE ______________________________ DATE ______________
Producer or Casting Director (indicate which)

PRINT NAME ______________________________ PHONE (____) ______________

Figure 7–8 SAG extra Taft-Hartley report

MILEAGE LOG

NAME: ______________________________ WEEK ENDING ______________

SHOW: ______________________________ PROD # ______________

DATE	LOCATION		PURPOSE	MILEAGE
	FROM	TO		

TOTAL MILES: __________

______ MILES @ ______ ¢ Per Mile = $ ______________

Approved By: ______________________________ Date: ______________

Pd. By Check # ______________ Date ______________

Figure 7–9 Mileage log (Reprinted by permission of ________)

CHECK REQUEST

DATE: ____________________

DATE NEEDED: ____________________

AMOUNT: ____________________

TO: ________________________________

ADDRESS and PHONE: ________________________________

____

____

SSN OR FED-ID #: ________________________________

DESCRIPTION: ________________________________

REQUESTED BY: ________________________________

APPROVED BY: ________________________________

- -

ACCOUNT: ________

CHECK# AND DATE: ____________________

PO#: ____________

Figure 7.10 Check request form

PETTY CASH ENVELOPE

Date: ____________

Name: ____________

Position: ____________

Picture: ____________

Check No: ______	Check/Cash Received: ______
RECEIVED BY:	

	DATE	TO WHOM PAID	PURPOSE	ACCOUNTING USE ONLY	AMOUNT	
1						
2						
3						
4						
5						
6						
7						
8						
9						
10						
11						
12						
13						
14						
15						
16						
17						
18						
19						
20						
21						
22						
23						
24						

UPM:	Prod'n:	TOTAL RECEIPTS			
Audit:	Dept:	PETTY CASH ADVANCED			
		CHECK/CASH ENCLOSED			
Show #		CHECK/CASH DUE			

TRANS. # ____________

VENDOR # ____________

VOUCHER # ____________

Figure 7–11 Petty cash envelope

RAW STOCK INVENTORY

SHOW________________________________ PROD# ____________________

WEEK ENDING ____________________

EPISODE/WEEKLY TOTALS	52_____	52_____	52_____	52_____
Print	_____	_____	_____	_____
No Good	_____	_____	_____	_____
Waste	_____	_____	_____	_____
Total **	_____	_____	_____	_____

PURCHASED				
Previously Purchased	_____	_____	_____	_____
Purchased This Episode/Week	+ _____	_____	_____	_____
Total Stock Purchased	_____	_____	_____	_____

USED				
Stock Used To Date	_____	_____	_____	_____
Used This Episode/Week**	+ _____	_____	_____	_____
Total Stock Used	_____	_____	_____	_____

Total Purchased	_____	_____	_____	_____
Total Used	– _____	_____	_____	_____
Estimated Remaining Stock	_____	_____	_____	_____
(Remaining Stock As Per Assistant Cameraman)	_____	_____	_____	_____

RAW STOCK PURCHASES MADE DURING THIS EPISODE/WEEK:				
P.O. #__________	_____	_____	_____	_____
P.O. #__________	_____	_____	_____	_____
P.O. #__________	_____	_____	_____	_____
P.O. #__________	_____	_____	_____	_____
TOTAL	_____	_____	_____	_____

NOTES:

(continued)

Figure 7–12 (a) Raw stock inventory form (Reprinted by permission of________)

DAILY RAW STOCK LOG

SHOW ______________________________ PROD # ______________

DATE ______________________________ DAY # ______________

CAMERA	ROLL #	GOOD	N.G.	WASTE	TOTAL

	DRAWN	GOOD	N.G.	WASTE	TOTAL
PREVIOUS					
TODAY					
TOTAL					

UNEXPOSED ON HAND	TOTAL EXPOSED

Figure 7–12 (b) Daily raw stock log (Reprinted by permission of________)

WALKIE-TALKIE SIGN-OUT

Date	Walkie-Talkie #	Signed out by:	Time Out	Time Returned

Figure 7–13 Walkie-talkie sign-out sheet

them at the appropriate locations. If you plan to shoot in a residential neighborhood after designated filming hours (as established by the local film commission), you will need permission from both the film commission and surrounding neighbors. An example of a location/filming notice is shown in Figure 7–20.

Personal Releases. If you are filming or will have a still photographer at a location while it is open to the public, you must secure a signed personal release from anyone who appears in a shot. An example of a personal release statement is shown in Figure 7–21.

Vendor Lists. Compile a list of vendors and rental houses as you rent or purchase equipment and materials. The vendor list should include contact names, addresses, telephone and fax numbers, cell numbers, and any other pertinent information. It is appropriate to list banks, labs, copy shops, caterers, emergency numbers, hospitals, parking lot information, weather forecast phone numbers, and similar information on the vendor list. On the first page of the list, be sure to include the production office's address and telephone and fax numbers, the film's title, and the date. Have updated lists printed out and available for crew members. An example of a vendor list is shown in Figure 7–22.

Daily Office Responsibilities Checklist

The following are items you should keep on top of daily:

- Review to-do lists; update with office staff.
- Have petty cash on hand.
- Issue checks per check requests.
- Compile pickup and return lists for pre-production needs.
- Check in with the director regarding schedule and equipment needs.
- Check in with each department head regarding schedule and budget.
- File all paperwork in office files at day's end.
- Prepare a daily cost overview sheet.
- Actualize the budget for pre-production costs when quotes for equipment, vehicles, locations, lab, food, and so on come in.
- Remember to eat and sleep.
- Thank the crew.

LOCATION AGREEMENT

Dear

You have advised the undersigned that you are producing a ______________________________ tentatively entitled ____ (the "Picture"). In consideration of your payment to the undersigned for the sum of$ _____________ you and the undersigned hereby agree as follows:

1. The undersigned hereby irrevocably grants you and your agents, employees, licensees, successors and assigns:

   (a) The right to enter and remain upon the property, which shall include not only real property but any fixtures, equipment or other personal property thereat or thereon, located at: ____ (the"Property"), with personnel and equipment (including without limitations, props, temporary sets, lighting, camera and special effects equipment) for the purpose of photographing scenes and making recordings of said Property in connection with the production of the Picture on the following date(s): Prep:________________________ ; Shoot: _________________________ ; Strike: ______________________ . If the weather or other conditions are not favorable for such purpose on such date(s), the date(s) shall be postponed to __________________________ .

   (b) The right to take motion pictures, videotapes, still photographs and/or sound recordings on and of any and all portions of the Property and all names associated there with or which appear in, on or about the Property.

   (c) All rights of every nature whatsoever in and to all films and photographs taken and recordings made hereunder, including without limitation of all copyrights therein and renewals and extensions thereof, and the exclusive right to reproduce, exhibit, distribute, and otherwise exploit in perpetuity throughout the universe (in whole or in part) such films, photographs and recordings in any and all media, whether now known or hereafter devised, including without limitation in and in connection with the Picture and the advertising and other exploitation thereof.

2. You agree to indemnify and to hold the undersigned harmless from and against all liability or loss which the undersigned may suffer or incur by reason of any injury to or death of any person, or damage to any property (ordinary wear and tear excepted), directly caused by any of your agents or employees when present on the Property or by reason of the use by any of your agents or employees or any equipment brought by them on to the property.

3. The undersigned warrants and represents (as a condition to the payment of the compensation referred to above), that the undersigned has the full right and authority to enter into this agreement and grant the rights herein granted, and that the consent or permission of no other person, firm, or entity is necessary in order to enable you to exercise or enjoy the rights herein granted.

4. The undersigned hereby releases you from, and covenants not to sue you for, any claim or cause of action, whether known or unknown, for defamation, invasion of his privacy, right of publicity or any similar matter, or any other claim or cause of action, based upon or relating to the exercise of any of the rights referred to in Paragraph 1 hereof; provided, however, that the foregoing shall not affect your obligations to indemnify the undersigned pursuant to Paragraph 2 hereof.

5. The undersigned further warrants neither he/she or anyone acting for him/her, gave or agreed to give anything of value, except for use of the Property, to anyone at _______________________________________ or anyone associated with the production for using the property as a shooting location.

Figure 7–14 Location agreement

6. This agreement shall inure to benefit of and shall be binding upon your and our respective successors, licensees, assigns, heirs and personal representatives. You shall not be obligated actually to exercise any of the rights granted to you hereunder; it being understood that your obligations shall be fully satisfied hereunder by payment of the compensation referred to above. The agreement constitutes the entire agreement between the parties with respect to the subject matter hereof and cannot be amended except by a written instrument signed by the parties.

Very truly yours,

ACCEPTED & AGREED TO:

By ______________________________

____
(Signature)

____
(Please print name)

____
(Title)

____
(Address)

____

____
(Phone Number)

____
(Business Phone)

____
(Fed. ID # or Soc. Sec. #)

Figure 7–14 Location agreement (continued)

Neighboring Location Agreement

I understand that PRODUCTION COMPANY, Inc., its employees, assigns, or other representatives will be using a nearby location in the production of their upcoming film "TITLE." I also understand that this project may involve crew members and their accompanying equipment. I understand that this crew may create some noise, both during the day or night, and agree not to hold PRODUCTION COMPANY, Inc. responsible for any discomfort, physical or otherwise, that they, their employees, assigns, other representatives, or equipment may cause me between the dates of ___________ and ___________.

I have read the foregoing and fully understand the meaning and effect thereof and, intending to be legally bound, I have signed this release.

____
RESIDENT

____
PRODUCTION COMPANY, INC.

____
DATE

____
DATE

____
ADDRESS

Figure 7–15 Neighboring location agreement

"PRODUCTION COMPANY", INC./LLC
CREW DEAL MEMO
"TITLE"

NAME: ____________________

ADDRESS: ____________________

CITY: ____________________ STATE: ____________________ ZIP: ____________________

PHONE: (____)____________________ FAX: (____)____________________

SS# ____________________ FED.I.D.# ____________________

LOAN OUT CORP.: ____________________

POSITION: ____________________

START DATE: ____________________ EST. FINISH DATE: ____________________

WEEKLY RATE: ____________________

ADDT'L TERMS: ____________________

SCREEN CREDIT: [End Credits]____________________

Subject to the terms and conditions of this agreement, PRODUCTION COMPANY, INC., ("Producer") hereby engages you and you accept such engagement in the position stated above, in connection with the production of the feature film tentatively entitled "TITLE," (the "picture"). You agree to perform any and all services required by the Producer in your position to the best of your abilities as such services are commonly performed in the motion picture industry. You shall supply all the necessary tools, equipment and supplies commonly used in the industry to perform such services. Producer shall have the right to request, and you agree to provide to Producer or Producer's representative a written, catalogued inventory of all tools, equipment and supplies you supply, if any. Producer is not liable for loss or damage of such tools, equipment, or supplies as you provide.

If you shall provide your own transportation to and from the locations at which your services are to be rendered in connection with the Picture, and/or if you use your own vehicle in connection with the production of the Picture, then you further agree that any personal vehicle used will be adequately insured for collision damage, liability damage and property damage belonging to third parties, all in such amounts as are reasonably necessary. You agree to provide Producer with proof of insurance and valid driver's license. You hereby indemnify Producer and Producer's representatives against any and all liability and claims whatsoever in connection with your automobile or transportation during the term of this agreement.

All items purchased for the Picture, whether directly or indirectly, by the Producer, shall remain Producer's property. You warrant that you have not entered into and shall not enter into any agreements to perform work during the term of this agreement which could in any way interfere with the rendering of your services hereunder. Producer or Producer's representative retains the right to terminate this agreement at any time for any reason.

All out of pocket expenses incurred in connection with the Picture will be reimbursed only to the extent that they are pre-approved by the department head, line producer and verified by original receipt. There will be no exceptions. Also, all purchases and rentals must be by Purchase Orders. Purchase Orders must be approved by department heads.

In full consideration of your fully performing your obligations under this agreement, Producer agrees to pay you and you agree to accept a combination of cash compensation and deferred compensation (if any) as per the sum(s) listed above. Deferred compensation (if any) shall be paid at the same time as and on a pari passu basis with all other crew deferrals. You accept that said compensation is based on a _______ work week. The _______ day work week may be working days or working nights or a combination of the two. Compensation for any work week consisting of less than _______ day shall be based on a daily rate equal to _______ the weekly compensation rate paid for each day actually worked.

(continued)

Figure 7–16 Crew deal memo

The screen credit, accorded to you hereunder shall be positioned at Producer's discretion. No casual or inadvertent failure to accord such credit, nor any breach of any third party contract with Producer concerning such credit shall be a breach hereof by Producer.

Your services will be performed as a specifically ordered or commissioned work made-for-hire, and Producer shall own all results and proceeds of your services rendered hereunder in perpetuity to use for all purposes, including without limitation to the exploitation of the Picture or otherwise. This agreement may be assigned to any entity by Producer provided such entity assumes all executory obligations. You may not assign this agreement. You agree to maintain the secrecy of all Producer's confidential information which comes into your possession by virtue of your participation in the Picture.

A waiver of any breach provision shall not be deemed a waiver of any preceding or subsequent breach of the same or any other provision. This agreement contains the full and complete understanding between Producer and yourself with reference to the within subject matter, supersedes all prior agreements and understandings, written or oral, and cannot be modified except by the written instrument signed by both parties. This agreement is governed by the laws of the State of California. This agreement is not valid until signed by Producer.

FOR PRODUCTION COMPANY, INC.:

____

Producer

____

Date

AGREED TO AND ACCEPTED BY:

____

Employee

____

Date

Figure 7–16 Crew deal memo(continued)

CREW DEAL MEMO

PRODUCTION CO. ______________ DATE ______________
SHOW ______________ PROD # ______________
NAME ______________ SOC. SEC. # ______________
ADDRESS ______________ PHONE (Home) ______________
______________ (Beeper) ______________
START DATE ______________ (Fax) ______________
JOB TITLE ______________ ACCOUNT # ______________
UNION/GUILD ______________ GUARANTEE ______________ weeks
RATE (In Town) ______________ Per [Hour] [Day] [Week] for a [5] [6] ____-day week
(Distant Loc.) ______________ Per [Hour] [Day] [Week] for a [5] [6] ____-day week
ADDITIONAL DAY(S) PRO-RATED @ ______________ (th) Of a week
OVERTIME ______________ After ________ hours ______________ After ________ hours

BOX RENTAL ______________ Per Day/Week
EQUIPMENT/VEHICLE RENTAL ______________ Per Day/Week
MILEAGE ALLOWANCE ______________ Per Day/Week

NOTE: Box & Equipment rental & mileage allowance are subject to 1099 reporting. Any equipment rented by the Production Co. from the employee must be listed or inventoried before rental can be paid.

TRAVEL/ACCOMMODATIONS ______________
____
EXPENSES/PER DIEM ______________
____
OTHER ______________
____

☐ LOAN OUT
CORP. NAME ______________ FED. ID # ______________
ADDRESS (If Different From Above) ______________
____
AGENT ______________ AGENCY ______________
ADDRESS ______________ PHONE # ______________
______________ FAX # ______________
EMPLOYER OF RECORD ______________
ADDRESS ______________ PHONE # ______________
______________ FAX # ______________
IF AWARDED SCREEN CREDIT, HOW WOULD YOU LIKE YOUR NAME TO READ ______________
____

APPROVED BY ______________ TITLE ______________
ACCEPTED ______________ DATE ______________

Form **W-4** — Department of the Treasury, Internal Revenue Service

Employee's Withholding Allowance Certificate

▶For Privacy Act and Paperwork Reduction Act Notice, see reverse.

OMB No. 1545-0010 — 19

1 Type or print your first name and middle initial — Last name — 2 Your social security number

Home address (number and street or rural route) — 3 ☐ Single ☐ Married ☐ Married, but withhold at higher Single rate.
Note: If married, but legally separated, or spouse is a nonresident alien, check the Single box.

City or town, state, and ZIP code — 4 If your last name differs from that on your social security card, check here and call 1-800-772-1213 for more information . . . . ▶ ☐

5 Total number of allowances you are claiming (from line G above or from the worksheets on page 2 if they apply) . 5

6 Additional amount, if any, you want withheld from each paycheck . . . . . 6 $

7 I claim exemption from withholding and I certify that I meet BOTH of the following conditions for exemption:
• Last year I had a right to a refund of ALL Federal income tax withheld because I had NO tax liability; AND
• This year I expect a refund of ALL Federal income tax withheld because I expect to have NO tax liability.
If you meet both conditions, enter "EXEMPT" here . . . . . ▶ 7

Under penalties of perjury, I certify that I am entitled to the number of withholding allowances claimed on this certificate or entitled to claim exempt status.

Employee's signature ▶ Date ▶ , 19

8 Employer's name and address (Employer: Complete 8 and 10 only if sending to the IRS) — 9 Office code (optional) — 10 Employer identification number

Figure 7–17 Crew deal memo and W-4 form

STATION 12: DEAL START:

BY: DEAL SET:

CAST DEAL MEMO

SHOW TITLE:

DIRECTOR: PRODUCERS:

ARTIST NAME: ROLE:

ADDRESS: AGENT:

CITY, ZIP:

AGENCY:

ARTIST PH#:

SS#: FAX:

CORP. NAME: MANAGER:

FED ID#:

START DATE:

LOCATION:

COMPENSATION: $ + 10% PER WEEK FOR ________ WEEKS. ANY ADDITIONAL DAYS WILL BE PRORATED BASED ON A SIX (6) DAY WEEK.

$ + 10% PER DAY FOR_____3_____DAYS.

LOOPING:

BILLING/CREDIT:

TRANSPORTATION:

ADDITIONAL NOTES:

APPROVED:

____

____
PRODUCTION COMPANY, INC.

____
AGENT

Figure 7–18 Cast deal memo

PURCHASE ORDER

DATE ______________________ P.O. # ______________

SHOW ______________________ PROD # ______________

COMPANY ______________________

ADDRESS ______________________ PHONE # ______________

______________________ FAX # ______________

VENDOR ______________________ PHONE # ______________

ADDRESS ______________________ FAX # ______________

____

CONTACT______________________

VENDOR SS # OR FED. I.D. # ______________________

☐ PURCHASE ☐ RENTAL ☐ SERVICE

DESCRIPTION	CODING	AMOUNT

INCL. TAX IF APPLICABLE: ______________

SET #(s) ______________________ **TOTAL COST: $**______________ Per Show ☐ Day ☐ Week ☐ Month ☐

IF TOTAL COST CANNOT BE DETERMINED
AT THIS DATE, ESTIMATE OF COSTS WILL
NOT EXCEED $______________________

IF P.O. IS FOR A RENTAL, PLEASE ESTIMATE DATE OF RETURN ______________________

ORDER PLACED BY ______________________ DEPT. ______________

APPROVED BY ______________________ DATE ______________

cc: Vendor (Orig.) Accounting Dept.
Production Manager Department Head

Figure 7–19 Purchase order (Reprinted by permission of________)

ATTENTION:

Please be aware that by entering this establishment and/or its environs, you are granting "PRODUCTION COMPANY Inc.", its employees, agents, and assigns, the right to photograph you and use your picture, silhouette, and other reproductions of your physical likeness (as the same may appear in any still camera photograph and/or motion picture film), in and in connection with the exhibition, theatrically, on television or otherwise, of any motion pictures in which the same may be used or incorporated, and also in the advertising, exploiting, and/or publicizing of any such motion picture, but not limited to television motion pictures without any compensation, monetary or otherwise. You further give the said company the right to reproduce in any manner whatsoever, any recordation made by said company of your voice and all instrumental, musical, or other sound effects produced by you.

By entering this establishment and/or environs you hereby certify and represent that you have read the foregoing and fully understand the meaning and effect thereof and accept this agreement as legally binding.

Figure 7–20 Location/filming notice

RELEASE

AUTHORIZATION TO REPRODUCE PHYSICAL LIKENESS

For good and valuable consideration, the receipt of which from ______________ is acknowledged, I hereby expressly grant to said ______________________ and its employees, agents, and assigns, the right to photograph me and use my picture, silhouette, and other reproductions of my physical likeness (as the same may appear in any still camera photograph and/or motion picture film), in and in connection with the exhibition, theatrically, on television or otherwise, of any motion pictures in which the same may be used or incorporated, and also in the advertising, exploiting, and/or publicizing of any such motion picture, but not limited to television motion pictures. I further give the said company the right to reproduce in any manner whatsoever any recordation made by said company of my voice and all instrumental, musical, or other sound effects produced by me.

I hereby certify and represent that I have read the foregoing and fully understand the meaning and effect thereof and, intending to be legally bound, I have hereunto set my hand this ____________ day of _________, _______.

WITNESS:

____

_____________________________ _____________________________

Figure 7–21 Personal release statement

SWINGERS

Double Down Productions
4692 Olympic Blvd. Los Angeles, CA 93628
phone: 213-555-6767 213-555-4676 fax

VENDOR CONTACT LIST

9/5/95 white

AIRPORT	LOS ANGELES AIRPORT	310-555-4765
ANIMALS	AMERICAN HUMANE 1534 Higgins St. Sherman Oaks, CA 91234 Contact:Bobbi Berns	818-555-9878
BAKERY	FLUFFIN' MUFFINS 234 Oakwood Dr. San Simente, CA 98987	323-555-5654
BANK	CENTURY FIRST 4545 American St. Holsby Heights, CA 95676	310-555-7879
CAMERA EQUIP.	VISIONQUEST USA 167 Willowbrook Ave. Century City, CA 98456	213-555-9084
CATERING	BIG FAT DADDY-O'S Stephenson Allley Inglwood, CA 95656	323-555-4453
COPIERS	DOUBLE DITTO 3298 Ninth Street Beverly Hills, CA 95612	310-555-3987
DRUG STORE	THE BIG FIX 345 Alamo Station Complex Hollywood, CA 99567	323-555-0978
EXTRAS	BABES-R-US 1314 La Tunera St. Silverlake, CA 99678	310-555-7698
FILM STOCK	EXPOSURE 9845 Wilson Drive Beverly Hills, CA 90213	213-555-0989
FLORIST	POCKET FULL OF POSIES 657 Emilie Ave. Los Feliz, CA 94875	323-555-3456

Figure 7–22 Vendor list

Details of the Daily Office Responsibilities Checklist

To-do Lists

To stay on top of everything you will need to do each day (and each week), compile a daily to-do list for yourself. To-do lists will help ensure that you remain on schedule, on budget, and on top of everything that needs to be accomplished. Compile your to-do list from the pre-production checklists. Go through each checklist, identify items that must be dealt with that day, and put them on your list. Each person working in the office should have his or her own personal to-do list. Check the lists with your colleagues to be certain there is no overlap and that all the bases are covered. It is extremely important to review the to-do lists at the end of each day with each office member so that everyone is prepared and ready to go the next day. Cross off only the items that have been completed. Transfer the items that must still be addressed to the next day's to-do list.

Petty Cash

It will save everyone time if you have enough petty cash on hand to issue to crew members. Review petty cash requests so that you know how much you should have on hand and when.

Check Requests

Empty the check request box at the end of each day, and prepare any checks that will be needed for the next day. Write the check number and the date of the check on the check request, and file it in the appropriate file. Occasionally, a check must be cut right away. When this happens, fill out a check request so that you have a record of the check number, amount, and date issued. File it.

Pickup Lists

As pre-production heats up, equipment, expendables, vehicles, and supplies will have to be picked up and made ready for production. Have a separate pickup list for each day that pickups are scheduled, and for each person who is making a pickup. Do the same for when returns need to be made. Indicate the date and time of return on the return list and be sure the proper paperwork is received. Check with rental houses to find out what time equipment can be picked up. Put pickup times down on the list next to each destination. Do not pick up anything too soon! Wait until you need it, because many rental houses charge by the day. An example of a pickup and return list is shown in Figure 7–23.

Review each person's pickup list each day to see where he or she will need to be and when. Make sure he or she has a beeper or a mobile phone during pickups in case you have to send him or her on another run or add something to the pickup list. Gather any checks, cash, POs, and insurance certificates needed for a given set of pickups and issue them to the person facilitating the pickup. The person making the pickup must obtain paperwork from each vendor that indicates whether the pickup has been paid for or that a deposit has been made. All paperwork should be handed in to the office at the end of each day, and filed accordingly.

Director Check-in

It is important that you remain in constant communication with the director. Make sure that his or her needs are attended to. During pre-production, the director must meet with department heads, the casting director, and the cast, and he or she must also scout potential locations. Know the director's schedule. Discuss with him or her all equipment needs, location setups or concerns, changes to the shooting schedule, casting decisions, and other issues.

Department Check-ins

Checking that each department is on schedule and on budget is extremely important as pre-production heats up. Meet with all department heads each week. Make sure they are successfully securing the materials and equipment they need, that they have updated schedules and recent script changes, and that their departments are on budget. All department heads should meet with the director and discuss the needs of the film during their first week of work.

Checking in with department heads lets them know that you are there if they need any help, and allows you to stay on top of the budget for each department and know that everything will be ready for production. Having a weekly meeting with key staff members is also useful for informing them of any demands particular to a location (see the *"Locations Checklist" section*) or any other issues that arise that relate to their work. When discussing the budget with department heads, reduce the figure of their departmental budgets by about 25 percent, because odds are they will go overbudget and this way you are covered.

Filing Paperwork

Each day you will accumulate myriad pieces of paper, including POs, invoices, pickup paperwork, contracts, and letters. It is essential you file all paperwork at the end of each day. Allowing paperwork to pile up on your desk will

PICKUP & RETURN LIST

VENDORS	PICKUP	RETURN	DEPOSIT
ART RENTALS Art Supply USA 112 Fullerton, L.A.	4/15 After 9:00 am Table	5/9 Before 8:00 AM	$1,000
CAMERA EQUIP. Hollywood Camera 324 Cahuenga, H'wood	4/12 After 10:30 am Camera, accessories	5/8 Before 9:00 AM	$25,000
DOLLY/TRACK Chapman Rentals 657 Arlington St., S. Pedro	4/12 After 9:00 am Dolly, track, jib arm	5/8 Before 9:00 AM	$8,000
ELECTRIC EQUIP. Dan's Electric 3912 Eden Ln., H'wood	4/15 After 10:00 am 5-ton truck, loaded	5/9 Before 5:30 PM	$5,300
CRANE Panacrane West 16 E. Nicole, Bev Hills	Delivery	Pickup at wrap	$2,300
DAILIES FROM LAB Monochromatic 87 E. Burbank, Van Nuys	4/17-5/8 8:30 PM SHARP!	At wrap daily	*
GRIP EQUIP. Adolf Gassme 42 Market St., Alameda	4/15 After 11:15 am (see electric)	5/9 Before 8:00 PM	$5,000
CAMERA SUPPLIES Kim's Cam 341 Columbus, Azusa	4/15 After 2:30 PM Air, chamois, sharpies	5/9 Before 12:30 PM	$1,000
WARDROBE JC Penney 413 MCA Ave., How'd	4/12 After 3:00 PM Costumes	5/10 Any time after 12 noon	$1,500
SOUND EQUIPMENT Free Quency 989 Allstar Lane, L.A.	4/15 After 9:30 am Walkies, nagra, slate	5/9 Before 9:00 AM	$2,000

Figure 7–23 Pickup and return list

ultimately result in a big mess. You will need to refer again to much of this paperwork, and if you secure a distributor for the film you may be required to deliver paperwork such as cast and crew contracts to the distribution company.

Daily Cost Overview Sheet

Track your costs for budget purposes. A daily cost overview sheet will help you actualize your budget and track money you have spent and money that is available. It is essential you know where you are over- and under-budget. A typical cost overview sheet, an example of which is shown in Figure 7–24, has designated spaces for certain common costs that might arise. There is also space on the sheet to account for any unanticipated costs incurred, such as electric or grip equipment costs or fringes. Once you have prepared your cost overview sheet, file it with the other daily cost sheets.

Actualizing Your Budget

When actualizing your budget, track original costs against current costs (see Figure 6–3). This is how you will account for over- and underspending. Figure into your current costs any completed petty cash envelopes. (Be sure you code them according to your chart of accounts to ensure that you account for them properly.) Do not close out any budget accounts if costs will still be incurred in that category. Actualize the budget when all of the above- and below-the-line accounts have been closed and the final costs have come in. If you used Movie Magic Budgeting to compile your budget, you can easily actualize it by going into the Tools menu and selecting the Compare command. Enter your current costs in the box provided, and the program will calculate the variance.

Schedules and Lists Checklist

You will have to compile, organize, and arrange schedules, lists, and meetings as you hire cast and crew members, secure locations, negotiate with vendors, and hold department meetings. Attend to each of the following items daily, as necessary.

- Update, color-code, and distribute schedules, day-out-of-days sheets, strip boards, and script changes.
- Prepare office memos; distribute them to the crew or put in crew boxes.
- Compile crew, cast, and vendor packs.
- Compile production expendables list; place orders with vendors. (Include expendables for makeup, prop/art department needs, wardrobe, craft service, and catering.)
- Start compiling a thank-you list; write thank-you notes and/or purchase gifts.
- Start compiling main and end title credits.
- Compile a list of days on which only a skeleton crew will be needed.
- Compile a list of days on which a second-unit crew will be used.
- Once you have made a lab deal, compile a schedule for picking up dailies from the lab and delivering them to the editor.

Details of the Schedules and Lists Checklist

Schedule Updates

Any schedule, list, or script page that is changed or updated (such as the day-out-of-days sheets, shooting schedule, strip board, and script board) must be redistributed to all cast and crew members. Changes to the script and schedules are reflected by color-coding the updated pages (printing them on paper of different colors). The white copy (of a script, schedule, day-out-of-days sheet, and so on) is the first shooting version. The industry-standard color-coding order for subsequent changes is blue, pink, yellow, green, goldenrod, gray, buff, and salmon. Put the date in a header at the top of each page.

Changes to the script or schedule may prove necessary for a variety of reasons, including falling behind schedule, not being able to secure a location for the time you originally anticipated, actor unavailability, and weather problems. It is imperative that there be communication regarding any change in schedule among AD, production manager, line producer, and cast and crew. If anyone is unaware of the schedule change, it will cause mishaps that can cost time and money. The production office is responsible for making sure that the schedule changes are printed according to color code and immediately distributed among all crew members and all affected cast members.

Office Memos

It is essential that all crew be alerted to any changes, delays, meetings, and so on, so that the show can remain on schedule and everyone will be on the same page. During pre-production the crew is not usually in the office all day. Putting memos in each crew member's box or hanging manila folder will ensure that crew will be advised of anything that comes up. Often, one member of each department will check in to the office each day to pick up any memos, script and schedule updates, and petty cash or checks, and will alert their department to any memos.

DAILY COST OVERVIEW

SHOW ______________________ PROD # ______________________

DATE ______________________ DAY # ______________________

START DATE ______________

SCHEDULED FINISH DATE ______________

REVISED FINISH DATE ______________

	PER CALL SHEET	SHOT	AHEAD/BEHIND
# OF SCENES			
# OF PAGES			

	AS BUDGETED AND/OR SCHEDULED	ACTUAL	COST (OVER)/UNDER
CAST OVERTIME	______	______	______
COMPANY SHOOTING HOURS	______	______	______
MEAL PENALTY	______	______	______
EXTRAS & STAND-INS	______	______	______
CATERING	______	______	______
RAW STOCK	______	______	______
UNANTICIPATED EXPENSES:			
______	______	______	______
______	______	______	______
______	______	______	______
______	______	______	______
		TOTAL FOR TODAY	______
		PREVIOUS TOTAL	______
		GRAND TOTAL	______

PREPARED BY ______________________ APPROVED BY ______________________

Figure 7–24 Daily cost overview sheet (Reprinted by permission of ________)

Crew and Vendor Packs

Crew and vendor packs help ensure that all goes well during pre-production and production. Crew and vendor lists contain addresses, phone numbers, and contact information. A master vendor and crew list, updated as new information comes in, should be kept on the production manager's or coordinator's computer. These packs should be distributed among crew. Date them so that when you print new ones the old ones can be thrown away. You can also print updates on colored paper. This is important so that everyone remains on the same page and can do his or her job properly. For example, you do not want the DP trying to contact a lab you once planned to use when you have made a better deal at a different lab and have forgotten to replace the old lab information with the new.

Production Expendables

Expendables are items that can be either purchased or rented, depending on what they are and what they will be used for, and are usually items other than heavy equipment. For instance, craft service and catering will need tables, chairs, coolers, extension cords, and urns. The makeup and hair department will need chairs and a makeup mirror and table with lights. The wardrobe department may need a rolling rack and a steamer. These items are considered expendables, and can most often be rented from the same facility and often are inexpensive. They should be picked up prior to production, and either the production department or the member of the department the expendable is rented for can facilitate the pickup. Compile an expendables list for each department. Many of your departments will need items that can be rented from the same vendor. Make sure all production expendables rented from the same facility are referenced on the same purchase order, and are all accounted for at the end of each filming day.

Thank-you List

Start compiling a thank-you list at the beginning of pre-production. Include individuals and businesses that have made in-kind donations or have somehow been a "friend" of the production (contributed time, money, materials, services, and so on). Determine whether each person or business should receive a thank-you note, a small gift, or a thank-you credit at the end of the film. Do not take any one's goodwill for granted. Creating an ongoing thank-you list with a brief note of what each person contributed and where he or she works will greatly assist you. If you send a thank-you note or a gift to someone who has helped out, note that on your list. Silly as all of this may sound, it is unlikely you would be able to retain this information in your head; inevitably someone would be forgotten.

Crew and Cast Credits

On crew and cast contracts, include a line that indicates how the person's name will appear in the film's credits, or create a simple form (see Figure 7–25) on which each cast and crew member prints out this information. File these forms and have your coordinator put the list in the computer. This is not an urgent task; if the pace slows during production, do it then.

Skeleton Crew List

Low-budget shows often have several days when only a skeleton crew is needed. Determine which days may be skeleton crew days based on the schedule. If you are paying your crew daily rates, using a skeleton crew on some days will save you money. Do not do this with your key department heads, however, and be fair about limiting crew members' days, especially if you are paying them little to begin with. If you are paying your crew on a weekly basis, it may not be worth scheduling skeleton crew days unless the location dictates it. The best way to organize skeleton crew days, while still being fair to crew members, is to schedule them at the end of the shoot so that the crew does not have to come on and off the job.

Second-Unit Filming List

During filming, there may be days when no actors are required and a limited crew, called a second-unit crew, can be used. Often, second-unit filming days are scheduled at the end of the shoot. Make sure you have budgeted for the costs involved by accounting for equipment, raw stock, locations, and crew you will need for each second-unit filming day.

Dailies Pickup

It is important that dailies be picked up from the lab each day so that the director, the editor, and the producer(s) can view the footage from the previous day and the editor can begin assembling the film. If possible, one person should oversee picking up of dailies. This way, you are sure that dailies will be picked up and delivered to the editor. Find out what time dailies are ready each day, and notify the editor as to when to expect them. Secure a contact name at the lab for the person handling dailies in case there is a problem.

"TITLE"
Credit List

Please confirm that your name and credit are as you would like them to appear on screen. If your name is as you wish it to appear (i.e., spelling, nicknames, etc.), please initial. Thank you. We love you.—Production Office

1st AD "NAME OF CREW MEMBER"

____

Production Manager

____

2nd Assistant Director

____

Production Coordinator

____

Editor

____

Assistant Editor

____

Figure 7–25 Credit form

Crew Checklist

Crewing should begin in week 1 of pre-production. The hiring order indicated in the following checklist is based on a four- to six-week pre-production period.

- Hire a production manager or production coordinator (week 1).
- Schedule meetings with key crew members and the director.
- Hire an office production assistant (week 1).
- Hire a director of photography and members of the camera department (weeks 1 and 2).
- Hire members of the locations department (week 1).
- Hire an assistant director and other members of the department (week 2); start scheduling and filling out paperwork two or three weeks before production begins and as locations are secured.
- Hire crew for the art, prop, and production design departments (week 1 or 2).
- Hire crew for the wardrobe department (week 2); get cast sizes and set up fittings.
- Hire other office and set production assistants (weeks 1 to 4).
- Hire electricians and grips (weeks 2 and 3).
- Hire members of the makeup and hair department (week 3); schedule meetings with cast and makeup and hair artists.
- Hire sound department crew (week 3).
- Hire transportation department crew (week 3).
- Hire editing department crew (week 3); discuss lab and editing facility needs.
- Hire a script supervisor (week 3).
- Secure crew deal memos as the crew is hired; send copies to the payroll company.
- Have crew members fill out W-4 forms, I-9 forms, and Start forms as they are hired; file forms and send copies to the payroll company.
- Have the department heads fill out kit rental forms as needed.
- Have the heads of the prop/art, makeup, and wardrobe departments and the script supervisor start their continuity notebooks.
- Set up mailboxes or hang manila folders for each crew member as he or she is hired.
- Compile a list of extra crew members (day players) for larger shoot days.
- Make petty cash available to all departments with sign-out slips and petty cash envelopes.
- Ascertain any special meal needs or dietary requirements of crew members.
- Schedule a pre-production meeting with all crew members the week before production; arrange for a place to hold the meeting.

Details of the Crew Checklist

Hiring

Crewing should begin in week 1. (See Chapter 6 for a description of each crew member's responsibilities.) If you do not have contacts or leads for every department you need to crew, there are many ways to locate gifted crew members:

- Post listings on film school Web sites.
- Post signs at local film schools.
- Post listings on your local film support organization Web site (such as the IFP), and look through the online classifieds.
- Ask people you know in the business or people you have already hired for recommendations.
- Post signs at equipment rental houses.
- Contact the local film commission. This is a great way to locate competent crew, but they will most likely be quite experienced and therefore somewhat expensive.
- Contact the producer of a film in your budget range and ask for recommendations and resumes.
- Post signs at art schools for the art and props departments.
- Post signs at cosmetology schools for the hair and makeup departments.
- Look in the classified section of the trades.
- Post a notice in the classified section of the trades.

All of the foregoing should be done either online or the more traditional way (posting a sign on a bulletin board). It will be for you to determine which strategy will be most effective given the community you are in.

Hiring Process and Interviews

It is essential that the director be involved in hiring crew members, especially department heads. Gather sample reels of people's work, portfolios that display work they have done, and references of people with whom they have worked in the past. This is particularly important for hiring department heads. You may want to conduct an initial round of interviews and then submit a smaller group of select individuals to the director. How you involve the director in the hiring process will depend on the relationship you have with the director and the extent to which he or she is available to participate in the process. The following are the most important things to establish when interviewing potential crew members:

- The crew member knows what is expected of him or her and is qualified for the job.
- He or she is a team player who will get along with other crew members.
- You have made clear to the crew member the long hours required and the pay being offered.
- The philosophy of the shoot is clear (e.g., this is a nonunion shoot, four six-day weeks, and so on).
- The crew member is responsible and punctual.
- The crew member has a vehicle or transportation to and from work each day.

Without question, if you are hiring people you do not know, especially department heads, call at least one of their references. We have learned the hard way that sometimes applicants misrepresent themselves on their resumes and really are not qualified for the job.

Crew Deal Memos

Have each crew member fill out a crew deal memo (see Figure 7–16). Make sure the deal memo is completed in full and that the crew member's rate is clearly indicated. Start and finish dates and any deferral arrangements should also be included. Give the crew member a copy, file the original in the contract book, and place another copy in the production files. Create your own deal memos, or purchase a standard form from any production supply and form store. If you are using a payroll company to prepare crew payroll, send the company a copy of each crew member's deal memo.

Department Head Meetings

It is essential that each department head meet with the director to discuss the vision, look, feel, and equipment needs of the film. Schedule an initial meeting. Thereafter, department heads can check in with the director on their own. The DP, the production designer or art director, the gaffer, the AD, the location manager, the key grip, and the electrician will need to scout locations with the director as they are secured.

W-4 Forms and Start/I-9 Forms

When hired, each crew member must fill out a W-4 form with important information, including name, address, Social Security number, and the number of deductions for tax withholding purposes. Crew must also fill out Start/I-9 paperwork (see Figure 7–26) that indicates the dates for which they will be employed by the company, Social Security number, and the number of deductions they are claiming. For the payroll company to process and pay the employee, all of these forms will need to be completed. This information will be reported to the government. Make copies for the office files, and attach them to the crew member's deal memo. Send the originals to the payroll company.

Kit Rental Forms

If you are paying kit rental fees to crew members who rent their own supplies or equipment to the production, have them fill out a kit rental form, an example of which is shown in Figure 7–27. Kit rental fees are nontaxable and are usually paid on a weekly basis or as a one-time flat fee. File each kit rental form in the office files, and attach a copy to the crew member's deal memo. Send another copy to the payroll company with the crew member's time card. (See Chapter 6 for more on kit rentals.)

Continuity Notebooks

It is essential to have some record of how actors and sets look for a given scene to reference for continuity. Continuity notebooks will allow you to recreate how an actor was dressed and made up so that when script days need to be recreated, they will match. The costume designer, set designer or prop master, production designer, script supervisor, and makeup and hair artists will need instant or still film and notebooks to catalog wardrobe, makeup and hair, and the props and set design. The notebooks belong to the production when the show wraps. The editor will be given the script supervisor's notes each day and will receive the notebook he or she has compiled, which includes all script notes, at the end of production. The editor will refer to the notes while assembling the film.

Crew Mailboxes

Set up a box or hang a large manila envelope for each crew member on one of the office walls. Put any paperwork (such as schedules and updates, memos, script pages or changes, and contracts) and any messages in crew members' boxes or folders. This system is efficient and helps ensure that the office remains neat and organized and that crew members receive the necessary paperwork.

Extra Crew

Often there are days during production when departments may need extra help due to lighting needs particular to a location, heavy lifting or operating of equipment, time constraints at a given location, if there will be a lot of extras or cast on set, and so on. You will want to have a list ready of crew members you may be able to hire by the day (often referred to as day players). Keep resumes of those you did not hire because they were unavailable at the time, or ask department heads

I01349969

U.S. Department of Justice
Immigration and Naturalization Service

OMB No. 1115-0136
Employment Eligibility Verification

Please read instructions carefully before completing this form. The instructions must be available during completion of this form. ANTI-DISCRIMINATION NOTICE. It is illegal to discriminate against work eligible individuals. Employers CANNOT specify which document(s) they will accept from an employee. The refusal to hire an individual because of a future expiration date may also constitute illegal discrimination.

Section 1. Employee Information and Verification. To be completed and signed by employee at the time employment begins

Print Name: Last | First | Middle Initial | Maiden Name

Address *(Street Name and Number)* | Apt. # | Date of Birth *(month/day/year)*

City | State | Zip Code | Social Security #

I am aware that federal law provides for imprisonment and/or fines for false statements or use of false documents in connection with the completion of this form.

I attest, under penalty of perjury, that I am (check one of the following):
- ☐ A citizen or national of the United States
- ☐ A Lawful Permanent Resident (Alien # A______
- ☐ An alien authorized to work until ___/___/___
  (Alien # or Admission #______

Employee's Signature | Date *(month/day/year)*

Preparer and/or Translator Certification. *(To be completed and signed if Section 1 is prepared by a person other than the employee.) I attest, under penalty of perjury, that I have assisted in the completion of this form and that to the best of my knowledge the information is true and correct.*

Preparer's/Translator's Signature | Print Name

Address *(Street Name and Number, City, State, Zip Code)* | Date *(month/day/year)*

Section 2. Employer Review and Verification. To be completed and signed by employer. **Examine one document from List A OR examine one document from List B and one from List C** as listed on the reverse of this form and record the title, number and expiration date, if any, of the document(s)

	List A	OR	List B	AND	List C
Document title:	______		______		______
Issuing authority:	______		______		______
Document #:	______		______		______
Expiration Date *(if any)*:	___/___/___		___/___/___		___/___/___
Document #:	______				
Expiration Date *(if any)*:	___/___/___				

CERTIFICATION - I attest, under penalty of perjury, that I have examined the document(s) presented by the above-named employee, that the above-listed document(s) appear to be genuine and to relate to the employee named, that the employee began employment on *(month/day/year)* ___/___/___ **and that to the best of my knowledge the employee is eligible to work in the United States. (State employment agencies may omit the date the employee began employment).**

Signature of Employer or Authorized Representative | Print Name | Title

Business or Organization Name | Address *(Street Name and Number, City, State, Zip Code)* | Date *(month/day/year)*

Section 3. Updating and Reverification. To be completed and signed by employer

A. New Name *(if applicable)* | B. Date of rehire *(month/day/year) (if applicable)*

C. If employee's previous grant of work authorization has expired, provide the information below for the document that establishes current employment eligibility.

Document Title:______ Document #:______ Expiration Date (if any):___/___/___

I attest, under penalty of perjury, that to the best of my knowledge, this employee is eligible to work in the United States, and if the employee presented document(s), the document(s) I have examined appear to be genuine and to relate to the individual.

Signature of Employer or Authorized Representative | Date *(month/day/year)*

Form I-9 (Rev. 11-21-91) N

Figure 7–26 Employee I-9 form

BOX RENTAL INFORMATION

PRODUCTION COMPANY ____________________

EMPLOYEE ____________________ S.S.# ____________________

LOAN OUT COMPANY ____________________

FEDERAL ID# ____________________

RENTAL RATE: $ ____________________ PER WEEK/DAY

(Must be recorded on employee time card each week)

RENTAL COMMENCES ON: ____________________

INVENTORY (Attach additional pages if necessary):

____

____

____

____

____

____

____

Employee/Loanout agree that the equipment listed herein is rented to Production Company for use under Employee/Loanout's direction and control. Employee/Loanout are solely responsible for any damage to or loss of such equipment and hereby waive any claims against Entertainment Partners for any loss or damage of any kind and agree to look solely to Production Company to resolve any such claims. Entertainment Partners shall have no obligation to indemnify Employee/Loanout against any losses or damage, or to provide any insurance coverage for the benefit of Employee/Loanout covering the equipment herein described.

I attest that the above-described equipment represents a valid rental for this production.

____

EMPLOYEE SIGNATURE DATE

____

APPROVAL SIGNATURE DATE

Figure 7–27 Kit rental form

for recommendations of crew they have worked with before and like. You do not want to be scrambling at the last minute to find crew.

Petty Cash

As crew members are hired, explain how petty cash is handled and discuss their needs and responsibilities. Whenever petty cash is distributed, have the crew member sign a petty cash receipt. Issue a petty cash envelope. Generally, petty cash envelopes should be filled out in pencil by the crew member spending the money so that changes can be made if there are any mistakes. Ask your crew to tape receipts to an 8–1/2" by 11" sheet of paper, number each receipt, and highlight the total on each. Your job will be infinitely easier if the numbers on the receipts match the numbers on the outside of the envelope. It is customary to retally the numbers on the front of the petty cash envelope on a calculator that has a paper feed and to tape the paper feed to the envelope and highlight the matching totals. Check the math whenever a petty cash envelope is handed in. Encourage crew members to submit check requests whenever possible rather than paying for anything expensive with cash. The only time cash is preferable is when the vendor or merchant is cutting you a major deal on a cash-only basis. If you are uncertain how the petty cash situation is going to work with your crew or if you have never worked with someone before, dole out only a small amount of money at a time.

Special Meal Needs

Members of your crew may have dietary needs that can be easily accommodated. Make arrangements with craft service and catering for any special meals, beverages, or snacks that crew members have (within reason).

All-Crew Pre-production Check-in Meeting

Schedule an all-crew check-in meeting for the last week of pre-production either at the office or in a space large enough to accommodate the entire crew. (See "The Last Week of Pre-production" later in this chapter.)

Cast Checklist

The following are items to attend to in regard to cast:

- Hire a casting agent (week 1 or before).
- Determine under which contract you will sign with SAG. Fill out and file SAG paperwork; post bond (weeks 1 and 2).
- Prepare for auditions: secure a casting space, arrange for beverages and food, prepare sides, make copies of the sign-in sheet, and forward head shots to the casting director (weeks 1 and 2).
- Have the casting director fill out cast contracts and deal memos; file them and send them to SAG as the cast is hired.
- Have cast members fill out W-4 forms, I-9 forms, and Start forms as they are hired; forward copies to SAG and the payroll company.
- Have the casting director "Station-12" cast members as they are hired.
- Ask the insurance carrier about required medical exams; schedule medical exams for four or five principal players as they attach and before production begins; schedule a medical exam for the director if required.
- Ensure that wardrobe fittings and makeup tests are scheduled (weeks 3 and 4).
- Compile the cast list as cast members are hired.
- Secure rehearsal space; schedule rehearsal time with the actors and the director.
- Arrange for extras, or hire an extras casting agent; determine how many location extras will be needed and when.
- Give the AD the SAG paperwork and forms that will be filled out on the set.
- Have the SAG payroll time cards on hand to be filled out weekly and forwarded to SAG and the payroll company.
- Make travel arrangements for out-of-town actors if necessary and determine how they will be transported to and from the set.
- Ascertain special meal needs or dietary requirements of any actors.

Details of the Cast Checklist

Casting Agent

If your film is largely cast already, you may not need a casting agent until the second week of pre-production. On the other hand, if you have to attach name talent or any talents to secure your financing, you may have to bring a casting director on board earlier. The time frame will depend on the project, but it may be as much as 12 months before your film is given the green light.

SAG Paperwork

Request and begin filling out the SAG paperwork package immediately! (See the "Legal, Financial, and Accounts Checklist" section.) SAG guidelines and the rule handbook are provided in the package. It is not a bad idea to enlarge the pages of the SAG agreement that outline the daily responsibilities of the signatory and post them in the production office for quick reference. The Guild requires that you include the film's budget and shooting schedule with your signatory paperwork. (The package specifies what to include and when.) Your casting director, if you have one, can be helpful with much of the SAG paperwork. SAG production forms are also included in the package and should be copied for use during production (Exhibit G forms, Taft-Hartley forms, casting data reports, and so on). Give copies to your AD to fill out each day on the set. These forms may be purchased in bulk at a production form supply house.

Auditions

Before you begin casting sessions, secure a space to hold auditions. Beverages should be provided at all casting sessions. What you can or want to do beyond providing drinks will be based on your budget. Sides are the pages of dialogue that are read by actors auditioning for a part. Choose scenes from the script that give the actors a fair amount to work with and will allow you to see their potential. Sides should be copied before auditions are held and should be made available to actors before their auditions.

If yours is a SAG show, each actor is required to sign a SAG sign-in sheet, shown in Figure 7–28, which must be sent to SAG. Even if yours is not a SAG production, a sign-in sheet will be useful for recording who has read, for what part, and how he or she can be reached.

The casting director, the director, and the production office all refer to head shots. The casting agent will likely forward a large number of head shots to the director or producer for approval on whom to call in to read. You can solicit head shots by running a breakdown through breakdown services. A breakdown in this instance refers to a list of each of the principal characters you seek to cast and a description of what they are like, such as personality, age, ethnicity, and so on. Expect to receive many unsolicited head shots from actors responding to the listing. Forward them to the casting director if you have one.

Cast Contracts and Deal Memos

Each cast member must fill out a SAG weekly or daily contract and a deal memo with the production company. Copies of each must be given to SAG, the payroll company, the actor, and the actor's agent and filed in the contract notebook and office files. The deal memo should include the actor's name, contact information, start and finish dates, pay rate, deferred compensation (if any), transportation and accommodations to be provided, looping dates, and Station 12 information. The contracts are standard SAG employment agreements that can be obtained from SAG or purchased from a production supply house. If you have a casting director, he or she will help with filling out and securing contracts and deal memos from performers as they are hired. If you are making any deals with your performers above and beyond SAG scale, you will likely have long-form agreements with each of your key players and will have contracts your attorney will help negotiate. Figures 7–29 and 7–30 show, respectively, a SAG freelance contract and a SAG daily contract.

W-4 Forms and Start/I-9 Forms

Cast members must also fill out W-4 forms and Start/I-9 forms. Attach these forms to each cast member's contract and forward copies to the payroll company and SAG (see Figures 7–17 and 7–26).

Station-12

SAG requires that an actor's status be cleared with the Guild before beginning work on any production. The production must "Station-12" an actor within 15 days of hiring him or her. SAG requires that members of the Guild pay yearly dues. If they have not paid their dues, they must do so before working on your set. The production company will pay a fine for any actor working on a set whose status has not been cleared with the Guild. The SAG package outlines how to Station-12 an actor. If you have a casting agent, he or she will usually handle this task. Fill out the Station-12 status on the production company deal memo you have with the actor.

Cast Medical Exams

To secure production insurance, medical exams for a few of your principal players and the director are often required. As you attach your principal cast members, schedule physical exams. Physical exams must be concluded before production begins. Have the physician send the examination records to the production office, and then forward the records to your insurance carrier. Make sure you budget properly for this expense.

Wardrobe Fittings and Hair and Makeup Tests

Wardrobe fittings and makeup tests are important and must be scheduled prior to production. Leave ample time to replace, make, or alter any items of wardrobe; to cut, dye, and fit wigs; to test prosthetics or masks; and to determine the makeup needs for each cast member. Ideally, the costume designer and makeup and hair artists will facilitate these meetings. The degree of support required from the production office will vary. Make sure a space for fittings and tests is arranged for. The line producer should ensure that these meetings occur, and that all wardrobe will be ready and any hair and makeup needs have been tended to and will be ready when filming begins.

Cast List

As cast members come on board, start compiling a cast list similar to the list you have compiled for the crew. Include each actor's name, address, telephone and cell phone numbers, and agent information. This list will be useful for myriad reasons, including securing cast members for rehearsal time, wardrobe fittings, and makeup and hair tests.

Rehearsals

The AD, in conjunction with the director, is often responsible for scheduling rehearsal time and pairing actors who need to rehearse with each other. The production office is responsible for securing the rehearsal space.

SCREEN ACTORS GUILD THEATRICAL & TELEVISION SIGN-IN SHEET

PRODUCER: ______________________
PROD'N CO: ______________________
PROD'N OFFICE
PHONE # ______________________

CASTING REP: ______________________
CASTING REP. PHONE: ______________________
PRODUCTION TITLE: ______________________
EPISODE: ______________________

AUDITION DATE: ____________ ______________________
Casting Director's Signature

CASTING REP:
Please fill in <u>time seen</u>
for each actor

(1) NAME	(2) SOCIAL SECURITY OR SAG MEMBER NUMBER	(3) ROLE	(4) AGENT	(5) PROVIDED?		(6) ARRIVAL TIME	(7) APPT. TIME	(8) TIME SEEN **<u>(Cast. rep.)</u>**	(9) TIME OUT	(10) TAPED?	(11) ACT. INI
				PARK	SCRIPT						

Figure 7–28 SAG sign-in sheet

THE PERFORMER MAY NOT WAIVE ANY PROVISION OF THIS CONTRACT WITHOUT THE WRITTEN CONSENT OF SCREEN ACTORS GUILD, INC.

SCREEN ACTORS GUILD
MINIMUM FREE LANCE CONTRACT
FOR THEATRICAL MOTION PICTURES

Continuous Employment—Weekly Basis—Weekly Salary
One Week Minimum Employment

THIS AGREEMENT, made this_________________ day of ____________, 19____, between ______________________, hereafter called "Producer", and ______________________, hereafter called "Performer".

WITNESSETH:

1. PHOTOPLAY, ROLE, SALARY AND GUARANTEE. Producer hereby engages Performer to render services as such in the role of ____________________, in a photoplay, the working title of which is now ____________________, at the salary of $____________ per "studio week" (Schedule B Performers must receive an additional overtime payment of four (4) hours at straight time rate for each overnight location Saturday). Performer accepts such engagement upon the terms herein specified. Producer guarantees that it will furnish Performer not less than _________________ week's employment (if this blank is not filled in, the guarantee shall be one week). Performer shall be paid pro rata for each additional day beyond guarantee until dismissal.

2. TERM: The term of employment hereunder shall begin on

on ____________________

on or about* ____________________

and shall continue therafter until the completion of the photography and recordation of said role.

3. BASIC CONTRACT. All provisions of the collective bargaining agreement between Screen Actors Guild, Inc. and Producer, relating to theatrical motion pictures, which are applicable to the employment of the Performer hereunder, shall be deemed incorporated herein.

4. PERFORMER'S ADDRESS. All notices which the Producer is required or may desire to give to the Performer may be given either by mailing the same addressed to the Performer at____________________ or such notice may be given to the Performer personally, either orally or in writing.

5. PERFORMER'S TELEPHONE. The Performer must keep the Producer's casting office or the assistant director of said photoplay advised as to where the Performer may be reached by telephone without unreasonable delay. The current telephone number of the Performer is ____________________.

6. MOTION PICTURE AND TELEVISION RELIEF FUND. The Performer (does) (does not) hereby authorize the Producer to deduct from the compensation hereinabove specified an amount equal to _________________ per cent of each installment of compensation due the Performer hereunder, and to pay the amount so deducted to the Motion Picture and Television Relief Fund of America, Inc.

7. FURNISHING OF WARDROBE. The (Producer) (Performer) agrees to furnish all modern wardrobe and wearing apparel reasonably necessary for the portrayal of said role; it being agreed, however, that should so-called "character" or "period" costumes be required, the Producer shall supply the same. When Performer furnishes any wardrobe, Performer shall receive the cleaning allowance and reimbursement, if any, specified in the basic contract.

Number of outfits furnished by Performer _____ @ $_____
(formal) _____ @ $_____

8. ARBITRATION OF DISPUTES. Should any dispute or controversy arise between the parties hereto with reference to this contract, or the employment herein provided for, such dispute or controversy shall be settled and determined by conciliation and arbitration in accordance with the conciliation and arbitration provisions of the collective bargaining agreement between the Producer and Screen Actors Guild relating to theatrical motion pictures, and such provisions are hereby referred to and by such reference incorporated herein and made a part of this Agreement with the same effect as though the same were set forth herein in detail.

9. NEXT STARTING DATE. The starting date of Performer's next engagement is____________________.

10. The Performer may not waive any provision of this contract without the written consent of Screen Actors Guild, Inc.

11. Producer makes the material representation that either it is presently a signatory to the Screen Actors Guild collective bargaining agreement covering the employment contracted for herein, or that the above-referred-to photoplay is covered by such collective bargaining agreement under the Independent Production provisions of the General Provisions of the Screen Actors Guild Codified Basic Agreement as the same may be supplemented and/or amended.

IN WITNESS WHEREOF, the parties have executed this agreement on the day and year first above written.

PRODUCER____________________ PERFORMER____________________

BY____________________ Social Security No.____________________

*The "on or about" clause may only be used when the contract is delivered to the Performer at least seven days before the starting date. See Codified Basic Agreement, Schedule B, Schedule C, otherwise a specific starting date must be stated.

Production time reports are available on the set at the end of each day, which reports shall be signed or initialed by the Performer.

Attached hereto for your use are the following: (1) Declaration Regarding Income Tax Withholding ("Part Year Employment Method of Withholding") and (2) Declaration Regarding Income Tax Withholding. You may utilize the applicable form by delivering same to Producer. Only one of such forms may be used.

NOTICE TO PERFORMER: IT IS IMPORTANT THAT YOU RETAIN A COPY OF THIS CONTRACT FOR YOUR PERMANENT RECORDS.

Figure 7–29 SAG freelance contract

THE PERFORMER MAY NOT WAIVE ANY PROVISION OF THIS CONTRACT WITHOUT THE WRITTEN CONSENT OF SCREEN ACTORS GUILD. INC.

SCREEN ACTORS GUILD

DAILY CONTRACT
(DAY PERFORMER)
FOR THEATRICAL MOTION PICTURES

Company ____________________ Date ____________________

Date Employment Starts ____________________ Performer Name ____________________

Production Title ____________________ Address ____________________

Production Number ____________________ Telephone No.: (____) ____________________

Role ____________________ Social Security No. ____________________

Daily Rate $____________________ Legal Resident of (State) ____________________

Weekly Conversion Rate $ ____________________ Citizen of U.S. ☐ Yes ☐ No

COMPLETE FOR "DROP-AND-PICK-UP" DEALS ONLY:

Firm recall date on ____________________

or on or after * ____________________

("On or after"recall only applies to pick-up as Weekly Performer)

As ☐ Day Performer ☐ Weekly Performer

*Means date specified or within 24 hours thereafter.

Wardrobe supplied by Performer Yes ☐ No ☐

If so, number of outfits __________ @ $__________

(formal) __________ @ $__________

Date of Stunt Performer's next engagement: __________

The employment is subject to all of the provisions and conditions applicable to the employment of DAY PERFORMER contained or provided for in the Producer-Screen Actors Guild Codified Basic Agreement as the same may be supplemented and/or amended.

The performer does hereby authorize the Producer to deduct from the compensation hereinabove specified an amount equal to _____ percent of each installment of compensation due the Performer hereunder, and to pay the amount so deducted to the Motion Picture and Television Relief Fund of America, Inc.

Special Provisions:

PRODUCER ____________________ PERFORMER ____________________

BY ____________________

Production time reports are available on the set at the end of each day. Such reports shall be signed or initialed by the Performer.

Attached hereto for your use is Declaration Regarding Income Tax Withholding.

NOTICE TOPERFORMER: IT IS IMPORTANT THAT YOU RETAIN A COPY OF THIS CONTRACT FOR YOUR PERMANENT RECORDS.

Figure 7–30 SAG daily contract

Extras
Compile a list of the locations where extras are needed and calculate approximately how many you will need to create the desired atmosphere. If you will need to hire a number of extras for many of your locations, it is advisable that you hire an extras casting agent. If many of your locations will be open to the public while you are filming, or there are a limited number of days for which a limited number of extras are needed, it may be more cost efficient to hire extras a few days before through an extras casting company. Remember to have all extras fill out W-4 forms (see Figure 7–17), Start/I-9 forms (see Figure 7–26), and an extras voucher. Forward these forms to both SAG and the payroll company.

SAG Paperwork for the Assistant Director
There are some forms included within the SAG package that will need to be given to the AD and filled out on the set either daily or when necessary. Forms, such as the Exhibit G (the actor's daily time report), Taft-Hartley forms, extras contracts (if there will be extras on a particular day), day players contracts if they have not yet been signed for any reason or there is a last-minute hire, and accident forms in case there are any cast injuries will need to be completed. These forms when completed should be turned in to the office each day and forwarded to SAG every week. Make sure the necessary SAG paperwork is in the AD's kit before production begins.

Time Cards
Cast members' time cards must be forwarded to SAG and to the payroll company each week, which you keep track of via a talent worksheet, an example of which is shown in Figure 7–31). The Guild requires that actors be compensated for rehearsal time, just as they are paid for shoot days, travel days, and looping days.

Travel and Transportation for Actors
If you have hired actors who will need to travel from out of town to the production, you will need to make the necessary travel arrangements. Make flight reservations early on for any out-of-town actors, and compile a master list of each actor who will be flying. On low-budget shows, try to make the same arrangements for each actor. However, depending on who the actor is, first-class flight accommodations may need to be booked if stipulated in the actor's contract. Make sure that arrangements have been made to have them picked up and returned to the airport.

You will also need to make transportation arrangements to and from the set for any out-of-town actors. If possible, designate a production assistant or "talent liaison," who is responsible for getting the necessary actors to and from the set on the days they are needed. Often, actors may request that the production rent them a car while they are working on location, if the budget can afford it, and may want to drive themselves to and from the set.

Locations Checklist

The following are items to attend to in regard to locations.

- Have the location manager begin scouting and photographing locations (weeks 1 and 2).
- Compile a list of possible locations and assemble folders for location photos; show them to the director and the producer.
- Arrange and schedule location scouts with the necessary crew.
- Secure permits as locations are locked; notify the film commission.
- Secure signed location contracts and releases as the locations are locked.
- Arrange to have insurance certificates sent to each secured location.
- Determine whether a generator will be necessary or whether you will tie in for power at each location.
- Arrange through the film commission for police officers and firefighters as necessary.
- Arrange for security as needed.
- Prepare filming notices, personal and still releases, neighbor sign-off releases, and notice of filming; add to the AD kit.
- Determine the setup of each location; make necessary arrangements for crew parking and cartage, bath rooms, dressing rooms, holding areas, production office, and craft service and catering areas.
- Compile a list of expendables needed for each location, and place other items on hold (layout board, cones, rope, bullhorn, chairs, tables, tents, and so on).
- Have extra keys made for the locations if necessary.
- Draw a map to each location.
- Secure a stage if needed; organize strike, rig, and prelight days.
- Update the shooting schedule and strip board as locations are locked.

Details of the Locations Checklist

Scouting for Locations
If you have a four-, five-, or six-week pre-production period, the location manager should begin work in week 1 or 2 of pre-production, depending on how many locations have to be secured, whether you will be filming at any out-of-town

PRODUCTION COMPANY: ______________________ NAME: ______________________ WEEK ENDING: ______________

PRODUCTION TITLE: ______________________ EMPLOYEE #:: ______________________

G/L CODE	DATE	WORK STATUS SW R W WF H SWF TR / DAY	LEAVE MOTEL	ARRIVE MAKE-UP/ WARDRBE	ARRIVE ON SET	NDB	FIRST MEAL From	FIRST MEAL To	SECOND MEAL From	SECOND MEAL To	DISMISS on SET	DISMISS Make-Up Wardrobe	ARRIVE at MOTEL	STUNT ADJUSTMENT	ACTUAL HOURS	TRAVEL TIME 1 1/2X	OT 1 1/2X	OT 2X	6th DAY PREMIUM	MEAL PENALTY	FORCE CALL
		SUN																			
		MON																			
		TUE																			
		WED																			
		THU																			
		FRI																			
		SAT																			
														TOTAL HOURS							

G/L CODE	PAY CODE#	SAG PENSIONABLE	HOURS	TOTAL
	472	Base Salary		
	415	Daily OT (1.5x)		
	420	Daily OT (2x)		
	416	Travel (1.5x)		
	490	Weekly OT		
	474	6th Day Prem.		
	437	Holiday Prem.		
	476	Stunt Adj.		
	473	Guarantee		
	447	Location Allow		
		Other / Misc.		

G/L CODE	PAY CODE#	NON PENSIONABLE	TOTAL
	449	Meal Penalty	
	430	Forced Call	
	488	Wardrobe	
	452	Drive - to	
	464	Per Diem NT	
	465	Per Diem TX	
	464	Per Diem NT	
	465	Per Diem TX	
		Other / Misc.	

Schedule: ______________

Daily Rate: ______________

Weekly Rate: ______________

Days / Weeks Guaranteed: ______

Days Paid: ______________

Last Day Worked: __________

Theatrical/ Motion Picture ☐
Division ☐

TOTAL DUE: ______________________

SAG P&W DUE: ______________________

Figure 7–31 Talent worksheet

locations, and the budget's limitations. After an initial meeting with the director and producer to discuss the look of the locations, the dates when the locations will be needed, the budget, and any other concerns, the location manager will compile a list of all scripted locations. If there are multiple locations, you may have to hire an assistant location manager for a few weeks to assist with paperwork, notices that have to be posted, and permits that have to be secured and filed.

Finding appropriate locations that are affordable and available when you need them is not always easy, and you may need an extra week or several days to scout for locations, especially if they are out of town. If there is little time to lock locations and the location manager is having trouble finding suitable options, inquire at a location rental office, which will have listings and photos of locations that are regularly used and available for filming for a fee. Check local film guides, or contact the film commission in your area.If the locations that have been scripted actually exist, it is ideal to lock those locations if possible, in that they are likely to best serve the film's look. However, make sure the scripted locations are convenient for the production in terms of access and travel. As with any other location, they must be affordable and available to you when you need them.

If necessary, find a substitute location that will better serve the needs of the film, or build the location on a stage. *Swingers* was set in Los Angeles, and we filmed in most of the actual bars and other locations Jon Favreau scripted. We were fortunate to secure those locations at an affordable price when we needed them. Other bars we shot in were not the actual bars scripted. We shot in these substitute bars because of budget limitations, availability, or other production-related concerns. For example, the Treasure Island Casino was scripted, but it was completely out of our budget range. We locked another casino that was available and that we could afford.

Location Files

As the location manager scouts for potential locations, he or she will photograph them (interiors, exteriors, and specific areas of the location that will be used for filming). Create a file for each potential location, and include such pertinent information as the address, cost, how power will be provided (generator or tie-in), names of contacts, and the dates the location is available. The director and producer will go through the files to determine the suitability of potential locations and to decide which locations the director should scout. The production office is responsible for housing the files. Be sure your location manager has ample instant or still film and enough petty cash for gas, phone calls, and food while scouting.

Location Scouting with Crew

Try to keep scouting to a minimum. It is best that the location manager narrow down the location choices based on what would best serve the film's needs (proximity, dates available, and cost) before bringing options to the director. Once the majority of your locations have been locked (some may not be locked until production if they are difficult to find or secure), the location manager and line producer will schedule scouts of each location. The director, producer, first AD, DP, gaffer, key grip, sound recordist, production designer, and location manager will scout locations for setups, equipment needs, power issues, lighting needs, sound, and other concerns. Sometimes the production designer or art department representative will not have to attend the final scout because he or she will have looked at scouted locations and been prepping the locales long before this final scout. In an early "Project Greenlight" they're shooting under the Chicago "L" train. It is unlikely that had an experienced sound recordist prescouted that location that he or she would have approved it as a realistic choice. Because it's so loud, it's almost impossible to read dialogue.

Schedule locations that are within the same vicinity on the same day. Be sure to have enough instant film on hand. Be prepared to pay crew members for the days they scout and to reimburse them for meals and mileage or gas (the latter only if you are not renting a passenger van large enough to accommodate everyone, which is usually a good idea so that discussion and ideas can be exchanged between locations). On *Swingers*, we were able to scout several of our locations on the same day because they were located near one another. We did not have an overwhelming number of locations to secure, and most of the locations scripted were actual places, so the location manager was able to lock many of them quickly, with minimal scouting. We scouted several potential locations just to be sure we had not missed a location that would better serve the look of the film. For instance, although the Derby was the scripted location, we scouted several other possibilities because we were concerned about the high ceilings, the cost, the lighting, and the power issues in the Derby. We were also not sure if we would be able to film on the days we needed to. Ultimately, we made the right deal and the majority of the footage was shot while the Derby was open to the public, which saved us money on extras and the site rental itself.

Permits

Once your locations have been determined, you will have to obtain permits for each one. The location manager should obtain the contact information for the local film commission. The city or state film commission will often issue all of the permits for the production. You may be able to secure a blanket permit if your locations are all within the same city and near one another. (See Chapter 6.) The production can be shut down if you fail to have the proper paperwork and permits on hand. The location manager will contact the city permit office to determine which locations require permits and the fees involved, which will be determined by such factors as where on the premises you will be shooting, whether a location will be open to the public, and whether a location is also used as a public thoroughfare. The permit office will issue the production permits once the permit fees have been paid and will tell you whether a firefighter or police officer will be required at any of your locations. It takes time to secure permits and to fill out the necessary paperwork, so the location manager should contact the permit office as locations are locked. Be sure the production office has copies of each permit issued and that the AD has a copy of each permit on the set.

Location Contracts and Releases

Once your locations have been locked, your location manager must secure location contracts (see Figures 7–14 and 7–15). Whether you are filming in a bar, a restaurant, a private home, a car dealership, or a park, you must have the owner, the manager, or another representative sign a contract with the production company agreeing to the terms set forth. Fill in the dates of filming, the production company's name, the film's title, the address of the location, the site rental fee to be paid, any screen credit that has been promised, and the name of the location contact. The contract protects the production in case of a dispute as to whether a fee was paid or permission was given to film at the location. The permit office may want to see your signed location contracts before issuing a permit. If you are scheduled to film at a location in a residential area, you must abide by certain rules. For instance, there are specific filming hours for residential neighborhoods, and if you intend to film after the city's filming hours an extended- hours filming release (see Figure 7–32) from the permit office will be required. Contact the permit office for the filming rules and guidelines in your area. Signatures must be gathered from local residents to acknowledge that they have been notified that filming will take place in their neighborhood on certain days and during certain hours. You will need a minimum number of signatures before permission can be granted. Copy all permits, releases, and contracts in triplicate: one for the office file, one for the AD kit, and one for your personal notebook.

Insurance Certificates

Each location must be covered under the production insurance policy, and the representative of each location must receive an insurance certificate. Ask your insurance carrier to send a certificate to each location as it is locked. The certificate indicates that the production is covered for any loss or damage that may occur at the location during filming. Proof of insurance for each location must be on hand during filming, and make sure it is filed in the AD kit. The permit office may want to verify that you have insured each location before it issues permits.

Generator and Tie-ins

The location manager, together with the gaffer, will identify the locations for which a generator must be rented. Ideally, a generator should be rented for the entire show, if you can afford it, to provide ample power for running lights, charging walkie-talkies and batteries, and plugging in coffee urns, hot plates, microwaves, irons, and the wardrobe steamer. Your locations may allow you to tie in for power, which means that you can run your lights and other equipment (without a generator) from the location itself. Be prepared to pay electrical costs if they are above the norm for the location (a tie-in will typically drive up an electric bill). The gaffer will be able to determine if a tie-in is an option, and if limited lights will be used this may be preferable. (It may save you money in terms of gas purchases and generator rental, it will be less noisy, and you may not need a firefighter present.) You will need to identify your power source so that the permit office can instruct you about fire personnel requirements in order to make the necessary rental arrangements.

Police Officers and Firefighters

Depending on the location at which you are filming, whether you have a generator or special equipment on the set, whether you are using equipment that will be set up on the sidewalk at a location, whether you are filming any type of special effect or stunt (fire, car chase, gun fight, and so on), and whether your locations are open to the public while filming, the permit office may require a city official be present on your set. When your location manager is permitting each location, based on the information given to the permit office about each location the permit office will determine for which locations and for how long you will need a police officer and/or firefighter present. These officers are on set to ensure the safety of the cast, crew, extras, passersby, and anyone who is affected by the production. They will also help keep the public off your set and will block off parking and traffic lanes if necessary. The rate they are paid is determined by the union.

COUNTY & CITY OF LOS ANGELES - FILM PERMIT
SIGNATURE SURVEY FOR EXTENDED HOUR,
WEEKEND AND/OR LONG TERM FILMING

Dear Resident/Merchant/Business Representative,

We are planning to film scenes of ______________________ at ______________________.

Proposed date(s): ______________ hours: from ______________ a.m./p.m. to ______________ a.m./p.m.

Description of scenes & parking:

____

____

____

____

We have applied for the necessary permit and maintain all legally required liability insurance. If a permit is granted, all personnel required to ensure public safety will be on location. We agree to abide by all County or City filming rules and any specific guidelines applicable to your neighborhood.

We will make every effort not to disturb you and will not arrive earlier or vacate the neighborhood later than the specified time. Thank you, in advance, for your cooperation and hospitality while we are filming in your neighborhood.

If you have any questions or concerns regarding this request, please contact us at the production office or by pager. Please don't hesitate to call us.

____
Production Company

____
Production Office phone#

____
Location Manager

____
Production Manager

Or you may contact:

EIDC/Los Angeles Film Office
7083 Hollywood Blvd.
Los Angeles, CA 90028
213.957.1000
Office Hours: 8am - 6am Mon. - Fri.

AFTER HOURS HOTLINE: (24 hours a day)
800.201.5982
Give the operator your name, phone no.,
and a brief message.

I DO NOT OBJECT to the filming permit.

I DO OBJECT to the filming request. Reasons (optional)

____

I DO NOT OBJECT but prefer not to sign my name.

____
Signature

____
Print Name

____
Address

____
Phone (optional-for verification purposes only)

In multiple unit buildings, managers may sign on behalf of tenants but must notify all tenants.

Total no. of units in building ________
Addresses signed for ________

I, as manager of the above building, have notified all of the tenants and know of no substantial objection to the proposed filming activity.

____
Manager, Address

Figure 7–32 Film permit for extended hours

Security

You may find it necessary or preferable on certain days to hire private security personnel when filming large party scenes, outdoors, or at night. On *Swingers*, we hired two security guards while filming the party scene. We shot at a friend's house and knew there would be many people going in and out. Having hired security reduced the risk of damaging the house we filmed in, of people being injured, and of equipment and materials being lost, broken, or stolen. The security guards helped us maintain order in what might otherwise have been an uncontrollable situation. If you will be filming in a dangerous neighborhood or will be leaving equipment overnight at a location, security is a must. As the line producer, you will not be able to oversee everything, but you are responsible for the location, equipment, and materials.

Filming Notices and Personal Releases

The location manager is responsible for posting filming notices at locations that will be open to the public while you are filming (see Figure 7–20). Filming notices alert patrons that you are filming on the premises and that they may be in a shot. The local film commission and the permit office require that you post notices. Check with each permit office for guidelines for each of your locations. Make sure notices have been posted where they can be seen easily. You may want to post several. On *Swingers*, we posted notices in all of the bars we filmed in while they were open to the public. We also secured personal releases from patrons whom we specifically asked to be in the background of a shot. Have both types of notices and releases on the set and in the AD kit.

Setup

The location manager should determine the setup of each location before you are scheduled to film there. The location manager should photograph or sketch the layout of each location. After the AD and the location manager have discussed the needs of the scenes being shot at each location, they will determine how to best use the space. For example, will a trash receptacle have to be rented, and if so, where will it be placed? Will the location accommodate dressing areas for the actors and a makeup station? If not, you may have to rent a motor home to use as a bathroom, an office, a changing area, and a makeup station. Where will the motor home be parked?

Determine where each department will keep its materials and where department personnel will work. Where will crew and production vehicles park? Will you have to rent a parking lot? You will need a designated craft service area and a place where tables, chairs, and catering can be set up. Determine where the restrooms are and where equipment can be stored. Figure out the best place to run the generator, keeping in mind both size and noise. Is there a place to house the production office? Will you view dailies at the location, and if so, where? All of these factors must be considered, and your location manager, together with the AD, should be prepared to direct crew members to the appropriate place when they arrive at the location so that no time is wasted. A floor plan of the location will allow the necessary personnel to answer these questions beforehand and to direct the crew accordingly during production.

Expendables

You may need to purchase or rent certain items for your locations. Compile a list of expendables that may be needed at each location. (See the "Schedules and Lists Checklist" section.) Consider the following:

- Rope for sectioning off areas
- Parking cones for directing cars to parking areas or for blocking off areas
- Bullhorns if the location is large or if there are several actors, crew members, and extras on the set to direct
- Butt cans for cigarettes (you can save empty coffee cans to use as butt cans), trash cans, and trash bags
- Tables and chairs for catering and workstations
- Director's chairs for cast, crew, and extras while on the set
- Coffee urns, coolers, chafing dishes, tablecloths, thermoses, hot plates, and extension cords for craft services and catering
- Portable fans or stationary heaters, as the weather dictates
- Wardrobe racks and a steamer for the wardrobe department
- Flashlights, batteries, a fire extinguisher, and a first aid kit
- Makeup mirrors, chairs, and tables for the makeup and hair department
- Bungee cord for securing equipment in production vehicles
- Hand carts or dollies for transporting heavy equipment
- Tents for changing rooms or eating areas, as the weather dictates
- Layout board for the safety of the cast and crew and for the protection of the location floor

Keep a list of all rented expendables, or post the purchase orders for these rentals on a bulletin board in the office. Many of these items are small (and inexpensive) and could easily be lost or confused with other similar items owned by crew members. You will have to replace or purchase whatever items end up lost or damaged. Production expendables should be kept together if possible when they are collected at the end of each day, and it is safest to store them in one production vehicle. Designate a production assistant who will account for all expendables. He or she should keep a checklist of expendables and make sure that each item on the list is accounted for when wrapping each day.

Keys

The AD and the location manager should have a key to every location unless arrangements have explicitly been made for a manager or owner to let you in. The production office should have a key on file so that if your location manager will not be on the set at call or if your AD is stuck in traffic and running late someone else will have a key to the location. Keys are often lost, so it is best to have copies. When filming is complete, return all copies of keys to the location, or destroy them.

Maps

Maps of each location and travel directions should be drawn by the location manager and attached to the call sheet for each location. The page number in the street atlas on which the location appears should also be indicated on the map, and the name of the nearest hospital, its phone number, and the address should be noted.

Update Shooting Schedules

As discussed in Chapter 5, the shooting schedule is always subject to change. The availability of locations and cast members are variables that will affect the schedule. Try to lock your locations based on your preliminary shooting schedule, which was compiled based on multiple factors (easy transition between day and night filming, actor availability, location proximity, and out-of-town filming). You may find, however, that locations are not available when you need them. Change your schedule based on location availability only when the location in question is the location that will best serve the needs of the film. Keep in mind that changing the schedule to accommodate locations will have repercussions, so be sure that actors and other locations are all available based on the updated shooting schedule. (See the "Schedules and Lists Checklist" section.)

On *Swingers*, we updated the shooting and one-line schedules several times. We were unable to lock many of our locations for the time we had originally scheduled them and therefore had to revise the schedule based on location availability. For instance, we originally scheduled filming in the Dresden Room for two nights, but the Dresden Room was only able to accommodate us for one day, which did not correspond with the date we had tentatively scheduled. We knew it was important for the look of the film to shoot at the Dresden Room, so we figured out how to make it work based on the availability of other locations and actors. We wanted to do all of our out-of-town filming at the end of the shoot. We did not want to put our actors on hold or break up the flow of shooting at the Los Angeles locations. We also knew it would be fun for the crew to have a change of pace, spend our last few production days in Vegas, and wrap the show there.

Camera Checklist

The following are items to attend to in regard to cameras.

- Rent camera package (when the director of photography comes on, weeks 2 and 3).
- Schedule camera and film tests (week before production). If you are shooting on a DV format you should still plan for tests. If you plan to transfer to 35-mm film you may want to test the transfer. Consider engaging a transfer lab in the pre-production stage. They will be able to help you shoot your DV film so that it is "transfer ready."
- Arrange to have an insurance certificate sent to the camera house.
- Rent monitors, VCR, video tap, special equipment, and so on.
- Rent a camera bag or camera van.
- Compile a camera supply list; give the second assistant camera operator petty cash to purchase supplies; pick up cores, bags, cans, and camera reports (week 4).
- Schedule camera prep day for the first assistant camera operator (week before production).
- Purchase film stock (week 3).

Details of the Camera Checklist

Camera Package

The camera package you choose should suit the needs of your shoot. When renting, keep the budget, the DP's shooting style, and the types of locations in which you will be filming in mind. It makes the most sense to wait until your DP comes on board before you cut a deal on the camera package. Get a list of the equipment the DP would like included (with the caveat that the budget may not be able to sustain everything requested). Ask the DP if there is a camera house with which he or she has a relationship (that is, a rental house that will make you a deal if you mention the DP's name or the DP orders the package him- or herself). Secure multiple quotes before you make a final decision on a package.

Camera and Film Test

When you make the deal on your camera package, negotiate a day, about a week before production begins, to do some test shooting to ensure that the camera, lenses, and film stock are what is needed. As we stated earlier, you must perform camera and lighting tests if you are shooting in a digital formats. Do not imagine that shooting in digital means you can be sloppy or cavalier in your preparation. If you have a cinematographer who has shot primarily on film and is shooting for the first time in a digital format, you have to be even more careful than usual. Lighting concerns and camera settings are often very different for a digital production. Whether or not you plan to transfer to film is another concern to be carefully considered at the outset.

Insurance Certificate

Most likely, you will have to set up a vendor account with the camera house. This is also the appropriate time to arrange to have an insurance certificate, or "cert," sent to the rental house. Establish with the insurance company who will send the insurance certs to your vendors. If the insurance company will be sending off the certificates, compile a list of certs that need to be issued, and fax it to the insurance company toward the close of each workday.

Monitors and VCRs

You may want to rent a monitor and a VCR for screening dailies, or a video tap for viewing scenes as you are shooting. It is usually most efficient to rent as much of your equipment as you can from as few rental houses as possible. This reduces the number of pickups and returns, POs, and so on you will have to handle.

Camera Bag or Camera Van

Rent a camera bag or camera van, depending on the needs and budget of your shoot. A camera van is a convenience but is not essential. Remember that the camera department will require a changing bag and a sturdy table to work on, at the very least. On *Swingers*, we used a camera bag and a table, which was both cost and time efficient because our lightweight Aaton camera took only 400-foot loads, and the magazines had to be loaded frequently. Having the changing bag nearby helped us maintain our pace. Neither a camera bag nor camera van will be required if you are shooting in a digital format. Depending on how much equipment you have, you may still want a designated vehicle for camera equipment, but that vehicle need not have a darkroom in it. Typically, an SUV-size vehicle would hold all the necessary equipment for a DV shoot.

Camera Expendables

The second AC is usually responsible for purchasing expendables for the camera department. Sometimes, the production office will receive a detailed list of expendables from the camera department, and a production assistant will make the purchases.

The same is true for a production assistant picking up cans, cores, bags, and camera reports, all of which can be had, usually free of cost, from the laboratory that will be processing your film. Extra film cans are required for downloading film, short ends, recanning, and so on. Cores are what go in the center of the film roll and keep the film rolled properly, and bags are for storing the film as a precaution to keep the film from being exposed to light. Often, the lab will print information specific to your production on the camera reports. This should be arranged in advance. As a courtesy to the lab and to other productions, be sure to return the unused cans, bags, and cores to the lab, along with any unused, uncustomized camera reports, at the end of the shoot.

Camera Prep

The first AC will prep the camera package just before the shoot. This process can take up to eight hours. Ask the rental house what time your AC can start prepping the camera. Make sure that he or she has a vehicle large enough to transport the equipment when finished prepping and that he or she knows where the equipment should be stored to ensure its safety. If necessary, arrange for a production assistant to meet him or her with a production vehicle to transport the camera equipment when prepping is complete.

Film/Tape Stock

Refer to your budget to determine how many feet of stock have been budgeted for and whether it is 16-mm film, 35-mm film, or tape stock if you are shooting digitally. Ask the DP and the director which stocks will be required for the shoot. Call the company that manufactures the stock (Kodak, Fuji, and so on) and several film stock houses to compare prices. If you are a student or a member of the IFP or a local independent film organization, you may be entitled to a discount. Ask the vendor. Be careful to store the film in a cool, dry place.

Purchasing film stock is simple if you have the money to purchase factory-unopened stock. If you are purchasing recans or short ends, your task is less straightforward. As soon as the DP and the director have determined which stocks will be required for the shoot, call film stock houses that deal in recans. (In Los Angeles, try Dr. Rawstock and Steadi-Systems.) If you are shooting somewhere other than New York or Los Angeles, you will probably have to deal through these vendors. Plan to pay shipping. Let vendors know which film stocks you will need and how many feet you require. If they do not have the total footage you need for the shoot (and they probably will not), establishing a good working relationship with someone who works there is essential. On *Swingers*, we had to call several recan raw stock houses each day to find the film stock we needed.

Another possibility is to purchase recanned film stock directly from another production that is wrapping. If you know of any such productions, contact the production manager or line producer and find out if the production will sell its recanned stock to you at a reduced rate. If you are accumulating film stock in this piecemeal manner, it will be necessary, and somewhat more difficult, to track all of your footage. (Recans are usually not standard loads. For example, a recan may be a 380-foot load or a 750-foot load, as opposed to factory-unopened stock, which is sold in loads of 100, 400, and 1,000 feet.)

Regardless of whether the film you purchase is factory-unopened or recanned, keep a record of the raw stock purchased, the raw stock issued to the camera department, and the raw stock shot. (The latter will be calculated and recorded by the camera department on each day's camera report.) On *Swingers*, our raw stock purchase continued from the first week of pre-production through the final week of production. It was a constant quest for Kodak 5298 stock, most of which we managed to purchase at incredibly low prices from various vendors in Los Angeles. We also shot Kodak 5248 for exterior daytime shots, which was somewhat less expensive. If you have any questions about a particular film stock, ask the manufacturer.

Tape Stock

If you are shooting in a DV format, you will be purchasing tape rather than film stock. Generally, tape stock is much less expensive than film. Often, purchasing your tape stock in bulk will bring the overall cost down. Try to negotiate a deal on your stock.

Grip and Lighting Checklist

During the second or third week of pre-production, discuss the film's grip and lighting needs with the director, DP, the key grip, and the gaffer.

- Rent a grip and electric package and a truck, or hire department keys with their own equipment and trucks.
- Rent a dolly and a crane, and hire operators as needed.
- Purchase grip and electric expendables.
- Schedule a scout for each location for the director, the key grip, and the gaffer.
- Discuss with the gaffer which generator to rent and at which locations you may be able to tie in.
- Arrange to have insurance certificates sent to the rental houses.
- Schedule prelight/prerig days for locations during production.
- Discuss special equipment needs.

Details of the Grip and Lighting Checklist

Grip and Electric Package

Ideally, hire a key grip or a gaffer who owns his or her own equipment and has a truck you can rent for the production. If not, you will have to rent the equipment and vehicle from a rental house. After a discussion with the director, the gaffer, and the key grip and a scout of the locations that have been locked, secure the lighting and grip equipment lists from the respective department heads. Make sure both department heads know that you may not be able to secure everything on their lists. Even if you are renting the bulk of your equipment from a crew member, you may still need to rent some items from a rental house. Considerations to bear in mind when deciding on a rental house or vendor are cost, quality, if they have the bulk of your needs, and accessibility from your location or production headquarters.

Dolly and Crane

Among the items you may need to rent are a dolly (do not forget the track) and a crane. You will want to have a dolly grip for those days when you are using the dolly. This can be someone who is already on the crew if he or she can be spared. Cranes often come with an operator. If not, make sure someone in the department is familiar enough with the equipment that he or she can operate the crane efficiently and safely. If a crane operator must be hired, ask your department head for recommendations, and inquire with the rental house. Send an insurance certificate to all vendors.

On *Swingers*, we used a wheelchair as a dolly for most of the shots that required one because that was the least expensive option that still enabled us to secure the shots we wanted. This "doorway dolly" served us well because our locations were small and dolly track would have taken up too much space. We rented a dolly for one day, for the shot at the diner in which the boys are sitting at a large round table and a dolly with circular track was required to shoot the scene. Another less expensive option is a golf cart. Wheelchairs and golf carts both work great, depending on what shots you need.

Expendables

As with the camera department, lighting and grip expendables can be purchased either by the production or by the lighting and grip departments themselves. Sometimes, department members include expendables as part of their kit; the production pays for the expendables either as part of the kit rental or through an invoice the crew member submits. Otherwise, you will need to secure a detailed list of supplies from the key grip and gaffer or make sure the departments have ample petty cash to cover their needs. If the departments are responsible for purchasing these items, make sure they know their total budget for expendables and that they submit their receipts to the production office.

Location Scout

The scout is of extreme importance to ensure the feasibility of a location in terms of grip and electric concerns, and to determine which equipment will be essential. If your locations are not locked by week 3, you will need to consider which locations are available to scout. Have your grip and electric departments scout locations as they are locked, but do not ask them to inspect one location a day if they are not yet on the payroll. Instead, have them scout several locations at a time unless you are in a bind and need their input immediately to determine which location to secure.

Generator and Tie-ins

As discussed earlier, scouting will reveal which locations will require a generator, where you may tie in, and for which locations existing power is ample.

Prelight/Prerig Days

Depending on the lighting needs of the show and the rental arrangements for a given location, if possible have your lighting and/or grip departments prelight/prerig a location before filming there. This day of setup allows the shoot day at a given location to get off to a quicker start. At some locations, prelighting/prerigging will be mandatory to ensure you do not waste everyone else's time on the production day. Try to assess on the scout which, if any, of the locations will require a prelight/prerig day. Make sure both the location and the crew are available for prelight/prerig days. You may need to bring on extra crew members (day players; see the "Schedules and Lists Checklist" section) for these days so that you maintain the necessary crew on the set and avoid overtime.

Sound Checklist

The following are items to attend to in regard to sound.

- Secure the sound package; arrange to have insurance certificates sent to the sound house or the sound mixer if you are renting equipment directly from your sound mixer (week 4).
- Purchase or rent sound supplies and expendables: slate, walkie-talkies, microphones, batteries, cable, tapes, magnetic stock, and so on.
- Arrange for playback if needed.
- Arrange for bands, musicians, and live music if needed.
- Gather sound reports and sound tape.

Details of the Sound Checklist

Sound Package

Once the sound mixer has been hired, identify the film's sound package needs. Based on your locations (that is, large interior space or exterior highway), the setup of each scene, and the number of characters in each scene, your sound mixer will determine with the director the types of microphones and other equipment that will be needed. Because sound equipment can be costly, rent only the equipment that is essential, and keep the equipment only for the days you need it. You can always rent a piece of equipment again later if it turns out you need it. Whether you rent your sound package from the sound mixer or a sound house, an insurance certificate must be provided.

If possible, hire a sound mixer who can provide his or her own equipment. On *Swingers*, our sound mixer had his own equipment and a van to transport it. We made a flat deal with him for both. His kit included all of the necessary mics, booms, cable, batteries, a slate, and a mixing board.

Sound Supplies and Expendables

The sound department will need a variety of supplies, such as DAT tapes, batteries, extra booms, magnetic stock for each day, and markers. Provide the sound mixer with blank sound reports. A copy of each sound report is submitted to the lab attached to the corresponding sound roll. Find out if the sound mixer has a relationship with a sound house that will make you a deal on supplies or equipment.

Playback

If you are filming a scene that requires sound or music playback, discuss the required equipment with the sound mixer and the director. Playback is the recording of a song that will be used in the final mix on DAT tape, with time code, a stereo, and speakers, on which to literally play the song back on the spot and a smart slate so that you can synchronize the recording. On *Swingers*, we needed to film a band live while shooting in a location that was open to the public, so we arranged for playback on the set, and later synchronized the band's lyrics of the recording to the picture.

Sound Reports and Sound Tape

At the end of each filming day, collect the sound rolls and their corresponding sound reports, and send them to the lab with the film and the camera reports. The lab will match the sound to the footage based on the information recorded on the sound reports. One copy of the sound report should stay with the sound mixer, one copy should be given to the editor the following day along with the script supervisor's notes and camera reports, and copies should be filed in the production notebooks.

Travel and Transportation Checklist

Arrange for the following as needed in accordance with your budget, cast, crew, locations, and equipment.

- Call the film commission in the city or state in which you are filming.
- Arrange travel to distant locations.
- Prepare per diems for nonlocal cast and crew.
- Rent motor homes, dressing rooms, and honey wagons as needed.
- Rent production vehicles as needed.
- Have extra keys made for truck locks and for each production vehicle.
- Arrange for drivers of production vehicles (weeks 3 and 4); file copies of the drivers' licenses.
- Have mileage sheets and petty cash on hand.

Details of the Travel and Transportation Checklist

Film Commission

The first thing you should do if you are filming on location is contact the local film commission. (See "Permits" in the "Locations Checklist" section.) Determine the local guidelines, rules, permit requirements, and so on. Ask for a listing of local crew members, and establish a contact person at the film commission who can help you with your needs. If you will be on location for an extended period, a local bank account will facilitate many tasks, including renting equipment and securing locations.

Travel Arrangements

Start organizing travel arrangements early on if you will be filming out of town. Making reservations well in advance may save you money. Make flight reservations for the cast and crew, or rent passenger vans or cars. You may be able to make a package deal with an airline if a significant number of people will be traveling. Whenever possible, transport actors to distant locations via airplane rather than by car, in that it is a far more comfortable and faster means by which to travel, and the actors' needs can be catered to.

If you will be on location for several nights, make hotel or motel arrangements for the cast and crew. Determine lodging costs as early as you can to secure the best rate and to ensure availability.

Accommodate your cast and crew according to the travel and lodging terms negotiated in their contracts. For instance, if a cast member was guaranteed a first-class flight and a suite in a hotel, you must honor those terms. On low-budget shows, try to establish a favored-nations policy that prohibits any elaborate arrangements for any one cast or crew member. If special arrangements have not been guaranteed, ask crew members to share rooms. If you have hired nonlocal cast or crew members, the production will need to accommodate their travel to the city in which you will be filming, and you may need to rent a vehicle for their use while working on the show. (You must also pay per diems for nonlocal cast and crew members.)

On *Swingers*, we traveled to Las Vegas for three days and three nights to film the casino scenes. We rented a passenger van for 14 members of the crew. Two crew members transported equipment and film stock in their own cars, which also provided us with smaller vehicles for getting around Las Vegas. Traveling by passenger van saved us gas, valet, and gratuity costs. We booked flights for the four cast members who were needed in Las Vegas and picked them up at the airport. Hotel rooms were provided for each cast member at a reasonable rate, and the crew (including the director and producers) shared ten hotel rooms (two crew members to a room). We did not screen dailies while in Las Vegas, so it was not necessary to ship the film and sound tape back to Los Angeles for transfer. We brought ample raw stock with us so that we were able to get the coverage we needed while we had the casino, because we knew we could not afford to go back for reshoots. Arrangements were made to store both the footage and the camera equipment in a cool, secure place within the hotel.

On *Kissing Jessica Stein*, the scenes at Jessica's parents' home in Westchester were shot on location in Connecticut, in the hometown of one of the writers and co-stars. Because we had a great deal of support locally, we were able to arrange housing in homes of friends and family. We scouted in Guilford two or three times and made all of our arrangements in advance of the trip. The house that served as the location for Jessica's parents' home was donated to us, and therefore we had to shoot when it was convenient for them. It turned out that they would be out of the country in the beginning of our shoot, so Connecticut was the first location of our shoot. Ideally, we would normally not have had travel involved in the first week, when crew was getting to know one another and nerves were high. However, we did it because we had no choice. Needless to say, it worked out fine.

Per Diems

If the production will be filming at a distant location, it will be necessary to pay per diems to the nonlocal cast and crew. (Try to hire local crew members if you will be filming at a distant location for some time.) Check with SAG for the current minimum per diem rate paid to cast members while on location. At the time this book went to press, the SAG per diem rates were $12 for breakfast, $18 for lunch, and $30 for dinner, totaling $60. The government per diem rate on location for crew is $32.50 (breakfast $6.50; lunch $9; dinner $17).

On *Swingers*, we paid per diems to the four cast members according to SAG rates. The crew received what the budget could sustain, which was $25 per day to cover miscellaneous expenses such as meals, tips, and so on. The per diem is not meant to cover personal expenses such as snacks or phone calls. If the crew is working for low money, the production company should consider picking up the hotel room charges in the interest of good working relations. We treated the crew to dinner with production funds on two nights in addition to the on-set meals provided during filming.

Motor Homes and Dressing Rooms/Honey Wagons

Based on your locations, budget, and cast contracts, you may need to rent motor homes or star trailers for the course of the show or for particular locations. If you will be at a given location for some time, production may need a designated workspace. If there is no space within the location itself and it is neither cost nor time efficient for crew members to drive back and forth between the office and the set with paperwork, film stock, messages, supplies, and so on, rent a motor home if it can easily be parked nearby. Motor homes usually come with a driver, an office setup, a makeup station, a wardrobe area, and a bathroom. They can be costly, but it may be worthwhile to rent one for a few of your locations for convenience sake.

Dressing rooms are often provided to cast members either because their contracts stipulate so or because suitable changing rooms are not available at the location. Renting tents is a cost-effective way to provide dressing rooms for your cast, a makeup station, and so on, if there is enough space at the location to set them up. On low-budget shows, the cast is typically hired on a favored-nations basis, and motor homes, star trailers, or honey wagons are provided only if required for the show to run smoothly.

On *Swingers*, we did not budget for any motor homes or star trailers. The cast and crew were hired on a favored-nations basis, and the budget could not sustain such accommodations. When we scouted our locations, we determined where the cast would change and where makeup would be applied. The production office was located at our house, so there was ample room for wardrobe and makeup to be done at the office if space was not available on location. Most of our locations were within 20 minutes of the production office, and it was convenient for both cast and crew to drive between the set and the office. When necessary, the cast dressed at the production office and then drove to the location, where the wardrobe and makeup departments were able to set up small workstations for any needs the cast had during filming. Production was able to deliver paperwork, call sheets, supplies, and so on several times each day between the set and the office.

Department Vehicles

Refer to your budget to determine which departments will need production trucks or cube vans. Often, the grip and electric department heads have their own trucks, or you can rent your grip and electric equipment by truck size (that is, a 5- or 10-ton truck that comes loaded with grip and electric equipment). If possible, combine the materials rented by your set design department, prop department, and art department onto one production truck. (Be sure that pickups and drop-offs are coordinated carefully among the departments sharing a production vehicle.) See if the head of the wardrobe department can use his or her own vehicle or can fit the wardrobe racks on the production truck. The production vehicle will be used to store craft service and catering items, production expendables, and, if need be, sound equipment and makeup and hair expendables. The sound mixer should be able to fit the sound equipment in his or her own vehicle or in the production truck. On *Swingers*, the art director and the sound mixer had their own trucks or vans, which were used to pick up and transport most of their materials and equipment. Any expendables they needed were picked up and returned by production.

When a vehicle must be rented will depend on which department will use it. Place the maximum number of vehicles you anticipate needing on hold during the first or second week of pre-production. The prop and art departments may need their vehicle a few weeks before production, depending on the quantity of equipment and materials that need to be picked up. These departments may need to build, assemble, and transport items. Determine if one production truck can suffice early on for pickups for multiple departments. This will save you money.

Purchase key or combination locks for the back of each production truck so that the equipment and materials left on your trucks are safe. Arrange for secured overnight parking for your production vehicles.Keep in mind when renting production trucks, vans, or cars that the rental company may give you a certain number of miles at no extra charge. If you exceed the given number of miles, you will be charged per mile at a prenegotiated rate. Negotiate in advance how many miles will be included at no charge and what the rate per mile thereafter will be. (Try to get unlimited free miles in exchange for a screen credit.) The rental house you rent your production vehicles from will record the current mileage on the truck or van before you drive it off the lot. Get a copy of the paperwork on which the mileage is recorded for each vehicle, and also be sure that any damage previously done to the vehicle has been noted.

On *Swingers*, we rented one production truck a week and a half before production for small prop and art pickups, production expendables, and wardrobe. We stored materials and equipment either on the truck, which was locked and safely parked each night, or in the production office, where there was always a crew member around to ensure the safety of the equipment. We did not have a camera truck, so the camera equipment was taken to the set with wardrobe, production expendables, craft service, and catering items on the production truck. We always loaded all camera equipment onto the truck last so that it could easily be taken off each night and stored in the production office.

Locks

You must make copies of keys to any locks used on production trucks and cube vans! Keys are often lost or damaged, and it will cost you money and time to have locks broken or new keys made. If a driver misplaces the key to the truck's lock, having copies on hand will ensure that the equipment can be readily accessed. Copies of keys should be left in the office in a file, and a duplicate set of all keys should be put in the AD kit.

Drivers

Determine how many drivers you will need for production vehicles and who they will be. On *Swingers*, we had department heads drive their department's vehicles, and a PA drove the production truck. Make sure that anyone who is asked to drive a production vehicle is comfortable with driving a truck and that he or she is able to do pickups; many trucks, depending on their size, require special driver's licenses. If not, you may need to hire extra crew members to drive vehicles and do pickups. If you are a union show, you will need to hire Teamsters to drive your vehicles and to handle all pickups and returns. Copies of drivers' licenses should be filed in the office and in the AD kit.

Mileage Sheets

If you will be paying mileage to crew members who use their personal vehicles for pickups, returns, or other errands, have mileage sheets available. (See the "Office Setup Checklist" section.) It is also best to issue petty cash to those persons who will be running errands in case a last-minute purchase is needed or gas costs need to be covered.

On *Swingers*, Jon Favreau owned the Comet Caliente that served as Trent's car. We paid for some minor repairs on the car to be sure it was in proper working order for filming.

If you need some of your vehicles for only a few days and they are fairly common and readily available cars, try to borrow them from a friend or secure a flat-rate deal on them from a neighbor or local auto shop. Picture vehicle rental houses can help you locate the vehicle you need, but they can be costly. Do not forget that insurance certs will be needed when you borrow or rent picture vehicles.

Craft and Catering Checklist

The following are items to attend to in regard to craft and catering.

- Hire a craft service person and have him or her prepare food and expendables lists (week 3).
- Have craft service approach local cafes and restaurants regarding donations.
- Identify the eating areas at each location.

- Secure a caterer (a catering company, restaurants, and so on); sort out the menu so that there is a variety.
- Compile a list of local restaurants near each location that might be able to provide second meals or extra food on larger set days.
- Have petty cash available daily for second meals or extra meal needs.
- Arrange for special meal needs if necessary.
- Arrange for catering and craft service at distant locations.

Details of the Craft and Catering Checklist

Catering refers to the actual on-set meals, as opposed to craft service, which refers to the snacking and beverage station available throughout the shoot day. How you provide meals and snacks to the cast and crew will depend on your budget.

Craft Service

Make sure your craft service person is committed and understands the importance of providing healthy snacks and sustenance for the cast and crew who will be working long hours. Have the craft service person prepare both a grocery list and an expendables list. Review the grocery and supply list, and make sure there are plenty of affordable options. As for rentals, craft service will need a table and chairs, at the very least, and may require coolers, thermoses, urns, a hot plate or microwave, a toaster oven, a cutting board, a first aid kit, and extension cords. If the craft service person has a lot of these items, rent them from him or her as a kit rental. If not, add them to your production expendables list.

Soliciting Donations

It is almost always possible to get some food donated to your production. Have the craft service person, the production coordinator, or an intern speak to local cafes, restaurants, coffee shops, and so on. Manufacturers are sometimes interested in making a donation in exchange for product placement. On *Swingers*, we solicited donations of soft drinks, bottled water, coffee beans, cigars, and some second meals. On another film, we managed to get all of our coffee, daily bagels, and day-old pastries from a local bakery. If you are on a tight budget, these donations will help you keep costs down. On *Kissing Jessica Stein* we had Krispy Kreme donuts cleared for product placement and they donated 12 dozen donuts a day to our craft service. Very dangerous and unhealthy!

Identify the Eating Areas

The craft service person can help determine where food will be set up at each location and can assist, if necessary, with serving the catered meals. He or she should arrange to have adequate craft service each day, based on the number of cast and crew bodies on the shooting schedule. That is, you will need more food for days when many extras are scheduled or visitors are expected.

Catering

The meals you feed people on a low-budget show can range from professionally catered meals to home-cooked meals. In addition to keeping your cast and crew energized, healthy, and ready to work, feeding them on the set keeps everyone together in one place and ensures that the workday proceeds without delays. Figure out how much money you can spend per person per meal. Call caterers and see if you can come to an arrangement that works for both of you. For example, tell them you have $10 per person and must feed 30 people for 15 days; what type of menu can they provide for that amount of money?

On *Swingers*, we had $5 per person per meal. In exchange for $5 per head and a production credit, we found six restaurants who were willing to provide meals. Some of the restaurants agreed to deliver the food to the set; others required that we pick it up. We signed contracts with each establishment that stipulated the terms of the agreement. The paperwork was turned over to the craft service person, who orchestrated pickup or delivery of the food and payment.

Restaurant List and Petty Cash

You will want to have a list of affordable and convenient restaurants handy when filming at each of your locations. Often a filming day will go into overtime and a second meal will need to be provided, or there will be visitors or extras on the set for whom you may want to make other meal arrangements. For extras, it is often cheaper to provide what is called a "box lunch" from local inexpensive restaurants than to have such meals catered. Your AD, if possible, should alert the craft service person and the production office about three hours in advance of needing a second or extra meals if overtime is anticipated on a particular day. Make sure that craft service has enough petty cash to purchase second or extra meals and has an accurate count of how many meals will need to be provided.

Special Meal Needs

There may be days when certain actors are working who may be on a special diet or make a particular request for a meal. Certain crew members may also need to abide by a particular diet. When you arrange set meals with your caterer, try to provide choices that will hopefully accommodate everyone's needs. For instance, both hot and cold foods should be available, as well as protein-rich foods (chicken, fish, meats, or tofu, as some of your cast and crew members may be vegetarians). Arrange for any special meal requirements with your caterer and craft service person in advance. Accommodate any special meals needed within reason, keeping in mind that it is best to be fair to everyone and to avoid setting lavish standards.

Distant Location Craft Service and Catering

Prior to filming at any distant location, arrange for your set craft service needs and catered meals. Call the locations at which you will be filming or the local film commission and ask for recommendations for craft service companies or persons and caterers if you will be filming at a distant location for some time. If you will be filming at a distant location only for a few days, it may be cheaper to take the crew to lunch at a local restaurant determined in advance, or to have preordered meals picked up by your craft service person or a production assistant or delivered by the restaurant. You may want to hire a local craft service so that they are able to have a day to prepare items and rent expendables before production arrives. Investigate your options carefully to determine what is most convenient, affordable, and best for your cast and crew.

Still Photography Checklist

The following are items to attend to in regard to still photography.

- Hire a still photographer; secure film and processing deals, and issue petty cash if necessary.
- Select specific filming days for the still photographer to shoot.

Details of the Still Photography Checklist

Lack of decent action production stills is an oversight of many independent productions. These photos are indispensable in press kits, fliers, posters, festival programs, industry magazines, and more. Do not forget that production stills are shots of the action occurring in front of the camera, not you and a grip standing at the craft service table. Some behind-the-scenes photos can be useful for recording the making of your movie but are not mandatory the way production stills are.

Still Photographer

Once your schedule is set, secure a still photographer. Take a look at the photographer's portfolio and get references to make sure you will not end up with poor-quality pictures that will prove useless. Most professional photographers process their work and purchase their supplies through a particular lab and supply house, usually at a reduced rate. If your still photographer is amenable, have him or her purchase expendables and arrange for processing. Reimburse any of his or her purchases or dole out petty cash and have receipts returned. Otherwise, call around to various labs and get quotes. Have the photographer shoot both black-and-white and color slide film.

Key Shoot Days

If your funds are limited, select several key production days for the photographer to shoot on set. Select these days according to which scenes and which actors will make the most useful publicity shots. Discuss this briefly with the director and possibly with the cinematographer. If you have any name actors in your film, have the photographer present when those actors are working.

AD Kit Checklist

The AD kit should include the following items:

- Call sheets
- Production reports
- Exhibit G forms
- Taft-Hartley forms
- Meal allowance sheets
- Location permits
- Location insurance certificates and blanks
- Location contracts and blanks
- Security guard and parking lot information
- Extras vouchers
- Copies of signed cast contracts
- Blank SAG contracts (weekly and daily)
- Cast, crew, and vendor packs
- Cell phone numbers
- Maps
- Extra keys to locations and vehicles
- Walkie-talkie sign-out sheets
- Still releases, personal releases, filming notices, extended hours releases, and neighbor releases
- Schedules, day-out-of-days sheets, and strip board
- W-4 forms, Start/I-9 forms, and time cards
- Check request forms
- Petty cash envelopes
- Purchase orders
- Petty cash
- Accident reports
- SAG rule book
- Current shooting copy of the script

Details of the AD Kit Checklist

The AD kit is a portable file box the AD brings to the set each day. In it, forms, schedules, contracts, reports, lists, and other paperwork are kept. It is important that the AD have the necessary paperwork on the set at all times. Production assistants and office staff should not have to drive back and forth between the set and the office to deliver and retrieve paperwork all day long. In addition, SAG, the film commission, permit officers, firefighters, and police officers may come to your set and ask to see your paperwork, permits, and so on.

The set is the AD's office during production, and the AD kit functions as a mini filing cabinet with paperwork the AD may need to refer to, fill out, or provide while on the set. The following are examples:

- The AD may need to refer to a cast member's contract when filling out Exhibit G forms, call sheets, or the production report. Copies of cast contracts, blank Exhibit G forms, and call sheets should be kept in the AD kit.
- If yours is a SAG show, Taft-Hartley forms must also be on the set so that any nonunion actors can fill them out when they begin work.
- The AD or second AD will need to refer to a copy of the shooting schedule when filling out the next day's call sheet.
- The AD or second AD must have cast members fill out W-4 forms and Start forms on the first day they report to work. Any extra crew members who are hired must also fill out these forms.
- If yours is a SAG show, the AD should have a copy of the SAG handbook on the set so that he or she can refer to SAG's rules and guidelines.
- Copies of filming notices and releases should be kept in the AD kit so that the AD can post them as necessary.
- Crew members may have to fill out petty cash envelopes. Having them on the set in the AD box saves crew members time.
- Vendor lists should be on hand so that crew members can quickly locate the phone numbers of equipment houses and vendors in case additional equipment is needed during filming. Equipment may be broken or damaged and have to be replaced immediately.
- Cast and crew lists are important in case someone must be contacted.
- A shooting copy of the script is handy in case the AD has to refer to a scene.
- Additional equipment, materials, or expendables are often needed during filming, and having POs on the set makes it easy to account for items and rent them immediately.
- The AD may have to issue certificates of insurance for any last-minute equipment ordered.
- It is essential that the AD have immediate access to extra keys to locations and vehicles in case keys are lost or damaged.
- POs, insurance certificates, Start forms, Exhibit G forms, releases, Taft-Hartley forms, or other paperwork that is filled out on the set by the AD department should be turned in to the office each day for copying, filing, and distribution.

Send to Set Checklist

The following items should be prepared during the last week of pre-production and sent to the set on the first day of production:

- Extra office supplies
- First aid kit
- Flashlights
- Extra instant film and camera
- Street atlas or local maps and guides
- Three-ring binder
- Local film guide (such as LA 411 or NYPG)
- Batteries
- Extension cords
- Rope

Details of the Send to Set Checklist

The set should function like a mini office. Crew members will be spending most of their time on the set while in production, and supplies, books, forms, and other items should be on hand. (See also the "Office Setup Checklist" section.)

Post-production Checklist

The following tasks must be taken care of during the third and fourth weeks of pre-production.

- Interview post-production supervisors.
- Arrange for an editing facility and equipment; discuss needs with the editor (week 2 or 3).
- Arrange for lab needs: dailies, transfers, developing, and processing (week 2 or 3).
- Purchase videotape for transfers, mag stock, and so on.
- Purchase stock footage if necessary.
- Purchase supplies for the editing facility.
- Compile a calendar or timeline of screenings, picture lock dates, mix dates, ADR recording, titles, music meetings, festival deadlines, and so on.

Details of the Post-production Checklist

Editing Facility

Arrange during pre-production to rent editing space and equipment so that they are available when the editor comes on board, most likely during the first or second week of production. Call several facilities for quotes and a list of their equipment. Determine the medium on which the film will be cut (Avid, flatbed, or D-Vision), and discuss equipment needs with the editor. Find out if the editor prefers to work at a particular facility.

Try to make a combined flat deal on equipment and the editing suite if possible. Editing equipment and suites are usually priced on a weekly basis, and additional equipment is often priced separately. Find a facility that is conveniently located to the production office or the lab where the film will be processed for easy delivery and pickup. Ask for a few parking spaces if they are designated, and try to include that cost in the overall cost of the facility.

On *Swingers*, we were able to strike a deal at our editing facility. We made a flat deal paid in two installments: one upon striking the deal during pre-production and the second toward the end of our rental period. This was in lieu of a weekly rate. The deal included the Avid system, hard drives, a VCR, a television, two parking spaces, and any additional equipment or accessories needed during the editing process that the facility could provide. The only additional expenses were for phone calls, food, and supplies for the editor and assistant editor. We anticipated needing the edit system and suite for 12 weeks, and we cut our deal accordingly. Ultimately, though, we needed an additional 8 weeks of editing time, and we were given a reduced rate for the subsequent rental.

On *Kissing Jessica Stein* we made an all-in deal with an editing facility that was in the business of editing high-end commercials but wanted to break into film. This worked out in terms of our budget, but the drawback was that we were limited to their pool of editors and we felt confined to the number of weeks they felt they could afford to have us editing virtually for free in their high-end facility. This ultimately did not serve our editing process and we ended up raising more money to open an edit suite of our own and hiring another editor.

Determine the number of editing weeks you will need carefully. If you need additional weeks, you may find that the facility has committed your room to another production and you are unable to continue using the space or the equipment.

Lab

Arrange and determine your lab needs in week 2 or 3 of pre-production. Your footage will need to be developed and processed for it to be viewed and assembled. Determine if you will have dailies made for each day of filming and when transfers of footage videotape (1/2-inch and a Betacam) will need to be made. Lab costs are expensive; secure quotes from several facilities before deciding on one. Finding the best price will take time. Ideally, your film will be developed and processed after the first day or two of shooting. Your director, DP, or editor may have a relationship at a particular lab with which a deal could be negotiated. Make sure to establish a contact person at the lab who will be responsible for your dailies and paperwork, and for scheduling all of your film's needs. You will want to discuss your film's needs with your editor and the director to properly communicate them to the lab. In some instances you may want the editor to speak directly with the lab.

Videotape

If you will be transferring your footage to video, it is cheaper to purchase 1/2-inch or Betacam tapes from a videotape supply house than to have the lab provide them to you at their cost. You will also need 1/2-inch or 3/4-inch tapes during the editing process if you will be using an Avid editor to output transfers of rough cuts to the music crew, festival committees, dialogue and sound editors, producers, director, and others. Purchasing videotapes by the case is usually cheapest, and if any are unused you can sell them back to the store where you purchased them (usually at a reduced rate).

Stock Footage

On low-budget independent films, there are often scenes that are expensive to shoot but important to the look and feel of the film. For instance, if a movie requires a car chase, a car accident, a building being blown up, or a fire, it may be most cost effective in such instances to purchase stock footage (footage that has already been shot). There are stock-footage houses at which you can purchase such footage. Call around for the best quotes.

Supplies

Have either a production assistant or the assistant editor purchase supplies so that the editing room is equipped when the editors begin work. Pens, markers, tape, notebooks, paper, disks, videotapes, DATs, and so on will be needed. The editing staff will also need petty cash (dispensed weekly) for food purchases.

Calendar

It is important to compile a calendar of deadlines and dates so that you can properly determine and schedule your post-production needs (or if you have a post-production supervisor, he or she will know how to schedule the film's needs). Determining the schedule of events during post-production will keep you on track and on budget. The producer(s), director, and editor should determine when the editor's version of the film will need to be locked, when the director's cut will need to be locked, and when the ADR, foley, and mix should be scheduled. Determine when trial prints or answer prints will ideally be struck. The timing of these elements is often determined (and may need to change during post-production) based on festival deadlines and the amount of money budgeted for post-production.

Miscellaneous Needs Checklist

Depending on your script, you may have to secure and organize the following:

- Licensed weaponry person/weapons
- Welfare worker/children's tutor
- Animals and an animal trainer/wrangler (see discussion in "Budget" section)
- Stunts and a stunt coordinator
- Special effects, computer-generated images (CGI)
- Electronic press kit (usually referred to as an EPK)

Details of the Miscellaneous Needs Checklist

Weapons

If your script calls for guns, swords, knives, or other types of weapons, you may need to have a licensed weaponry person on the set, depending on how the scene will be shot and if you will be using real weapons. You may be able to hire a prop master who has a weapons license, which will save you money. It may be a wise idea to contact stunt coordinators for some advice as to how to best deal with any weapons called for in your script.

Welfare Worker

If you will be employing minors, you must first contact the Child Labor Laws division of the State Labor Commissioner's office to be sure that you comply with the laws governing the employment of minors. A welfare worker and/or teacher will be required, depending on the time of year (if school is in session) to ensure the safety and treatment of minors.

Stunts

Hopefully, on a low-budget show you will have few, if any, elaborate stunts that will require the cost of a stunt coordinator, but it is best to hire one for safety purposes if you do. You may have a gun scene, a fight, or someone jumping out of a window. This may require a stunt person who is familiar with how to fall out of a window, throw a punch, or take one, and what type of materials will be needed for certain stunts, such as break-away glass or body pads. If you are a SAG show, you will need to pay your stunt coordinator SAG rates, so be sure to properly budget this expense.

Special Effects

Arrange early on for any special effects that may be required in your film. Depending on the effect, it may be done in post-production by computer-generated images (CGI). An on-set special effect may be fireworks, a fuse box explosion, or spark, smoke, or rain. Call around to special effects houses to help determine your needs and costs. Discuss your special effects needs with your production and art departments, DP, gaffer, director, and prop master. They may be helpful in figuring out the most cost-efficient and safest way to perform an effect, or they may know someone who can be helpful. Special effects can be costly, so be sure that they are imperative to the film and that you approach them creatively in order to keep costs down.

Electronic Press Kit

An EPK is video footage of the "behind the scenes" making of your film. Typically it includes interviews with key cast and crew as well as more vérité-style footage of the making of the movie. If your dream comes true and you secure a distribution deal for your film, you will be pleased that you had the foresight to make an EPK. If you have the budget for it, you can hire an outfit that specializes in making EPKs. If money is tight, perhaps you can find a film school student or someone starting out, but who has some experience with shooting and sound on DV. These tapes need not be edited right away. It is the type of material a distributor may be very happy to utilize and edit for the marketing campaign of your film. You may want to secure releases from any interviewees you do not already have them from (usually anyone other than cast).

THE LAST WEEK OF PRE-PRODUCTION

The final week of pre-production is extremely important. Equipment, vehicles, materials, and so on will be picked up; all crew members will come on board; last-minute arrangements, deals, and adjustments will be made. Stop!

Go back to the pre-production checklists and review every item on every list to see what must still be done. Make sure that nothing has been overlooked. Double check all arrangements, contracts, paperwork, and deals. Make calls to cast, crew, caterers, locations, permit offices, rental houses, and so on to confirm arrangements. Are all of your locations (or at least the locations needed for the first two weeks of production) locked and secured by contract, and have all permits been obtained? Is everyone on schedule? Check the weather forecast for the first week of filming. Should you adjust the schedule based on weather or other production concerns? You do not want to begin principal photography on the wrong foot. Reviewing the checklist and confirming deals and arrangements will ensure that you account for everything.

Review your contracts and paperwork to be sure that everything has been sent to the appropriate organizations and individuals, and that copies have been filed in the production office and included in the AD kit. Double check that all of your vendors and locations have received certificates of insurance. Prepare the AD kit and send it to the set or with the AD so that it is ready for the first day of filming. Actualize the budget for those costs you are certain about to ensure that you have ample funds for filming and post-production (and some padding for unanticipated costs that arise). Contact cast members working on the first day of principal photography with their call times, or verify that the AD or second AD has taken care of this.

The all-crew check-in meeting, which should already be scheduled, will take place during the last week of pre-production. Make sure you have found a space large enough to accommodate the entire crew. The meeting will allow you to determine what is left to do; to troubleshoot any problems a crew member or department is having; to determine whether the shooting schedule must be changed because a location has not been locked, the art department is not ready, or equipment has not been secured; and to ensure that everyone is prepared and on schedule.

Go through the pre-production checklists during the meeting to verify that each department has taken care of its responsibilities. Hand out the most current shooting schedule, and review each location and scene with the crew. The crew should be familiar with the shooting schedule and the order in which scenes will be shot. Address any questions or concerns. Discuss the events planned for the first day of filming and distribute and review the first day's call sheet. Make sure everyone has a ride to the set and knows how to get there. Thank the crew for their continuing hard work and dedication.

8 PRODUCTION

"Production—it's like going to war. You're dealing with a group of people that's like the size of a platoon. Everybody knows what they have to do. You get in, you get out, you make home wherever it is. You have to deal with what the situation throws you, and it's very stressful, and you can't sleep at night. And the more involved you are with the outcome of it, the more twisted up you are inside."

—*Jon Favreau, on* Swingers

During production, the line producer monitors both the set and the office, staying on top of all details and operations. It is the line producer's responsibility to ensure constant communication between the office and the set; that is, he or she instructs the office about the set's needs, and vice versa. This is vital to a smooth show.

If you have done your job thoroughly during pre-production, the actual shooting period should be a bit calmer for you. Your job will be to ensure that every item on every checklist is taken care of and to troubleshoot as necessary. Refer daily to the production checklists in this chapter (see also the companion CD-ROM).

TROUBLESHOOTING

Inevitably, something will go wrong during production, regardless of how well you did your job during pre-production. Lenses get dropped, people get hurt, things happen that are beyond your control. Perhaps you need a piece of equipment that was overlooked, or maybe something has been damaged and the entire shoot is waiting for a replacement, or perhaps a location has fallen through at the last minute.

If something unexpected comes up, remain calm. Have the coordinator or unit production manager (UPM) begin to make phone calls immediately to price out your needs while you determine how best to deal with the circumstances. Refer to your budget to determine from which line item you can draw money. Perhaps you spent too much in certain departments but saved money in other areas that will allow you to pay for unexpected expenses. Do not forget to keep the cast and crew apprised of your progress in resolving any problems or delays. Gather as much information as you can, and consider all options before making a decision. It is important for the show to remain on schedule, but making hasty or rash decisions will be more time consuming and expensive in the long run.

MONITORING THE SET

During production you will likely work on set while remaining in communication with the office. You must be available in the event that questions, problems, or concerns arise or decisions must be made, and you will have to oversee the set to ensure that the production is on schedule.

Set Checklist

The following are items to attend to in regard to set.

- Check in with the director and the AD. Obtain the set update, check that the day is on schedule, and resolve any problems that have come up.
- Check in with department heads: ask if they need anything, ensure that they are on schedule, and collect petty cash envelopes or issue petty cash as necessary.
- Check that meals are served on time.
- Check in with the cast to see if anyone needs anything.
- Decide about going into overtime, renting special equipment, scheduling changes, providing second meals, and other issues.
- Bring supplies to the set, and replenish the AD kit.
- See that all SAG forms, Exhibit G forms, Start/I-9 forms, and so on are properly filled out and collected.
- See that call sheets are distributed.

- Deliver and sign checks and paperwork.
- Make sure department heads are compiling continuity notebooks as necessary (makeup, wardrobe, art department).

OFFICE RESPONSIBILITIES AND FUNCTIONS

The office is the lifeline and the communication center of the shoot during production. For the set to function smoothly and efficiently, the office must be organized and stay one day ahead of the set. Ideally, the office should be open at least an hour before call time and an hour or so after wrap each day. If you are filming nights, keep in mind that businesses are generally open only during the day; therefore, the office may have to be open at least part of the day, and phone calls may have to be made then. Throughout the shoot, the office and the set should be in communication so that the office is prepared to fulfill any requests or directives that come from the set.

Office Checklist

The office may have to organize, arrange, and facilitate the following items during production:

- Acquire any additional equipment needed during filming; immediately replace equipment that has been damaged.
- Gather and send to the set paperwork, materials, equipment, and anything else needed during the day.
- Notify the lab if there will be a delay in delivering film; make sure the lab's phone and fax numbers and hours of operation are posted in the office.
- Be sure it is clear who will deliver and pick up film from the lab each day.
- Organize and pick up equipment and materials needed for the next filming day. Organize equipment pickup and return lists; notify those who are responsible for pickups and returns and review lists.
- Check the weather forecast for the next filming day; have the AD note the forecast on the call sheet.
- Make sure the next day's call sheet is distributed either at lunch or at the end of the day; file copies in the production notebooks and office files.
- Coordinate the transportation of actors who must be brought to the set.
- Collect and file any paperwork regarding vendor pickups and returns at end of each day.
- Collect sound and camera reports and the script supervisor's notes for the editor at the end of each day.
- Collect completed petty cash envelopes from the crew, and actualize the budget in whichever line item this may be possible.
- Check the status of dailies with the lab each day; arrange a pickup.
- Schedule the screening of dailies with the director and the producers.
- Purchase film stock or videotape as needed.
- Schedule and coordinate prelight/prerig days.
- Organize and plan any company move days.
- Replenish petty cash; prepare per diems if necessary.
- Confirm with the still photographer which days he or she is needed on the set; fax the still photographer a call sheet with directions to the location the day before.
- Replenish forms and have them available when crew members come into the office (stationery, fax sheets, check requests, petty cash envelopes and requests, and so on).
- Update the calendar or whiteboard with important dates, pickups, and returns; distribute updated schedules, day-out-of-days sheets, memos, and strip board.
- Update and distribute script changes (colored pages).
- Update and continue to compile the thank-you list.
- Compile the credit list showing how the credits will run; add new vendors, crew members, and so on.
- Send Exhibit G forms, Taft-Hartley forms, production reports, time cards, contracts, and other paperwork to SAG at the end of each filming week.
- Fill out SAG time cards at the end of each filming week; send them to SAG and the payroll company with appropriate on-set reports (production reports, Exhibit G forms, and so on).
- Make or finalize arrangements for out-of-town filming (travel, accommodations, food, and so on).
- Check in with the editor daily: Are the script notes clear and accurate? Has the editor received dailies? Are there any questions or messages regarding footage shot or additional footage needed that the editor wants communicated to the director?

WRAPPING OUT A SHOOT DAY

Because wrapping out of a location takes time, remember to allow enough time so that you avoid having to pay overtime. Check in with the AD toward the end of the day to see if the set is on schedule and to ascertain when he or she anticipates beginning to wrap.

End-of-Day Checklist

The following checklist for wrapping out a shoot day ensures that you are prepared and organized for the next filming day. Note that the items that follow are not all performed by the line producer. However, you should make sure everything on this list is covered by the appropriate crew person.

- Review shooting schedule for the next shoot day; make sure all arrangements have been made.
- Confirm arrangements for the next day's location with the location manager.
- Confirm catering arrangements with the craft service person or the caterer. Total the number of people to be fed the next day.
- Check with the AD to make sure that the cast and additional crew needed for the next day's shoot have been notified of their call times and have a map or directions.
- Distribute the next day's call sheet if it was not done at lunch.
- Check in with department heads.
- Purchase more raw stock or videotape stock as needed; dole out raw stock for the next day to be sent to the set.
- Return or pick up equipment or materials as necessary.
- Properly store perishable craft service and catering items.
- Load vehicles with equipment, bearing in mind the order required for unloading.
- Clear out and clean up the location; have the trash removed.
- Collect copies of the camera and sound reports.
- Take the film and sound rolls directly to the lab after the shoot day wraps.
- Lock production vehicles after the equipment has been loaded; park all vehicles safely overnight. Collect and copy script notes.
- File script notes, sound reports, and camera reports in the production notebooks and the office files, along with call sheets, Exhibit G forms, production reports, Taft-Hartley forms, and other paperwork.
- Collect any completed petty cash envelopes from the crew.
- Screen dailies if not screened during the lunch break.
- Replenish forms needed in the office or the AD kit.
- Review the to-do list with the office staff.
- If shooting on DV, have clones made of the tape.

DAILY/WEEKLY COST OVERVIEW

A daily cost overview is a one-page sheet that allows you to compare what you anticipated spending and what you actually spent (see Figure 8–1). The cost overview usually includes information about how many scenes were shot in a given day, how much you anticipated paying actors and crew (here you account for any overtime or meal penalties), catering, raw stock, and miscellaneous unanticipated expenses. If you are not reporting to anyone else, such as a production company or investors, these daily cost overviews are for your own information so that you know where you stand in terms of the budget. If another entity is involved with the show—such as a mini-major, an executive producer, or a bond company—you may be required to turn in a cost overview sheet each day or weekly. Figure 8–1 will help you to actualize your budget. If you are working with a bond company, they will tell you exactly what is required.

ACTUALIZING THE BUDGET

Throughout the show you will accumulate final receipts and paperwork for all equipment and services rendered. At the end of the show, after all returns have been made and final invoices have been received, you will have to actualize your budget, comparing how much money you have actually spent and how much you anticipated spending for each line item.

If you created your budget with Movie Magic Budgeting, select Compare under the Tools menu in the control bar at the top of your screen. This will add two new columns to your budget, one labeled *Original* and the other labeled *Variance*. When you insert an actual cost to the budget column labeled *Current*, you will see your original projected cost, the actual cost, and the variance between them.

Because you will have to actualize your budget, it is essential that you collect paperwork from vendors and keep it organized. Once you have entered an invoice or receipt into the budget, mark it so that you do not lose track of what you have done. If your daily cost overviews are for your own purposes only, you may want to actualize your budget as current numbers come in and leave the more formal cost overview sheet aside. You will determine which approach best serves your needs. The point is to be aware of how much you are spending so that you feel confident about making decisions. On low-budget shows this is particularly important because you have such limited funds.

It is also essential that you are able to discuss confidently where the film stands financially with other key members of your team. If your film is bonded, the bond company will require that you submit weekly cost reports. The accountant usually prepares this document with the line producer's assistance.

DAILY COST OVERVIEW

SHOW ______________________ PROD # ______________________

DATE ______________________ DAY # ______________________

START DATE __________

SCHEDULED FINISH DATE __________

REVISED FINISH DATE __________

	PER CALL SHEET	SHOT	AHEAD/BEHIND
# OF SCENES			
# OF PAGES			

	AS BUDGETED AND/OR SCHEDULED	ACTUAL	COST (OVER)/UNDER
CAST OVERTIME			
COMPANY SHOOTING HOURS			
MEAL PENALTY			
EXTRAS & STAND-INS			
CATERING			
RAW STOCK			
UNANTICIPATED EXPENSES:			

TOTAL FOR TODAY __________

PREVIOUS TOTAL __________

GRAND TOTAL __________

PREPARED BY ______________________ APPROVED BY ______________________

Figure 8–1 Daily cost overview

COMPANY MOVE DAYS

Company move days are notoriously difficult because they require that the production pick itself up, move to an entirely different location, and set up for filming again the same day. Whenever possible, organize company moves so that the new location is near the current one. Company moves are not altogether different from personal moves—they are a pain in the butt, and they are exhausting. That said, the better organized the company move is the less painful and time consuming it will be. If company move days are well organized, they can save your production time and money.

Company Move Checklist

Company moves need to be carefully planned. Refer to the following list to ensure that you properly organize any company move days.

- Load the equipment into the production trucks, bearing in mind what will have to be unloaded from the truck first at the new location. This should be coordinated in advance.
- Make sure all cast and crew members have directions, a map, and transportation to the new location.
- If possible, send a production assistant ahead of the rest of the production to post parking and bathroom signs, to familiarize him- or herself with the space, and to determine where to unload equipment and set up tables, chairs, and other items.
- If possible, have the craft service person leave a small cooler at the old location with drinks and snacks, and send him or her to set up at the new locale before the rest of the company arrives so that there are coffee, cold drinks, and snacks awaiting them.
- Have the AD ensure that every last bit of equipment, paperwork, and supplies has been loaded into the trucks. The AD and the location manager should be the last ones off the set. Send the second AD to the new location.
- Make sure the location is left in proper order (see the "End-of-Day Checklist" section).
- Whenever possible, have the company movc to a location where you will do more than one day of shooting, to avoid having to wrap out the second location that same day (too tiring).
- If you have equipment the vendor must deliver and pick up, inform the vendor in advance that you will need the equipment moved. (This is often the case with cranes, generators, and other heavy equipment.)
- Provide any cast and crew members who were not needed at the previous location with a call sheet for the new location.
- Determine in advance to which location the caterer will report on the company move day.
- Indicate clearly on the call sheet that there are two locations for that day; include maps and directions to both locations.
- Call the office to check in when the crew arrives at the new location.

DISTANT LOCATIONS

As discussed in Chapters 6 and 7, you must make the necessary arrangements well in advance for filming at distant locations. You will need all of the same elements when shooting at a distant location as you do when you are shooting locally, but you usually will not have the same support infrastructure of contacts or the same easy access to equipment at a distant site. Depending on the scale of the shoot, you may want to hire a local coordinator or production manager to assist you and to ensure that all goes smoothly. If this extra expense is unrealistic for the size and budget of your film, make sure you have taken all of the elements of the shoot into consideration and have determined how best to deal with them.

Distant Locations Checklist

You will need to deal with the following items if you will be filming at a distant location:

- Travel arrangements and living accommodations for cast and crew
- Parking arrangements for crew vehicles and production trucks
- Catering and craft service
- Transportation of crew, materials, and equipment to the location
- Equipment storage
- Office space and setup
- Insurance if you are filming in a different state
- Film stock purchase if needed; a proper place to store film
- Equipment rental if additional equipment is needed
- Local unions
- Shipment of film to the lab if necessary
- Screening of dailies

Details of the Distant Locations Checklist

Travel and Living Accommodations

Confirm the lodging arrangements made for the cast and crew. Let the hotel or motel know when you anticipate arriving, ask for directions, and get the name of a contact person. Prepare maps for the crew. Make sure there is secure, ample space in which to park crew vehicles, picture cars, and production trucks, and find out where you will be able to store equipment, materials, and film safely. Ask the hotel or motel to fax you a list of local restaurants and hospitals near your shooting location.

If you will be flying to the location, call the airline to confirm your reservations. Make sure the airline tickets are in hand and that you coordinate with the cast and crew how each person will get to the airport and at what time and where the crew will meet. Arrange cast and crew transportation from the airport to the location or lodging facility. When traveling, have petty cash on hand for tips. If any cast or crew members will be reporting to the distant location at a different time or day than the rest of the production, arrange to pick them up from the airport.

Per Diems

As discussed in Chapter 7, you will have to provide per diems to all nonlocal cast and crew members. Be prepared to distribute per diems the day you arrive at the location. Because per diems are usually distributed in cash, you will have to withdraw cash beforehand from your local bank.

SECOND-UNIT FILMING AND PICKUPS

Basically, a second unit is a scaled-down crew that usually includes the director, the director of photography, the AD, the assistant camera operator, the second AC, the camera operator, and a production assistant. You may need prop or art department personnel; special effects people; wardrobe, makeup, and hair; and a gaffer. All of this depends on the nature of the shoot. On larger-budget productions, a second unit sometimes has its own director, and the camera operator becomes the second-unit DP. On occasion, an entirely different crew is hired.

A second-unit crew is most appropriate on low-budget shows for shooting exteriors, inserts, and other scenes that do not require principal cast members or a great deal of lighting. An example of when a second-unit crew might be used would be if you were to shoot in Los Angeles interiors scripted as Las Vegas locations and the exteriors of Las Vegas are needed. In this case, it makes most sense for a second-unit crew to travel to Las Vegas to shoot the necessary exterior shots. Second-unit shooting can save you time and money and is quite efficient when carefully planned. Depending on how the editing process evolves, you may find that you need pickup days to shoot more coverage of a given scene, or that you need different footage than you have.

Second-unit filming on a low-budget shoot should be scheduled for the final days of production if possible. This enables you to wrap the majority of the crew while a handful of people stay on board for several days of second-unit filming.

THE LAST WEEK OF PRODUCTION

Wrapping out the show must be carefully planned and organized. A week before completing principal photography, begin to compile return lists, and be sure you have budgeted for a PA or two to remain on for a week of wrap to return equipment, vehicles, materials, and expendables that department heads do not need to return themselves. The production manager or coordinator should also remain on for a week or so of wrap to close out vendor accounts, finalize vendor and SAG paperwork, facilitate getting deposits back, coordinate returns, organize and store paperwork and materials for the production company, and secure final numbers from vendors so that you can actualize the budget through the production period and know how much money is available for post-production. A few department heads may need several days to wrap out their respective departments. Paperwork, equipment returns, petty cash envelopes, continuity notebooks, and so on must be completed and turned in to the office.

Checklist for the Last Week of Production

The following items must be dealt with in the last week of production, with an eye toward wrapping:

- Make sure that the post-production supervisor is on board.
- Compile return lists for equipment, vehicles, and expendables.
- Coordinate and organize pickup days and second-unit filming.
- Organize vendor and SAG paperwork.
- Complete the crew credit list; make sure all crew members have signed off on it.

- Close out vendor accounts; collect final paperwork and numbers from vendors.
- Collect outstanding petty cash envelopes from the crew as appropriate.
- Organize the wrap party.
- Send thank-you notes and gifts.

During the final week of production, start scheduling the film's post-production needs. The producer (or line producer) may have already secured some initial bids on items needed to complete the film, such as ADR, foley, mixing, festival deadlines, and so on.

As discussed in Chapter 6, if you can afford a post-production supervisor, it is advisable that you hire one, even if just for the initial few weeks of post-production. During the first few weeks of post-production, you will have to continue handling the final wrap of production. The timing of events during the editing process is very important. Deadlines must be met, and it is important that the elements be properly planned and carefully organized. The supervisor's familiarity with the requirements of post-production will save you time and money. It is possible, however, to navigate through post-production on your own if the budget does not allow for a post-production supervisor. (See Chapter 9.)

Wrap Party

If the budget cannot sustain a blowout wrap party for the cast and crew, come up with a creative way to celebrate finishing the show and to thank the cast and crew for their hard work and dedication. Whether it is a dinner at someone's house, a party, or a gathering at a local bar (a no-host bar, if necessary), it is important to show the cast and crew how much you appreciate them. You may want to invite the cast and crew to screen dailies to see how all of their hard work has paid off.

On *Swingers*, we could not afford a wrap party, but we did invite the cast and crew for cocktails and dailies. When we sold the film, we had a "deferral" party and handed out deferral checks.

WRAPPING OUT PRODUCTION

Officially, the line producer's job ends when all of the production's loose ends are wrapped up. With your low-budget film, the division of labor may not be as clearly delineated as it is here; that is, you may be the post-production supervisor or the producer as well as the line producer.

As the line producer, you will oversee the return of equipment, close out paperwork, finalize cast and crew payroll, complete and file SAG paperwork, close vendor accounts and secure final numbers, collect production and continuity notebooks, and actualize the budget. Wrapping out the show should take no more than two weeks, but you may not receive final numbers, paperwork, and deposits back from vendors for a few weeks after you have wrapped. The budget must be actualized as the final numbers and deposits come in. This is the time to be sure that all paperwork, contracts, and forms are in order and properly filed. They may have to be delivered to a distributor later.

Final Wrap-out Checklist

You will have to handle the following items when wrapping out the show:

- Shoot inserts and pickups if necessary.
- Return equipment, expendables, and materials.
- Return all production trucks, rental cars, and picture vehicles.
- Store any purchased equipment, props, and materials in a storage facility.
- Close out vendor accounts and secure final numbers.
- Close out and code petty cash envelopes; actualize the budget.
- Finalize cast and crew payroll.
- Complete and file vendor paperwork.
- Check festival deadlines; make VHS dubs of the film for festival prescreenings and use.
- Give the script supervisor's notes and continuity notebook to the editor.
- Select still photos to be printed from the still photographer's contact sheets for festival use and publicity.
- Give the editor petty cash for supplies and food.
- Collect the continuity notebooks from the various departments; give them to the production company.
- Complete the production notebooks with production forms and SAG forms; give them to the production company.
- Finalize SAG paperwork that must be completed at the end of the show and send it to SAG; get the bond back once the cast payroll has been completed.
- Get deposits back from vendors.
- Pick up from the lab any leftover film stock or videotape; sell back excess film stock and videotape to vendors.
- Make sure the editor has everything from the lab and all of the necessary equipment.

- Return cores, bags, and cans to the lab.
- Cancel phone and fax lines no longer needed.
- Return rented or borrowed office equipment and furniture.
- Actualize the budget through the production period.
- Send final thank-you notes.

Details of the Wrap-out Checklist

Returns to Vendors

Returning rentals to vendors on time is essential to keeping your costs down, because most likely you will be charged for every day beyond the expected return date. If you have your pickup and return lists in order, the process should be fairly painless. Check in with all department heads and make sure they are conducting their own returns, and ask if they need assistance. It may be less expensive to have a production assistant return art department materials, for example, than to have art department personnel do the returns themselves. On the other hand, it may be more efficient for each department to do its own returns because department members know which equipment is from which vendor.

Make sure that when the production truck is loaded consideration is given to the order in which the equipment will be unloaded. That is, the first item to be returned should be the last item loaded on the truck. Otherwise, whoever is returning the equipment is going to have a horrible time when he or she arrives at a vendor and must find equipment buried toward the front of the truck.

Whenever a return is made, the vendor must provide paperwork confirming receipt of the returned items, a list of any items damaged or missing, a deposit check if one was issued, and a final invoice. If necessary, the person making the return should ask that the final invoice be faxed to the production office as soon as possible and that a hard copy be sent through the mail. Always attach a hard copy of the final invoice to the purchase order to which it belongs, and file it.

Closing Out Production Accounts

If you have the funds in your production account to pay bills directly, issue checks to close out production accounts as soon as possible after receiving final invoices. Most vendors expect payment on a net-30 cycle (within 30 days), so it is not essential that bills be paid right away. However, if you are trying to wrap out a production, the sooner bills are paid the sooner you will be officially wrapped and able to actualize your budget. Vendors sometimes issue the deposit upon return of the equipment, but more often they keep the deposit until the final payment has been made. If you are working with a large company that has an accounting department, hand over all of your POs with the final invoices attached, and the accounting department will facilitate payment to the necessary parties.

9 POST-PRODUCTION

"Few Filmmakers adequately budge post, which is why most of them have to find more money to finish their films . . . "

—Peter Broderick

ORGANIZING THE FILM'S POST-PRODUCTION NEEDS

We recommend hiring a post-supervisor if at all possible. If a post-production supervisor has not been hired, you will have to determine who will be the point person for scheduling and organizing all of the technical aspects of post-production. If it is one of the producers and he or she has limited experience with the technical aspects of post-production, it is imperative to work closely with the assistant editor to figure out what should happen when. Ideally, begin determining the post-production needs of the show during the final weeks of production. If you have a post-production supervisor, he or she will be able to help you arrange the scheduling of all elements at the appropriate time during the editing process.

Post-production Checklist

The following items must be handled during post-production:

- Create a tentative post-production schedule with preliminary deadlines (editor's assembly, director's cut, sound mix, music meetings, color timing, festival deadlines, ADR, foley, titles and opticals, final answer print, screenings, and so on).
- Hire the music supervisor and composers.
- Map out festival deadlines.
- Meet with publicists.
- Schedule ADR.
- Schedule foley.
- Arrange for titles and opticals.
- Schedule sound mix.
- Assemble press kits (should include still photos, synopsis, bios, and so on).
- Arrange for the MPAA rating, a title/research clearance report, and E&O insurance.

EDITING

Ideally, as the line producer your job will end when the "wrap" period following production ends, typically about two weeks after the last day of shooting. This scenario assumes you are not the producer of the film and that your budget allows you to hire a post-production supervisor. If there is no budget for such a person, your role during post-production is as the post-production supervisor, which essentially means pulling together and organizing all of the necessary elements of post in a timely and affordable way. The producers, the director, and the editor will confer during the first week of post and discuss the film's post-production schedule.

A calendar of important dates—such as festival deadlines, director's cut, screenings, ADR, foley, and mix dates—will be compiled. Most likely, there will be deadlines to meet, and being organized and meeting those deadlines will help you remain on budget. Post-production does require a certain degree of technical understanding, so if you do not have it, make sure to do some "informational interviews" with an experienced post-super to get your bearings. This is essential because post-production is expensive and having the right elements at the right time will aid you in keeping your costs down. As we suggest previously, the assistant editor is often a good person to work in conjunction with.

TIPS ON POST-PRODUCTION

The trick during post-production is to be as organized, efficient, and thorough as possible without rushing or compromising the film. It is costly and time consuming to have to reschedule any of the post-production events. The sections that follow explore creative ideas and tips on dealing with a few post-production needs.

Automated Dialogue Replacement (ADR/Looping)

If possible, schedule just one session of ADR if the actors are available. Ask actors to come in and record ADR only if it is absolutely necessary for a scene. Recording ADR on a stage is expensive, but it may be the best option if there are several days of ADR and several actors to record. Investigate your options carefully.

On *Swingers,* we spent two days recording ADR in the producer's living room. Our ADR needs were few because our production tracks were relatively clean. Because our resources were limited, this was the most viable option. We compiled a list of all lines we needed to re-record and all of the additional lines we needed from each actor, and we scheduled ADR within a two-day period. We cued the dailies to the relevant scene so that the actors could sync their lines while viewing the scene. Our sound mixer was equipped with the necessary sound equipment and microphones, and he cued the actors with their lines at the beginning of each take.

Sound Mix

On *Swingers,* because we cut on an Avid system, we were able to do a temp mix, which not only saved us time and money required for a temp mix in a studio, but also saved us time and money on our final mix because we were as ready as we could have been. All of the elements—dialogue, music, and effects—were premixed; the levels just needed to be adjusted in the final mix.

Titles and Opticals

Titles can be expensive. It depends on how long the end credit crawl is on the film, how many single cards will be run in both the main and the end titles, and how elaborate the credit sequence is. On *Swingers,* we compiled our main and end title credits exactly as we wanted them to run on the film, printed them from a computer (we installed the fonts we wanted onto our computer), and then photographed them. This saved us a tremendous amount of money compared with having a title house create, photograph, and then print the credits, and then have them processed at a lab for an additional cost.

Music

While assembling the film, the director and the editor will set various songs and pieces of music to the film to establish which choices best suit the story and set the mood. If you are cutting on an Avid system, sync the music to the picture at least temporarily.

A music supervisor is an extremely worthwhile investment if you plan to use licensed music rather than an original score. He or she can assist you with music licensing, publishing rights and fees, and festival licenses if needed. If your budget is too limited, seek help from people who have some expertise in this field, and refer to guidebooks in navigating through the film's music needs.

The music supervisor's job is multifaceted. He or she suggests songs, score, source cues, and a composer, and arranges for recording facilities for any score composed for the film. If the film will be playing at festivals, festival master use and synchronization licenses must be secured for any music used in the film. Unless it is an original score, festival licenses are generally inexpensive and negotiable (sometimes free), and are far more affordable than broad distribution master use licenses and sync fees. While the music supervisor is negotiating and securing the festival rights to songs, he or she will ideally also be securing quotes on broad distribution rights. If the film secures distribution, the distributor will want to know how much it will cost to purchase the rights to the music in the film. Often, songs you may want to use are not affordable. A music supervisor who is familiar with securing rights and licenses and negotiating fees will help you find songs that are within the film's price range and still work for the film.

A music supervisor can also assist in attracting the interest of music labels that might want to package the film's sound track. Having a label involved or interested can be advantageous because the label can help pay for some of the music in the film. The label might also want to put some of its songs or artists on the sound track and in the film at no cost to you. Having a label interested in packaging and releasing the soundtrack can be an attractive selling point with a distributor.

MOVING TOWARD A COMPLETED FILM: BEFORE YOU LOCK THE PICTURE

Filmmaking is a collaborative process, and this an important time to listen to the advice and opinions of others. Seek the opinion of trusted outsiders before you lock the picture and cut your negative. We highly recommend conducting some "test" screenings of your picture and holding focus groups so that you can really get a sense of how your picture is playing. It is important to have more than one test screening. One thing we have learned is that when you conduct several of these screenings you start to recognize patterns in what people are saying. It is important not to ignore these patterns, particularly if they are things like: "I don't understand how this character made the transition from A to B" or "I'm confused by what happens at the end of the second act."

If the line producer is still involved just before the picture is locked, it is most likely as post-production supervisor or because he or she is the producer of the film. For the director, there is a distinct line between remaining auteur of the film while considering the opinions of others and relinquishing creative control to accommodate the whims of those who may not know what is best. The time just before your picture is locked is crucial because the director's decisions during this period ultimately shape the movie. When you have been through the editing process multiple times, it becomes evident that the director and the editor could cut the footage together three or four ways, resulting in three or four different films.

Certainly, not all of these options will work, but it is hoped that one of them does. For example, in an early cut of *Swingers*, there was very little of Vince Vaughn's performance. This would not have been a favorable version of the film. In fact, almost all of us involved in the film at that point were disappointed when we viewed that cut of the film. Fortunately, the team knew there was a film to be unearthed in the coverage they had seen in the dailies. Further input came several times, closer to locking the picture, when several of the team members' agents viewed the film. Had the film not been working, we would have cast our net slightly wider and solicited advice from elsewhere.

There are professionals who consider themselves independent film specialists and who have watched hundreds of cuts of independent films and given advice at this crucial point. In many instances, this advice enables the films to become movies that could really play to an audience, as opposed to a film that only plays to you, your friends, the cast, and the crew (see the Peter Broderick interview on the companion CD-ROM).

The period just before the picture is locked is your final chance to make changes. You may be too myopic at this point in the process to be able to tell how the film is playing and what could and should be changed. Do not assume that to ask the advice of others is to give up your creative control.

ROUGH CUTS: WHAT TO SHOW TO WHOM

Call us paranoid, but we believe that as few copies of rough or fine cuts of your film should be floating around as possible. We also believe it is best to conduct some informal test screenings of your film before you decide if it is ready to send to the selection committee of a major festival. If your film really is not ready, it is not worth rushing. Often, if a selection committee has screened your film and passed on it, it will not look at it again. And no matter how many times we have heard that someone is experienced at looking at rough cuts of films and can see the potential of something even if it is not finished, we have learned the hard way that it is often not the case. Sundance rejected *Swingers* and *Kissing Jessica Stein.* Both films were submitted as rough cuts. Perhaps neither film would have gotten in even if it had been submitted in its final form, but that we will never know.

We recommend inviting people to screenings but giving out as few videotapes during your editing process as possible. On *Kissing Jessica Stein,* we held at least five separate screenings in our editing room before we locked the picture. After each of these "test screenings," we had audiences fill out questionnaires and attend informal focus groups. This was invaluable to our creative process.

LOCKING THE PICTURE

The final weeks of post-production will be spent locking the picture. Final changes will be made, the final sound mix will be completed, the color-corrected prints of the film will be struck, and video copies of the locked picture will be made. If you are no longer the line producer but are now the post-supervisor, this is the time to make sure everything is in order and accounted for. Following are the tasks that may need to be accomplished.

Once the picture is locked, arrange for the negative to be sent from the lab to a film vault. Both the A- and B-roll negatives must be safely and properly stored in a climate-controlled film vault, along with the sound rolls. If you cannot afford a film vault, make space in a cool, dark, dry closet. Make sure the dailies, the continuity notebook, and the editor's notes are in a safe place (you will need to refer to them if you find a distributor and have to go back and make changes to the picture), along with any other equipment and materials that belong to the production.

During the final weeks of post-production, the producers and the post-supervisor will begin to wrap out the show completely. If you have not had time to complete and file paperwork, now is the time to do so. Clearly label files and organize them so that paperwork can be easily found later. If the production office will be shut down after post-production, arrange for a safe place to store all of the files and any office equipment that belongs to the production. Usually, all of the show's paperwork belongs to the entity that made the film. As the producer or the line producer, you may want to keep copies of some files or paperwork for your own records.

Once all accounts have been closed, all equipment and materials have been stored, and all bills have been paid, actualize the budget. There may be a few outstanding final numbers, but you will most likely be able to actualize the budget in its entirety. If you have remained on the show through post-production, part of your job is to provide the production with the final accounting of the show. (See "Actualizing the Budget" in Chapter 8.)

10 FESTIVALS AND DISTRIBUTION

". . . you have to be judicious in showing your film to potential reps and by the same token you have to be even more judicious about how to expose the film to potential buyers . . ."

—John Sloss, producer's rep. and attorney

INTRODUCTION

Once your film is complete, preparing a strategy for selling your film is crucial. Considering the best way to give your film exposure in the right area and generating a press kit is the next step.

Preparing a strategy for selling your film is crucial. For most independently made films, the festival circuit is the best way to gain exposure, generate press materials, and make an acquisitions deal with a distributor. These are steps that may be best achieved with the help of others (sales rep and publicist).

It is advisable to have a festival strategy for your film, rather than applying to as many festivals as you can download applications for. Assuming you are new to the process and do not have a consultant or sales rep working with your team, the best way to develop your festival strategy is to look at festival Web sites and speak to filmmakers who have recently screened their films at the festivals you are considering. Some festivals have a reputation for treating filmmakers well. Others pay little attention to smaller films and your film can easily "get lost" at these festivals. Certain festivals have a reputation for attracting sales because acquisitions executives from distribution companies attend the festival (e.g., Sundance and Berlin), whereas other festivals are tailored more for those films that already have a distributor in place, or that have already had their premiere (see "The World Premiere" later in this chapter).

DEVELOPING A FESTIVAL STRATEGY

Get the submission dates for festivals to which you may want to submit the film. Almost all festivals provide information on their Web sites about the festival and application deadlines. Even if you submit the application online, you may have to snail-mail a copy of your film to the festival. Some may prefer that everything be submitted at once. Compile a list of festival deadline dates and identify the festivals to apply to based on the estimated date for completing post-production.

Depending on which festivals the film is being submitted to and what the requirements are, prints may need to be struck or 1/2-inch video copies of the film made. Check deadlines and read applications and the submission requirements carefully. Be prepared to send a check so that the application can be processed. When submitting an application you may also be required to provide still photos of the actors, bios of the filmmakers and key cast, and a synopsis of the film, which essentially forms your press kit. An attractive, informative, and organized press kit may help distributors distinguish your film from the rest, as distributors see many films when traveling the festival circuit. (If you are considering distributing a rough cut of your film, see "Rough Cut: What To Show to Whom" in the material that follows.) The following are a few important questions to address when planning the film's festival strategy:

- What is the goal of the film?
- Which distributors should see the film?
- Does anyone in the core filmmaking team know any of those distributors personally, or does anyone know someone who does? In other words, who can make a call on the film's behalf and ask that a distributor see the film?
- Should a publicist be hired to help promote the film at the festival before securing distribution?
- What type of deal do the filmmakers want?

- Who in the core filmmaking team is savvy enough to discuss and negotiate a deal, or should a producer's rep be engaged?

SALES AGENTS

Having a sales agent or producer's representative to help you in the sale of your film can be invaluable. These are people who (should) have a fair amount of experience selling films. They know the buyers and they know how to negotiate a deal. They have contacts and access to people and companies, where filmmakers often do not. Sometimes a sales rep will charge an upfront fee that you have to pay regardless of whether the film is sold or not. Some reps take a percentage of the sale price if and when the film is acquired. This is usually a more attractive scenario because if no sale is made no money changes hands.

John Sloss's Cinetic Media is a renowned sales company for independent films. Although Cinetic (based in New York City) may be at the top of your list, there are many sales agents out there. You can research them on the Web and, as always, talking to filmmakers who have been through the sales process recently will help you determine who you may want to work with.

PUBLICISTS

We strongly recommend making an investment in a publicist for the world premiere of your film and possibly beyond that, depending on what festival course you have chosen for your film.

A publicist will be helpful on multiple fronts. He or she will help you develop press materials for your film, and compile bios of the filmmaking team. This is important because it is often the case that a journalist writing about your film may refer to the press materials and draw copy for an article, verbatim, from your press materials. The filmmaker plays an important role by helping to generate these materials. However, it is exceedingly helpful to work in conjunction with an experienced publicist. As a more objective, knowledgeable party, a publicist is often able to finesse the materials in ways you might not think of.

Second, a publicist will leverage all of his or her contacts to get certain press to attend your screening. They will help create a sort of "buzz" about the film to the public and industry via radio interviews and other media. The publicity generated for a film is hugely important to your film's success. If it is a festival screening, you are likely to want to hold full reviews from all press other than the trade publications. For example, you may not want your *New York Times* review to be out of a festival, but you might be happy to have a "capsule" included in the overview of the festival the paper is writing. It can be valuable to get a sense of how certain press will review your film down the line, when it is being fully reviewed. This information can be a powerful tool in helping sell the film, and is often only disclosed to those publicists who have good relationships with the press.

In the ideal world, you will sell your film after the first festival you attend and no longer be solely responsible for the publicity of your film. This happens to a miniscule number of very lucky filmmakers. Most films take much longer to find a distributor. It may be helpful to keep your publicist on board beyond the first festival. Your publicist will help ensure that these goals are met and that the press you get is the press you want.

Your publicist will also help ascertain which trade publication reporters are attending the festival and know which reporters should cover your film. The publicist can then try to ensure that the best reviewer of your film comes to your screening. Publicists also help get media interviews for filmmakers, further helping to generate word-of-mouth about the film and making sure it is getting exposure.

CHOOSING A PUBLICIST

Do some research before contacting publicists. Speak to filmmakers who have taken a similar film (e.g., genre, feature versus documentary) to the festival you are going to, and find out who they used as a publicist. Find out what they liked and did not like about the relationship. Were expectations met? Did they feel the publicist earned his or her fee? Would they work with him or her again? Talk to more than one filmmaker so that you can compare experiences.

After creating a short list of publicists you would like to work with, contact them and let them know that you have been accepted to a given festival and are looking for a publicity firm. Usually, you will give a potential publicist a tape of your film. After they have watched it, you will have a nuts-and-bolts discussion about the film and the best strategy for marketing it, what the publicist thinks their firm could accomplish for your film at a festival, how much that would cost, and so on.

One key element in hiring a publicist is ensuring that your point person at the firm is the person you want publicizing your film. You are hiring the company, but there may be a specific publicist you really want to work with.

If you know you want to work with someone in particular, make sure you establish that at the outset.

The publicist's fee will depend on the publicist, the type of film, and what you hope to accomplish. When negotiating the fee, you may agree that the publicist will work for one festival, for a month or several months. The fee will be established based on the specifics of your scenario.

THE WORLD PREMIERE

The world premiere of your film is the first screening of the film for the public. It is essential to think carefully about where and under what circumstances your film will world premiere. You may want to consider using a sales agent and/or publicist, who should assist you with the ins and outs of getting your film seen by the right buyer, as well as getting in a few back doors you may not have access to or even known about. If you do not have a distributor, you will want your film to premiere at a festival that is well attended by acquisitions people and that has a track record of filmmakers walking away with a sale.

Kissing Jessica Stein had its world premiere at the Los Angeles Film Festival, which had just been purchased by IFP Los Angeles. The festival did not have a history of films being sold from it. We decided to have our world premiere screening there for several key reasons. First, we were very ready to screen the film. Our process had been long and intense and we needed that release of actually completing the film and showing it to a wider audience. Second, the festival engendered our trust and confidence by expressing how much they wanted our film, backed with how they would help us position it and give us good screening slots. We felt we were not only in good hands but really wanted. Finally, even though the festival did not have a history of sales being made from it, because it was in Los Angeles we believed we could get more acquisitions executives to the screenings because many of them live and work in L.A. We did this through strategically placed e-mails, calls, and mailings.

On *Kissing Jessica Stein*, we did engage both a publicist and a sales agent for the world premiere. Having a strong team behind the film was essential to our success. Although we do not know what might have happened had we gone it on our own, we have felt that the money spent on both our sales agent and publicist was worth its weight in gold. There were multiple interested parties after the first L.A. Film Festival screening. We had to send the print to Harvey Weinstein in Connecticut and many distributors sent upper-level acquisitions executives to the second screening of the festival. Our sales rep also set up a few private screenings during that week. The final deal with Fox Searchlight did not close until Cannes, almost three weeks later. Our sales rep was instrumental in facilitating and regulating the sale of *Kissing Jessica Stein*.

IF YOU DO NOT GET INTO A FESTIVAL

If attending a festival with your film does not seem to be in the cards, you may want to organize a distribution screening. A well-thought-out strategy is essential. The following are a few things to keep in mind: Does anyone from the key team of filmmakers know any agents or other filmmakers who have useful contacts? Would these contacts be willing to attend a screening of the film? Compile a list of distributors to invite to the screening. Talk to other filmmakers who have had a distribution screening and get their list of distributors who attended. Choose distributors you think would respond favorably to the film and would best market and promote it. (See the "Distributor" section of Appendix A for a list of contacts.)

The scheduling of your distribution screening is also very important. Do not schedule a screening on a night when there are other screenings or premieres distributors may be attending. Do not organize a distribution screening during major festivals. Most distributors will be attending the festivals and will not be able to attend your screening. Unless you want to organize individual screenings for distributors (which can be costly and time consuming) or make video copies of the film to send to distributors, the distribution screening will most likely be a one-shot deal, so do it right.

When organizing a distribution screening, send invitations, postcards, or fliers to distributors via e-mail, snail-mail, or fax at least two weeks before the scheduled screening. Include pertinent information on the invitation, including an RSVP e-mail or phone number. If you know agents or managers who are willing to help with the film, ask them to make calls to some of the distributors on your wish list. Compile a list of people who plan to attend the screening as they respond.

Have press kits made up to give to distributors at the screening. Have a poster created for the film to hang at the theater. Even with limited means, there are a fair number of affordable options for creating a poster (you might make your own) and other graphically appealing support materials for the film. On *Swingers*, we created both the poster we hung for our distribution screening and the postcard we sent out as our invitation to the event. We purchased a computer graphics program, pulled a frame of negative to use as the photo, and generated an appealing and recognizable design. Make sure the venue for the screening is accessible, can accommodate the number of people invited, and that ample parking is available.

You may want to invite the cast and crew to attend the distribution screening. By combining the screenings, distributors and cast and crew will all see the film. Mixing these two audiences has a further advantage: the cast and crew will be an extremely friendly audience and will provide a beneficial atmosphere for agents, distributors, and others at the screening.

Designate someone to stand by the door and check the names of attendees as they arrive. This is important because it will provide information to producer(s) who saw the film, so that they can follow up. Someone should be available to speak with distributors after the screening. If you do not have a producer's rep, this would most likely be the producer or the person best able to discuss the film and a potential deal.

IF YOU DO NOT GET A DISTRIBUTOR

If you do not get a distributor, you have a couple of options. Self-distribution is a tough row to hoe, but it may be worth the effort to get your film out to the world. Most likely, self-distribution will mean semi- or nontheatrical bookings, as opposed to real theatrical bookings. In today's market, it may be close to impossible to self-distribute a theatrical release. (We do not like to say that anything is impossible, but this may well be pretty close to it.) Because the marketplace is so glutted with films, it can even be difficult for the smaller distributors to get their slate of films booked in theaters. The mini-majors have more money to spend on their print and advertising budgets and can provide the exhibitor with a steadier flow of material. The larger distributors have the most bargaining power with theaters. However, if your film has had a successful run in the festival circuit, it is possible to book it at universities, colleges, museums, and organizations that have a particular interest in your film.

Another option is to self-distribute your film on video (or if it is a short, on the Internet). This is probably easier than self-distributing in theaters because you can access underground video rental stores all over the United States. Further, depending on the film, you may be able to make some sales to television, both domestic and foreign. If you have no contacts in this area, it is worth your while to commission a foreign sales agent or producer's representative to assist you with such sales. Although sales of independent films to foreign television are not as lucrative or widespread as they were in the early 1990s, this is still a feasible option, and it is a way for your film to be seen and possibly to recoup its costs, if only just a little. Often, the fees for television sales are negotiated on a per-minute basis. (See Appendix A for more on this subject.)

RECUTTING

Go back to the cutting room if you can afford it. See if you can make a deal with your editing facility or with another film that is still cutting their film for the use of their Avid for a week. With luck, your media is stored on drives and it may be easy enough to go back in and see what you can fix. Take some of the constructive criticism from audiences who have screened your film and see if reworking your film makes a difference. There are films that end up not getting out into the world as we might have hoped they would. You will have to determine when it is appropriate to stop trying to get the film out into the world and start on your next project.

DELIVERY LIST

Each distributor and/or cable or television outlet will have its own delivery list of all items they require you hand over to them once you have signed a contract. Typically, a delivery date will be established, and at least a portion of an advance would be paid once delivery is complete. Often, especially with a studio, the delivery list is long and involved, and some of the items on the list will be quite expensive to generate. If your original budget did not include deliverables, make a budget for the delivery items. They may cost as much as $300,000, depending on your music and other factors. The following list is an idea of the types of items that might be on a delivery list when you sell your film:

- Timed answer print
- Interpositive
- Internegative
- Continuity script
- TV/video master (some times in high-definition video)
- Trailer
- All music publishing and master licenses
- Errors-and-omissions (E&O) insurance
- Publicity materials: all production stills, production stories for press articles, and a list of full credits

The previous is not a complete list, but it should give you a sense of the types of items you will need to come up with for delivery.

11 A FINAL WORD

"If you want to make a movie and you have a dream, you do whatever you can to get it made. And if you have that kind of perseverance, the films will ring true because they are such an honest effort. It becomes a part of your life. If you follow through, usually those kind of films are the ones that surprise people out of left field. And you can look at Slacker *or* Crumb, In the Company of Men, *as just a few. Movies like* Safe, Welcome to the Dollhouse, *all of these people put these movies together on shoestrings and had tremendous success and launched careers. But it was probably the worst nightmare of their lives getting the money for the movies. It seemed to make the filmmaking even better because they had to be more creative."*

—Tom Bernard, president, Sony Pictures Classics

BREATHE—IT'S OVER

If you've completed your film, that is a huge feat. Don't underestimate what you have done. Now, grow thick skin, and do it quickly. No matter what your film is, there will be those who like it and those who do not. It is important to try to have some perspective on what you've done and to maintain an inner sense of accomplishment despite what may become of the project and despite what other's opinions about it may be. Opinions are just that.

It is hoped that your goals for the film, whatever they may be, will be realized. But if they aren't, assess what is realistic for the project (Lock a video deal? Make a cable television sale?), and move on to your next film. There is never any guarantee as to how a film will turn out. It is essential that we learn from the process and enjoy the journey. Focusing too much on results can lead to disappointment. Ideally, we continue to grow and learn as filmmakers and as people with each film we make, and from each experience we gain perspective, insight, experience, and a sense of accomplishment.

RELIEVE SOME STRESS

"All you can talk about is the movie. The movie, the movie, the movie . . ."

—Jon Favreau, Swingers

Need a break? If you're feeling stressed out and in need of a break from whatever chaos you're in the midst of, you may enjoy reading a couple letters that came through the *Swingers* production office.

Both letters are from Joan Favreau, Jon's grandmother, who played the Blue-Haired Lady at the $5 table in Las Vegas. Her participation in the film warmed all of our hearts. The first letter is one she sent to us right after production (Figure 11–1), and the other letter followed the *Swingers* premiere, which she traveled from Queens, New York, to Los Angeles to attend (Figure 11–2).

September 23, 1995

I was indeed surprised and actually thrilled to be asked to do a small part in Jonathan's movie. My son Charles, hearing this, immediately obtained a round-trip ticket to Las Vegas. On Tuesday, Charles drove me to the airport, but before we arrived he made a stop at an old-fashioned ice cream parlor. He ordered my favorite ice cream, topped with nuts and whipped cream. I enjoyed the surprise treat, and off we went to the airport. We arrived in plenty of time. Charles chatted with me and then wished me a pleasant trip.

The air trip was pleasant. I ordered a gin and tonic, making the flying trip a lark. Upon my arrival in Las Vegas, a handsome young man with windblown hair called out, "Joan Favreau!" as he was walking down the ramp towards me. I, with such relief, waved back at him and smiled. He introduced himself as Wally, and he tenderly took my hand and walked me through the terminal.

Outside the terminal was a cute red car with a stunning young lady called Nicole, who greeted me with a warm embrace. I knew right then and there this was going to be a great stint. They drove me through the Vegas strip, describing the large hotels and huge display of lights.

Upon arriving at the casino, the crew was having their evening meal. At my entrance, they all greeted me simultaneously, "Hi, Grandma Favreau!" I felt a warm and friendly feeling. Standing there was my grandson Jonathan, handsome and full of enthusiasm. He walked over to me after the crew gave me that warm welcome, and he hugged me tenderly They immediately fed me and told me I was to do my scene in about an hour.

Being well fed, I was turned over to the makeup man. I told him to make me beautiful. He tried. The wardrobe person dressed me in a lovely lavender-color suit. She then tied a white chiffon scarf around my neck, giving the entire outfit a smart look.

Not knowing much about the movie, Jon had a young man coach me. He coached me well. The scene was well done. The crew stood up clapping loudly and reassured me again and again. The cast continued shooting other scenes through the night.

What a delightful crew. All young, good looking, and willing to work hard. What amazed me most was the support and loyalty they have for Jon. I noticed just the reason: communication.

The next day was my big scene. We rehearsed over and over again at the blackjack table. At last, it was cast and done well. It truly was a joy doing that scene. The participants were a jolly group. We laughed and joked about Jon and Vince's part in the scene. It got so that each one had a story or an incident to tell. I pitched in, too.

Thursday was my free day. Jon made sure he left time from his busy schedule to take me to the famous strip. He called a cab, and we left for the sights on the strip. We arrived and walked along, looking in amazement at the bright lights, brilliant marquees, and signboards. To make the tour complete, we entered Caesar's Palace. It was magnificent. I thought I was back in Italy. The statues, the fountains, the boutiques, the blue-clouded moving ceiling—I was in awe of the grandeur of this superstructure. To complete this lovely visit to the strip, Jon ordered dinner. We sat under the lovely blue sky and in full view of the magnificent sights. Jon ordered an Italian meal for us, which was the typical order for the day. We ate and enjoyed. We now had to return to the hotel, where the crew was waiting for Jon for a scheduled scene. His crew reminds me of the Energizer Bunny. It keeps going, and going, and going . . .

I was now on my own. I gambled a bit, then remembered that I had a 6:30 A.M. plane flight. It was now 11:30 P.M., and a knock came at the door. I slipped on my robe and opened the door. It was one of the crewmen inviting me to join them in the room opposite my room. I went in and was served cake and a Coke. I watched them work. It was 3:30 A.M. When I realized I had to get to bed, but it was too late.

The wake-up call came through, so I dressed in a hurry. I met Wally and Nicole at the main desk. Nicole handed me a large container of orange juice, which I drank on my way to the airport. I said my good-bye to Nicole. Wally affectionately took my hand and again walked me through the terminal. He sat me down at my proper spot and kissed me good-bye.

It was a delightful trip back. At the end of the Kennedy terminal was my son Charles. He embraced me tenderly and was anxious to sit me down in the car and turn me on. I spoke the entire trip home, never stopping to take a breath, and my son Charles loved every moment of it.

Later the next day, I missed Jonathan's telephone call, but the tape said it all. He was pleased with my performance, concerned about the long and tiring trip home, and told me he loves me. I really was touched by his affection for me.

Love,

Grandma Favs

Figure 11–1 First letter from Joan Favreau

Swingers (The Premier)

March 21, 1996

Hi!!

When Charles and I stepped out of the car we noticed long lines of young and old people waiting to get into the theater. Never for one moment did we think they were waiting to see "SWINGERS". The theater was large. It soon was filled to capacity. Seated at least 1,000 and soon standing room only. We were escorted to our reserved seats. I felt a bit important. We met Nicole, she looked stunning with her new hairdo and her leather outfit. We also met with Cary Woods, the Producer and many others.

Soon the lights dimmed and all went silent. On the huge screen appeared MIRAMAX. It was very impressive. Then the opening credits. When JON FAVREAU'S name flashed alone on the big screen, his name seemed larger than life itself. My son Charles squeezed my hand which he was holding at the time. I was so moved for I knew I was surely blessed.

As the movie opened, the music was perfect. It was loud and a catching tune setting the audience up for a fun show. MIKE, who was Jonathan, did a remarkable performance. He was a down-hearted young man making the audience feel his pain. MIKE was a jilted lover. His friends tried very hard thruout the movie to change his moody attitude to a "Happy go lucky guy". They were so overly concerned that it made MIKE irritable thruout the picture.

TRENT, a handsome young man did a superb job of acting, specially his torrid love scene. At the height of one of the love scenes, MIKE was so desperate he wanted to make a phone call to see if his loved one had a kind word. He knocked at the very door that a heated love making was going on. TRENT opened the door, partly naked and threw a condom out to MIKE thinking he too was in a heated situation. The audience went wild. It was also a good laugh when the four cars followed one another after an unsuccessful evening with dames at the bars. We did laugh when MIKE went to the answering message machine to get repeated responses that continued to drive him mad. The audience loved him in that scene. No news for MIKE was not easy to live with. That gun scene was a bit frightening but it was done well.

As for my small part in the movie, I sure was no raving beauty but I can assure you my lavender suit looked great.

When MIKE finally made out with some dame and did some fast stepping on the dance floor, his friends and the audience cheered. Finally they saw a bright spark in the life of their friend. They now knew their job was well done. MIKE was back in the fold and ready to start living it up again.

I enjoyed,

Grandma

Figure 11–2 Second letter from Joan Favreau

APPENDIX A: RESOURCE GUIDE

REFERENCE BOOKS

Handbooks and Manuals

Carroll, Bonnie. *The Reel Directory: Northern California Guide to Film, Video, Multimedia.* Catati, CA: Reel Directory, 2002.

Honthaner, Eve Light. *The Complete Film Production Handbook,* Boston: Focal Press, 2001.

Mackaman, Julie. *Filmmakers Resource.* NY: Watson-Guptill, 1997. A guide to workshops, conferences, artist's colonies, and academic programs.

LA 411 Resource Guide. Professional reference guide by LA 411, 2002.

MPE Hand Guide. A semi-annual motion picture, TV, and theater directory. Tarrytown, NY: MPE Publications, Inc., 2003.

NYPG Handbook. New York: NYPG, Ltd, 2003.

Production Support Manuals

Litwak, Mark. *Contracts for the Film and Television Industry, Second Edition.* Beverly Hills, CA: Silman-James Press, 1998.

Litwak, Mark. *Dealmaking in the Film and Television Industry, Second Edition.* Beverly Hills, CA: Silman-James Press. Covers everything from negotiations to final contracts, 2002.

Singleton, Ralph S. *Film Budgeting.* Los Angeles: Lone Eagle Publishing, 1996.

Levison, Louise. *Filmmakers and Financing: Business Plans for Independents.* Boston: Focal Press, 2003.

Singleton, Ralph S. *Film Scheduling.* Los Angeles: Lone Eagle Publishing, 1997.

Singleton, Ralph S. *Film Scheduling/Film Budgeting Workbook.* Los Angeles: Lone Eagle Publishing, 1989.

Singleton, Ralph S. *Movie Production and Budget Forms . . . Instantly!* Los Angeles: Lone Eagle Publishing, 1985.

Festivals

Gaydos, Steven. *The Variety Guide to Film Festivals.* New York: Berkley Publishing, 1998.

Gore, Chris. *The Ultimate Film Festival Survival Guide,* 2001.

Langer, Adam. *The Film Festival Guide.* Chicago: Chicago Review Press. A guidebook for filmmakers, film buffs, and industry professionals. Includes the background of each festival and what premiered there, how to submit films, interviews with festival directors, and top-ten festivals, 2000.

Distribution

AFMA Member Profile Annual. Yearly report on member acquisition, production, and development. *www.afma.com/members.*

Hollywood Creative Directory. Santa Monica, CA, *www.hcdonline.com*

Mookis, Ioannis. *Self-Distribution Toolkit.* New York: AIVF, *www.aivf.org/resources/aivf_books.html.*

Legal

Donaldson, Michael. *Clearance and Copyright.* Beverly Hills, CA: Silman-James Press, 2003.

Litwak, Mark. *Contacts for the Film and Television Industry.* Los Angeles: Silman-James Press, 1998.

SUPPORT ORGANIZATIONS

Academy of Motion Picture Arts and Sciences
8949 Wilshire Blvd.
Beverly Hills, CA 90211-1972
Phone: 310/247-3000, Fax: 310/859-9619
Web site: *www.oscars.org*
E-mail: *ampas@oscars.org*

American Cinematheque
1800 N. Highland Ave., No. 717
Los Angeles, CA 90028
Phone: 323/466-3456, Fax: 323/461-9737
Web site: *www.americancinematheque.com*
E-mail: *info@americancinematheque.com*

American Film Marketing Association (AFMA)
10850 Wilshire Blvd., 9th Floor
Los Angeles, CA 90024-4321
Phone: 310/446-1000, Fax: 310/446-1600

Web site: *www.afma.com*
E-mail: *info@afma.com*

Anthology Film Archives
32 Second Ave.
New York, NY 10003
Phone: 212/505-5181, Fax: 212/477-2714
Web site: *www.anthologyfilmarchives.org*

Association of Independent Video and Filmmakers (AIVF)/
Foundation of Independent Video and Filmmakers (FIVF)
304 Hudson St., 6th Floor
New York, NY 10013
Phone: 212/807-1400, Fax: 212/463-8519
Web site: *www.aivf.org*
E-mail: *info@aivf.org*

Association of Independent Feature Film Producers,
Inc. (AIFFP)
P.O. Box 38755
Hollywood, CA 90038
Phone: 530/658-6061
Web site: *www.aiffp.org*
E-mail: *info@aiffp.org*

California Lawyers for the Arts
1641 18th St.
Santa Monica, CA 90404
Phone: 310/998-5590, Fax: 310/998-5594
Web site: *www.calawyersforthearts.org*
E-mail: *usercla@calawyersforthearts.org*

Filmmakers Alliance
965 North Fair Oaks Ave.
Pasadena, CA 91103
Phone: 626/791-6114
Web site: *www.Filmmakersalliance.org*

Film Arts Foundation
145 Ninth Street, No. 101
San Francisco, CA 94103
Phone: 415/552-8760, Fax: 415/552-0882
Web site: *www.filmarts.org*
E-mail: *info@ filmarts.org*

Filmmaker's Collaborative
29 Greene St.
New York, NY 10013
Phone: 212/966.3030, Fax: 212/965-9253
Web site: *www.filmmakers.org/projects.htm*
E-mail: *info@filmmakers.org*

Film Forum
209 W. Houston St.
New York, NY 10014
Phone: 212/627-2035, Fax: 212/627-2471
Web site: *www.filmforum.com*
E-mail: *filmforum@ filmforum.com*

Film/Video Arts
462 Broadway, Suite 520
New York, NY 10013
Phone: 212/941-8787, Fax: 212/219-8924
E-mail: *filmforum@filmforum.com*

Hudson Valley Film and Video Office
40 Garden St., 2nd Floor
Poughkeepsie, NY 12601
Phone: 914/473.0318, Fax: 914/473.0082
E-mail: *HVFF@aol.com*

Image Film & Video Center
75 Bennett Street
Atlanta, GA 30309
Phone: 404/352-4225, Fax: 404/352-0173
Web site: *www.imagefv.org*
E-mail: *imageinfo@imagefv.org*

IFP/Chicago
33 East Congress Parkway, Room 505
Chicago, IL 60605
Phone: 312/435-1825, Fax: 312/435-1828
E-mail: *infoifpmw@aol.com*

IFP/Los Angeles
8750 Wilshire Boulevard, 2nd Floor
Beverly Hills, CA 90211
Phone: 310/432-1200, Fax: 310/432-1203
E-mail: *www.ifp.org*

IFP/Miami
210 2nd Street
Miami, FL 33139
Phone: 305/538-8242
E-mail: *ifp.miami@bigfoot.com*

IFP/Minneapolis - St. Paul
401 N. 3rd St., Ste. 490
Minneapolis, MN 55401
Phone: 612/338-0871, Fax: 612/338-4747

IFP/New York
104 West 29th Street, 12th Floor
New York, NY 10001-5310
Phone: 212/465-8200, Fax: 212/465-8525
E-mail: *general information: ifpny@ifp.org*

IFP/Seattle
P.O. Box 20307
Seattle, WA 98102
Phone: 206/860-8490
E-mail: *general information: seattleinfo@ifp.org*

International Documentary Association
1201 West 5th Street, Suite M 320
Los Angeles, CA 90017-1461
Phone: 213/534-3600, Fax: 213/534-3610
Web site: *www.documentary.org*
E-mail: *info@documentary.org*

Independent Television Service (ITVS)
501 York Street
San Francisco, CA 94110
Phone: 415/356-8383, Fax: 415/356-8391
Web site: *www.itvs.org*
E-mail: *itvs@itvs.org*

Jerome Foundation
125 Park Square Court
400 Sibley Street
St. Paul, Minnesota 55101-1928
Phone: 651/224-9431, Fax: 651/224-3439
Web site: *www.jeromefdn.org*
E-mail: *info@jeromefdn.org*

The National Alliance for Media Arts and Culture (NAMAC)
145 Ninth St., Suite 250
San Francisco, CA 94103
Phone: 415/431-1391, Fax: 415/431-1392
Web site: *www.namac.org*
E-mail: *namac@namac.org*

National Video Resources, Inc.
73 Spring St., Suite 403
New York, NY 10012
Phone: 212/274-8080, Fax: 212/274-8081
Web site: *www.nvr.org*
E-mail: *NVRInfo@nvr.org*

New York Foundation for the Arts
155 Ave. of the Americas, 14th Floor
New York, NY 10013-1507
Phone: 212/366-6900, Fax: 212/366-1778
Web site: *www.nyfa.org*
E-mail: *nyfaweb@nyfa.org*

Public Broadcasting Service
1320 Braddock Pl.
Alexandria, VA 22314
Phone: 703/739-5000, Fax: 703/739-0775
Web site: *www.pbs.org*

Sundance Institute
8857 West Olympic Blvd.
Beverly Hills, CA 90211
Phone: 310/360-1981, Fax: 310/360-1969
Web site: *www.sundance.org*
Email: *la@sundance.org*

Utah Office Sundance Institute
P.O. Box 3630
Salt Lake City, UT 84110-3630
Phone: 801/328-3456, Fax: 801/575-5175
Web site: *www.institute@sundance.org*

Guilds and Unions

Directors Guild of America, Inc.
7920 Sunset Blvd.
Los Angeles, CA 90046
Phone: 310/289-2000, Fax: 310/289-2029
Web site: *www.dga.org*

Screen Actors Guild (Los Angeles)
5757 Wilshire Blvd.
Los Angeles, CA 90036
Phone: 323/954-1600, Fax: 323/549-6603
Web site: *www.sag.com*

Screen Actors Guild (New York)
360 Madison Avenue
New York, NY 10017
Phone: 212/944-1030, Fax: 212/944-6774

Writers Guild of America, East
555 W. 57th St., Suite 1230
New York, NY 10019
Phone: 212/767-7800, Fax: 212/582-1909
Web site: *www.wgaeast.org*
E-mail: *info@wga.east.org*

Writers Guild of America, West
7000 W. Third Street
Los Angeles, CA 90048
Phone: 323/951-4000, Fax: 323/782-4800
Web site: *www.wga.org*

U.S. DISTRIBUTORS

Angelika Entertainment Corp.
1261 Madison Ave.
New York, NY 10128
Phone: 212/996-8215, Fax: 212/876-4365
Web site: *www.angelikafilm.com*

Arrow Entertainment, Inc.
25 West 45th Street
New York, NY 10036
Phone: 212/398-9511, Fax: 212/398-9558
Web site: *www.arrowentertainment.visualnet.com*
E-mail: *arrow@arrowfilms.com*

Artisan Entertainment (Los Angeles)
2700 Colorado Avenue, 2nd floor
Santa Monica, CA 90404
Phone: 310/449-9200

Artisan Entertainment (New York)
157 Chambers St., 12th Floor
New York, NY 10007
Phone: 212/577-2400, Fax: 212/577-2890

Artistic License Films
101 West 79th Street, Suite 21C
New York, NY 10024
Phone: 212/265-9119, Fax: 212/262-9299
E-mail: *info@artlic.com*

Cowboy Pictures
13 Laight Street, 6th Floor
New York, NY 10013
Phone: 212/925-7800, Fax: 212/965-5655
E-mail: *info@cowboypictures.com*

Fine Line Features (Los Angeles)
116 N. Robertson Blvd., No. 200
Los Angeles, CA 90048
Phone: 310/854-5811, Fax: 310/854-1824
Web site: *www.FLF.com*

Fine Line Features (New York)
888 Seventh Ave., 20th Floor
New York, NY 10106
Phone: 212/649-4800, Fax: 212/956-1942

Fireworks Pictures
421 South Beverly Drive, 7th Floor
Beverly Hills, 90212
Phone: 310/789-4700, Fax: 310/789-4747
E-mail: *info@fireworkspix.com*

Fox Searchlight Pictures (Los Angeles)
10201 W. Pico Blvd., Bldg. 38
Los Angeles, CA 90035
Phone: 310/369-4402, Fax: 310/369-2359

Fox Searchlight Pictures (New York)
1211 Ave. of the Americas, 16th Floor
New York, NY 10036
Phone: 212/556-8258, Fax: 212/556-8606

IFC Films
11 Pen Plaza
New York, NY 10001
Web site: *www.ifcfilms.com*

Lions Gate Entertainment
4553 Glencoe Ave., Suite 200
Marina Del Ray, CA 90292
E-mail: *feedback@lgecorp.com*

Lot 47 Films
116 West 23rd Street, Suite 500
New York, NY 10011
Phone: 646/375-2189, Fax: 646/375-2342

Miramax Films (Los Angeles)
8439 Sunset Blvd.
West Hollywood, CA 90069
Phone: 323/822-4200, Fax: 323/845-4211

Miramax Films (New York)
375 Greenwich St.
New York, NY 10013
Phone: 212/941-3800, Fax: 212/941-3949

New Line Cinema (Los Angeles)
116 N. Robertson Blvd., No. 200
Los Angeles, CA 90048
Phone: 310/854-5811, Fax: 310/854-1824

New Line Cinema (New York)
888 Seventh Ave., 19th Floor
New York, NY 10106
Phone: 212/649-4900, Fax: 212/649-4966
Web site: *www.newline.com*

New Yorker Films
85 5th Avenue, 11th floor
New York, NY 10003
Phone: 212/645-4600, Fax: 212/645-3030
Web site: *www.newyorkerfilms.com*
E-mail: *info@newyorkerfilms.com*

Newmarket Films (Los Angeles)
202 North Canon Drive
Beverly Hills, CA 90210
Phone: 310/858-7473

Newmarket Films (New York)
1180 6th Avenue, 14th Floor
New York, NY 10036

Palm Pictures (Los Angeles)
8981 Sunset Blvd. No. 102
Los Angeles, CA 90069
Phone: 310/278-3071, Fax: 310/278-3091

Palm Pictures (New York)
601 W. 26th Street, 11th floor
New York, NY 10001
Phone: 212/320-3600, Fax: 212/320-3709

Paramount Classics
5555 Melrose Ave.,
Chevalier Bldg., No. 212
Hollywood, CA 90038
Phone: 323/956-2000, Fax: 323/862-1212

Phaedra Cinema
5455 Wilshire Blvd.
Los Angeles, CA 90036
Phone: 323/938-9610, Fax: 323/938-9731

Regent Pictures
1401 Ocean Ave., No. 300
Santa Monica, CA 90401

Samuel Goldwyn Films, LLC (Los Angeles)
10203 Santa Monica Blvd.
Los Angeles, CA 90067

Samuel Goldwyn Films, LLC (New York)
560 W. 43rd St., No. 32E
New York, NY 10036
Phone: 212/594-3334, Fax: 212/268-9289
E-mail: *bijou@ix.netcom.com*

Screen Gems
1223 North 23rd Street
Wilmington, NC 28405
Phone: 910/343-3500, Fax: 910/343-3574
Web site: *www.screengems-studios.com*

Seventh Art Releasing
7551 Sunset Blvd., No. 104
Los Angeles, CA 90046
Phone: 323/845-1455, Fax: 323/845-4717
Web site: *www.7thart.com*
E-mail: *seventhart@7thart.com*

SoHo Entertainment, Inc.
105 Greene St.
New York, NY 10012
Web site: *www.sohoent.com*
E-mail: *HKsoho@aol.com*

Sony Pictures Classics
550 Madison Ave., 8th Floor
New York, NY 10022
Phone: 212/833-8833, Fax: 212/833-8844
Web site: *www.spe.sony.com/classics*
E-mail: *sonyclassics@spe.sony.com*

Strand Releasing
1460 Fourth St., No. 302
Santa Monica, CA 90401
Phone: 310/395-5002, Fax: 310/395-2502
Web site: *www.strandrel.com*
E-mail: *strand@strandrel.com*

Stratosphere Entertainment
767 Fifth Ave., No. 4700
New York, NY 10153
Phone: 212/605-1010, Fax: 212/813-0300

Think Films
451 Greenwich Street, 7th Floor
New York, NY 10013
Phone: 646/214-7908, Fax: 626/214-7907

Troma Entertainment, Inc.
733 Ninth Ave.
New York, NY 10019
Phone: 212/757-4555, Fax: 212/399-9885
Web site: *www.troma.com*
E-mail: *troma.com*

Unapix Films
200 Madison Ave., 24th Floor
New York, NY 10016

United Artists
2500 Broadway Street, Bldg. B201
Santa Monica, CA 90404
Phone: 310/449-3370

Universal Focus (Los Angeles)
100 Universal City Plaza Bldg. 2160-7N
Universal City, CA 91608
Phone: 818/777-1000

Universal Focus (New York)
417 Canal Street, 4th Floor
New York, NY 10013

WinStar TV and Video
419 Park Ave. S.
New York, NY 10016
Phone: 212/686-6777, Fax: 212/545-9931
Web site: *www.winstarnewmedia.com*

Zeitgeist Films, Ltd.
247 Centre St., 2nd Floor
New York, NY 10013
Phone: 212/274-1989, Fax: 212/274-1644
Web site: *www.zeitgeistfilm.com*
E-mail: *mail@zeitgeistfilm.com*

Wellspring
419 Park Ave. S., 20th Floor
New York, NY 10016
Phone: 212/686-6777, Fax: 212/685-2625
Web site: *www.wellspring.com*

LEGAL INFORMATION

Barab, Vaughan, and Kline
Production Counsel: Handles acquiring rights, incorporation, dealing with unions, hiring actors, music, distribution, and so on. Serves as production counsel for about 25 movies per year but does not do securities work; 20-percent discount to IFP members.
Phone: 310/859-6644.

Michael Donaldson, Esq.
Flexible rates.
Phone: 310/273-5394.

Fredricks and Vonderhorst, Law Offices
Full-service law firm for production companies, including financing, production, and distribution. Specializes in finding European cofinancing for projects that already have small deals with American companies or have stars or recognizable names attached. Offers representation of writers and directors but not actors or musicians. 20-percent discount on all fees to IFP members.
Phone: 310/472-1122.

Mark Litwak Law Offices
20-percent discount on all fees to IFP members.
Phone: 310/859-9595.

Pierce Gorman
New open-door policy.
Phone: 310/788-3939. Fax: 310/778-3950.

Surpin, Mayersohn, and Edelstone
Entertainment Law: Flexible rates.
Phone: 310/552-1808.

Harris Tulchin
Full-service entertainment attorney. Offers representation of writers, directors, and actors. Financing and distribution agreements. Acts as producer's rep. Flexible rates, and 10-percent discount to IFP members.
Phone: 310/914-7979.

Other Resources

Beverly Hills Bar Association
Attorney Referral Center: 310/553-6644.

Los Angeles County Bar Association
Attorney Referral Center: 818/880-0120.

FILM FESTIVAL AND MARKETS CALENDAR

The information provided in this section is provided by Mark Litwak, attorney-at-law.

January

Gothenburg Film Festival
Box 7079 S-40232 G^teborg, Sweden
Phone: (46) 31 410 546, Fax: (46) 31 410 063
Web site: *www.goteborg.filmfestival.org*
E-mail: *goteborg@filmfestival.org*

Palm Springs International Film Festival
1700 E. Tahquitz Canyon Way, No. 3
Palm Springs, CA 92262
Phone: 760/322-2930, Fax: 760/322-4087
Web site: *http://www.psfilmfest.org*
E-mail: *info@psfilmfest.org*

Rotterdam International Film Festival
P.O. Box 21696 3001
AR Rotterdam, The Netherlands
Phone: (31) 10 890 9090, Fax: (31) 10 890 9091
Web site: *www.filmfestivalrotterdam.com*
E-mail: *programme@filmfestivalrotterdam.com*

Slamdance Film Festival
5634 Melrose Ave.
Los Angeles, CA 90038
Phone: 323/466-1786, Fax: 323/466-1784
Web site: *www.slamdance.com*
E-mail: *mail@slamdance.com*

Sundance Film Festival
P.O. Box 16450
Salt Lake City, UT 84116
Phone: 801/328-3456, Fax: 801/575-5175
Web site: *www.festival.sundance.org*

Festival submission: Feature Film Program Application, Sundance Institute, 8857 W. Olympic Blvd., Beverly Hills, CA 90211 (application available online)

February

American Film Market (AFM)
10850 Wilshire Blvd., 9th Floor
Los Angeles, CA 90024
Phone: 310/446-1000, Fax: 310/446-1600
Web site: *http://www.afma.com*
E-mail: *info@afma.com*

Berlin International Film Festival
5 D-10785 Berlin
Phone: +49· 30· 25 920 + ext., Fax: +49· 30· 25 920· 299
Web site: *www.berlinale.de*
E-mail: *info@berlinale.de*

Film entry: Internationale Filmfestspiele Berlin Abteilung Programm, Potsdamer Strasse 5 D-10785, Berlin
Phone: +49· 30· 259 20· 222, Fax: +49· 30· 259 20· 299
E-mail: *program@berlinale.de*
Contact: Dieter Kosslick, Director, Internationale Filmfestspiele Berlin / Berlin International Film Festival.

CineMart
P.O. Box 21696 3001
AR Rotterdam, The Netherlands
Phone: (31) 10890 9090, Fax: (31) 10 890-9091
Web site: *www.filmfestivalrotterdam.com*
E-mail: *cinemart@filmfestivalrotterdam.com*

Portland International Film Festival Northwest Film Centre
1219 S.W. Park Ave.
Portland, OR 97205
Phone: 503/221-1156, Fax: 503/294-0874
Web site: *http://www.nwfilm.org*
E-mail: *info@nwfilm.org*

March

New Directors/New Films
Film Society of Lincoln Center
70 Lincoln Center Plaza, 4th Floor
New York, NY 10023
Phone: 212/875-5610, Fax: 212/875-5636
Web site: *http://www.filmlinc.com*
E-mail: *sbensman@filmlinc.com*

Santa Barbara International Film Festival
1216 State St., No. 710
Santa Barbara, CA 93101
Phone: 805/963-0023, Fax: 805/962-2524
Web site: *www.sbfilmfestcal*
E-mail: *sbiff@west.net*

South by Southwest (SXSW) Film Festival
P.O. Box 4999
Austin, TX 78765
Phone: 512/467-7979, Fax: 512/451-0754
Web site: *www.sbfilimfestcal.com*
E-mail: *sxsw@sxsw.com*

April

Brussels International Film Festival
Chaussèe de Louvain 30 1210
Brussels, Belgium
Phone: (32) 2 22739 80, Fax: (32) 2 21818 60
Web site: *http://www.netribution.co.uk/festivals/-BrusselsintFF.html*
E-mail: *infoffb@netcity.be*

Gen Art Film Festival
New York
133 West 25th Street, 6th Floor
New York, NY 10001
Phone: 212/255-7300, Fax: 212/255-7400
Web site: *www.genart.org*
E-mail: *info@genart.org*

Los Angeles
292 S. La Cienega Blvd, Suite 317
Beverly Hills, CA 90211
Phone: 310/360-0141, Fax: 310/360-7032
E-mail: *losangeles@genart.org*

Miami
407 Lincoln Road, Suite 706
Miami Beach, FL 33139
Phone: 305/659-8200, Fax: 305/659-8220

Chicago
737 North May Street
Chicago, IL 60622
Phone: 312/228-1701, Fax: 312/2229-1703
E-mail: *Chicago@genart.org*

San Francisco
690 5th Street, Suite 105
San Francisco, CA 94107
Phone: 415/284-9400
E-mail: *info@genartsf.org*

Mip TV International Television Program Market Reed Midem Organization
P.O. Box 572
11 rue du Colonel Pierre Avia 75726 Paris
Cedex 15, France
Phone: (33) 1 4190 4580, Fax: (33) 1 4190 4570
Web site: *http://www.miptv.com*

San Francisco International Film Festival
39 Mesa Street, Suite 110, The Presidio
San Francisco, CA 94129
Phone: 415/561-5000, Fax: 415/561-5099
Web site: *www.sfiff.org*
E-mail: *info@sffs.org*

Taos Talking Picture Festival
1337 Gusdorf Road
Taos, NM 87571
Phone: 505/751-0637, Fax: 505/751-7385
Web site: *www.ttpix.org*
E-mail: *ttpix@taosnet.com*
Applications available online.

May

Cannes International Film Festival (Feature and short films)
3, rue Amelie 75007
Paris, France
Phone: 33 (0) 1 53 59 61 71, Fax: 33 (0) 1 53 59 61 70
E-mail: *maria.sjoberg@festival-cannes.fr*
Web site: *www.festival-cannes.com*

Seattle International Film Festival
911 Pine Street, No. 607
Seattle, WA 98101
Phone: 206/464-5830, Fax: 206/264-7919
Web site: *www.seattlefilm.com*

Tribeca Film Festival
375 Greenwich Street
New York, NY 10013
Phone: 212/941-2400, Fax: 212/941-3939
Web site: *www.tribecafilmfestival.org*

June

Banff Television Festival
1350 Railway Ave.
Canmore, Alberta T1W 3E3, Canada
Phone: 403/678-9260, Fax: 403/678-9269
Web site: *www.btvf.com*
E-mail: *info@banfftvfest.com*

Florida Film Festival Enzian Theater
1300 S. Orlando Avenue
Maitland, FL 32751
Phone: 407/629-1088, Fax: 407/629-6870
Web site: *www.floridafilmfestival.org*
E-mail: *filmfest@gate.net*

IFP Los Angeles Film Festival
8750 Wilshire Blvd., 2nd Floor
Beverly Hills, CA 90210
Phone: 323/951-7090
Web site: *www.lafilmfest.com*

Maui Film Festival
P.O. 790669
Paia, HI 96779
Phone: 808/579-9244, Fax: 808/579-9552
Web site: *www.mauifilmfestival.com*

Monte Carlo Television Festival and Market
4, Blvd. du Jardin Exotique MC98000 Monaco
Phone: 377/9310 4060, Fax: 377/9350-7014
Web site: *www.tvfestival.monaco.mc/*

Nantucket Film Festival
1633 Broadway, Suite 14-334
New York, NY 10019
Phone: 212/708-1278, Fax: 211/654-4784
Web site: *www.nantucketfilmfestival.org*
E-mail: *ackfest@aol.com*

Sydney Film Festival
P.O. Box 950 Glebe,
NSW 2037, Australia
Phone: 02 9571 6766, Fax: 02 9692 8793
Web site: *www.sydneyfilmfestival.org*
E-mail: *info@sydneyfilmfestival.cor*

Troia International Film Festival Forum
Luisa Todi Av. Luisa Todi, 65 2902 Setubal 2900-461
Portugal
Phone: (351) 65 525 908, Fax: (351) 65 525 681
Web site: *www.festoria.pt*
E-mail: *festoria@mail.eunet.pt*

July

Galway Film Fleadh Cluain Mhuire
Monivea Rd.
Galway, Ireland
Phone: (353) 91 751 655, Fax: (353) 91 770 746
E-mail: *gafleadh@iol.ie*
Web site: *www.galwayflimfleadh.com*

Karlovy Vary International Film Festival
Panska 1 Prague 1, 110 00 Czech Republic
Phone: (420) 2 2423 5413, Fax: (420) 2 2423 3408
Web site: *www.kviff.com*
E-mail: *festival@kviff.com*

Melbourne International Film Fest
P.O. Box 2206
Fitzroy Mail Centre, Victoria 3065, Australia
Phone: (61) 3 9417 2011, Fax: (61) 3 9417 3804
Web site: *www.melbournefilmfestival.com.au*
E-mail: *miff@melbournefilmfestival.com.au*

Wine Country Film Fest
Box 303
Glen Ellen, CA 95442
Phone: 707/996-2536, Fax: 707/996-6964

Web site: *www.winecountryflimfest.com*
E-mail: *wcfilmfest@aol.com*

August

Edinburgh International Film Festival Filmhouse
88 Lothian Rd. Edinburgh EH3BZ, Scotland
Phone: (44) 131 228 4051, Fax: (44) 131 229 5501
Web site: *www.edfilmfest.org.uk*
E-mail: *info@edfilmfest.org.uk*

Locarno International Film Festival
Via Luini Locarno CH-6601 Locarno, Switzerland
Phone: (41) 91 756 2121, Fax: (41) 91 756 2149
Web site: *www.pardo.ch*
E-mail: *headprogram@pardo.ch*

Montreal World Film Festival
1432 de Bleury St. Montreal, Canada H3A 2J1
Phone: 514/848-3883, Fax: 514/848-3886
Web site: *www.ffm-montreal.org/en_index.html*
E-mail: *info@ffm-montreal.org*

Venice Film Festival
La Biennale di Venezia Settore Cinema E Spetta Colo Televisivo CaíGiustinian,
1364 San Marco, 30124 Venice, Italy
Phone: (39) 41 521 8711, Fax: (39) 41 523 6374
Web site: *www.labiennale.org*
E-mail: *das@labiennale.com*

September

Boston Film Festival
P.O. Box 516
Hull, MA 02045
Phone: 718/925-1373, Fax: 718/925-3132
Web site: *www.bostonfilmfestival.org*
E-mail: *gemsad@aol.com*

Breckenridge Festival of Film
150 W. Adams
Breckenridge, CO 80424
Phone: 970/453-6200, Fax: 970/453-2692
Web site: *www.breckfilmfest.com*
E-mail: *programming@breckfilmfest.com*

Deauville Festival of American Films Le Public Systeme Cinema
40 rue Anatole Levallois-Perret Cedet Cedex 04 F-92594 France
Phone: (33) 1 41 34 20 33, Fax: (33) 1 41 34 20 77
Web site: *www.festival-deauville.com*

IFP Market (No Borders)
104 W. 29th St., 12th Floor
New York, NY 10001
Phone: 212/465-8200, Fax: 212/465-8525
Web site: *www.ifp.org*
E-mail: *ifpny@ifp.org*

Mipcom, Reed Midem Organization
P.O. Box 572
11 rue du Colonel Pierre Avia 75726 Paris Cedex 15, France
Phone: (33) 1 4190 4580, Fax: (33) 1 4190 4570
Web site: *http://www.mipcom.com*

New York Film Festival
70 Lincoln Center Plaza
New York, NY 10023
Phone: 212/875-5638, Fax: 212/875-5636
Web site: *www.filmlinc.com*

San Sebastian International Film Festival
Apartado de Correos 397 20080 Donostia-San Sebastian, Spain
Phone: (34) 43 481 212, Fax: (34) 43 481 218
Web site: *www.sansebastianfestival.ya.com*
E-mail: *ssiff@sansebastianfestival.com*

Temecula Valley International Film Festival
27945 Jefferson Ave., Suite 104A
Temecula, CA 92590
Phone: 909/699-6267, Fax: 909/301-1414
Web site: *www.tviff.com*

Telluride Film Festival (feature submissions only)
2600 10th Street, No. 438
Berkeley, CA 94710
Phone: 603/433-9202, Fax: 603/433-9206
Web site: *www.telluridefilmfest.com*
E-mail: *tellufilm@aol.com*

Toronto International Film Festival
2 Carlton St., Suite 1600
Toronto, Ontario, Canada M5B 1J3
Phone: 416/934-3232, Fax: 416/967-7669
Web site: *www.bell.ca/filmfest*

Vancouver International Film Festival/Film and TV Trade Show 410-1008 Homer Street
Vancouver BC, Canada V6B 2X1
Phone: 604/685-0260, Fax: 604/688-8221
Web site: *www.viff.org*
E-mail: *viff@viff.org*

October

Fort Lauderdale International Film Festival
1314 East Las Olas Blvd., No. 007
Fort Lauderdale, FL 33301
Phone: 954/760-9898, Fax: 954/760-9099
Web site: *www.fliff.com*
E-mail: *info@fliff.com*

Hamptons International Film Festival
3 Newtown Mews
East Hampton, NY 11937
Phone: 516/324-4600, Fax: 516/324-5116
Contact: Bruce Feinberg
Web site: *www.hamptonsfest.org*
E-mail: *hiff@hamptonsfest.org*

Heartland Film Festival
200 S. Meridian, Suite 200
Indianapolis, IN 46225
Phone: 317/464-9405, Fax: 317/464-9409
Web site: *www.heartlandfilmfest.org*
E-mail: *info@heartlandfilmfestival.org*

Hollywood Film Festival
433 N. Camden Dr., Suite 600
Beverly Hills, CA 90210
Phone: 310/288-1882, Fax: 310/475-0193
Web site: *www.hollywoodfestival.com*
E-mail: *awards@hollywoodfestival.com*

Mifed Fiera Milano Largo Domodossola
1 200 Rassenge Spa Foro Buonaparte 65 Milan, 20121 Italy
Phone: (39) 02 480 12912, Fax: (39) 02 499 77020
Contact: Elena Lloyd
Web site: *www.fmd.it/mifed*
E-mail: *mifed@fmd.it*

Mill Valley Film Festival
38 Miller Ave., Suite 6
Mill Valley, CA 94941
Phone: 415/383-5256, Fax: 415/383-8606
Contact: Zoe Elton, Director of Programming
Web site: *www.mvff.com*
E-mail: *info@finc.org*

Mipcom, Reed Midem Organization
P.O. Box 572
11 rue du Colonel Pierre 75726 Paris Cedex 15, France
Phone: (33) 1 4190 4580, Fax: (33) 1 4190 4570
Contact: Andre Vaillant

Sao Paulo International Film Festival
Al Lorena 937, CJ 303 01424-001 Sao Paulo, Brazil
Phone: (55) 11 883 5137, Fax: (55) 11 853 7936
Contact: Leon Cakoff
Web site: *http://www.mostra.org*
E-mail: *info@mostra.org*

Vancouver International Film Festival
410-1008 Homer Street Vancouver BC, Canada V6B 2X1
Phone: 604/685-0260, Fax: 604/688-8221
Web site: *www.viff.org*
E-mail: *viff@viff.org*

November

American Film Institute (AFI) Los Angeles International Film Festival
2021 N. Western Ave.
Los Angeles, CA 90027
Phone: 323/856-7707, Fax: 323/462-4049

French Film Festival
12 Sunbury Place Edinburgh EH4 3BY
Phone: (44) 131 255 6191, Fax: (44) 131 225 6971
Web site: *www.frenchfilmfestival.org.uk*
E-mail: *fff@frenchfilmfestival.org.uk*

Gijon International Film Festival
Paseo de Begona, 24, entlo. P.O. Box 76, 33201 Gijon, Spain
Phone: 34 (9) 8534 3739, Fax: 34 (9) 8535 4152
Web site: *www.gijonfilmfestival.com*
E-mail: *festivalgijon@telecable.es*

Hawaii International Film Festival
001 Bishop St., Pacific Tower, Suite 745
Honolulu, HI 96813
Phone: 808/528-3456, Fax: 808/528-1410
Web site: *www.hiff.org*
E-mail: *ale@hiff.org or media@hiff.org*

International Documentary Film Festival Amsterdam
(IDFA) Kleine-Gartmanplantsoen 10 1017 RR Amsterdam, The Netherlands
Phone: (31) 20 627 3329, Fax: (31) 20 638 5388
Web site: *www.ifda.com*
E-mail: *www.info@idfa.nl*

International Film Festival
Mannheim-Heidelberg Collini-Center Galerie, 68161 Mannheim, Germany
Phone: (49) 0 621 102 943, Fax: (49) 0 621 291 564
Web site: *www.mannheim-filmfestival.com*
E-mail: *ifmh@mannheim-filmfestival.com*

London Film Festival
National Film Theatre, South Bank, Waterloo, London
SE1 8XT UK
(44) 207 815 1322, Fax: (44) 207 633 0786
Web site: *www.rlff.com*
E-mail: *sarah.lutton@bfi.org.uk*

Northwest Film and Video Festival
1219 S.W. Park Ave.
Portland, OR 97205
Phone: 503/221-1156, Fax: 503/226-4842
Web site: *www.nwfilm.com*
E-mail: *info@nwfilm.org*

Southern African International Film and Television Market
P.O. Box 52120
Waterfront, 8002, South Africa
Phone: (27) (0)21 430 8160, Fax: (27) (0)21 430 8186
Web site: *www.sithengi.co.za*
E-mail: *info@sithengi.co.za*

Tokyo International Film Festival
Competitions Section
Nippon Cine Arts Co., Ltd.
2-5 Honmura-cho, Ichigaya, Shinjuku-ku Tokyo 162-0845, Japan
Fax: (81) 3 3268-5235
Web site: *www.tiff-jp.net*

December

Mip Asia Reed Midem Organization
P.O. Box 572
11 rue du Colonel Pierre 75726 Paris Cedex 15, France
Phone: (33) 1 4190 4400, Fax: (33) 1 4190 4409
Web site: *http://www.mipasia.com*

GLOSSARY

Above-the-Line Costs. In a budget, the expenses that relate specifically to the creative components of the film. The story rights, writer, director, producer(s), and cast are all considered to be above-the-line costs. (Compare *below-the-line costs.*)

Actualize. To compare actual costs against original anticipated costs. At the end of the show, after all returns have been made and final invoices have been received, you must actualize the budget to determine how much money you have actually spent compared to how much you anticipated spending for each line item. This is how you will account for any overages or shortages.

AD Kit. A portable file box that the assistant director brings to the set each day that contains forms, schedules, contracts, reports, paperwork, lists, and so on. The AD kit functions as a mini filing cabinet with paperwork that the AD may need to refer to, fill out, or provide while on the set.

ADR. See *Automated Dialogue Replacement.*

Agency Fee. The 10 percent fee that each cast member pays his or her agent. It is common practice within the industry for the production to pay the agency fee in addition to the actor's salary.

Allow. Money allocated for a given expense within a budget line item, the exact cost of which has not yet been determined. (Compare *Flat Fee.*)

Assistant Director (AD). The AD assists the director on the set and is commander of the set. The assistant director designs the final shooting schedule and works closely with the director. He or she communicates directly with the actors and the crew, organizes the set, and keeps the production on schedule. The AD is also responsible for call sheets, Exhibit G forms, production reports, schedule changes, meal breaks, overtime, accident reports, and so on.

Automated Dialogue Replacement (ADR). ADR substitutes or adds dialogue to your film after it has been shot. After you have been in the editing room, you can determine which lines of dialogue need to be rerecorded because they are unclear and which additional lines of dialogue are needed in the film. ADR sessions take place after the shoot has wrapped. You will need to determine which actors are needed for ADR after you determine your needs. (Also called *additional dialogue recording, advanced dialogue replacement,* and *looping.*)

Bag. A lightproof sack used to store the film as a precaution to keep it from being exposed to light.

Below-the-Line Costs. In a budget, the expenses that refer to the manual labor or technical aspects of the film. Crew, equipment, locations, props, wardrobe, sound, and transportation are all below-the-line costs. (Compare *above-the-line costs.*)

Blanket Permit. A single permit that is secured for filming at several locations within the city's filming zone and within close proximity to one another. A blanket permit can save you money because you will not need a separate permit for each of your locations. Contact the permit office of the city in which you are filming to determine if you can obtain a blanket permit for your locations.

Box Rental. See *Kit Rental.*

Breakdown. Identifying all of your characters, locations, extras, vehicles, props, and so on, for a given scene and putting this information on a breakdown sheet. You will break down each page of your script to account for and properly schedule and budget your film. Once you have a breakdown sheet for each scene in your script, you will be ready to begin creating your shooting schedule.

Call Sheet. A form used to log the daily call times issued to the cast and crew during production. The front of the call sheet lists the director, producer(s), location, weather, interior/exterior location, scene, cast, and special equipment needed for a particular day. The back of the call sheet lists each cast and crew member and the time he or she is needed on the set.

Can. A container for storing film. You will need extra film cans on the set for downloading shot film, short ends, recanning, and so on. Make sure that you have the right size cans for your film loads.

Catering. The meals provided to cast and crew members on the set during production. (Compare *Craft Service.*)

Chain of Title. Documents that show proof of ownership of a script or story from its beginnings. Among the documents that might be included in a chain of title are the certificate of copyright, the option/purchase agreement, and the writer's agreement, if there is one.

Chart of Accounts. A list of the account codes that correspond to each line item in the budget. Use these codes when actualizing the budget, writing checks, and coding petty cash envelopes.

Clone. A copy of a digital tape created as a backup to the original

Company Move Day. A day on which the production moves from one location to another. Company moves must be carefully factored into your schedule and well planned because they can require a fair amount of time.

Completion Bond. A bond that is often required when a film's financing is secured through an independent film company or a bank. This insurance policy serves as a guarantee to the financing entity that the film will be completed. A completion bond is usually computed at 3 percent of the budget total.

Contingency. Money, usually budgeted at 10 percent of the below-the-line costs, that the completion bond company requires that you have. Contingency serves as a cushion should there be cost overruns on your film. It also works as an insurance policy for the completion bond company. A higher contingency may be required for larger-budget films.

Continuity. Tracking and accounting for all of the details and elements within each scene shot, assuring the continuity of the film. Because films are not shot in proper order from the first scene to the last, special care must be paid to the continuity of the film. It is essential to have a record of the look of each actor and the design of each set for reference to maintain continuity.

Continuity Notebook. A notebook used to help maintain a film's continuity. It includes photos of actors and sets, the script supervisor's notes, and lined pages of the script, all of which are essential to the editor. A continuity notebook will allow you to recreate how an actor was dressed and made up so if you have reshoots, the script days will match.

Contractual Charges. The costs that are applied to the budget as percentages of the overall budget, such as the completion bond, contingency, overhead, and insurance.

Core. A hard piece of plastic found in the center of the film roll that keeps the film rolled properly.

Craft Service. The snacking and beverage station available on the set throughout production. (Compare *Catering.*)

Dailies. Either the work print or the digital version (depending on how the film will be edited) of all of the film shot in a given day. Typically, the director, the director of photography, the producer, and others may view the dailies each day.

Day-Out-of-Days Sheet. A form that indicates which days each element of a production will be needed. You can prepare a day-out-of-days sheet for your props, extras, vehicles, locations, actors, and special effects, for example.

Day Player. Any actor who works three or fewer consecutive days. (Compare *Weekly Player.*)

Deferral Agreement. An agreement between the producer and a crew or cast member in which money is deferred until a later date. A deferral agreement is a good way to signify to crew or cast members that *if* a low-budget film makes money down the line, they will be compensated. Arriving at an appropriate deferral amount for each crew member is somewhat arbitrary. We take the difference between what the crew member is actually paid and what we would have liked to have paid him or her had the budget been higher, and attach a small premium to compensate the crew member for contributing his or her time at a cut rate.

Delivery. The process of transferring a film over to a distribution company after it has been completed. In addition to the film itself, delivery requirements may include proof of errors-and-omissions insurance, paperwork and contracts, proof of chain of title, and documentation of music clearance.

Domestic Production-Distribution Deal (P-D deal). Financing given to a firm by a production company that can guarantee a theatrical release prior to production. If you can make a domestic distribution deal with a company, anticipate that the money they give you for the domestic rights to your film should cover between 40 percent and 60 percent of your negative cost.

Dubbing. The process of combining all of the various sound elements (dialogue, music, and effects) on a dubbing stage while watching the film. Most films are mixed into four analog channels (left, center, right, and surround). This is referred to as *matrix stereo.* (Also called *mix.*)

Equity Financing. Hard cash invested in a film by a company or an individual—be it a family member, friend, or professional investor—in exchange for either rights or profit points.

Errors-and-Omissions (E&O) Insurance. Insurance that protects the distributor against assuming any legal liabilities by purchasing the film. E&O insurance protects the production company or distributor from liability lawsuits for slander, unauthorized use of the film's title, using living people's names, and copyright infringement. If you secure a distributor, E&O insurance will be a delivery requirement.

Expendables. Smaller items, other than equipment, that can be rented cheaply, usually from the same vendor. You may need to purchase or rent certain items to shoot at a given location. Examples include items such as wardrobe steamers, wardrobe racks, cones, bullhorns, tables, chairs, desks, director's chairs, rope, bungee cords, coffee urns, coolers, craft service equipment, tablecloths, handcarts for carrying equipment, hangers, and makeup tables.

Extra. An actor who is required in a shot but has no speaking role. Extras are important to the look and feel of a film and create the atmosphere.

Favored Nations. A term used to indicate that a cast or crew member will receive treatment on par with the best that the producer is offering anyone else on the set, but not better. It refers in particular to pay and to perks (dressing rooms, travel, accommodations, and so on).

Fine Cut. The cut of the film before the final cut and after the rough cut.

First Composite Answer Print. A print that results from the first color timing pass and marries, or combines, the picture with any opticals and the soundtrack.

Flat Fee. When the cost remains the same regardless of how many weeks it ultimately takes to complete filming or of how much overtime is worked. Crew compensation and equipment rental can be arranged on the basis of a weekly fee or a flat fee. (Compare *Allow.*)

Foley. The sounds effects added to a film to help communicate the full effect of each scene, consisting of either sounds that were not clean off the production track and must be replaced, or sounds that must be added to the film. A foley artist uses props to create sounds such as kissing, rain, and footsteps on a sound stage while matching it to the picture.

Foreign Presales. The sale of the rights to a picture on a territory-by-territory basis before the film is actually shot.

Fringe. Any cost that is above and beyond a central cost. For example, sales taxes, employee taxes (.80% Federal Unemployment Insurance [FUI], 5.4% State Unemployment Insurance [SUI], and 6.20% Social Disability Insurance [SDI]), and agency fees are all considered fringes.

Gaffer. One of the cinematographer's key people, along with the key grip, in creating the lighting effects on the set.

Gap. The shortfall between the money you have and the money you need to cover the full cost of a picture. To obtain gap financing from a bank, you will need to present any presale contracts and guaranteed equity investment contracts, along with other items such as a budget and script.

Headboard. The top portion of a strip board. It contains key information about the production such as the picture title, director, producer, assistant director, etc. as well as character names and identification numbers and other information pertinent to the production. (See also *Strip Board.*)

Hold Days. Days when a principal player is not working but is being "held" by the production and is not free to take other work. You must generally pay actors for hold days. If you are working with one of the Screen Actors Guild low-budget agreements, this consecutive employment requirement may be waived.

Kit Rental. A fee paid for equipment or supplies that a crew member provides to the production. For example, you may need to budget a kit rental fee for a makeup artist who has his or her own makeup supplies. The fee depends on the department and the budget of the show. Fees paid for kit rentals are not subject to payroll taxes. (Also called *box rental.*)

L&D. See *Loss and Damage.*

LIBOR. London Interbank Offered Rate.

Loan-Out Company. A corporation that "loans" the services of its employees. Certain members of the above- and below-the-line staff may want to be paid as "loan-outs." When hiring a loan-out, the producer (or the producer's payroll company) does not deduct employee payroll taxes or add fringes to the loan-out's rate. Instead, the loan-out company is responsible for absorbing the tax liability on the income. Any employee whom you pay as a loan-out must provide you with papers of incorporation and a federal identification number or employee identification number (EIN).

Loss and Damage (L&D). Money that is budgeted to ensure that the production will be covered in the event that equipment or materials are lost or damaged during the course of the show. The most conservative way to handle budgeting for L&D is to set aside an amount in each department's budget equal to the amount of the deductible on the production insurance policy. For example, if your deductible is $1,200, you would budget $1,200 for L&D in each department category. (Insurance deductibles must usually be met on a per-occurrence basis.)

Magazine. The mechanism that attaches to the camera body that holds the film stock.

Mix. See *dubbing.*

MOS. A term used to describe scenes shot without sound. According to legend, this acronym is derived from a German director's order, "Mit out sound."

Motion Picture Association of America (MPAA) Certificate. The MPAA certificate certifies that the film has been rated by the MPAA and that its production meets the association's regulations and standards. The MPAA views the finished film and assigns it a rating, which is required if the film is to be released. The cost of the certificate is based on the budget of the film. The MPAA certificate is a delivery requirement for all distribution companies.

Negative Cutting. The process of conforming the negative to match the edited work print or digital "fine cut." Conform your negative only when you have locked your picture.

One-Line Schedule. A shortened version of the shooting schedule. The one-line schedule does not list props, set dressing, vehicles, and similar items, and characters are identified by number only.

On Location. Filming at a distant location where either cast and crew members are working as nonlocals and will need to be traveled around and paid pier diem. The production is required to pay for the traveling and living expenses of cast and crew members who must travel from their homes in Los Angeles, for example, to Park City, Utah, to work. If you hire your cast and crew in Park City, on the other hand, they are local hires, and you do not have to pay for their traveling and living expenses. On location is also used to distinguish a preexisting location where you are filming from a set that has been built on a stage or is on a lot.

Optical. A type of effect that is shot optically and placed into the film during post-production. You may need to correct shots in your film that need to be repositioned or made clearer, or you may need to place elements into the film that are not actually there, such as a creature, volcano, windstorm, laser beam, or falling star.

Overhead. Overhead can cover certain pre-production costs, office rental, utility costs, nominal development costs, and out-of-pocket expenses of those who are involved with the project for some time before the film is financed. On an independent film, overhead, if it is applied at all, is applied as a percentage of the overall budget; it might be anything between 1 percent and 10 percent.

P&A. See *Prints and Advertising.*

PC. See *Petty Cash.*

P-D Deal. See *Domestic Production-Distribution Deal.*

Per Diem. Money allocated to cover food and other out-of-pocket expenses of the cast and crew members while on location. Unions have minimum per diem (per day) rates. For nonunion cast and crew, set the per diem rate at a reasonable amount given the cost of living where you are shooting.

Permit. A certificate issued by the city in which you are filming that entitles you to shoot at a particular location. To obtain a filming permit, you will be required to pay a fee that will be determined by the city, your location or locations, and the zone in which you plan to film.

Petty Cash (PC). Money set aside for small purchases, such as gas, tolls, tips, parking, office supplies, inexpensive props, and food.

Pitch. To pique someone's interest in your firm so that will want to know more or read the script. A brief description of what your film is about.

Preference Claim. A penalty for having hired a nonguild actor,

Prelight/Prerig. Any day or portion of a day spent preparing a set, stages, or location for filming. Depending on the lighting needs of the show and the rental arrangements for the location, you might be able to have your lighting and grip departments prelight/prerig a location before filming. This day of setup allows the shoot day at the location to get off to a quicker start.

Principal Player. An actor needed for more than three days in a row. Also referred to as a weekly player.

Prints and Advertising (P&A). The costs of striking prints of a film and the advertising costs for promoting the film in the marketplace. These costs are typically absorbed by the distribution company and may be prenegotiated in your contract with a distributor.

Production Insurance. All independent productions must be insured to secure equipment, locations, transportation, props, wardrobe, cast, crew, and so on, and the policy must be purchased before the production period officially begins. Typically, production insurance is calculated at 1.5 percent to 3 percent of the budget depending on the budget and the life of the film.

Production Report. The production report accounts for the on-set events of a given shoot day. During production the assistant director fills out a production report daily. Crew times, crew meal times, camera call times, first shot, the quantity of footage shot, which scenes were shot that day, and which shots were retakes are all recorded on the production report. Production reports also list such information as faulty equipment, meal penalties, and on-set injuries.

Product Placement. Name brand products that are featured in a film, serving as advertising and promotion for the product as well as a source of revenue or in-kind donation to the production, depending on the arrangement with the manufacturer.

Raw Stock. Film stock that has not yet been shot and will be loaded into camera magazines when ready to be used.

Recan. Film stock that was loaded into a magazine but was never shot and then was literally recanned.

Rough Cut. An early cut of a film. Assembling a film and determining which footage best tells the story is what the editing process entails. After making extensive notes, incorporating new ideas and changes, and assembling several rough cuts, you will eventually be ready for the fine cut.

Scale. The minimum crew or cast payment established by a union

Schedule. To determine how many days it will take to shoot a film and then within each shoot day which scenes will be shot and in what order.

Scout. To explore a potential location to determine its ability to meet the film's needs. Initially, the location scout will search out and photograph potential locations to present options to the director and production designer. Once the majority of your locations has been locked, the location manager and the line producer will schedule scouts of each location to determine setups, equipment needs, power availability, lighting needs, and so on.

Second Unit Filming. Scaled-down crew that usually includes the director, assistant camera operator (AC), second AC, operator, and production assistant. (You may need a prop or art department person as well.) On bigger-budget productions, a second unit might have its own director. Sometimes, the camera operator becomes the second unit's director of photography, or an entirely different crew is hired.

Skeleton Crew. A scaled-down crew, most appropriate when shooting under conditions in which space or time is limited and a smaller crew would facilitate getting the shot.

Stand-in. An actor who takes the place of another actor and resembles him or her. A stand-in is most appropriate when you have name talent and are shooting scenes without sound or background shots. It may be less expensive to use a stand-in, and an actor sometimes requests one. The rate for stand-ins is usually the same as the rate for extras.

Station 12. To determine if an actor is in good standing with SAG, call the Station 12 desk at the guild, prior to allowing him or her to work on your set. If the actor has not paid SAG dues, he or she must do so before beginning work. The production company will pay a fine for any actor working on a set whose status has not been cleared with the guild.

Strip Board. Individual strips, each representing one scene, are arranged on a board creating the shooting schedule. (See also *Headboard.*)

Synopsis. A brief written description of what a script is about. It should grab the reader. It's not a scene-by-scene breakdown. A synopsis is often required for investors or financing companies in order to pique their interest, hopefully resulting in their wanting to read the script.

Titles. Main titles typically run at the beginning of the film and indicate the film's title as well as key credits. End titles run at the end of the film (also called credit crawl) and list all cast and crew, music, and often vendors who have participated in the film's making.

Top Sheet. The first page of a budget, which reflects the categories and their totals but does not show line-item detail.

Turnaround. The amount of time the cast and crew are given from the time they are released from work on a given day before they must return to work the next day. Guild and union guidelines typically require a 12-hour minimum turnaround for cast and crew members.

Vendor Account. An account that allows a production to rent equipment and be billed for it, rather than having to pay up front. A vendor account is established by filling out a credit application. It is favorable to establish a vendor account with any business from which you will be renting equipment or garnering services (e.g., lab or editing facility, wardrobe and prop houses, camera house, etc.).

Weekly Player. An actor who works under a weekly contract. If an actor is needed for more than three days in a row, he or she should be paid as a weekly player based on weekly rates set by SAG. (Compare *Day Player.*)

White Copy. The draft of a script when preproduction begins. White is the first color in the color-coding system used to identify different drafts of a script.

INDEX

ELSEVIER SCIENCE CD-ROM LICENSE AGREEMENT

PLEASE READ THE FOLLOWING AGREEMENT CAREFULLY BEFORE USING THIS CD-ROM PRODUCT. THIS CD-ROM PRODUCT IS LICENSED UNDER THE TERMS CONTAINED IN THIS CD-ROM LICENSE AGREEMENT ("Agreement"). BY USING THIS CD-ROM PRODUCT, YOU, AN INDIVIDUAL OR ENTITY INCLUDING EMPLOYEES, AGENTS AND REPRESENTATIVES ("You" or "Your"), ACKNOWLEDGE THAT YOU HAVE READ THIS AGREEMENT, THAT YOU UNDERSTAND IT, AND THAT YOU AGREE TO BE BOUND BY THE TERMS AND CONDITIONS OF THIS AGREEMENT. ELSEVIER SCIENCE INC. ("Elsevier Science") EXPRESSLY DOES NOT AGREE TO LICENSE THIS CD-ROM PRODUCT TO YOU UNLESS YOU ASSENT TO THIS AGREEMENT. IF YOU DO NOT AGREE WITH ANY OF THE FOLLOWING TERMS, YOU MAY, WITHIN THIRTY (30) DAYS AFTER YOUR RECEIPT OF THIS CD-ROM PRODUCT RETURN THE UNUSED CD-ROM PRODUCT AND ALL ACCOMPANYING DOCUMENTATION TO ELSEVIER SCIENCE FOR A FULL REFUND.

DEFINITIONS

As used in this Agreement, these terms shall have the following meanings:

"Proprietary Material" means the valuable and proprietary information content of this CD-ROM Product including all indexes and graphic materials and software used to access, index, search and retrieve the information content from this CD-ROM Product developed or licensed by Elsevier Science and/or its affiliates, suppliers and licensors.

"CD-ROM Product" means the copy of the Proprietary Material and any other material delivered on CD-ROM and any other human-readable or machine-readable materials enclosed with this Agreement, including without limitation documentation relating to the same.

OWNERSHIP

This CD-ROM Product has been supplied by and is proprietary to Elsevier Science and/or its affiliates, suppliers and licensors. The copyright in the CD-ROM Product belongs to Elsevier Science and/or its affiliates, suppliers and licensors and is protected by the national and state copyright, trademark, trade secret and other intellectual property laws of the United States and international treaty provisions, including without limitation the Universal Copyright Convention and the Berne Copyright Convention. You have no ownership rights in this CD-ROM Product. Except as expressly set forth herein, no part of this CD-ROM Product, including without limitation the Proprietary Material, may be modified, copied or distributed in hardcopy or machine-readable form without prior written consent from Elsevier Science. All rights not expressly granted to You herein are expressly reserved. Any other use of this CD-ROM Product by any person or entity is strictly prohibited and a violation of this Agreement.

SCOPE OF RIGHTS LICENSED (PERMITTED USES)

Elsevier Science is granting to You a limited, non-exclusive, non-transferable license to use this CD-ROM Product in accordance with the terms of this Agreement. You may use or provide access to this CD-ROM Product on a single computer or terminal physically located at Your premises and in a secure network or move this CD-ROM Product to and use it on another single computer or terminal at the same location for personal use only, but under no circumstances may You use or provide access to any part or parts of this CD-ROM Product on more than one computer or terminal simultaneously.

You shall not (a) copy, download, or otherwise reproduce the CD-ROM Product in any medium, including, without limitation, online transmissions, local area networks, wide area networks, intranets, extranets and the Internet, or in any way, in whole or in part, except that You may print or download limited portions of the Proprietary Material that are the results of discrete searches; (b) alter, modify, or adapt the CD-ROM Product, including but not limited to decompiling, disassembling, reverse engineering, or creating derivative works, without the prior written approval of Elsevier Science; (c) sell, license or otherwise distribute to third parties the CD-ROM Product or any part or parts thereof; or (d) alter, remove, obscure or obstruct the display of any copyright, trademark or other proprietary notice on or in the CD-ROM Product or on any printout or download of portions of the Proprietary Materials.

RESTRICTIONS ON TRANSFER

This License is personal to You, and neither Your rights hereunder nor the tangible embodiments of this CD-ROM Product, including without limitation the Proprietary Material, may be sold, assigned, transferred or sub-licensed to any other person, including without limitation by operation of law, without the prior written consent of Elsevier Science. Any purported sale, assignment, transfer or sublicense without the prior written consent of Elsevier Science will be void and will automatically terminate the License granted hereunder.

TERM

This Agreement will remain in effect until terminated pursuant to the terms of this Agreement. You may terminate this Agreement at any time by removing from Your system and destroying the CD-ROM Product. Unauthorized copying of the CD-ROM Product, including without limitation, the Proprietary Material and documentation, or otherwise failing to comply with the terms and conditions of this Agreement shall result in automatic termination of this license and will make available to Elsevier Science legal remedies. Upon termination of this Agreement, the license granted herein will terminate and You must immediately destroy the CD-ROM Product and accompanying documentation. All provisions relating to proprietary rights shall survive termination of this Agreement.

LIMITED WARRANTY AND LIMITATION OF LIABILITY

NEITHER ELSEVIER SCIENCE NOR ITS LICENSORS REPRESENT OR WARRANT THAT THE INFORMATION CONTAINED IN THE PROPRIETARY MATERIALS IS COMPLETE OR FREE FROM ERROR, AND NEITHER ASSUMES, AND BOTH EXPRESSLY DISCLAIM, ANY LIABILITY TO ANY PERSON FOR ANY LOSS OR DAMAGE CAUSED BY ERRORS OR OMISSIONS IN THE PROPRIETARY MATERIAL, WHETHER SUCH ERRORS OR OMISSIONS RESULT FROM NEGLIGENCE, ACCIDENT, OR ANY OTHER CAUSE. IN ADDITION, NEITHER ELSEVIER SCIENCE NOR ITS LICENSORS MAKE ANY REPRESENTATIONS OR WARRANTIES, EITHER EXPRESS OR IMPLIED, REGARDING THE PERFORMANCE OF YOUR NETWORK OR COMPUTER SYSTEM WHEN USED IN CONJUNCTION WITH THE CD-ROM PRODUCT.

If this CD-ROM Product is defective, Elsevier Science will replace it at no charge if the defective CD-ROM Product is returned to Elsevier Science within sixty (60) days (or the greatest period allowable by applicable law) from the date of shipment.

Elsevier Science warrants that the software embodied in this CD-ROM Product will perform in substantial compliance with the documentation supplied in this CD-ROM Product. If You report significant defect in performance in writing to Elsevier Science, and Elsevier Science is not able to correct same within sixty (60) days after its receipt of Your notification, You may return this CD-ROM Product, including all copies and documentation, to Elsevier Science and Elsevier Science will refund Your money.

YOU UNDERSTAND THAT, EXCEPT FOR THE 60-DAY LIMITED WARRANTY RECITED ABOVE, ELSEVIER SCIENCE, ITS AFFILIATES, LICENSORS, SUPPLIERS AND AGENTS, MAKE NO WARRANTIES, EXPRESSED OR IMPLIED, WITH RESPECT TO THE CD-ROM PRODUCT, INCLUDING, WITHOUT LIMITATION THE PROPRIETARY MATERIAL, AND SPECIFICALLY DISCLAIM ANY WARRANTY OF MERCHANTABILITY OR FITNESS FOR A PARTICULAR PURPOSE.

If the information provided on this CD-ROM contains medical or health sciences information, it is intended for professional use within the medical field. Information about medical treatment or drug dosages is intended strictly for professional use, and because of rapid advances in the medical sciences, independent verification of diagnosis and drug dosages should be made.

IN NO EVENT WILL ELSEVIER SCIENCE, ITS AFFILIATES, LICENSORS, SUPPLIERS OR AGENTS, BE LIABLE TO YOU FOR ANY DAMAGES, INCLUDING, WITHOUT LIMITATION, ANY LOST PROFITS, LOST SAVINGS OR OTHER INCIDENTAL OR CONSEQUENTIAL DAMAGES, ARISING OUT OF YOUR USE OR INABILITY TO USE THE CD-ROM PRODUCT REGARDLESS OF WHETHER SUCH DAMAGES ARE FORESEEABLE OR WHETHER SUCH DAMAGES ARE DEEMED TO RESULT FROM THE FAILURE OR INADEQUACY OF ANY EXCLUSIVE OR OTHER REMEDY.

U.S. GOVERNMENT RESTRICTED RIGHTS

The CD-ROM Product and documentation are provided with restricted rights. Use, duplication or disclosure by the U.S. Government is subject to restrictions as set forth in subparagraphs (a) through (d) of the Commercial Computer Restricted Rights clause at FAR 52.22719 or in subparagraph (c)(1)(ii) of the Rights in Technical Data and Computer Software clause at DFARS 252.2277013, or at 252.2117015, as applicable. Contractor/Manufacturer is Elsevier Science Inc., 655 Avenue of the Americas, New York, NY 10010–5107, USA.

GOVERNING LAW

This Agreement shall be governed by the laws of the State of New York, USA. In any dispute arising out of this Agreement, you and Elsevier Science each consent to the exclusive personal jurisdiction and venue in the state and federal courts within New York County, New York, USA.

WELCOME TO THE *IFP/LOS ANGELES* INDEPENDENT FILMMAKER'S MANUAL COMPANION CD-ROM

COPYRIGHT INFORMATION

This product is sold "as is" without warranty of any kind except that the magnetic disc on which the code is recorded is free from defects under normal use and service for a period of ninety (90) days from the date the product is delivered.

GETTING HELP

If you have questions or problems with the installation or use of this CD-ROM, please contact technical support:

Via phone: Call 1-800-692-9010 Monday – Friday, 5:30 a.m. – 7:00 p.m. Central Time
Via fax: Fax question or problem to 1-314-579-3316
Email: Send e-mail to technical.support@elsevier.com

Please help us solve your problem by having the following information available when you contact technical support:

- Type and speed of processor (e.g., Pentium 133 MHz)
- Amount of RAM (e.g., 32 MB)
- Video display settings (e.g., 800 × 600, 16-bit)
- Speed of CD-ROM drive (e.g., 8×)
- Size and free space of hard disk (e.g., 4.3 GB total, 250 MB free)
- Operating system including version and service packs (e.g., Windows NT Workstation 4.0 Service Pack 3)
- Version number of the browser, available from the help pull-down menu, under About (IE or Netscape)
- Version number of the browser, available from the help pull-down menu, under About (IE or Netscape)

For more information regarding other products, visit our Web site at *www.us.elsevierhealth.com*

HOW TO ACCESS THE DATA

All of the files on this CDR run through an **Adobe Acrobat PDF** interface. To access the forms and checklists, you must have either **Adobe Acrobat 5.0** or **Acrobat Reader 5.0** installed on your computer. An installer is available on this CD for **Acrobat Reader 5.0**

ADOBE ACROBAT READER

Installation for Windows 98/2000/ME/XP/NT

Double-Click **MY Computer** and select the folder titled **Software**. Open the **Acrobat Reader** folder and run the rp505enu.exe file to begin the installation.

Installation for MAC OS (8.5 or higher)

Open the **Acrobat Reader** folder and run the rp505enu.exe file to begin the installation.

SYSTEM REQUIREMENTS

PC

PC Based Pentium 266MMX
Windows 95 Release 2 and higher, 98/98SE, ME, 2000, NT 4.0 Service Pack 6 (SP6) or higher
32MB RAM
8X CD ROM Drive
Video Card with 16bit or higher color (24 or 32 bit is best)
Display Resolution of 800x600 or greater
Sound Card and Speakers

Macintosh

Power PC G3 300MHZ, I-MAC, I-Book
Macintosh OS 8.5 and higher
32MB RAM
8X CD ROM Drive
Video Card with 16bit or higher color (24 or 32 bit is best)
Display Resolution of 800 × 600 or greater
Sound Card and Speakers

INSTALLING A MEDIA PLAYER

To access the MP3/MPEG-1 audio and video interviews you need to have a media player installed on your computer. There are many players available for free or as shareware. For Windows, we recommend **Windows Media Player**. For MAC users go to *http://www.apple.com/quicktime/download/* to download the free Quicktime player.

Windows 98/2000/ME/XP/NT

To install Windows Media Player from this CD, run **D:\Software\Windows Media Player\mp71.exe** (where "**D**" is the designation of your CD drive).

MAC OS (8.5 or higher)

A free version of the Quicktime player can be downloaded online at *http://www.apple.com/quicktime/download/*

WELCOME SCREEN

Once you have successfully installed Acrobat or Acrobat Reader as well as the appropriate media player, simply open **Welcome.pdf**. Everything featured on CD has been linked to this opening screen.

POINTERS FOR SURFING THE CD CONTENT

- Accessing the interviews, checklists, forms, memos, reports, worksheets, and catalog is as easy as pointing and clicking to what you'd like to view.
- Use the VIEW pull-down menu to zoom in, out, or full-screen. To see the file contents, SHOW BOOKMARKS from the WINDOW pull-down menu.
- Press ESCAPE to exit full-screen mode.
- If you have purchased and installed the complete version of Acrobat 5.0, you can modify and save the forms and checklists to suit your specific needs; otherwise, use Acrobat Reader provided with this CD to view and print each form.
- Everything featured on this CD has been linked to this opening screen; however, you can also access each individual file from the file manager.

AUDIO INTERVIEWS

Peter Broderick, Film Consultant, Executive Producer *Manic, Following*...On Festivals and Distribution

Ted Hope, Founder of Good Machine and This Is That, Producer *In the Bedroom, American Splendor, 21 Grams*...On Filmmaking

Mira Nair, Director-*Vanity Fair*; *Monsoon Wedding, Mississippi Masala*; *Kama Sutra*...On Filmmaking

John Sloss, Founder of Sloss Law and Cinetic Media...On Selling Your Film

Gary Winick, Founder of Indigent, Producer *Pieces of April,* director of *Tadpole, 13 Going on 30*...*On Filmmaking and Digital*

Michelle Byrd, Executive Director, IFP in New York...*On Independent Film and IFP/New York*

Geoff Gilmore, Director of Programming, Sundance Film Festival...*On the Sundance Film Festival*

Marcus Hu, Co-President, Strand Releasing...*On Distribution*

Ang Lee, Director, *Wedding Banquet, Ice Storm, Crouching Tiger Hidden Dragon*...*On Directing*

All the audio interviews were derived from cassette tape recordings and though every effort was made to maximize sound quality, they do contain some background noise and tape hiss. All the audio interviews are monophonic, recorded at 64 kbps/44.1 kHz.

TEXT INTERVIEWS

Tom Bernard, Co-President, Sony Pictures Classics...*On Distribution*

Jon Favreau, Writer/Co-Producer/Actor...*On the Making of* Swingers

Geoffrey Gilmore, Director of Programming, Sundance Film Festival...*On the Sundance Film Festival*

Marcus Hu, Co-President, Strand Releasing...*On Distribution*

Ang Lee, Director, ***Wedding Banquet, Ice Storm, Crouching Tiger Hidden Dragon***...*On Directing*

Kasi Lemmons, Writer/Director...*On the Making of* Eve's Bayou

Kevin Smith and Scott Mosier, Director and Producer of *Clerks, Chasing Amy, Jersey Girl*...*On Working as a Team*

Mark Pogachefsky, President, mPRm...*On Working with a Publicist*

Billy Bob Thornton, Actor/Writer/Director...*On the Making of* Slingblade

Christine Vachon, Killer Films Producer, ***Far From Heaven, Boys Don't Cry, Velvet Goldmine***...*On Producing*

VIDEO INTERVIEWS

JON FAVREAU
- Filmmaking and Story Structure
- Protecting Your Script
- Keeping Creative Control
- Writing
- Festivals
- Screening for the Industry

KASI LEMMONS
- Writing *Eve's Bayou*
- Choosing the Right Director
- Working with Child Actors
- Postproduction
- Advice to Filmmakers

KEVIN SMITH and SCOTT MOSIER
- Financing *Clerks*
- Post-production for *Clerks*
- From *Clerks* to *Mallrats*
- Creative Control

BILLY BOB THORNTON
- Writing
- Creative Control
- Story Structure
- Success
- Directing

CHECKLISTS

All of the checklists on this CD have been reformatted for screen from those found throughout the book. To access a file, just point and click to the title you'd like to view. To tick completed tasks, just point and click on the appropriate box, then print. If you have Acrobat 5.0 installed, you can save the checklist to your hard drive to modify it to suit your specific needs; otherwise use Acrobat Reader to view and print each form.

TIPS: Use the **VIEW** pull-down menu to zoom in or out, **VIEW FULL-SCREEN,** or to see the complete contents **(SHOW BOOKMARKS).** Hit **ESCAPE** to exit full-screen mode.

- ☐ **Ad Kit**
- ☐ **Camera**
- ☐ **Cast**
- ☐ **Company Move**
- ☐ **Craft & Catering**
- ☐ **Crew**
- ☐ **Daily Office Responsibilities**
- ☐ **Distant Locations**
- ☐ **End-of-Day**
- ☐ **Schedules & Lists**
- ☐ **Send-to-Set**
- ☐ **Set**
- ☐ **Final Wrap-Out**
- ☐ **Grip & Lighting**
- ☐ **Last Week of Production**
- ☐ **Legal, Financial, & Accounts**
- ☐ **Locations**
- ☐ **Miscellaneous Needs**
- ☐ **Office Set-up**
- ☐ **Office**
- ☐ **Postproduction**
- ☐ **Sound**
- ☐ **Still Photography**
- ☐ **Travel & Transportation**

FORMS, MEMOS, REPORTS, & WORKSHEETS

All of the forms on this CD duplicate the blank forms found within the bound book. To access a file, just point and click to the title you'd like to view. If you have Acrobat 5.0 installed, you can save the form to your hard drive to modify it to suit your specific needs; otherwise use Acrobat Reader to view and print each form.

TIPS: Use the **VIEW** pull-down menu to zoom in or out, **VIEW FULL-SCREEN,** or to see the complete contents **(SHOW BOOKMARKS).** Hit **ESCAPE** to exit full-screen mode.

- ☐ **Box Rental Information**
- ☐ **Call Sheet**
- ☐ **Production Requirements**
- ☐ **Cast Deal Memo**
- ☐ **Check Request**
- ☐ **Credit List**
- ☐ **Crew Deal Memo**
- ☐ **Crew Deal Memo with W-4**
- ☐ **Daily Cost Overview**
- ☐ **Daily Production Report**
- ☐ **Daily Raw Stock Log**
- ☐ **Employee Verification / I-9**
- ☐ **I-9 Instructions**
- ☐ **List of Acceptable Documents**
- ☐ **Employee Start/Form PA**
- ☐ **PA Instructions**
- ☐ **Location Agreement**
- ☐ **Location/Filming Notice**
- ☐ **Mileage Log**
- ☐ **Neighboring Location Agreement**
- ☐ **Personal Release Statement**
- ☐ **Petty Cash Envelope**
- ☐ **Pickup and Return List**
- ☐ **Product Placement Release**
- ☐ **Purchase Order**
- ☐ **Raw Stock Inventory**
- ☐ **SAG Daily Contract**
- ☐ **SAG Freelance Contract**
- ☐ **SAG Exhibit G**
- ☐ **SAG Sign-In Sheet**
- ☐ **SAG Taft-Hartley Report**
- ☐ **SAG Taft-Hartley Report Extra**
- ☐ **SAG Talent Worksheet**
- ☐ **Vendors List**
- ☐ **Walkie-Talkie Sign-Out Sheet**

EXTRAS

Focal Press Web Link

A link has been provided for the Focal Press Web site.

Movie Magic Budgeting Demo

This CD-ROM also includes a demo version of the software used to create the sample budgets in Chapter 6. Please note that saving, exporting, library, and printing features have been disabled in this demonstration version. Go to the **Welcome Screen** to install.

We wish to thanks the following for their contributions on this CD-ROM:

Elinor Actipis—Developmental Editor
Marcy Barnes-Henrie—Production Project Manager
Bruce Robison—Multimedia Producer
Ryan Sullenberger—Associate Producer

Progressive Information Technologies Team:

Ann Chisnell—New Media Leader
Dan Murren—Project Manager